Bioetн

33.

Sexuality, Gender & Education

Edited by

Giorgia Brambilla and Joseph Tham

IF Press

Originally published in Italian as *Temi scelti di bioetica: Sessualità, gender ed educazione* © 2015 by Edizioni Scientifiche Italiane s.p. a., Napoli

IF Press srl - Roma, Italy
info@if-press.com - www.if-press.com

ISBN 978-88-6788-141-3

CONTENT

PREFACE TO THE ENGLISH EDITION

A couple of years ago, political forces were seeking to impose a certain sexual "education" agenda over and above parental roles in Italy, a situation that caused a good amount of alarm and unease.[1] Since the public is uninformed about the science and philosophical currents undergirding the questions of gender and sexuality, our university Pontifical Athenaeum *Regina Apostolorum* organized an academic symposium "*Sapere per Educare*" (*Knowledge for Education*). We involved many pro-life and pro-family associations and there was an overwhelming participation of parents, educators, students, religious and pastoral personnel.

Inspired by the urgent need and the widespread interest in the education of gender and sexuality, Giorgia Brambilla eventually published this bioethics text in Italian. Even though the authors are all Italians, we believe an English translation that reaches a broader readership is nonetheless beneficial.

The debates on gender and sexuality are strangely controversial today. There is a claim that two camps are waging a cultural war—between conservatives or so-called "traditionalists" who uphold the time-honored values of family and sexuality, and those who are pushing a "liberal" agenda of change to redefine these traditional roles. The former camp complains about the undemocratic tactics of media and law-makers imposing changes and "gender ideology" on society, an idea that is still far from being commonly accepted. The latter complains of injustice and discriminations against LGBT groups by homophobes, bigots and those who are grossly intolerant and discriminatory towards their lifestyles. This division is global. These discussions are heated in Europe as different authors of this volume attest. Across the Pacific, the US Supreme Court judgment was a watershed moment, galvanizing both sides to greater activism, particularly because of "judiciary activism"—that a federal bill, Defense of Marriage Act (DOMA) voted in by elected officials, was struck down by the difference of one judgment.[2] Judge Scalia's minority dissent laments that this verdict has ironically stifled democratic debates:

---

[1] See A. Manotovano, "Gender a scuola e ddl Cirinnà. La svolta Lgbt si nasconde nei dettagli", in *Tempi*, July 18, 2015, http://www.tempi.it/gender-a-scuola-e-ddl-cirinna-la-svolta-lgbt-si-nasconde-nei-dettagli#.WgbJXmhSwus (accessed Nov. 11, 2017).

[2] D. Davenport, "Is Gay Marriage The Product Of Judicial Activism?" in *Forbes*, July 2, 2013, https://www.forbes.com/sites/daviddavenport/2013/07/02/is-gay-marriage-the-product-of-judicial-activism/#5077b8e33642 (accessed Nov. 11, 2017).

> By formally declaring anyone opposed to same-sex marriage an enemy of human decency, the majority arms well every challenger to a state law restricting marriage to its traditional definition… The result will be a judicial distortion of our society's debate over marriage.
> In the majority's telling, this story is black-and-white: Hate your neighbor or come along with us. The truth is more complicated. It is hard to admit that one's political opponents are not monsters, especially in a struggle like this one, and the challenge in the end proves more than today's Court can handle… But the Court has cheated both sides, robbing the winners of an honest victory, and the losers of the peace that comes from a fair defeat. We owed both of them better.[3]

Unfortunately, the observation of Scalia has borne out, and there seems to be an insurmountable difference between the two sides of the divide. Robbie George points out, for example, that the tactic of demonizing your opponent has worked well for the progressives to effect cultural changes:

> By vilifying their opponents, sending a message that no one who supports the idea of marriage as a conjugal union can be a reasonable person of goodwill, they sent a clear signal—a threat, really to anyone who might even consider standing up to them. It was a strategy of intimidation—and it worked. And when strategies work, be they in politics, business, sports, or anywhere else, they are quickly copied. And that is what is happening now.[4]

A recent example of this intimidation played out on the campus of Georgetown University. An LGBT student group accused another group, Love Saxa, of discrimination and hate because it promotes "traditional marriage as defined between a man and a woman." Since Love Saxa promoted this restricted definition of marriage, which incidentally is the one espoused by the Catholic university itself, the school newspaper editorial considered them "fundamentally intolerant and hateful," and asked that the university end the group's funding.[5]

---

[3] UNITED STATES V. WINDSOR, 570 U. S ___ (2013) Scalia, J. dissenting, p.24-26.

[4] M. E. BUNSON, "Robert George on US Society: 'Our Divisions Are Very Deep'" in *National Catholic Register*, July 19, 2017, http://www.ncregister.com/daily-news/robert-george-on-us-society-our-divisions-are-very-deep (accessed Nov. 11, 2017).

[5] EDITORIAL BOARD, "Defund Intolerance", in *The Hoya*, (October 20, 2017) http://www.thehoya.com/editorial-defund-intolerance/ (accessed Nov. 11, 2017); Mary Hui, "Georgetown students have filed a discrimination complaint against a campus group promoting heterosexual marriage," in *Washington Post,* Oct. 25, 2017, https://www.washingtonpost.com/news/acts-of-faith/wp/2017/10/25/georgetown-students-file-a-discrimination-complaint-against-a-campus-group-that-promotes-heterosexual-marriage/?utm_term=.5267856b9649 (accessed Nov. 11, 2017).

In this debate, scientific and empirical studies are often summoned to defend respective positions. Recently two long papers, "Sexuality and Gender" in *The New Atlantic* and "Sexual Orientation, Controversy, and Science" by Bailey et al. have come up with different interpretations with divergent conclusions about these questions.[6] It is interesting to note that the style of these arguments is what we called "public," based on empirical data rather than humanistic disciplines like philosophy. The fact that both these public reasonings come up with drastically different conclusions demonstrate the inadequacy of this approach.[7] While we acknowledge the importance of science in addressing these issues, we are also aware that even scientific disciplines like psychology and sociology are inexact with many theories and points of view. Interestingly, Bailey's article did not wish to address the question of whether SSA is natural or unnatural from a perspective outside of science, that of philosophy and natural law.[8] At the same time, Judge Alito noted in his dissenting opinion that gender is "a question that philosophers, historians, social scientists, and theologians are better qualified to explore."[9]

Hence, this book wishes to offer a supplement to this lacuna in the debates by taking on an interdisciplinary approach so dear to bioethics. The authors have professional degrees in medicine, neuroscience, psychology, psychiatry, history, philosophy, moral theology, biblical studies, law, bioethics, or pedagogy. They approach the issues from many angles, ranging from medical to psychodynamic to legal and social.

We wholeheartedly agree with Fr. James Martin's recent invitation to build bridges between the Catholic Church and the LGBT community, by fostering a relationship of compassion, sensitivity, and mutual respect.[10] However, as some his critics mention, real bridges also require honesty and not being afraid of offending the other with truth claims. In today's contentious atmosphere, society might label any criticism of the LGBT lifestyle and defense of the traditional model of the family as "hateful." In that sense, this book would

---

[6] L. Mayer, P. McHugh, "Sexuality and Gender," *The New Atlantis*, no. 50 (Fall 2016), p.4–143; J. M. Bailey et al., "Sexual Orientation, Controversy, and Science," *Psychological Science in the Public Interest* 17, no. 2 September 1, 2016, p.45–101, https://doi.org/10.1177/1529100616637616.

[7] Bioethicist Robert Veatch writes about the difficulty of being value-neutral in science, especially in controversial debates. R. M. Veatch, *Value-Freedom in Science and Technology*, Scholar's Press, Missoula, Montana 1976.

[8] Bailey et al., "Sexual Orientation, Controversy, and Science," p.64.

[9] United States v. Windsor, 570 U. S ___ (2013) Alito, J. dissenting, 14.

[10] See J. Martin, *Building a Bridge: How the Catholic Church and the LGBT Community Can Enter into a Relationship of Respect, Compassion, and Sensitivity* HarperOne, USA 2017.

not be politically correct. We need to warn that the style of argument might seem forceful and blunt in this work, but this is not due to self-righteousness but rather a passion for the truth. We believe that truth is universal and that every individual can access it. These ideas and arguments are rational and are open to corrections. The strong Catholic views are not meant to be an attack on any LGBT persons but are invitations to a sincere dialogue based on truth. Truth can be uncomfortable, mainly when it affects personal conducts. Truth calls us to change and correspond to the reality, which can be liberating.

While we translate this book into English for a global audience, it is primarily addressed to Catholics and those who seek a greater apprehension of human sexuality and gender. Philosophy, biblical theology, and religious wisdom can help science and humanity to appreciate the complexity of these goods better. In the Catholic and personalist approach of bioethics, the natural law tradition distinguishes the person from his or her acts. In the case of same-sex attractions, the teaching of the Church is clear that the inclination in itself is not sinful, and that persons have full dignity deserving respect and compassion. However, same-sex acts are considered "intrinsically disordered." Once again, this scholastic terminology might sound offensive to the modern ear, but it is a judgment not on the person but any wrongful act.[11]

Accordingly, there are five parts in this book. Each section ends with an interview by an expert in that area.

Part one addresses the thorny issues of human sexuality: contraception, medicalizing sexuality, and gender dysphoria. These chapters aim not only to raise awareness of various problems but above all to provide arguments to judge these issues adequately. Giorgia Brambilla explains the biological mechanism of human conception, starting from the menstrual cycle leading up to ovulation and ending with implantation and pregnancy. She wishes to highlight the little-known facts of how contraceptives at times work against implantation of the embryo causing loss of human life. Medicalization of human sexuality is the topic Gennaro Bruno wishes to raise. Starting from a historical discussion, this medical specialist in andrology delineates the societal change in its understanding of sexuality—moving from its link to procreation and formation of the family to a hedonistic concept of pleasure. In this trajectory, sex is no longer a wonder to behold in conjugal love, but a market-

[11] See J. Finnis, "Natural Law and Unnatural Acts", *Heythrop Journal* 11, 1970: 365-387; Id., "Sex and Marriage: Some Myths and Reasons," in *Human Rights and Common Good*, Collected Essays: Vol III, OUP, Oxford 2011, p.353-388; J. Tham, "The Decline of Natural Law Reasoning: The Influence of Recent Cultural and Intellectual Currents on the Tradition", in *National Catholic Bioethics Quarterly* 14.2, 2014, p.245-255.

able commodity with enhancement drugs like Viagra. He discusses how this change in perspective has deviated the core values of the medical profession by relabeling a physiological diminution of function a disease that requires "treatment." Paradoxically, on the opposite end of the process of medicalization, there is the tendency to declassify sexual disorders as pathologies. Alberto Capriolo analyzes the reclassification of these diseases in the world of psychiatry and psychology, especially in the cases of gender dysphoria and gender reassignment surgeries. This young jurist also expounds the legal ramifications of changing one's gender on birth certificates with or without surgical operations in different countries. Finally, the interview with neurosurgeon Massimo Gandolfini touches on the hot topics of gender theories and deconstruction of sexual identity, and how such changes affect child development and parenting.

According to philosophical anthropology, sexuality is a constitutive dimension of the human person. The second part, therefore, analyzes the question of sex differences from philosophical, exegetical and scientific points of view. Biblical scholar Laura Paladino approaches this topic with an exegesis of the Book of Genesis. Her analysis of the etymological root of the Hebrew words Adam and Eve sheds light on the deeper meaning on several biblical themes: God's image and likeness, masculinity and femininity, stewardship and lordship, identity and difference, generation and sexuality, corporeality and transcendence, paternity and maternity. These topics so hotly disputed today will benefit from such insights. Philosopher Susy Zanardo analyzes the meaning of the terms masculine and feminine to understand better what lies behind sexual differences. Without falling into stereotypes, she traces the difference from the bodily, to its symbolic, relational, and social dimensions, without ignoring the importance of one's cultural background and biographical data. The question is ultimately related to the perception of marriage, procreation and having a family with children. Chiara Atzori proceeds to look at sexual differentiation from a biological and medical angle. She looks at the basis of this difference derived from the studies of genetics, epigenetics, development (during and post gestation), secondary characteristics, hormonal makeup, psychology, and neuroscience. Finally, Carlo Rochetta's interview examines the question of love, as an abused and misunderstood word today. This theologian responds to the question as to whether love is still related to marriage, given the present socio-cultural and legal environment where we can no longer take monogamy and stable relationships for granted.

After an analysis of this dual reality of the human person, part three of the book looks at gender theory and its cultural implications. The first chapters examine the philosophical roots of sexual difference, by critically analyzing the evolution of the concept of gender identity, their claims and gradual acceptance in social and health sciences, and eventually its transition into legal reality. Pierluigi Pavone traces the history of philosophical thought from Plato to Marx and sees in Gnosticism the key to unlocking today's enigma in gender theories. In it, this Italian philosopher believes that Gnostic humanism emphasis on self-determining and absolutizing perception of the self against any objective nature, truth or religion as a seedbed of these theories. Brambilla also wonders about the strategies to label those who are non-conformant with gender ideology as intolerant and homophobes. She sees in this approach an underlying relativistic mentality that questions authority, a desire to deconstruct traditional understanding of sex, and a promotion of an overly spiritualized, depersonalized and liquid selfhood with practical results. Educator and pedagogy specialist Giuseppe Mari warns about the impact on education. While it is crucial to root out discrimination and bullying from schools, it is another story to inflate diversities and negate all "stereotypes" of social roles in the (sexual) education of the young. The jurist Gianfranco Amato recounts how these theories are making inroads in Italian laws, through media influence and the effects of education reform. He appeals to the recuperation of the category of beauty as a possible antidote to these errors.

Part four of this volume tackles the thorny issue of same-sex attraction. We know that it is impossible to exhaust the subject, but we also believe that we can still say something with intellectual honesty. Alessandro Fiore analyzes the meaning of "nature" and "natural" philosophically. He explains that nature should not be identified with biology, but is the way things are, intrinsically ordained towards its goal or finality. Morality enters the picture with freedom: one can freely choose to do good acts (moral) or acts deprived of good (immoral). He argues that the nature of human sexuality is dimorphic and complementary. So, any action that contradicts the finality of sex (the good of human sexuality) is morally disordered. Psychologist Giancarlo Ricci delineates the different psychological profiles of persons with SSA. This diversity can many times be traced back to one's relationship with mother and father figures in his or her upbringing. Childhood traumas could have affected maturity and development of one's sexual identity. It would be a disservice to persons with SSA when these roots causes are ignored or passed over.

Lawyer and philosopher Gabriella Gambino recognizes the need to fight against homophobia as well as the need to protect the physical and moral integrity of the LGBT persons. However, she is concerned about recent legislation that is logically and legally incoherent in redefining marriage. Most of these decisions view human sexuality with a reduction to its functionalist reproductive dimension. The law is the guardian of the proper evolution of relationship dynamics based on sound anthropological principles regarding marriage, family and procreation, parentage and filiation. It cannot disregard the substance of human co-existence and the foundation of society. Roberto Marchesini, psychologist and psychotherapist, reiterates the Catholic Church's teaching on same-sex attraction through different papal pronouncement and church documents. The Church does not condemn persons with SSA as an inclination or orientation and must accept them with respect, compassion, and sensitivity. She should avoid every sign of unjust discrimination in their regard. However, same-sex acts are considered disordered.

Bioethicist Miriam Fiore analyzes the history of the debate on reparative therapies on persons with same-sex attractions. She notices an uneasy relationship of treatment of SSA persons in the early days of psychoanalysis, but modern approaches have moved away from Freud. Today, there is a growing emphasis on the subject's relational, environmental, familial, and social factors, thereby offering a more psychodynamic model. A positive self-vision and formation of habits resulting from specific interactions with parents and peers is the basis of all reparative psychotherapies. Rather than making a change in sexual orientation, its goal is a maturation of gender identity. The patient *becomes* the primary agent of the therapeutic process. When modern psychiatry rejects reparative psychotherapies, these individuals become victims of reverse discrimination paradoxically. Dina Nerozzi, a specialist in pediatric neuropsychiatry and endocrinology, laments that political correctness has prevented honest discussion on SSA behind the screen of intolerance and bigotry. She believes that we ought to frame this question within a coherent worldview attuned to scientific reality.

Since this book is catered to teachers and parents, part five addresses the increasingly sophisticated forms of education emerging today. The chapters examine the family from the legal and socio-cultural perspectives within the context of diminished roles of fathers and mothers in the family. Aside from weaknesses and the dangers facing the family, there are also strengths and opportunities. They offer best practices and achievable proposals dedicated to the affective education of youths. Education specialist and historian Furio

Pesci is concerned with the emphasis on autonomy and creativity in today's educational approaches that does not help youth grow into mature adults. He proposes to reestablish the links between ethics, virtues, and happiness which implies an emphasis on duty, moral living, and character formation. In the Christian tradition, the gift of self in love is the real source of happiness and the fulfillment of desire. Educational systems require the presence of role models, be they teachers, coaches or parents. Those who grow up in happy families founded on love, respect and trust will flourish. Hence, the so-called gender-sensitive education proposed in Italy and elsewhere is detrimental to child development, causes identity confusion, and may create difficulties of relations between the sexes in the future.

Giancarlo Cerelli, jurist and canon lawyer, engages in a historical account of the development of Western legal tradition. Lamentably, he notices that laws are no longer aimed at the common good, but are open to manipulation by the powerful. Ideological lobby groups hijack even human rights. He relates the weakening of the family in different historical moments—the Reformation, the French Revolution, communism, and the sexual revolution of the 60s. They paved the way to permit divorce initially and now attempts to redefine marriage and family under the influence of gender theories. Educator Donatella Mansi looks at the current situation of the affective-sexual education for the youth. There is a need to recuperate the real meaning of love and being loved. She proposes this by chastity education through a discovery of the wonder of the teenager's own body.

Finally, for Franco Nembrini, education is the path that leads a person to his or her destiny through beauty. Unfortunately, educators too often forget this and prefer the use of threats, reprimands, and punishments. Instead, attraction to the beauty of a good life moves the human heart and inspires us to live up to our potential. Educational approaches err when they implicitly accept a view of self-sufficient human development, without any help from without, including education. Given the current educational crisis, more and more parents want their rights to be the primary teachers of their children respected.

In conclusion, we hope that this book will also be a resource for those in the LGBT academic community who wish to understand the Catholic position better. In our limited engagement in interreligious dialogue in bioethics, we believe that differences are not detrimental but essential to the process of building bridges. Only through respectful conversation can we achieve such appreciation.[12] Bridges require understanding the predicaments and languages of the opposite side. Tolerance is much valued today, but it could ironically become a one-way street with intolerance towards those with whom we disagree.[13] We hope there will be tolerance on a two-way street of this bridge, where these chapters could be read with open-mindedness and not censure, even by those who disagree with their conclusions.

Joseph Tham
Giorgia Brambrilla

[12] See J. Tham, A. Garcia, G. Miranda, (eds.), *Religious Perspectives on Human Vulnerability in Bioethics*, Springer, New York 2014; J. Tham, A. Garcia, K. M. Kwan, *Religious Perspectives on Bioethics and Human Rights*, Springer, Switzerland 2017.

[13] See D. A Carson, *The Intolerance of Tolerance,* William B. Eerdmans Pub., Grand Rapids, Mich. 2012.

PART I

ISSUES OF BIOETHICS AND SEXUALITY

GIORGIA BRAMBILLA*

WHAT YOUR GYNECOLOGIST WON'T TELL YOU

"That is the one eternal education: to be sure *enough that something is true that you dare* to *tell it to a child.*"
—G.K. *Chesterton*

In some lessons, my students stare at me wide-eyed, as if I had told them I know an Avatar (which is somewhat accurate, considering my son's latest attempt to use blue paint as moisturizing cream). Such happens when I explain to them the so-called "side effects" of contraceptives, which patients often take with very little awareness. My intention in this short piece is to recount what gynecologists typically do not say about contraceptives, starting with the basics of the ovarian cycle. I will not present a thorough or innovative treatise on contraceptives. My goal, rather, is to emphasize that, beyond the moral aspects of contraception itself, there is no real awareness about their mechanism of action and, therefore, of the consequences of using them. I will focus on those aspects a gynecologist should have told patients about, given their importance and simplicity, if only to offer them a more informed choice.

1. Physiological components in the ovarian cycle[1]

The female genital apparatus has four functions: to provide female germ cells (oocytes or egg cells); to synthesize female sex hormones; to allow the passage of and survival of sperm within the proximity of ovulation; and to create the most favorable condition possible for fertilization and maintenance of pregnancy.

Ovaries are those organs in which female germ cells mature. At birth, there are between 700,000 and 2,000,000 egg cells. In the ovary, we find follicles as the ovary's most basic units. The follicle is responsible for the growth

* Doctor in Bioethics and Moral Theology, a specialist in Family and Sexual Morality, Adjunct Professor in Bioethics at the Pontifical Athenaeum Regina Apostolorum.

[1] For an exhaustive treatment see G.B. Candiani, V. Danesino, A. Gastaldi (Eds.), *La Clinica Ostetrica e Ginecologica*, Masson, 1996²; M. De Felici et al., *Embriologia Umana*, Piccin, Padua 2014.

and release of egg cells, as well as producing the female sex hormones. In the ovary, the *corpus luteum* develops from the residual follicle following the release of the egg from the mature follicle (ovulation) and secretes estrogen and primarily progesterone.

The fallopian tubes are ducts that capture the egg released from the ovary. They guide the sperm that have swum up through the cervical canal and uterine cavity to the egg cell and carry the embryo to the uterus following conception. Fertilization and early embryo cell multiplication both occur within the fallopian tubes. After five to seven days, at the blastocyst stage, the embryo embeds in the lining of the uterine wall. The tubal mucosa is composed of cells producing substances needed for the survival of the zygote and ciliated cells. The latter cells, following conception, guide and facilitate the descent of the zygote to the uterus, whereas before fertilization they made it difficult for the sperm to travel.[2]

The uterus is a hollow muscular organ in the form of an inverted pear. It consists of two parts, the cervix and the corpus. The corpus is the upper, broader part of the uterus, shaped to welcome pregnancy. It has several layers. The inner layer is called the endometrium, subject to cyclical changes owing to hormones produced during the ovarian cycle. The cervix is the "gatekeeper" of the uterus, allowing the elimination of menstrual blood loss, the transit of sperm, and the passage of a newborn during delivery. The cervical canal runs along the cervix and is covered with crypts that have a glandular function.

The vagina is a muscular canal that enables sexual intercourse. It also communicates with the external genitalia—the vulva—and shields the internal genitalia. The external genitalia include the labia majora, labia minora, mons pubis and clitoris. The vulva's rich distribution of nerves enables women to detect the presence of mucus conducted from the cervix through the vagina to the external genitalia. This detection is of great importance for the regulation of natural fertility.

All these structures interact within the ovarian cycle—sequence of different stages of maturation (development of follicle, ovulation, formation, and regression of the corpus luteum) occurring cyclically in the ovary—in response to specific stimuli arriving along the central nervous system's "hypothalamic-pituitary-gonadic" axis.[3]

---

[2] I tell my students it is as if sperm swam "upstream."

[3] See A. Bompiani (ed.), *I metodi naturali per la regolazione della fertilità,* Centro studi e ricerche per la regolazione naturale della fertilità, Rome 2014.

This axis causes the release of a hypothalamic hormone, as well as two gonadotropin adenohypophysis hormones called luteinizing hormone (LH) and follicle-stimulating hormone (FSH), which regulate the secretion of sex hormones from the gonads. The gonadotropin-releasing hormone is called GnRH. During menstruation, ovarian hormones function at a shallow level. It is the lowering of hormone levels that causes the endometrium to shed. The hormonal message produced by the pituitary gland is FSH.

When FSH reaches the "threshold level," the targeted follicles start to mature. This maturation causes the release of estrogen from the ovary. When FSH reaches an "intermediate level," estrogen quickly tells the pituitary gland to block further follicular stimulation. This inhibitory effect is called negative feedback. From that moment onward, just one follicle, the dominant one, proceeds to mature while the rest regress. A significant amount of estrogen produced by this follicle stimulates the cyclical activity of the hypothalamus. We call this positive feedback. LH and FSH reach peak levels during a period lasting 24 to 48 hours.

Ovulation is the effect of LH on a mature follicle, occurring about 17 hours after the LH surge. If there is no fertilization, the egg fails to survive more than six to twelve hours. Not only does LH provoke the egg cell's release, but it also transforms the residual follicle into the corpus luteum responsible for the production of estrogen and progesterone. The combined action of these two hormones permits embryo implantation as well as maintenance of pregnancy.

Again, high levels of progesterone and estrogen block the hypothalamic-pituitary axis, constituting a negative feedback. It is thus impossible for ovulation to occur. In fact, biovular twin pregnancy occurs when two egg cells—which practically mature at the same time and are released by the same LH surge—become fertilized.[4]

If pregnancy does not happen, the progesterone and estradiol plasma levels collapse and reach their lowest levels at the end of the post-ovulatory or luteal phase. Intrauterine mucosa, no longer supported by hormones, begins to shed, and menstruation occurs. If, instead, conception takes place, the corpus luteum is kept active by the hormone HCG (Human Chorionic Gonadotropin), which turns the corpus luteum into a "corpus luteum gravidarum," essential to hormone production and maintenance of pregnancy.[5]

---

[4] R.M. Berne, M.N. Levy, *Principi di Fisiologia*, Ambrosiana Publishing House, Milan 2010.[6]

[5] See G. Pescetto, L. De Cecco, D. Pecorari, N. Ragni, *Ginecologia e Ostetricia*, SEU, Rome 2009.[10]

This event takes place in the ovaries. Meanwhile, simultaneous to hormonal changes, a necessary mucus alteration occurs within the cervix. Cervical mucus is a hydrogel composite of 90% water together with electrolytes, sugars, protein, fat and enzymes. Specific cells in the cervix sensitive to estrogen and progesterone produce it. This mucus has unique characteristics with thread-like quality. In 1945 Clift described this phenomenon as "spinnbarkeit," noting that this mucus forms filaments 10 to 12 centimeters long halfway through the menstrual cycle, while at the start and the end of the period, they are just a few centimeters long.[6] Iser's classification of "spinnbarkeit" is still used today. Another important feature is its fern-like quality, a tendency to crystallize when left to dry. Observing cervical mucus through a microscope, Papanicolau noticed this typically fern-leaf crystallization.[7]

Using slides, it is possible to observe the "spinnbarkeit" and ferning phenomena in the process of forming crystal dendrites and producing channels. The number of channels increases the closer a woman is to the time of ovulation, causing an increase of mucus permeable to sperm. Oldeblad's studies reveal how throughout the menstrual cycle there are different types of mucus, produced by various cells in the cervix.[8] Crypts located in the lower part of the cervical canal produce type G mucus (in a process called gestagenic action), which close the external cervical orifice and block access to the uterine cavity. This process reveals ovarian inactivity and, thus, an absence of cervical stimulation associated with dry feeling at the vulva. Type G mucus behaves as a net of chaotically distributed protein molecules within 0.1-0.2 μ (micron). As a sperm head is 3.5 μ in size, type G mucus acts as a sperm barrier.

At the beginning of follicular maturation, increasing levels of estrogen stimulate the secretion of type L (Loaf) mucus, the quantity of which increases daily. Type L mucus is secreted in crypts spread throughout the cervical canal, concentrated mainly in the middle section. When a woman perceives a change and detects the presence of mucus, it means estrogen produced by the follicle has begun to stimulate the cervix. As the mucus barrier gradually dissolves, it permits sperm to enter and survive. In fact, the intermicellar spaces in type L mucus measure 1-3 μ. These areas facilitate the passage of sperm but not their progress.

---

[6] See P. Castellucci, "Il muco cervicale: fattore ed indicatore di fertilità," in A Bompiani (ed.), *I metodi naturali per la regolazione della fertilità,* Centro studi e ricerche per la regolazione naturale della fertilità, Rome 2014, p.37-50.

[7] *Ibid.*

[8] *Ibid.*

The crypts found in the upper part of the cervical canal secrete type S (Strings) mucus. The production of this mucus begins a few days before ovulation and is stimulated not only by a high level of estrogen but also by neurohormonal substances like noradrenalin. As type S mucus microcells are wider than the sperm heads, they permit sperm to pass through. Besides, type S mucus offers a natural means of transport for sperm so they can swim and survive for up to three to five days.

On the day of ovulation, mucus secretion consists in 30-40% type S mucus, 50-60% type L mucus and 5% type G mucus. As the days wear on, sensation in the vulva increases in intensity as mucus becomes increasingly fluid and aqueous. This phenomenon is related to peak estrogen levels preceding ovulation. Another type of mucus, called type P (Peak), is imperceptible till five days before ovulation, when it reaches 3%, before falling and then rising again on the day of ovulation, or peak day. Type P mucus is produced in those crypts highest in the cervical canal and delivers mucolytic action. The estrogen level decreases while progesterone increases after ovulation, thus causing a gradual increase in type G mucus that within three days will constitute 100% of mucus secretion. This phenomenon carries over into the whole post-ovulatory phase. Progesterone induces the formation of a barrier that within three days closes the cervical canal and blocks the passage of sperm.

2. Contraceptives or anti-implants?

Following this summary, it is easy to see how the ovarian hormones estrogen and progesterone act on multiple levels of the female reproductive system. To believe that the administration of progesterone for contraceptive use merely inhibits ovulation, or that the insertion of an IUD only "intercepts" sperm, impeding its movement, is reductive if not absurd. We need further clarification. We commonly define pregnancy to be "the period from conception to birth."[9] Hence, pregnancy is calculated from the date of the last menstrual period—the only specific date a woman remembers typically. When we compare this datum with the actual age of the child, we can calculate the presumed day of conception, when pregnancy begins.

There is thus a variance of two weeks (40 or 38 weeks) depending on whether one calculates from the last period or the moment of conception. It has never been the practice to contemplate pregnancy of 37-week duration beginning with implantation of the embryo. Whereas with in vitro fertiliza-

[9] B. Mozzanega, *Da vita a vita*, SEI, Rome 2013, p.223.

tion (IVF), the woman *apparently* cannot be regarded as pregnant within that span between IVF, the growth of the embryo and implantation in the uterus. For this reason, the American Congress of Obstetricians and Gynecologists (ACOG) and the American Medical Association (AMA) have proposed and established that pregnancy begins with implantation.

According to this logic, if abortion is the ending of the pregnancy, and pregnancy begins at implantation, anything occurring before implantation cannot be considered abortion. (Nevertheless, as any embryology manual can tell you, the embryo is already a full-fledged living human being.) Correspondingly, anything that acts to impede the implantation and not the union between gametes is "contra-ceptive," even though its action, whether primary or secondary, does not aim to "contra-conceive" but rather acts against the newly conceived being that already exists. I have described these mechanisms in detail because I believe any professional who informs a patient about "contraceptives" should do so with intellectual honesty, offering that patient the chance to confront her conscience genuinely. Changing nomenclature does not change the reality of things.

To understand the operation of anti-implantation products, commonly referred to as "contraceptives," we will start by explaining the effects of the known estrogen-progesterone pill, which, in addition to blocking ovulation, induces the following processes:[10]

a) Changes in tubal motility through obstruction or early interference in the descent of the oocyte *and* embryo
b) Modification of the endometrium, with impediment of embryo implantation
c) Alteration of the cervical mucus, which becomes impenetrable to sperm

As ultrasound demonstrates, there is follicular activity when taking the contraceptive pill. Therefore, the peripheral effects listed above are by no means secondary but rather reinforce the primary ones. Let us start with the first action. In the tube, progestin influences secretion and especially contraction. While normal movement makes it more difficult for sperm to ascend, it favors the descent of the zygote to the uterus.

A change in motility can cause—when there has been conception during the use of the pill—a desynchronized arrival of the embryo to the uterine cav-

[10] See P. Castellucci, "Il metodo Billings alla sospensione dei contraccettivi orali," in A Bompiani (ed.), *I metodi naturali per la regolazione della fertilità*, Centro studi e ricerche per la regolazione naturale della fertilità, Rome 2014, p.138.

ity relative to the "implantation window," resulting in an anti-implantation effect. Progestin changes the structure of the endometrium, rendering it unsuitable for embryonic implantation. Besides, by reducing glycogen production, it decreases energy available to the blastocyst for survival in the uterine cavity.[11] In particular, the actions carried out by progestin include the following: blocking the neo-synthesis of estrogen and progesterone receptors, gland atrophy, decreased cell proliferation, decidualization and transformation with an incomplete and transitory secretion of the endometrium.[12] It is interesting to compare this product with others, such as the IUD, that aim to make the uterus inhospitable. It is a device placed near the bottom of the uterus, occupying the entire cavity. Its use causes an inflammatory reaction that renders the uterine cavity inhospitable to the embryo.

To increase the toxicity of the uterine "environment," some devices release progesterone and contain copper. In fact, the IUD's precursor, Ota's ring, initially was sheathed in silver and, later, in plastic material (polyethylene). By the 1960s scientists discovered that adding copper increased its effectiveness, resulting in second-generation devices releasing biologically-active amounts of copper. There are also devices that release progesterone. We currently distinguish two types of devices: medicated (using copper or progesterone) and non-medicated ones (using polyethylene). The Population Council has developed an IUD offering Levonorgestrel graduated-release lasting from five-to-seven years. The device may also be used as so-called "emergency contraception" (EC). It is inserted within five days from presumed fertilization, with an effectiveness rate of 99%.

In this regard, it is important to talk about emergency contraception.[13] It is crucial to understand that the sperm, deposited deeply into the vagina during pre-ovulatory fertile days, reaches the cervical canal within a few seconds and continues traveling to the uterus and fallopian tube in the presence of fertile cervical mucus. There are two ways to prevent pregnancy in this case: block ovulation or else inhibit implantation of an embryo that has reached the uterus. We define EC as the intake of hormones or the application of an IUD to avoid unwanted pregnancies within 72 to 120 hours after unprotected sex, as a remedy to a failed contraceptive method.

---

[11] See S.S.C. Yen, R.B. Jaffe, R.L. Barbieri, *Endocrinologia della riproduzione. Fisiologia, fisiopatologia e aspetti clinici*, Verduci, Rome 2000, p.725.

[12] See L. Speroff, P.D. Darney, *A clinical guide for contraception*, Lippincott-Williams & Wilkins, Philadelphia 2000.

[13] See L. Romano, M.L. Di Pietro, M.P. Faggioni, M. Casini, *RU-486 - Dall'aborto chimico alla contraccezione di emergenza*, ART, Rome 2008.

According to the International Federation of Gynecologists and Obstetricians (FIGO), high doses of Levonorgestrel (LNG) play both these roles. In fact, scientific literature shows that LNG can inhibit ovulation only if taken before the beginning of the most fertile phase of the cycle and not in the pre-ovulatory days.[14] Ovulation after taking LNG presents a lack of progesterone during an inadequate luteal phase. We already know what this causes in the endometrium—an inhospitable environment. Thus, the primary effect of the "Morning-After Pill" is not properly anti-ovulation, but anti-implantation.[15]

Ulipristal acetate is even more misleading. It is the active ingredient of "Ella," and is commonly known as the "Five-day After Pill." Manufacturers present it as being able to delay ovulation through an anti-ovulatory effect. Instead, scientific studies indicate that, within the fertile window, this is only true on those days preceding the LH surge. [16] During the most fertile days, e.g., the peak day, Ulipristal cannot prevent ovulation. Its effectiveness rate at close to 80% is very high. [17] How does it work if it can be taken up to five days following the presumed date of fertilization, even if sexual intercourse may have taken place the day before ovulation, and after the LH surge it can no longer block ovulation? Ulipristal is a selective modulator of progestin receptors. It belongs to the same category as Mifepristone, an active ingredient in RU486. A single dose of Ulipristal alters progestin receptors in the endometrial tissue, rendering it inhospitable. Once again, this is an anti-implantation agent, not a contraceptive.[18]

Our last point concerns a different matter. It does not address anti-ovulation effects. I believe it is noteworthy, considering today's upsurge of infertility. Estro-progestin artificial hormones exert a decisive action on cervical mucus. They change the mucus produced in the cervical glands by increasing its viscosity and reducing its thread-like characteristics, rendering it less penetrable to sperm. The progestin component of the pill stimulates the production of thick mucus obstructing the penetration and survival of sperm,

---

[14] B. Mozzanega, *Da vita a vita*, SEI, Rome 2013, p.200.

[15] See P.J. Yeung, E. Laethem, S.J. Tham, "Argument Against the Use of Levonorgestrel in Cases of Sexual Assault," in *Catholic Health Care Ethics: A Manual for Practitioners*, National Catholic Bioethics Center, Philadelphia 2009, p.143-150.

[16] B. Mozzanega, *Da vita a vita*, p.200.

[17] *Ibid*, p.203.

[18] See J. A. Keenan, "Ulipristal Acetate: Contraceptive or Contragestive?," *The Annals of Pharmacotherapy* 45, no. 6 (June 2011), p.813-815, https://doi.org/10.1345/aph.1Q248; R. P. Miech, "Immunopharmacology of Ulipristal as an Emergency Contraceptive", *International Journal of Women's Health* 3 (November 22 2011), p.391-397, https://doi.org/10.2147/IJWH.S25887.

creating a barrier that reduces the chance of fertilization. Odeblad has demonstrated that the pill causes uterus atrophy of cells in the upper part of the cervix, those producing types S and P mucus. [19] The longer a woman takes the pill, the more significant the damage to the crypts, until they are progressively replaced by type G mucus ones that block the sperm. We will need to study further what determines these changes in the cervical crypts. We can say the primary aggravating factor is time, as the probability of this occurring increases in proportion to the gap between a woman's first intercourse and first childbirth.

3. The moral aspects of a choice

Following this brief excursus, it is evident that we cannot consider contraception as a single topic from a scientific point of view since some products are treated as contraceptives even when they are not. From a moral point of view, we are confronting very different actions. In fact, the illicitness of contraception itself lies in a perversion of the sexual act that intrinsically has two meanings: unitive and procreative. When using anti-implantation products, the moral consideration includes their abortifacient effects, which, as we have already seen, are directly intended and do not occur as "side effects." This abortifacient action thus takes on a more severe connotation, as it is anti-life. Let me say in no uncertain terms that we are talking about abortive effects here: if conception were to occur, these substances might end a pregnancy.

It is interesting to note that contraception is presented as a symbol of freedom of choice, whereas most women do not even know what they are doing when they choose not to get pregnant. What do gynecologists fear? Perhaps, with increased awareness, many patients might take a step back, deterred by the knowledge that their "sexual freedom" may cause the loss of human life. If gynecologists are so sure of the advantages of avoiding pregnancy, which perhaps is unwanted, and if they claim that before implantation there is no real pregnancy, or that a child formed of just 36 cells holds no real importance—then why boycott such information? Why not tell the truth as it is?

As Chesterton said: "That is the one eternal education: to be sure *enough that something is true that you dare* to *tell it to a child.*"[20]

---

[19] P. Castellucci, "Il metodo Billings alla sospensione dei contraccettivi orali," in A Bompiani (ed.), *I metodi naturali...*, p.139.

[20] G.K. Chesterton, Excerpts from "Education: Or the Mistake About the Child," in *What's Wrong with the World?* 1910, http://humanumreview.com/articles/whats-wrong-with-the-school. [accessed September 30, 2017]

GENNARO BRUNO*

MEDICALIZING SEXUALITY

1. The definition and development of sexuality in the history of modern thought

By "sexuality," I mean that set of biological, anatomical, physiological and psychological features which distinguishes and characterizes a person as male or female in society. It is a mutual relationship between the two sexes in every respect, including affectivity, unitive and communicative ability, the potential to plan and realize a life project and a mandate to perpetuate the species.

As numerous studies reveal, "sexuality" is the balance of an interaction between natural and cultural processes that function as "constructors" of a person's delimited sexual identity. Sexual identity is relational and adaptive. Biological difference constructs the "self" enmeshed within relational, cultural and social networks. The psyche (along with its biology, including conscious and unconscious sexual reactions, in addition to genotypic and phenotypic components) and culture (shaped by relationships, education and all that proceeds from them) enter in a wonderfully integrative interaction of all these aspects. "Nature" and "nurture" intersect with each other, inseparable always. Individually extrapolating them from the rest will shatter a person's very identity.

We could call sexuality that remarkable aspect of a human consisting of a "nature" formed by the complex of hormones and genes, by a sexed brain and by prenatal and postnatal exposure that structures behavior. "Nurture" is the socio-environmental and cultural sense in which a person relates to parents and peers. The individual shares his or her positive experiences within an environment where affection, attention, the opportunity to be heard, and role models are present. This setting would include families in which the individual can quickly identify specific roles assumed by men and women, for instance, the particular traits of fatherhood and motherhood. It includes schools that give the student's personality pride of place, and where the stu-

* Assistant Medical Director at S. Giovanni Calibita – Fatebenefratelli (Tiber Island, Rome). Andrologist, sexologist, a permanent deacon of the Diocese of Rome.

dent receives positive educational and scientific attention in essential matters such as sexuality. Where the school handles this in an age-appropriate way, it respects one's sense of modesty and accurate interpretation of the same, as well as educates one to respect both one's own body and those of others. Unfortunately, contrary experiences of sexual violence, pornography, or other possible traumas may also occur as part of the "nurture" that defines sexual identity, including its pathologies.

In this way, nature and nurture, temperament and environment, in mutual and reciprocal interaction, generate or, better put, characterize sexual impulses. In the human being, sex drive is not an automated and irresistible mechanism. It may be modulated, controlled and directed by that capacity proper to a sentient and intelligent being—the ability to offer a rational explanation of reality and the ability to choose, shaped by liberty and will power. Choices can structure and determine behavior.

We must say something about what neurobiological sciences have discovered regarding the human brain. It is a wondrous, mysterious organ displaying an extraordinary plasticity and vulnerability that last a lifetime. It is influenced by a large number of factors, from behavior to repetition and memory, from volition to human conditioning. The brain is affected by chemicals such as drugs, hormones, abusive or superfluous substances, and (metabolic, infectious, etc.) diseases. Thus, when determining sexual identity, neurophysiological elements expressed by cerebral and psychological mechanisms interact—genes, postures, skills, behaviors are "internalized" without awareness as circuits and are triggered and activated by empathy (according to mirror neuron theory). We now better understand how specific behavioral and media manipulation techniques propose role models that, when repeated continuously, can affect the persons exposed to them.

Is there a proper sexual model for humanity, as well as a behavior which ultimately is respectful of nature and truth? During modernity, many theorists and scholars of sexuality have ventured toward a limited and specific definition of this complex and essential aspect of human behavior.

Human sexuality—more specifically, those pathologies related to or associated with it—has long been treated by the scientific-academic community. In 1886 neurologist and psychiatrist Richard von Krafft-Ebing published the work *Psychopathia Sexualis* wherein sexual pathologies were related to psychiatric disorders. In the early 1900s Freud, father of so-called "pan-sexualist theory," published several works in which he examined sexuality in its influence upon specific mental disorders and in all its polymorphous expressions.

Freud's theory regarding the origin of neurosis caused an utterly new and explosive revolution in the scientific community as it represented a profound innovation in ways of thinking about sexuality. In his theory sexuality assumed the characteristics of a determinative and all-conditioning influence upon a person's life from the earliest stages of its development onward.

The Kinsey Reports on male[1] and female[2] sexual behaviors were published in the United States in 1948 and 1953, respectively. With this study on American sexual habits, Kinsey made a statistically documented original claim based on over 17,000 interviews conducted between 1938 and 1956, that reported detailed information (shocking for that time) on the sexual practices of men and women.[3]

Masters and Johnson published *Human Sexual Response*[4] in 1966 and *Human Sexual Inadequacy*[5] in 1970, texts in which they offer an in-depth study of human sexual physiology. Their aim, unlike Kinsey's statistical report, was to consider its subject from a clinical-therapeutic point of view. Tools used during the observation of anatomical and physiological responses (i.e., via masturbation and sexual intercourse) of about 700 volunteers over 11 years, included physiological reaction measuring instruments and photographic and cinematographic equipment to record the anatomical areas involved.

Helen Singer Kaplan, an American psychiatrist, proposed a new vision of sexology in the texts *The New Sex Therapy*[6] (1974) *Disorder of Desires*[7] (1979) and later did work on sex changes[8]. Her contribution consists in introducing a more "scientific-clinical" vision, one more consistent with modern "sexo-

---

[1] A.F. Kinsey, W.D. Pomeroy, C.E. Martin, *Sexual Behavior in the Human Male*, Saunders, Philadelphia 1948.

[2] A.F. Kinsey, W.D. Pomeroy, C.E. Martin, *Sexual Behavior in the Human Female*, Saunders, Philadelphia 1953.

[3] Kinsey's alleged findings (albeit broadly cited at the time and influential in revising American legislation in multiple U.S. states) were already considered suspect by the mid-1950's. They were subsequently "debunked" without any convincing refutation. See J. Reisman, *Stolen Honor, Stolen Innocence: How America was Betrayed by the Lies and Sexual Crimes of a Mad* "Scientist," New Revolution, Orlando 2012.[4]

[4] W.H. Masters, V.E. Johnson, *Human Sexual Response*, Little, Brown, & Co., Boston 1966.

[5] W.H. Masters, V.E. Johnson, *Human Sexual Inadequacy*, Little, Brown, & Co., Boston 1970.

[6] H.S. Kaplan, *The New Sex Therapy*, Brunner-Mazel, New York 1974.

[7] H.S. Kaplan, *Disorders of Desire*, Brunner-Mazel, New York 1979.

[8] H.S. Kaplan, M. Horwith, *The Evaluation of Sexual Disorders: Psychological and Medical Aspects*, Routledge Mental Health, New York 1983; H.S. Kaplan, *The Sexual Desire Disorders*, Taylor & Francis Group, New York 1995.

logical" science. She also presented a set of intervention techniques to treat sexual dysfunction with behavioral and psychoanalytic therapy. Recent studies on sexuality have highlighted how its constituting elements are essential to the formation of personal identity as well as the individual's socialization:

> Human sexuality is not only dictated by instinct or stereotypical behaviors, as it happens in animals, but is influenced on the one hand by the higher mental activities and on the other hand by social, cultural and educational characteristics of the environment in which subjects develop and fulfill their personality. The sexual sphere, therefore, requires an analysis based on the convergence of several lines of development, including emotions, affectivity, and relationships.[9]

Scientific research has not clarified exactly why sexual behaviors are so many and so varied—from the usual "sexual tastes" to rare or abnormal sexual behaviors, perversions and pathologies.

Their variety may owe to the fact that sexual pleasure relates to behaviors that are themselves so variable and specific to each person. That is to say, human sexuality exhibits highly individual dimensions. Research on these questions brings into play the study of human neuro-psychophysiology regarding what generates one specific pleasure perceived as sexual.

Research shows that the capacity and quality of this pleasure does not *depend* on specialized peripheral receptors, nor upon specific components of the Central Nervous System (CNS). The CNS processes and codifies everything in the cerebral cortex, beginning with the individual's entire sensorial and internal experience, as a product of structured thought.

This process explains the essentially psychological aspect of singular variability in sexuality—no one has the same brain, and men's minds differ from women's in their characteristics or manners of processing. Genetics determine the brain's form, yet its structuring and functionality depend upon experience, which varies from person to person. In fact, genetics alone cannot explain a human being. A biological basis influenced by the environment shapes the mind, and sexuality is one "special" dimension of the human mind that differs from subject to subject. This explains the connections between internal images (so-called "erotic imagination") and memories that condition sexual attraction, falling in love, arousal and orgasm.

Everything passes from and through the body as the decisive place of mediation, fruition and processing of sexuality and all emotions. Sexual life emanates from the mind as an extension, internalization and integration of

---

[9] See L. Boccadoro, S. Carulli, *Il posto dell'amore negato. Sessualità e psicopatologie segrete*, Tecnoprint, Ancona 2008.

corporeality. Abstract sexual identity does not exist any more than a body exists as a mere container of the psyche detached from the neurosensory dimension (hearing, smell, taste, touch and sight). The latter is characterized by a continuous progress because it is involved in an ongoing neurochemical "dialogue" with its environment.

Neurophysiological studies may seem to contradict this interpretation by demonstrating a massive involvement of the neural areas processing emotions. Can human sexuality then be defined as an "emotion," a simple processing of thought, and thus of psychological experience and imagination? Still, as with emotions, even sexuality with its many sets of feelings manifests somatically. Compared with all other emotions, human sexual emotion is peculiar in that its most substantial and most tangible somatic manifestation concerns genitalia in the arousal phase. Thus, the *soma*, the human body, returns to the center of debate and scientific speculation and remains at the center of a confluence and passage of human emotions.

Indications for therapy for sexual dysfunctions that are not merely pharmacological but also psychological derive from these studies.[10] Solely organic causes cannot explain sexual dysfunctions. They originate from and relate to an intrapsychic cause that has disturbed the normal function of the system it supports. This cause resides in the peculiar functioning of an individual in his or her own "sexual dimension," as well as his or her cultural, social and affective experiences. Clinical Sexology meets Sexual Medicine in a harmonious dialogue and consultation involving both psychological therapeutic techniques and a reasonable selection of medications helpful for alleviating sexual pathologies ordered toward the patient's well-being.

Another revolution, highly disruptive but with no absolute scientific basis, is the so-called "gender theory." Gender theorists affirm that reality is objectively unknowable and reject a distinction between anything normative or deviant, or between what is physiological and what is pathological. This theory amounts to a revolution that entirely disintegrates the person's structural unity through cultural and linguistic deconstruction, reducing everything to a decision detached from the biological. According to gender theory, sexuality is dependent on personal and subjective preferences and results from various reinterpretations of, and emancipation from, a sexual identity created by cultural and social structures.

---

[10] See A. Imbasciati, "La buona sessualità e le cosiddette disfunzioni sessuali in una prospettiva transgenerazionale. La 'salute sessuale' e le 'cure materne,'" in *Rivista di psicologia clinica online* 1, 2008, p.6-19.

We affirm, without fear of being contradicted by any other than purely ideological arguments, that this theory—which finds such eminent precursors as the philosopher Marcuse among others[11]—states that sexuality does not necessarily have any links to biological identity and may safely ignore it. It is a vision of sexuality modulated according to one's individual, fluid, ever changeable and indefinable desire.

How do we define this type of human being? What is this alienated kind of human being if not one who merely needs to consummate and satiate his preferences? His sexual desires thus respond to a categorical imperative to react to induced incitements for satisfying aesthetic criteria, grafted onto a disrupted, soulless human being.

How could industries or markets—for which an undefined body is dragged along by impetus or uncontrolled impulse—ever fear an animalized human existing for the satisfaction of his or her desires? What ethical question could ever arise for such a divided and atomized being?

For one thing, it is easy to manipulate this human being. In the name of an imaginary liberty (and courtesy of a wild and illusory liberation of senses), she becomes codependent upon anything—a drug, medication, a habit, or the manipulation of her existence by a screen. A screen that makes her feel that she, and others like her, are rejected as useless for being unable to satisfy a desire or right to parenthood in the name of mere wish-fulfillment. The screen demands a right to indulge such alleged needs. Precisely for this reason, science, at first vilified and humiliated (a theoretical construction subordinating it), is then instrumentalized to create responses proportional to these alleged needs. Some examples of this are IVF, embryo selection, wombs for rent by hetero or same-sex couples, and surgical or hormonal treatment of institutionalized transgenderism, etc.

Science is first reduced until rendered useless to ideology, then submitted to manipulative processes, and finally harnessed to the fantasy of an entirely new being. What does the increasing medicalization of this strategy, and its issue for a new mentality, signify? Does the support for such theories—constituting a revolution not merely for the concept of sexuality but also for the idea of "person"—by national governments and international institutions such as the WHO conceal less lofty motives? Are these incentives perhaps linked to financial profits consequent upon implementing these strategies?

---

[11] H. Marcuse, *Eros and Civilization: A Philosophical Inquiry into Freud*, Routledge & Kegan Paul, Ltd, London 1956.

2. Viagra and the medicalization of male sexuality.

Viagra is one of the most striking examples of the medicalization of sexuality. By medicalization, we mean a process of encroachment by a scientific discipline, i.e., medicine, aiming to swamp its boundaries. In this way, it no longer defines itself as the "art of healing," or as that process and capacity of organizing the knowledge and practices needed to manage and cure an individual's maladies. Instead, it is a science overextending its boundaries, constructed by knowledge and practices that since the 1700s have been directed to specific issues (till that time not always thought to be of medical interest) concerning the community, with the aim of establishing the defense and improvement of health on a broader societal scale.[12]

The physical well-being of the population, as well as the improvement of its health, came to be seen as a fundamental duty for political, economic and financial authorities. They not only sought solutions to poverty and marginalization (in themselves acceptable) but often created a social model of organization and problem-solving in which an aloof and technocratic understanding increasingly regulates, generates and exacerbates the satisfaction of artificial needs.

Through a gradual and ongoing pathologization of a typical, temporal and natural physiological event like senescence, Viagra became a forced and induced *need* for an "enhancement of performance" that more and more involves men of every age. In this way, imposed social models propose men as more and more imbued with a therapeutic virility that, in our opinion, derives from a utopian progressivism. Linked to the old and ever-recurring dream of a functionally perfect being, this progressivism creates a pornocratic society.[13] The great dream of perfection needs "chemical" promises and safety, as well as increasingly advanced techniques, to ensure for one's entire life efficient and assured physical performances, based on a male sexual model that finds in the phallus its reason for being.

In 1998, the year of Viagra's release, a vast marketing operation associated with the "Modernization Act" of the U.S. Food and Drug Administration paved the way to direct consumer advertising for pharmaceuticals with prescriptions offered in America. Using contrived language with connotations of an emergency, the operation made its way into the pharmacological and therapeutic quest for a circumscribed and vital need, i.e., a probable genital

---

[12] See M. Foucault, *The Birth of the Clinic: An Archaeology of Medical Perception*, Vintage, New York 1993. Trad. Fr. *Naissance de clinique*, 1963.

[13] See A. Del Noce, *I cattolici e il progressismo*, Leonardo, Milan 1994.

dysfunction. In other words, it "induced" a more general and extended need that involved specific segments of the population, i.e., the male population, to which, until then, the industry had not paid much attention. When elaborating the causes of Erectile Dysfunction (ED), the definition of "impotence" as an existential condition characterized by discomfort and involving psychological and relational problems transformed, thanks to linguistic manipulation, into an aseptic and mechanistic definition of erectile dysfunction as a symptom with only an organic cause generated by a vascular pathology.

Andrology for the Clinician[14] defines ED as an "insufficient penile rigidity" failing to facilitate sexual intercourse. Such absence of rigidity may be complete or partial, or else erection can be lost prematurely. In the case of premature loss of erection, the problem is classified as ED if it occurs before ejaculation. It is possible to assign a rating to the severity of the problem using the International Index of Erectile Function (IIEF).

Therefore, the quality of male erection has become an element to measure the satisfaction of male erection and sexual performance. We now witness a massive expansion of the diagnostic and therapeutic horizon. The potential targets now include not only patients suffering chronic severe diseases (such as diabetes mellitus), complicated hypertension, or prostate cancer (ED is a troublesome side effect for them) but also a vast population of men of all ages, including young men who until now have never presented problems. They all line up for phosphodiesterase type 5 *inhibitors* (*PDE5i*), the category to which Viagra belongs, as they are now dissatisfied with their erectile ability.[15] According to statistics from the Italian Andrology Society, ED "affects" 13% of males between the age of 18 and 70 (about 3 million men) in Italy, and of these only 450,000 currently use medication.[16]

In keeping with official estimates from those monitoring the aging of the Italian population, over the next 20 to 30 years, ED will expand voraciously, afflicting 50% of the male population from ages 40 to 70.[17]

The privileged therapeutic substance to treat this presumed sexual "epidemic" is phosphodiesterase type 5 *inhibitors* (*PDE5i*). In physiological terms,

[14] W-B. Schill, F. H. Comhaire, T.B. Hargreave (eds.), *Andrology for the Clinician*, Springer-Verlag, Berlin Heidelberg 2006.

[15] See M. Loe, *The Rise of Viagra*, New York University Press, New York 2004.

[16] See C. Basile Fasolo, *La comunicazione medico-paziente in sessuologia*, Kurtis, Milan 2004.

[17] See F. Bevere et al., "Criteri di appropriatezza strutturale, tecnologica e clinica nella prevenzione, diagnosi e cura delle patologie andrologiche," in *Quaderni del Ministero della Salute*, 13, 2012.

relaxation of the smooth muscles of the *corpus cavernosum* of the phallus, followed by arterial vasodilatation, causes an erection. The parallel constriction of veins involves capillary blockage, causing an erection. The relaxation of the smooth muscles of the *corpus cavernosum* is a phenomenon mediated by nitric oxide. It activates the guanylate cyclase enzyme, which catalyzes the conversion of guanosine triphosphate (GTP) into cyclic guanosine monophosphate (cGMP), inducing muscular relaxation. Phosphodiesterase degrades cGMP, a catalyst for which we have at least six known isoenzymes. The phosphodiesterase involved in the *corpus cavernos*um is phosphodiesterase type 5 (PDE5).

Sildenafil (Viagra) works by inhibiting the PDE5, causing an increase in blood flow, followed by a rise of cGMP levels and an enhancement in erection. In therapeutic doses, sildenafil does not produce an erection without sexual stimulation or desire. There are other drugs on the market which inhibit PDE5: tadalafil (Cialis), vardenafil (Levitra) and avanafil (Spedra). The first drug in this series of specialized molecules is Viagra, which has enjoyed great success. Pfizer, the firm producing the medication, reports that by 2008 alone Italy was (following England and Germany) in third place among European countries for Viagra usage, with 60 million tablets sold over 10 years, with an average of 4,300 Viagra pills purchased per 1,000 men over 40 years of age.[18]

In 2014 the world witnessed a new boom in the sales of approximately two million packs. This owed to the fact that the multinational's drug patent for Italy had expired. As a result, many other companies started to produce generic competitors.

> Generic companies started synthesizing sildenafil in their labs before the middle of 2013 when Pfizer lost its exclusivity in our country. Now in drugstores, there are 12 alternatives to Viagra having the same active ingredient, and offering consumers a product half the cost of the original brand: €22 instead of €54 for four tablets of 50 mg. Savings are a bit less for those buying packages of 100 mg: €38 instead of €64. Sales are so profitable that this has become a case of great interest. The Italian Medicine Agency has recently revealed that, among the firms that have lost their patent, generics account for only 30% of the market. In general, Italians prefer to spend a few more euros for a brand name product, helping multinational companies to earn over 710 million euros by the end of each year. But when the problem is impotence, everything changes. In fact, last November, a generic variant on Viagra cornered about 70% of the market.[19]

---

[18] See www.pfizer.it/cont/pfizer-italia/pfizer-italia.asp [accessed June 13, 2015.]

[19] See M. Bocci, "Il Viagra riconquista gli italiani: assalto al clone che costa la metà," in *La Repubblica*, January 30, 2015.

Direct consumer advertising of drugs is banned in Italy, as it is in the rest of Europe. Awareness campaigns became the chief marketing method for andrological pathologies. We can recall such propaganda, including "Get help" (*Chiedi aiuto*) in 2012. "Love without worries" (*Amare senza pensieri*) soon followed in 2013, succeeded by yet another called "Enough excuses" (*Basta scusa*) and, finally, "Men and health" *(Uomo e salute*). Incidentally, pharmaceutical company Eli Lilly, producer of Cialis, financed all of them. In recent years the Italian Andrological Association has extensively used these campaigns and received support from major pharmaceutical companies, as well as the Italian Ministry of Health.

Awareness and prevention campaigns, together with an overwhelming amount of information on the web, reveal a structured strategy never seen before—to medicalize male sexual health by using Italian scientists to impart a robust social undertone to the andrological matters in question. It is clear to us that men's health is becoming an area subject to intense tensions and conflicts among professionals. The legitimacy of a profession, i.e., that of urology, demands more attention to the prevention and solution of other medical issues studied in that discipline.[20] This urgency probably arises from the fact that, until that moment, the various medicalization trends in our country had not influenced the field of male sexuality. It is undoubtedly true that Italian men have very little disposition to seek medical attention regarding their sexual health. This likely is due to a neglect of their bodies, as well as ignorance of possible therapeutic solutions available. It is most definitely related to cultural attitudes typical of Latin (Southern European) males. All of this encourages and pushes the medical profession to address them using strategies which, as we have seen, often forces the issue. They present ED as a vascular and purely organic condition resolvable with the use of medications. This pathology is propagated as a grave health problem, which more than 50% of Italian males between the ages of 40 and 70 suffer.

The message of various campaigns becomes less "precise" as ambiguous language is used, such as, "It is not surprising that most men experience erection problems at some point in life." Evidently, the number of potential medication users expands accordingly.

[20] G. VICARELLI (eds.), *La dominanza medica*, Franco Angeli, Milan 2002.

3. International Index of Erection Function (IIEF)

There is a "measurement tool," a self-assessment questionnaire, that increases such open-ended feeling by inquiring about the quality of penetrative intercourse. Five graduated questions produce a benchmark for the culmination of maximum erectile function and the degree of pleasure experienced. And yet they are wrenched out of context in that they fail to consider the importance of the subject's relational ability, his environment and his general health condition. This questionnaire is the IIEF-5 or International Index of Erection Function.

Sexual health measured and standardized in this way refers to the functionality of the male reproductive organ and reduces the male world to a homogeneous conception of efficiency resembling an android. Performance is what matters. Following IIEF-5 parameters, everything regarded as suboptimal performance becomes dysfunctional, and so a measurement is developed that identifies optimal and standard according to functional or dysfunctional parameters.[21] This tool favors that massive medicalization of male sexual health which, from the view of underperformance, urgently calls for a potentially endless pursuit of human enhancement.[22]

When a patient resolves the psychological aspect of this problem by appealing to the functional-organic understanding of ED, he no longer "has bats in the belfry." As a result, he need not feel ashamed of not living up to expectations or fear being a "screwball." It's just a "vascular issue," and so can be treated like any other disease with the use of a single drug! Since the entry of PDE5i into the market, there has been an impressive increase in ED diagnoses. This increase is not due to a numeric growth of the pathology but the effectiveness of media campaigns. This "Quick-Fix Technological Solution"[23] is now available on the market.

Is there an ongoing attempt to change human sexuality, with the help of medications like PDE5i, that encourages a progressive "hyper-enhancement" of performance-erection as an indicator of masculinity? Is this a push beyond the normal standard, when appearance and physical performance become the parameter? Is Viagra truly the new "elixir of the gods" rendering men immortal or omnipotent? Is it an elixir of eternal youth for those deluded enough to seek triumph over the inexorable march of time? Has it become a security

---

[21] See S. Katz, B. Marshall, "Is the Functional 'Normal'? Aging, Sexuality and the Biomarking of Successful Living," in *History of the Human Sciences*, 17, 2004, p.53-75.

[22] See A. Maturo, *La società bionica*, Franco Angeli, Milan 2012.

[23] See M. Loe, *The Rise of Viagra*.

blanket for patients and young consumers with existential uncertainty and without stable points of reference, who are struggling with sexual and relational inexperience mired in performance anxiety?

Who are the real patients that require treatment? We do not exclude *a priori* the goodness of these medications or deny that in many carefully evaluated cases they can improve the health of patients who need them. But we deplore awareness-raising initiatives in the media that tend to broaden and expand diagnostic limitations, thereby shifting the boundaries between normality and pathology and raising the bar of sexual performance. This shift results in the medicalization of the quality of sexual performance, enhancing it indefinitely.

These performance-enhancing drugs have two sides to it. On the one hand, they can be "therapeutic," on the other hand doctors are prone to sidetrack the necessary diagnostic process. Often my colleagues will prescribe the drug while skipping the preliminary and needed diagnosis, saying, "Try this and see what happens, then come back and we'll see." In my opinion, this way of prescribing is often unwarranted. The drug is too often given for "recreational" reasons, thereby raising the standard of sexual performance to an idealized and visionary model of functionality. It induces many consumers to use such drugs in dangerous cocktails with alcohol and other substances, reducing the doctor to a mere prescriber. Viagra and its siblings are considered "magic potions" with aphrodisiac capacity that enhance the consumer's love skills. Apart from young consumers, patients between 50 and 60 years of age ask for them when dating younger partners, impelled by the fear and dread of "failure." When not medically indicated, physicians should categorically refuse to prescribe the drug and encourage the patients to make the sexual relationship "qualitatively" better by working on mutual comprehension.

The fine line between a consumer and a patient—between one who feels he has a right to improve his performance due to the media propaganda of eternal sexual youth, and one who is genuinely and legitimately in need—still needs to be defined. Serious questions remain regarding the management of men conditioned by powerful but unrealistic commercial promises, who nonetheless experience failures due to physiological decline with age.

Personally, I agree with my colleagues that simplification and trivialization of the male sexual universe is a form of "biological reductionism." I believe we should locate the topic of sexual health within the context of a patient's existential experience. He is a human being who relates, has a personal history and, above all, responds to a cultural reference point that began with his family and his education. Sexual pathologies may consist partially, though not exclusively, in organic-functional signs and symptoms. As an internist, the andrologist must study each case carefully to produce a differential diagnosis through clinical signs, lab works and diagnostic imaging to identify the possible causes of the symptoms, which could be related to etiology like diabetes. The physician then has the responsibility to elaborate an appropriate course of treatment, which can include changes in lifestyle, nutrition, a better understanding of his life events, and, if indicated, prescription of a pro-erection medication.

It is paramount to explain to the patient that erectile function consists of a range of possible measurements and is not merely an on-off mechanism. In the physiology of phallic erection, the variations correspond to those found in human sexuality, and we cannot reduce them to mere genitality. Male sexuality is not just erection and ejaculation, power and control over physiological mechanisms. It presupposes a desire that is necessary and fundamental, yet variable and contextualized—the relationship with his partner.

Male and female relational and sexual desire begins in the brain and moves through the senses, from the innermost, wondrous recesses and motions of the soul to the body—across the extraordinary diversity of privileged relationships, perfectly complementary, between males and females. We cannot reduce the desire to physiological impulse or "pure instinct." Man is not the "sex machine" some wish to create.[24] He is not someone with a desire-instinct that requires an enormous technocratic effort to satisfy his longings with anyone anywhere. A relationship should be at the center of desire as a constituent element of human sexuality, formed by an encounter with the Other. It should be an awe-inspiring universe to explore and immerse oneself in, a universe that for the man is a woman, and for the woman is a man.

Where is the woman when discussing issues of male sexuality? When facing discomfort in ED, it is always good to relate this to the couple's health seen from the perspective of a holistic model (except, of course, in single patients with occasional partners).[25]

---

[24] See F. Camoletto et al., "Italians (Should) Do It Better?", in *Modern Italy*, 4, 2012, p.433-448.

[25] E.A. Jannini, A. Lenzi, M. Maggi, *Sessuologia medica*, Masson, Milan 2007.

4. Viagra for woman—The pill of desire

Now and then, we read in the news about the release of a drug that would help women increase their sexual desire. The Italian newspaper *Il Fatto Quotidiano* reported in an article by Stefania Prandi on June 18, 2013, that:

> Following the treatments for pain from penetration and hypoactive sexual disorder, there is now a testosterone-based nasal spray to bring women to orgasm. Liz Canner, the author of an investigative documentary on the pharmaceutical industry, warns that "First, someone will invent a dysfunction, then they will sell the remedy."

"Viagra-mania-for-women" is bursting. After the marketing of Osphena (a drug for the treatment of dyspareunia, or pain during penetration which affects some menopausal women) in the United States, the company "Emotional Brain" announced that it would market a drug called Lybrido in 2016. It will treat hypoactive sexual desire disorder (HSDD), a condition characterized by a sharp drop in sexual desire and fantasies. In recent months a new arrival has been announced: Tefina, a testosterone-based nasal spray that, taken two hours before intercourse, guarantees orgasm.[26]

> Canner, who took nine years to complete her investigation and documentation, explains that after the marketing of Viagra, the search for a female equivalent began. To authorize the development and testing of a new drug, the [U.S.] Food and Drug Administration wanted a precise definition of the disorder. And so, they found the description of "female sexual dysfunction."[27]

And how would female sexual dysfunction be diagnosed? Prandi writes that the tests

> are not very scientific, as there is no objective way to establish the parameters of individual sexuality and the degree of pleasure they feel. Some may have never experienced an orgasm because of a lack of proper stimulation or because of past traumas. Apparently, if they imply that we must have an orgasm every time we have relations, or that when we are 60 years old we must have the same libido we had when we were 20, a lot of us would think that there is something wrong with us and that we need a cure.[28]

Canner emphasizes that according to American statistics, 43% of women suffer from sexual dysfunction. In the U.S. they have invented the "orgasma-

---

[26] See S. PRANDI, "Viagra per le donne, è mania negli USA. Ma il calo del desiderio non diventi malattia," in *Il Fatto Quotidiano*, June 18, 2013.

[27] *Ibid.*

[28] *Ibid.*

tron," a spinal device to cause an orgasm by an external stimulus regulated by remote control. A documentary reports the story of a woman who installed the gadget by means of a painful operation, with the only result being that she experienced uncontrolled shocks in her right leg.

5. Conclusions

As a conclusion to my analysis, I propose what Karol Wojtyla writes regarding sexuality in *Love and Responsibility*:

> Sexology formulates principles and standards that acquire moral force because of the high importance attached to health... [T]he sexual urge [i]s a specific orientation of the whole human being resulting from the division of the species Homo into two sexes. It is directed not toward sex as an attribute of man, but towards a human being of the other sex... The existence of somatic differences and the activity of sex hormones release and direct the sexual urge, which, however, cannot be completely reduced to a combination of anatomical and somatic or physiological factors. The sexual urge is a special force of nature for which those factors are only a basis... Sexology introduces us, in a much more detailed fashion than has been done here, to the complex of somatic and physiological factors conditioning the sensual reactions in which the sexual urge manifests itself in human beings... [These] manifestations of the sexual urge can be converted in the interior of a person into the real ingredients of love.[29]

[29] The first line of this quotation is translated from the Italian version. K. Wojtyla, *Amore e Responsabilità*, Marietti, Genova 1980, p.198. The rest comes from, Id., *Love and Responsibility*, Ignatius Press, San Francisco 1993, p.268.

ALBERTO CAPRIOLO*

TRANSSEXUALISM: NEW BIOETHICAL AND BIO-JURIDICAL QUESTIONS

1. Framing the problem and making distinctions

Psychopathology is the discipline that offers the first conceptualization and definition of transsexualism. David Cauldwell coined the term in 1949,[1] and Harry Benjamin disseminated this description of the transsexual as someone "who feels and wants to be and to act as a member of the opposite sex."[2]

The contextualization of transsexualism within successive editions of the *Diagnostic and Statistical Manual of Mental Disorders* (DSM) is indicative of the evolution of its psychiatric nosography. It classifies transsexualism within the pathological sphere, more precisely as a psychiatric syndrome in the DSM III. In the DSM IV, this condition becomes Gender Identity Disorder, defined as a "strong and persistent identification with the opposite sex, accompanied by persistent discomfort with their sex or with the sexual role of their sex."

The most recent edition (DSM V, 2013) introduces a new diagnostic classification for the purpose of outlining transsexualism as Gender Dysphoria. This latest definition emphasizes the concept of "gender incongruence" rather than "identification with the opposite sex," as well as a simultaneous weakening, at least linguistically, of any connotation of a pathological condition.[3] However, a marked discrepancy remains between the gender one experiences

* Doctoral student in Bioethics, Pontifical Athenaeum Regina Apostolorum, as well as Philosophy of Law Major at Rome's LUMSA University.

[1] D.O. Cauldwell, "Psychopathia Transexualis," in *Sexology*, 16, 1949, p.274-280.

[2] H. Benjamin, *The Transsexual Phenomenon*, Ace Pub. Co, New York, 1966; C. Lorè *Per una ricostruzione dei primi studi sul transessualismo*; P. Martini, *Aspetti e problemi medico-legali del transessualismo*, Milan 1991, p.35 ff.

[3] See the following for significant information on the issues in defining *gender dysphoria*, B. Fabris, S. Bernardi, C. Trombetta, "Cross-sex hormone therapy for gender dysphoria," in *Journal of Endocrinological Investigation*, 38, 2015, p.269-282; J. Marchand, E. Pelladeau, F. Pommier, "From transsexualism to gender dysphoria: conceptual clustering or confusion," in *Evolution Psychiatrique*, 80, 2, 2015, p.331-348; T. Steensma, J. Van der Ende, F. Verhulst, P. Cohen-Kettenis, "Gender variance in childhood and sexual orientation in adulthood: a prospective study," in *J Sex Med*, 10, 2013, p.2723.

and a "gender assigned" at birth; or, better put, a discrepancy between gender identity and biological sex.[4] It is important to note that Italy's National Health System uses another classification system. The ICD (International Classification of Diseases) classifies transsexualism as a gender identity disorder.[5] To be more precise, we must distinguish transsexualism from the intersex states and transvestism or cross-dressing. "Intersex" refers to a multiplicity of clinical conditions characterized by the dissonant development of specific components of one's biological sex (genetic, gonadal, genital).[6] A person seeking a "transitional path," however, need not present chromosomal abnormalities, endocrine deficiency, or signs of hermaphroditism. Comparatively, transvestism as a disorder falls within the paraphilia category. Unlike transsexualism, transvestism is a lewd behavior which involves dressing (episodically or over extended periods of time) in the clothing of the other sex, albeit without identifying with the latter.[7]

Still, it is more problematic to demarcate a dividing line between "transsexualism" and "transgenderism." The word "transgender" introduced in the social sciences refers to one who, though living a gender identity at odds with his or her biological sex, may still not wish to submit to treatments or interventions to amend primary or secondary sexual characteristics.[8] Instead, this

---

[4] See A.A. LAWRENCE, "Gender Assignment Dysphoria in the DSM-5," in *Archives of Sexual Behavior*, 43, 2014, p.1263. He observes, "the DSM-5 conceptualization of GD as reflecting an incongruence between gender identity and 'assigned gender' necessarily renders the new diagnostic criteria semantically incorrect as written, because it is biologic sex, not gender, that is recognized—and is 'assigned' only in accordance with that recognition—at birth."

[5] Paragraph F64.0 defines transsexualism as the "desire to live and be accepted as a member of the opposite sex, usually accompanied by a sense of discomfort with, or inappropriateness of, one's anatomic sex, and a wish to have surgery and hormonal treatment to make one's body as congruent as possible with one's preferred sex."

[6] I.A. HUGHES, "Disorders of sex development: a new definition and classification," in *Best Pract. Res. Clin. Endocrinol. Metab.*, 22, 2008, p.119-134; B. DALLAPICCOLA, "Genetica della determinazione sessuale," in *I Quaderni di Scienza e Vita*, 2, 2007, p.11-13; M.L. DI PIETRO, "Aspetti clinici, bioetici e medico-legali della gestione delle ambiguità sessuali," in *Medicina e morale*, 50, 2000, p.51-83.

[7] A. CERETTI, I. MERZAGORA, "L'istinto sessuale e le sue alterazioni," in *Trattato di medicina legale e scienze affini*, 4, Padua 2009, p.349.

[8] See F. GARGIULO, E. ORLANDO, R. ROMEO, "Transgenderismo come luogo del postmoderno," in P. VALERIO, R. VITELLI, P. FAZZARI (eds.), *Figure dell'identità di genere*, Rome 2013, p.190 ff.; Y. TAYLOR, S. HINES, M. CASEY, *Theorizing Intersectionality and Sexuality* (Genders and Sexualities in the Social Sciences), Palgrave Macmillan, Hampshire UK, 2010. About the philosophical foundations of transgenderism, even if from conflicting views, see

person claims to channel a feeling of *man* or *woman* that transcends anatomical structure via behavior and personal relationships. The term, in a broader sense, also refers to a condition marked by the fluidity of gender identity, an identity which might not readily correspond to either masculine or feminine genders.[9]

2. Misunderstanding "gender reassignment"

In recent years the question of transsexuality has been pervaded by an insistent demand—made to medical science and to legislative bodies alike—to shrink from any medical or therapeutic approach to this condition. As we will see further on, the transition process from the operative phase is already an option in many places. However, given the exercise of that choice, where legalized, there remains recourse to a modification of primary sexual characteristics with the aim of a best possible match between *soma* and *psyche*.

For this reason, despite new avenues made possible by transitioning, it does not seem inappropriate to examine the question of interventions altering the phenotypic sex in light of clinical ethics. Coordinates of reference for this brief survey include contributions made by personalist bioethicists in recent years.

First, a surgical correctional intervention does not assign masculinity (when female) nor femininity (when male) to those who seek it. Sexuality is an original dimension: the person who has undergone treatment will present the opposite sex merely phenotypically, offering only a semblance of the same, but is unable to ground a new sexual identity. There remains, on the one hand, a discrepancy between an "original" status (which is unavoidable) and on the other, a surgically constructed acquired identity. The first is not interchangeable with the second.

Accordingly, the phrase "gender reassignment" is inadequate. It is more appropriate to refer to this as "surgical and registry modification." We must now consider whether and under what circumstances this practice respects the therapeutic principle of the totality of health and the person.

J. Butler, *Undoing Gender*, Routledge, New York and London 2004, p.72 ff.; L. Palazzani, *Gender in Philosophy and Law*, Springer, Dordrecht 2012, p.84 ff.

9 P. Currah, "Gender Pluralisms under the Transgender Umbrella," in P. Currah, R.M. Juang, S. Price Minter (eds.), *Transgender Rights*, University of Minnesota Press, Minneapolis 2006, p.3-31.

Correct application of therapeutic interventions requires meeting some criteria.[10] First, a therapeutic intervention should aim at the good of the entire body and only eliminate the diseased part as a last resort when there are no other alternatives. In the case of transsexualism, the surgical operation is done on a physically healthy part, as the sexual organs of the subject in question are intact and not affected by diseases or abnormalities. It is, therefore, a mutilation and invalidating a body out of desires and purposes alien to it.[11] It introduces a new imbalance between chromosomal-gonadal elements and the exterior organs. Deprivation of copulative and procreative functions follow. For this reason, instead of offering a therapeutic value, this operation reveals a manipulative nature, not justifiable by the principle of totality.[12] The debate within the personalist bioethics community tends to conclude that psychiatric treatment is the most (clinically) appropriate as well as the most (ethically) opportune approach to reestablish the subject's psycho-physical harmony.[13]

Some scholars debate the admissibility of surgery, designating it in some instances as "palliative" in limited situations.[14] They permit the recourse to phenotypic correction as a palliative cure when the following risk factors are present:

[10] For more information: F. D'Agostino, L. Palazzani, *Bioetica: nozioni fondamentali*, La scuola, Brescia 2013; A. Sergio, *La libertà responsabile della ricerca*, Aracne, Rome 2010, p.30-32; M. Cozzoli, "La legge naturale a difesa della vita. Le ragioni e i limiti della difesa della vita fisica," in *La cultura della vita: fondamenti e dimensioni. Atti della Settima Assemblea Generale della Pontificia Accademia per la Vita*, Vatican City 2002, p.179-206.

[11] See E. Sgreccia, *Manuale di bioetica: aspetti Medico-Sociali*, Vita e Pensiero, Milan 2007, p.132 ff.

[12] M.L. Di Pietro, "L'educazione della sessualità e la procreazione responsabile," in E. Sgreccia, A. Spagnolo, M.L. Di Pietro (eds.), *Bioetica: manuale per i diplomi universitari della sanità*, Vita e Pensiero, Milan 2002, p.321; N. Tonti-Filippini, "Sex Reassignment and Catholic Schools," in *The National Catholic Bioethics Quarterly*, 12, 2012, p.85-90; E. Sgreccia, *Manuale di bioetica*, p.133; F. D'Agostino, *Sessualità. Premesse teoriche di una riflessione giuridica*, G. Giappichelli Editore, Turin 2014, p.154.

[13] S. Cipressa, *Transessualità: tra natura e cultura*, Citadella, Assisi 2010, p.61-63; M. P. Faggioni, "I disturbi della sfera sessuale", in E. Larghero, G. Zeppegno (eds.), *Dalla parte della vita. Itinerari di bioetica*, Vol.II, Effatta Editrice, Turin 2008, p.386; M. De Rosa, "Terapia medica del transessualismo maschio-femmina", in E.A. Jannini, A. Lenzi, M. Maggi (eds.), *Sessuologia medica*, Elsevier Masson, Milan 2007, p.94 ff.; E. Sgreccia, *Manuale di bioetica*, p.126 ff.

[14] See M.P. Faggioni, *I disturbi della sfera sessuale*, p.387-394; G. Russo, "Transessualismo", in *Enciclopedia di Bioetica e Sessuologia*, Elledici, Rome 2004, p.1708; S. Cipressa, "Transessualità", in S. Leone, S. Privitera (eds.), *Nuovo dizionario di bioetica*, Città nuova, Rome 2004, p.1186-1187; G. Russo, T. Forzano, "Problemi di bioetica sessuale", in G. Russo (eds.), *Bioetica della sessualità, della vita nascente e pediatrica*, Elledici, Turin 1999, p.203.

a) risk of severe and permanent impairment of mental equilibrium of the subject, due to the discomfort of belonging to the opposite sex to that of the perceived gender;
b) state of anguish enough to seriously undermine the subject's very survival;
c) the absence of valid and appropriate alternatives (e.g., psychiatric help and medication) to prevent or mitigate the behaviors deriving from this situation (e.g., suicide).

While we understand the delicate nature (and, at the same time, the drama) of these situations, there is still insufficient information to make a precise evaluation. We do not have clear indicators to decide what constitutes extreme circumstances, nor do we have a sufficient number of cases to evaluate. We will need them to delineate a hypothesis of admissibility for corrective surgery. Although it is easy to understand the nature and purposes of palliative cure, we cannot call this type of approach "therapy" in the genuine sense of the word, since they conflict with the therapeutic criteria indicated above.

3. Rectifying Registry without Surgery

We are witnessing locally and internationally an ongoing petition to allow modifying one's civil registry even without a "sex reassignment" operation. Most recently, these applications are receiving particular attention in the legislature, even when a full implementation has failed in several significant cases.

The success of *kleine Lösung* and *grosse Lösung* in the German legislation has progressively enriched an international framework with disciplinary measures to regulate the phenomenon.[15] The UK 2004 Gender Recognition Act is especially significant.[16] This provision allows people to alter their civil registries without the need for primary or secondary sex treatment, requiring merely a medical certificate stating the existence of a gender dysphoria. The Spanish law 3/2007, "Reguladora de la rectificatión registral de la mención relativa al sexo de las personas [Regulator of the registry rectification of the mention regarding the person's sex]" confers great importance on the "gender identity felt by the applicant or his psychosocial sex" (art. 4) and expressly excludes the need for surgery (Article. 4.2).[17]

[15] https://www.gendertreff.de/2013/09/10/kleine-losung-grose-losung/.
[16] http://www.legislation.gov.uk/ukpga/2004/7/contents.
[17] https://www.boe.es/buscar/pdf/2007/BOE-A-2007-5585-consolidado.pdf.

A more liberal approach marks the Argentine Statute 26,743 of 2012 on "derecho a la identidad de género de las personas [the right of gender identity of the persons]." It establishes the principle for everyone to be treated juridically in consonance with one's gender identity (art. 1). Presence or absence of prior genital reassignment surgery or medical evaluation does not condition the rectification of civil registry (art. 4).[18]

Two critical resolutions are emblematic of the legislative and political lines pursued by the EU. With n. 1728 of 29 April 2010, the Parliamentary Assembly of the Council of Europe exhorted the Member States to introduce new and appropriate regulations on procedures for alterations in civil registries due to sex changes, regulations that eliminate surgery as a necessary condition.[19] The European Parliament resolution on 12 March 2015, "Annual Report on Human Rights and Democracy in the World 2013," and the European Union policy are remarkable in that they ban "sterilisation as a requirement for legal gender recognition" (para. 164).[20] They allege an incompatibility of such medical treatments with the principle of self-determination. The European Parliament frames the requirement of surgery as a violation of human rights. More specifically, it is the "right to bodily integrity and of sexual and reproductive health and rights" (para. 164).

The latest trends in the law are similar. Of particular relevance is *ECHR, Y.Y. v. Turquie, 03.10.2015*.[21] The European Court regards as unacceptable the requirement of an applicant's prior sterilization as a condition for altering the civil registry. Explicitly, it considers illegitimate the provision of art. 40 of the Turkish Civil Code, which makes the inability to procreate a condition for authorizing sex change. The EU Court bases its decision on a violation of "personal freedom to choose one's gender" as guaranteed by a juridical principle of self-determination (para. 102: *la Cour observe que la procédure qui s'est déroulée devant les juridictions nationales mettait directement en jeu la liberté pour le requérant de définir son appartenance sexuelle, liberté qui s'analyse comme l'un des éléments les plus essentiels du droit à l'autodétermination*).

---

[18] http://www.ilo.org/dyn/natlex/docs/ELECTRONIC/90297/104004/F23938899/ARG90297.pdf.

[19] http://assembly.coe.int/nw/xml/XRef/Xref-XML2HTML-EN.asp?fileid=17853&lang=en.

[20] http://www.europarl.europa.eu/sides/getDoc.do?pubRef=-//EP//TEXT+TA+P8-TA-2015-0076+0+DOC+XML+V0//EN.

[21] J. Dute, European Court of Human Rights, ECHR 2015/14 Case of YY v. Turkey, 10 March 2015, no. 14793/08 (Former Second Section), Eur J Health Law, 2015 Jun;3)22):-297 300.

The current position of Italian courts regarding this matter is also significant. The most recent tribunals' decision concerning the rectification of civil registries to reflect a sex change is interesting both for the discontinuity with traditional juridical precedent and for its hermeneutical approach to interpret the wording of Statute No. 164/1982.[22]

Similar to other international experiences, one policy approach in Italy opposes the requirement of destructive-reconstructive intervention. It conserves the legality of a diverse but coexisting juridical, sexual and gender identity. There is a renegotiation of boundaries between the biological dimension and social construction.[23] In this way, the natural-organic dimension increasingly becomes disengaged from personal identity, and the focus centers on that which is purely volitional.[24]

As a result, the "right" to gender identity is devoid of any sexual connotation (i.e., denial that sexual characterization is constitutive of identity). This right presumes to transcend gender, reject conformity and will likely mutate several times over (in accord with the premise that gender is a continuum).[25] From here a novel self-determination paradigm develops. The primacy of choice unhinged from any relational or factual conditioning replaces the non-judgmental approach of the law (not to mention moral reflection). This paradigm merely involves acknowledgment and ratification of any option the subject chooses to embrace.[26]

---

[22] http://www.esteri.it/mae/doc/l164_1982.pdf.

[23] Court of Messina, sect. I, on Nov. 4, 2014: "In the present case the right to sexual identity is fully recognized and extended not only to those who, deeply feeling that they belong to the other gender, have modified their primary sexual characteristics, but also to those who without changing the primary sexual characteristics have built a different gender identity."

[24] Court of Trento, sect. I, on Aug. 19, 2014: "The interpretation of Article.1, first paragraph, of the law 14 April 1982 n. 164, requires that sexual rectification is to be excluded in the absence of the modification of primary sexual characteristics of the person; however, the right to choose one's sexual identity is subordinate to the modification of one's primary sexual characteristics and so, in irreparably jeopardizing the exercise of the right, has thus set itself at odds with the constitutional and conventional protection of a right to gender identity."

[25] Court of Trento, sect. I, on Aug. 19, 2014: "the fundamental fact is no longer the biological sex, but the gender that can be defined as a 'sociocultural variable' ... Gender may differ from biological sex, as well as mutate into various forms and directions over time." Along the same lines, see the Court of Rovereto, sect. I, May 2, 2013.

[26] On the juridical principle of self-determination and the right to gender identity, see, *among other things*, M. Cartabia, "Riflessioni in tema di eguaglianza e di non discriminazione," in M. D'Amico, B. Randazzo (eds.), *Alle frontiere del diritto costituzionale. Scritti in onore di Valerio Onida*, Giuffrè, Milan 2011, p.437; M. Ronco, "La tutela penale della

4. The issue of de-pathologization

Gender studies gradually validate, especially in the social sciences, a sexual identity status that transcends the masculine and feminine categories. This validation de-naturalizes the sexual binary while demanding the *naturalization* (and normalization) of the plurality and indefinability of gender experiences. The current debate on the de-pathologization of transsexualism derives from these theoretical premises. It is controversial not only from the standpoint of clinical ethics but also for its implications for politics and health. The latest version of *Standards of Care* from the World Professional Association for Transgender Health lends major support to the movement to declassify transsexualism from the list of psychopathological conditions. The document states that "the expression of gender characteristics, including identities that are not stereotypically associated with one's assigned sex at birth, is a common and culturally diverse human phenomenon [that] should not be judged as inherently pathological or negative."[27]

According to another thesis, the experience of gender dysphoria is not within the subjects themselves. Instead, they are victims of "minority stress"—difficult and prohibitive social adaptation is the cause of their psychopathological problems. In other words, it is not endogenous components but perceived social stigma that causes discomfort/disorder and subsequent need for medical care.[28]

This thesis, from a perspective detached from analysis and clinical evidence, affirms that the non-alignment of that identity with the "natural male-female binarism that characterizes the biomedical view" would have determined the pathological classification of the *trans* condition.[29] Even then, it is a

persona e le ricadute giuridiche dell'ideologia del genere," in F. D'Agostino (ed.), *Identità sessuale e identità di genere*, Giuffrè, Milan 2012, p.65 ff.

[27] http://www.wpath.org/site_page.cfm?pk_association_webpage_menu=1351.

[28] See H. Meyer, "Prejudice, social stress, and mental health in lesbian, gay, and bisexual populations: conceptual issues and research evidence," in *Psychological Bulletin*, 129, 5, 2003, p.674 ff.; V. Lingiardi, *Citizen Gay. Famiglie, diritti negati e salute mentale*, il Saggiatore, Milan 2007, p.74 ff.; A. Schillaci, "Dignità umana, comparazione e transizioni di genere. La lezione della Corte suprema dell'India," in *GENIUS*, 2, 2014, p.179.

[29] B. Busi, "Oltre la transizione, verso un modello polimorfico del genere," in C. Ballarin (ed.), *Esquimesi in Amazzonia: dialoghi intorno alla depatologizzazione della transessualità*, Mimesis, Milan 2013, p.25. Similmente, E. Arfini, *Scrivere il sesso: retoriche e narrative della transessualità*, Meltemi, Rome 2007, p.26 ff.; B. Preciado, *Manifesto contra-sessuale*, Il Dito e la Luna, Milan 2002, p.97-98.

thesis that defends the emancipation of transsexual and transgender persons from any psychopathological reference.

One objection comes precisely from movements that protect the rights of transgender persons.[30] In fact, deleting transgenderism from the list of disorders has reverberations in health policy. If a specific condition is no longer pathological, it is can no longer make demands or have free access to the national health services. In that case, health care will no longer cover psycho-diagnostic interventions, including surgical, endocrinological and pharmaceutical ones. As the condition is based on personal choice and no longer related to the subject's health, the burden of health cost will fall upon the applicant.

There are proposals to circumvent this difficulty in safeguarding access to free treatment, for example, by reframing the discussion with terms like *de-psychiatrization* instead of de-pathologization.[31] However, despite erasing the reference to pathology, transsexual and transgender persons continue to seek medical and pharmacological services not only during the transition period but also in the initial and successive phases. On the assumption that de-pathologization does not imply loss of health benefits, there is another proposal to "synthesize welfare policies that guarantee health rights to trans people, while stripping the label of illness from a dimension, such as that of trans, that must be socially and culturally seen as one of the variations of gender identity."[32]

Such policies of de-pathologization followed by procedural changes are logically inconsistent. First, there is methodological inconsistency. It transposes the categories of "pathology" and "care" from the clinical ambit to socio-cultural and biopolitical ones. When it encroaches on the medical field, this approach uses instruments that are alien to medicine. Second, regarding its goal, it does not seem that the de-pathologization model has developed strategies to protect the health of the transgender persons. Where such policies try to engineer a primacy of culture over nature, they seem more interested in ideological propaganda—for the full exercise of one's choice over biological ties—than real individuals' needs.

Pressure in favor of de-pathologization has come not only from associations or occasional scientific output but also from political and legislative bodies. The European Parliament's resolution of September 28, 2011, on *Hu-*

---

[30] See A. Lorenzetti, *Diritti in transito. La condizione giuridica delle persone transessuali*, FrancoAngeli, Milan 2013, p.80.

[31] In particular M.G. Toniollo, "Chi ha paura della depatologizzazione?", in C. Ballarin, *Esquimesi*, p.73-74.

[32] C. D'Ippoliti, A. Schuster, *DisOrientamenti. Discriminazione ed esclusione sociale delle persone LGBT in Italia*, Armando Editore, Rome 2011, p.29.

man rights, sexual orientation, and gender identity within the context of the United Nations, states in Section I, para. 13 that it:

Roundly condemns the fact that homosexuality, bisexuality, and transsexuality are still regarded as mental illnesses by some countries, including within the EU, and calls on states to combat this; calls in particular for the depsychiatrisation of the transsexual, transgender, journey, for free choice of care providers, for changing identity to be simplified, and for costs to be met by social security schemes.[33]

Finally, para. 16 of the same resolution "calls on the Commission and the World Health Organization to withdraw gender identity disorders from the list of mental and behavioral disorders, and to guarantee a non-pathological reclassification in the negotiations of the 11th version of the International Classification of Diseases (ICD-11)."

The aforementioned European Parliament Resolution of March 12, 2015 "calls on the Commission and the WHO to withdraw gender identity disorders from the list of mental and behavioral disorders; calls on the Commission to reinforce its efforts to end the pathologisation of trans identities; encourages states to ensure quick, accessible and transparent gender recognition procedures that respect the right to self-determination." (para. 163)

These measures are troubling. There seems to be a replay of the strategy that led the American Psychiatric Association at WHO's urging to remove same-sex attraction (SSA) from a list of mental disorders in 1974. The association adopted this indication in DSM III. Because of this, we must repeat—with no prejudice to legislative prerogatives—the inappropriateness of political bodies seeking to guide the nosology and classifications of psychosexuality.[34]

In fact, these areas belong, by their nature, to the competence of medical expertise. The tactic of politically engineering, more or less explicitly, a revision of diagnostic criteria and categories is an unwarranted interference that inevitably compromises the autonomy of the scientific community.

---

[33] http://www.europarl.europa.eu/sides/getDoc.do?pubRef=-//EP//TEXT+TA+P7-TA-2011- 0427+0+DOC+XML+V0//EN.

[34] P. Frati, E. Marinelli, S. Zaami, "Innovazioni legislative in tema di rettificazione di attribuzione di sesso", in *Rivista italiana di Medicina Legale*, 2, 2012, p.841-844.

AN INTERVIEW WITH MASSIMO GANDOLFINI*

Sexual identity is a fact of the human condition that was considered beyond debate until recently. When did the process of its deconstruction begin?

The biological and psychical structure of man, the development of the male and female personalities, and the subsequent relational, personal and social lives are closely linked and continuously interdependent throughout the entire life of every human being. Until the 1950's-60's, when "gender theory" began to emerge, sexual identity as a biological and anthropological given that characterizes every human being from the hominid onwards as male or female was a commonly accepted fact.

Momentarily setting aside the religious idea of creation, we affirm that biological evolution itself has shaped us this way, making us suitable for the inter-human and intersexual relationships that ensure the preservation of the species. The concept of the male and female sexes outlines a clear and straightforward idea of sexual identity. Each sex contains specific and unique differences whose integration perpetuates humanity. There are differences, in fact, but not diversity. Just as "sex" has its etymological root in the Latin verb *secare* (to differentiate, separate), "difference" finds its semantic and cultural root in the Latin verb *fero*, (to carry, bear). For this reason, it is correct to state that men and women "carry" specific characteristics that, taken individually, do not describe humanity as a whole but do when supplementing and completing each other.

In the late 1950s, Alfred Kinsey, Harry Benjamin and John Money—to mention only the most notorious "forefathers"—initiated a cultural process of "deconstruction" of the human being. They sought to reduce the biological sexual structures of the human person to insignificance and irrelevance, converting male and female to merely cultural phenomena. They reinterpreted biological corporeity as a sort of neutral structure, modeled and moldable by cultural conditioning and by self-determined free choice. Biological features, from this standpoint, have no say about one's gender, and sexual orientation

---

* Adjunct professor in neurosurgery. President of the Catholic Medical Association of Lombardia and National Vice-President of the "Scienza & Vita" Association.

is chosen instead by the individual. Culture vs. Nature: two-nil. Michel Foucault, one of the poststructuralist philosophers who most contributed to the concept of "no identity" or identity "without essence," effectively describes this new face of humanity. "Man's identity is like sand which the sea's waves rhythmically erase, like shifting figures entrusted from time to time to actualizing the decisions that history periodically lumps together and imposes as a wavering model of the human being." Not even the body possesses an essence but is constructed by culture.

But is this true? Or are we merely playing a dangerous game, the result of creative theories of denial with no scientific basis, aiming to "construct and deconstruct, do and undo the human being," as Judith Butler would say, "shaped by the performativity of action and being"?

On the contrary, science—genetics, biology, medicine, psychology and neuroscience—has a lot to say. Male and female sexuality is neither a choice nor a cultural product. Rather, it is structurally imprinted upon every cell of our body. The sex chromosomes, XX for female and XY for male, with their related hormone production (estrogen and androgen), are the genetic substances that regulate and develop all of our corporeity. Primary sexual characteristics, the gonads and genitals, and secondary sexual characteristics—the skeleton, muscles, breasts, subcutaneous fat, skin tissue, and hair—are structured and shaped by the sex chromosomes. The Y chromosome is the determinant of male biological sexual development; its presence affects masculinization while its absence causes feminization.

Primordial gonads are bi-potent up to the seventh week of gestation, at which time the presence of Y determines the development of the male gonads, while its absence allows the development of female sex organs (ovaries, fallopian tubes, uterus, etc.). In recent decades, owing to extraordinary growth in the field of neuroscience (a complex discipline that brings together neurology and classical neurophysiology, studies somatic functioning and explores the cognitive and symbolic workings that characterize the mind and the construction of thought), we are acquiring an understanding, based on pure empirical evidence, of the differences between the feminine and masculine personalities. We can now objectively define and describe the sexual dimorphism that involves the entire body, including the brain. Today we can speak of "brain sex," meaning that the female and male brains have different anatomical and functional specificities. Functional neuroimaging techniques allow us to "read" and "photograph" those areas of the brain involved in the execution of certain tasks or the performance of given functions, including complex symbolic functions such as language, emotions and feelings. They indicate that male and female brains have specificities that explain differences in personality (this is called "mind theory"). To the best of our knowledge, there are eight anatomical and functional regions of the brain that present sexed characteristics, almost all connected with complex tasks of the cognitive-emotional life. The amygdala, hippocampus, anterior cingulate cortex and prefrontal cortex, hypothalamus-pituitary axis and insula are parts of the "limbic system," a region involved in the structuring of memory, emotions, impulsive behavior, general cognition and empathic relations.

Isn't it true that all these functions plot our personality and significantly model our choices, conduct and daily behavior?

As a matter of fact, since the 1930's, studies in behavioral psychology portrayed masculine and feminine personalities as characterized by different ways of functioning. Concerning thought, for example, they described a "linear" mode in men and a "circular" one in women. Linear thinking means preferring to deal with one concrete or abstract task at a time. On the contrary, circular thinking is the simultaneous management of multiple tasks or functions. Today—thanks to the information presented above—we know the anatomical and functional interpretative bases that mediate these differences in behavior. The "female" brain is characterized by a lower hemispheric specialization (i.e., less anatomical and functional asymmetry between the two hemispheres of the brain), while the "male" brain has a marked asymmetry in favor of the dominant hemisphere (usually the left), along with a rigid lateralization. It entails, in the male, a strict dominance of the left hemisphere regarding language, for example, and of the right hemisphere regarding the visual-spatial functions. For the female, dominance of the left hemisphere is possible, but there would usually be functions in both hemispheres. With a touch of irony and drawing from computer language, some have distinguished women from men by their ability to "multitask."

Can we talk about "gender medicine"? What is it?

A precise and rigorous biological dimorphism is right at the base of what we call "gender medicine." Its existence and interpretation lie in the biological difference characterizing sexuality. Births are one example of this. More males are born than females (120/100), including both those born at term

(110/100) and those born alive (106/100). The opposite happens at the other end of the spectrum, death. The life expectancy for women is about 84.5 years, for men 80.1. Now even drug-genomics (the study of the interaction between genetic and individual drug treatments) suggests a gender difference. Take the case of levodopa, the drug used to treat Parkinson's. Given in equal doses, the unwanted side effects (dyskinesia and "on-off" phenomenon) are more frequent and appear earlier in men than in women.

Other aspects of great importance that neuroscience is interpreting and following with particular interest are the cognitive functions and, in particular, the study of the processes of psychical structuring, personal identity and the human personality during childhood (0 to 6 years). According to Gordon Alports, "personality is the dynamic organization within the individual of those psychophysical systems that determine his unique adjustments to his environment." From this definition, we can see the harmonious participation of several aspects and functions in the formation of one's personality, from relationships to co-parenting, from inter-corporeity to mental representation, and from haptonomy to identification.

How does all of this affect a child's development?

Relationships are the starting point. The human being, as a mammal, establishes a close inter-corporeal connection with the mother's body, which is not an inert and indifferent "container" for developing life, like an oven used to bake a cake. Rather, the maternal-fetal relationship is biologically active and integrated in such a way that some authors speak of a continuous and enriching "conversation" between mother and child. This dialogue consists of a complex exchange of fluids (mostly, but not only blood), proteins, cells, electrically charged ions, magnetic fields and neurotransmitters in a "Promethean" effort of mutual help and getting to know one another. Such an intricate and vibrant weave influences the very first structure of the child's psyche and, reciprocally, the mother's personality. Each one changes and somehow affects the other.

Another relationship of great importance is referred to as "inter-subjectivity" or "inter-corporeity," that is, the close acquaintance established between the child's and the parents' bodies. The bodies of the mother and father mediate the psychic world of personal identity that molds the child and which she grasps. Conversely, the child's physicality stimulates the mental structuring of the parents *qua* parents. Closely related to this process is inter-corporeity, which is the continuous and reciprocal interactions (present from the first days of the child's life) through which humans come to know themselves. It is the first step towards understanding another person's mind, which is the real "Rubicon" separating humans from all other living beings. We all know the child's cognitive abilities cannot develop from hypothetical mental categories, but require direct and concrete sensorial perception, mediated by the parents' bodies.

Knowing the mother's body—which conveys the female personality—and the father's body—which expresses the male personality—the child learns to identify herself somatically and, at the same time, structures her psyche and character. This structuring process has two channels: one of identifying with the parent of the same sex, the other of differing from the parent of the opposite sex. The instrument used unconsciously is the haptonomic ability (from the Greek *hapsis*, meaning "touch"), a form of proto-cognition (some authors speak of "proto-mimesis") occurring through touch. In early childhood the child is a haptonomic being *par excellence*: he needs to touch, smell, lick or eat the object of his attention to know it. The parents' affection for their child, expressed in words, actions, sounds, attitudes and facial expressions that necessarily vary between mother and father, is grasped by the child through body reading. In this way, he gradually becomes aware of the personality differences (and thus roles) of his mother and father.

Can we say then that corporeity gives the child a "mental representation" of his parents?

Inter-corporeity and inter-subjectivity are like wax seals impressing themselves upon the child's psyche, leaving an almost indelible mark we call mental representation, a fundamental concept in the history of psychoanalysis (e.g., Freud, Sandler and Rosenblatt). This stamp is the result of the child's concrete and objective experience, especially from birth to age three, and it will accompany him for the rest of his life as an original and indelible imprint. It involves two separate concepts: a stable and internal mental organization, and personal experience (real facts and unconscious fantasies). The further development of cognitive abilities, intellectual and cultural tasks and maturity can influence and even modify this imprint, but it is almost never entirely erased. For example, the mental representation of the concept "dog" comes from a concrete experience of a real "dog" from the early years of one's life. Someone who has had a negative experience—who has been attacked by a dog, for instance—forms a mental representation of "dog" as a dangerous animal that it is best to avoid. As she grows older, she may learn (through cognitive action) that things are not as they appear and may form a different idea of "dog." But the original mental representation remains. Therefore, when she spots a dog in the distance, her first reaction will be to avoid it. In conclusion, it should be quite clear that the internal psychodynamic organization (or "personality") is structured—not entirely, but significantly—during the early life of the child based on her inter-corporeal and inter-subjective experiences. For this reason, the environment within which the child grows during the first years of life is anything but irrelevant and neutral. It can influence, even profoundly, the structuring of his personality.

"Gender studies" try to ratify LGBT parenting as natural. What can we say about this position?

Concerning the harmonious and balanced mental development of the child, we readily understand how LGBT parenting seriously ignores all that science has said in the last century (from Freud till today). Freud writes in *Totem and Taboo* (1921) that, "Every human relationship formed with one's parents during childhood, whether consciously or unconsciously, will have a decisive influence on the development of the subject's personality."

A child who grows up with two mothers or two fathers is effectively deprived of an essential touchstone for the proper structuring of his personality. This physical and biological absence can only be an impairment of the inter-subjective process (since one of the two subjects with whom to relate—the female or male—is missing). It is also an element of confusion in the haptonomic/mental representation process given that the male body conveys the masculine personality and the fatherly role, while the female body expresses the feminine character and the maternal role. The adoption of a sound precautionary principle—universally accepted when it comes to defending the ecosystem of the biosphere and GMOs—should be the minimum countermeasure for avoiding social experimentation on children, whose supreme interest is undoubtedly that of having a father and a mother.

Gender ideology outlines and tells an entirely different story. From its perspective, biological sex (male and female) completely dissociates from sexual orientation and gender identity. The latter is the result of education, imposed through masculine and feminine "stereotypes" that condition the male to become a "man" and the female to become a "woman," and to belong to a different gender is considered socially unacceptable. Assuming the unproven axiom that biological sexuality has nothing to do with the structure of personality (is considered the result of culture and nature), everyone can and must make and unmake, build and deconstruct one's chosen gender based on desires and self-perception that can be experienced at any time and are, therefore, variable and changeable. In a short time, we have gone from four genders (LGBT), proposed in the sixties and seventies, to a growing list that today includes 58 different genders. It prompted Judith Butler to propose (in the late 1980s) "queer" as a kind of "fluid gender" that can include all possible and conceivable genders.

What are the origins of gender ideology?

Gender ideology was born in a medical environment (Kinsey, Benjamin and Money) and then in a political-philosophical one (Marcuse, Levi Strauss, Simone De Beauvoir, Foucault and Derrida) that created a historico-cultural blend with the radical feminist movement (Firestone, Witting, Butler and Kristeva). Its social pervasiveness was such that, in the academic world, colleges were founded and intended to study the sexual orientations present in populations. In this way "gender studies" was born. To be honest, this was nothing new or original, since Alfred Kinsey's famous "Reports," based upon empirical-statistical criteria and drafted between 1948 and 1953, claim that femininity and masculinity are cultural constructs that must be eliminated to establish genuine equality between human beings.

The first stage was the "linguistic revolution" from "sex" to "gender," with the explicit intent of relegating sexuality to a biological field that has nothing to say about social construction, which consists of roles related to the individual's self-determination. Thus, the human being could be asexual or pansexual because the only important thing is the free choice of identity and sexual orientation. "Gender studies" is, therefore, nothing more than an attempt—based on opinion polls—to prove that certain genders naturally exist among populations and are not the product of ideology or philosophy. Consequently, they should be naturally welcome and adequately developed in society. But the commonality between gender ideology and gender studies lies in the total absence of any scientific evidence. We are still waiting for someone to provide genetic, hormonal, phenotypic, neurological or some other type of evidence—as long as it is objective, intelligible and describable in scientific terms—of how a person can be "naturally" queer in the morning and gay or lesbian in the afternoon, after being heterosexual for the first twenty or thirty years of his or her life.

"In a time of universal deceit, telling the truth is a revolutionary act." Let's hope that Chesterton's words help us find each day the courage to swim against the tide of the "politically correct."

PART II

SEXUAL DIFFERENCES

LAURA C. PALADINO*

SEXUALITY, CONJUGALITY AND PROCREATION IN THE BIBLE

These reflections come from the opening chapters of Genesis and examine in depth sexual differences and related issues, such as procreation and the family. These themes presuppose a Biblical vision, the foundation of Judeo-Christian tradition. We outline a broad framework that, starting from the theological arguments of salvation and vocation to relational dynamics, examines the inherent symbolism in the stories of creation and explores the conceptual issues of conjugality and generativity. It analyzes the specific difference between male and female, along with their anthropological dimension of complementarity and reciprocity, reflected in the biblical texts and understood as the supreme expression of God's image. The human being manifests and reveals the vocation of being made in God's image and likeness as a creature capable of relation, fecundity and responsibly assuming motherhood or fatherhood.

1. A linguistic clarification: "separation" in the context of the Old Testament

As the great interpreter of Heidegger's philosophy, Luce Irigaray, wrote: "Sexual difference is one of the issues or the issue in our time... which could be our salvation, a new horizon of fertility not yet seen if we thought it through."[1]

We are not sure what Irigaray means by the word *salvation*. However, there is no doubt that in the Old Testament, the issues of difference and separation have much to do with salvation. The concept of separation, expressed by the root *badal* in Hebrew, is of capital importance in the post-Exilic biblical vision, as it is the best means of preserving the Chosen People and the favor of the Lord.[2]

* Biblical scholar, Professor of Biblical Theology and Biblical Historiography at the European University of Rome, and the Pontifical University Regina Apostolorum.

[1] L. IRIGAY, *Ethique de la différence sexuelle,* Minuit, Paris 1985. She wrote the work in parallel with a series of lectures she gave as the prestigious Jan Tinberg Chair at the Erasmus University of Rotterdam in 1982. We do not share all of Irigay's conclusions, but we have gladly mentioned a quote that maintains its significance and value in the contemporary context.

[2] It is a theological concept that actively operates in postexilic biblical texts and produces different currents of thought that I have examined in depth elsewhere. See L.C. PALADINO,

The salvific dimension of differentiation emerges clearly from the very first verses of the book of Genesis. It tells the creation of the world and describes God's intervention as one of order and the elimination of chaos through an act of separation and distinction. The distinction is considered a prerequisite for life even before man and woman, from the beginning of creation. In creating, God separates and orders. On the first day God separates the light from the darkness (Gen 1:1-5). On the second day God separates the waters above from the waters below. On the third day He separates the water under the firmament from the dry ground (Gen 1:9-13). On the fourth day He creates the sun and the moon to separate day from night and to distinguish light from darkness (Gen 1:14-19). On the fifth and sixth day, God makes all living creatures of the sea, sky and earth, separating and distinguishing them precisely according to their kind as He had done for the plants in the fourth day (Gen 1:12, 21, 25). God saw all creatures, day by day, and it was good. The Creator's specific gaze defines an implicit blessing that precedes and accompanies all the explicit blessings pronounced by God upon the animated creatures[3] that can listen[4] to his voice.

Tutelare l'identità. Studi storico-filologici sulle versioni antiche della Bibbia. Testo Ebraico Masoretico e Testo Greco dei Settanta, Pensa Multimedia, Lecce-Brescia 2012. It is interesting to underline how in the biblical language the root of the word "confusion"—*balal*—differs from that of "separation" in one letter: the central consonant. The Biblical message that also manifests through language is obvious: difference is order in chaos, while confusion is ambiguity. Even if it may seem that there are completeness and wholeness in confusion, in reality there is only disorder as an absence of difference.

[3] For this, see L.C. Paladino, "Dal creato all'uomo, dall'uomo alla storia: la benedizione nei racconti biblici", *in Coscienza,* 4-5, 2014, p.37-46; also see L.C. Paladino, *Dire bene di Dio, dire bene dell'uomo: le preghiere di benedizione nel Pentateuco e nei libri storici dell'Antico Testamento. Un confronto tra le versioni antiche* (TM – LXX), Arte Tipografica, Naples 2012.

[4] The importance of listening in the biblical context already emerges here, in the choice of differentiating the way of blessing from the existence of the sense of hearing: it is the ability that allows one to respond to God's call, to His blessing and His election. This ability is, therefore, the creatures' gift par excellence—they listen to the creator after seeing Him, recognizing *beauty* and covering themselves with His look of goodness and blessing. See, in this regard, the commandment of the good Israelite, who is invited to listen: "Hear O Israel, the Lord is our God, the Lord is one" (Deut. 6:4). Mark recalls this dispute of the great commandment in Mk12:29-30. We will later address the value of listening to the biblical texts and the symbolism inherent in it. For more information, see L.C. Paladino, *Dal creato all'uomo, dall'uomo alla storia, ...*; L.C. Paladino, *Dire bene di Dio, dire bene dell'uomo, ...*

2. "In the image and likeness of God": the vocation of humankind as male and female, guardian of the Garden of Eden, creatures in relation.

To seal the entire creation, God resolves to create humanity "in his image and likeness" on the sixth day (Gen 1:26). "In the image of God he created them; male and female he created them," as Gen 1:27 emphasizes.

In the Bible, "*'adam*," humankind, is conceived as sexually differentiated from the beginning. Two distinct possible expressions, the masculine and the feminine, reveal humankind's being in time. [5] Its existence is ontologically and inevitably denoted by a difference between male and female, even in the identity of their human nature in the one expression of *'adam*. Male and female together are called "man" by God since the day of their creation.[6]

As they receive their calling, they assume God's blessing and the vocation to be fruitful and increase in number, to tend the land and rule over the creatures, together in their condition of complementarity and reciprocity as evoked by their differences.[7] Humankind, male and female, is, therefore, created in God's image and serves to bring a beam of God's presence into the world through the senses. *'adam*, as the name itself recalls,[8] amounts to a gift for creation, which otherwise would not have a guardian "in the image of

---

[5] The two terms that define male and female in this step are *zacar* and *neqebâ*, which have an explicit sexual value, even in their etymology: the same words are used to refer to animals in many contexts in the Old Testament. The story of the great flood repeats these words in the entrance of every animal, "the male and his female" (Gen 7:2, 3:8-9) "to keep the species alive on the earth" (Gen 7:3).

[6] "This is the book of the generations of *'adam*. In the day that God created *'adam*, in the likeness of God made he him; Male and female created he them; and blessed them, and called their name "*'adam*," in the day when they were created." (Gen 5:1-2).

[7] Gen 1:28. We must point out the significance of the name in Hebrew sensitivity. It indicates a vocation, and its assignment or modification denotes an essential change in life itself. This calling is repeated in various contexts of the Old and New Testament, such as the call of Abraham (17:5) and Peter (Matt 16:18-19). Naming has a capital value in the Bible and is the prerogative of the father figure in the Jewish tradition (see also NT, about John the Baptist and Jesus: Lk 1:13-63; Matt 1:21. In the passage of Gen 5:1-2, God assigns a name to man, assuming in this way the dimension of creator and father. In return, the Lord gives the man the task to name the creatures (Gen 2:19), because *'adam* is the manifestation of God in the world, and holds the position of chief and guardian of creation, showing the paternal face of the Lord.

[8] Significantly, man, male and female, receives the name of "*'adam* " from God. In fact, in the name itself it is possible to identify the connection with the *'adamâ*, land, which must be guarded by man. Even linguistically and etymological *'adam* is the guardian of the *'adamâ*. See more on this aspect below.

God." It makes clear to the entirety of creation that, without humanity, creation itself would remain hidden.[9]

God confers upon all creatures differentiation, separation, ordering and salvific distinctions. However, in humans, this is conferred not according to kind,[10] as is the case for animals or plants, but in God's image. This image is explicitly identified in the sexual difference revealed by each human being, living and concretely existing as male or female.[11] Therefore, the relational dimension of *'adam*, ontologically related because made male or female in a limited and complementary condition, is made in the image of God. For this reason, the relational dimension of *'adam* is intended as a divine image. He is created as ontologically related in a condition of limited and reciprocal complementarity that simultaneously evokes and manifests a potential for completeness and wholeness.

Male and female bear within themselves the same relational dimension characterizing the God of Israel. This relationship is present in many contexts in the Bible. It is a prophecy of the Trinitarian dogma later institutionalized by Christianity.[12]

3. "It is not good for the man to be alone" (Gen 2:18): the woman and her difference, "a helper suitable for him."

This relational dimension, which is fundamental to human nature and, according to the Bible, appears as an expression of God's image in the sexually differentiated human being, is confirmed with an emphasis in different sections of Gen 2 (in a way more detailed than in Gen 1). This passage describes

---

[9] The prophecy fulfilled in Christ, "the image of the invisible God, the firstborn of every creature," as St. Paul says to the Colossians (Col 1:15), is already present in these passages of the Genesis.

[10] . This almost formulaic clause appears in the entire first chapter of Genesis when referring to the creation of all living things, plants (Gen 1:11-12), fish and birds (Gen 1:21), and land animals (Gen 1:24-25).

[11] On sexual difference see E. Roze, *Verità e Splendore della differenza sessuale,* Cantagalli, Siena 2014 and the extensive biography referenced in that work.

[12] Theology sees the relational dimension of the God of Jesus Christ, One in three Persons, foreshadowed in the abnormal plural content in Gen 1:26: "And God said, Let us make man in our image, after our likeness." The passage about Abraham encountering three men contains such a symbolic value (Gen 18:1-16). There is also a sudden change from plural to singular in the dialogue (Genesis 18:9-10) between Abraham and his guests. It ends with the prophecy, made by the three men, of Sarah's maternity.

the creation of man (*'adam*) from the dust of the ground (*'adamâ*),[13] man who is gifted with a spirit infused by the Creator, and placed as the only living being in the Garden of Eden "for him to work and take care of it" (Gen 2:15).

In the same context, *'adam* is commanded to not eat from the tree of knowledge, or he will die (Gen 2:16-17).[14] God creates all the animals for *'adam*, and after him, not before, as told in Gen 1. God leads all the animals, one by one, to man for him to name.[15] God finds a "helper suitable for him," since God saw that "it is not good for the man to be alone"(Gen 2:18). This presence of a denial is of great importance in the Bible. In the first chapter of the Genesis, God saw that every creature He called into existence "was good." Here instead, in total and deliberate contrast with the positive affirmations of creation, God sees that the loneliness of *'adam* is "not good." That is why He seeks "a helper suitable for him," who reveals himself (according to the translation that most fully expresses the richness of the root *nagad* in the Hebrew text).[16]

However, among "all the livestock, the birds in the sky and all the wild animals no suitable helper was found for *'adam* (Gen 2:21). Only when God forms the woman (*išâ*) from the rib He had taken out of *'adam* (Gen 2:22), *'adam* proclaims all her splendor and recognizes her as "flesh of his flesh and bone of his bones." For this reason, he reiterates that she shall be called a woman, *išâ,* for she originates from the man (*iš*). With this statement, through lexical contiguity, *iš* recognizes himself as guardian of *išâ*, just as God made *'adam* the guardian of *'adam*â.

---

13 . The etymologic similarity of terms translating "ground" and "man" is characteristic of Hebrew, and has theological value at different levels, as we have already mentioned and will see better further on. There is similar etymologic similarity in Latin, through the correspondence *humus-homo*.

14 For further information on the tree of life and on theological issues regarding the prohibition in the passage of Gen 2:16, see L.C. PALADINO, "'Dio non è dei morti, ma dei viventi' (Mt 22:32; Mk 12:27; Lk 20:38): vita e morte, immortalità e resurrezione nelle Scritture Sacre", in M. KRIENKE (ed.), *Morte e immortalità nel dibattito interdisciplinare, Atti delle conferenze di studio* (Lugano 2014), Messaggero, Padua 2015.

15 Man's position of superiority relative to creation and his role as a guardian of creation, assigned by God because made in His image and likeness, is seen in this operation. According to Gen 5:2, as the Lord gives a name to man, in the same way, man, as the manifestation of God in the world, is given the task of naming the creatures. The act of naming now assumes its primary value, the ultimate meaning and complex implications of which are understood further on.

16 For the meaning of "revealing" see, e.g., the occurrence of *nagad* in Isa 44:7. For this and other lexical references in this study, see as well, G.-J. BOTTERWECK, H. RINGGREN *Grande lessico dell'Antico Testamento* (ed. it. Edited by P.G. BORDONE), Paideia, Brescia 2007.

It is worth noting how in the biblical vision *iš* recognizes himself as such only when he meets the woman, *išâ*. In fact, the noun *iš* appears for the first time in Gen 2:22. After that, the term *išâ* appears in Gen 2:21 when the woman is made from the rib of *'adam*. In short, the identity of human nature is in *'adam*, but it necessarily differentiates into *iš* or *išâ*, which linguistically is identified by the same root declined to male and female, which are different but not radically diverse.[17] From a conceptual point of view, in the very moment the woman appears, characterized as *iš* and as *išâ*, we understand that masculine and feminine differences form *'adam*, or the human nature.

In these brief symbolic notations, the Hebrew mind perceives that sexual difference is marked precisely by the arrival of the woman. Her appearing reveals to man the very meaning of his sexuality, the value, meaning and purpose of his being male (*zacar*).

4. *So he made an išâ from the rib of 'adam: the identity, difference and sacredness of human sexuality in the Bible.*

The account of the woman's formation in Gen 2:21-24 is even more explicit. The woman is not created since God forms her nature at the very moment of creation of *'adam*. When referring to her, Genesis uses the verb of construction and generation,[18] instead of the verb of creation *bara'*. The Bible uses the verb of construction to describe the founding of cities[19] and homes,[20] places where the living dwell, or spaces consecrated to God.[21] It also refers to

---

[17] We can focus on the etymology of these two adjectives, which show how these are not equivalent in their meaning since they derive from two different Latin roots, that of *differo* ("to bring elsewhere," and so to extend) and *divorto/diverto* (to distance, or separate). Man and woman, distinct from the rest of creation in being made "in the image and likeness of God," are not offered a further separation or diversity of species but instead are given a sexual difference (*išâ*; *iš*) in the unity and identity of human nature (*'adam*).

[18] As we have already seen about *badal* and *balal*, the slight difference in the root always has a conceptual value in Hebrew. Here, too, there is a semantic shift, in the second consonant of the root, but this difference is essential, and it establishes otherness between the two concepts, partly contiguous, but different.

[19] See, e.g., Gen 10:11 on the foundation of Nineveh, Num, 13:22 on that of Heshbon, and Num 32 on that of the cities of the twelve tribes of Israel. See 2Sam 5 concerning the construction of the city of David in Jerusalem.

[20] Gen 33:17; Deut 8:12

[21] See, e.g., Gen 8:20 on the altar built by Noah after the flood, and Gen 12:7-8, 13:18 concerning the altars made by Abraham to thank God for the promise of the offspring and the land. Isaac (Gen 26:25), Jacob (Gen 35:7) and Moses (Ex 17:15, 24:4) built additional altars.

the procreative act of human couples, especially those of the patriarchs and matriarchs, and undoubtedly that of mothers.[22]

According to the Genesis account, the woman is formed from the rib (*ṣela'*) of *'adam*. It is a noun that appears about fifty times in the Old Testament and defines the side, the hip of the human body. It is the most important and significant part of the body since it is particularly strong. The woman comes out right from the side, as a help, support and column[23] for her man. The woman is robust and can offer help because she comes from the rib, a dynamic part capable of supporting the whole person.

This verse in Genesis seems to say that the woman is at the man's side to help and support him, to prod him beyond his inertia and share his vocation as guardian of the common good. The Bible assigns her this arduous task when appraising her, giving her the vocation to be a helper (*'ezer*), modeling after God. If she accepts and fulfills this task, she will inspire the man to realize the best of himself. Otherwise, her intervention can only contribute to his ruin.[24]

In addition to strength, *ṣela'* recalls the theme of sacredness in the Bible. Gen 32:32 recounts that after fighting with the angel and meeting God, Jacob limped in that part of the body identified by the noun *ṣela'*. It is in this condition that God manifested to the Patriarch. It is a presence to which no one is

---

See the use of the verb in 2Sam 7 about the claim of David to build a house for the Lord, and the altar made by David in 2Sam 24:25.

[22] The verb has this meaning for the first time in Gen 4:17, referring to Cain's wife, the mother of Enoch. It again appears with Sarah in Gen 16:2, referring to Hagar; see Gen 30:3 on Bila, Rachel's maid, and on Hagar in the stories of Jacob. Finally, see the use of the term in Ruth 4:11 concerning Rachel and Leah. It is a true and proper metaphor that unifies and clarifies all the meanings mentioned before.

[23] It is not a coincidence that the book of Sirach, undoubtedly recalling this passage from Genesis, designates woman as the help and pillar upon which a man can lean. The man who takes a wife has the makings of a fortune, a helper to match himself, a pillar of support (Sir 36:24). The book of Tobit echoes this belief, recovering and adding to the concept described above a reference to the story of creation: "You it was who created *'Adam* you who created Eve his wife to be his help and support. From these two the human race was born. You it was who said: 'It is not right that the man should be alone let us make him a helper like him'" (Tob 8:6).

[24] From here all the reflections contained in the biblical text warn against the wicked woman, often identified with the foreign woman, for reasons I have already discussed in L. C. PALADINO, *Tutelare l'identità...*: see only the passages of Proverbs (Prov 5, and the opposite praise of the wise woman, which closes the collection in Prov 31:10 ff.), or the significant and exemplary story of Jezebel, King Ahab's wicked wife, contained in the books of Kings (1Kings 21).

left indifferent.[25] Afterward, Jacob changed his name to the eponymous name of the people of Israel. The term appears again in Exodus 25-26 to define the sides of the Ark of the Covenant, God's dwelling, as well as in 1 Kings 6 to describe the temple walls supporting the architecture. For this reason, *ṣela'* describes the holy places *par excellence* in Jewish theology, first the Ark of the Covenant and then the Temple.

Christian theology finds a correlation between the rib of *'adam* and the side of Christ's body, the new temple and place of the new covenant,[26] as well as of the final generation of life[27] and man. Just as *išâ*, the spouse of *iš* and mother of the living, is born from the rib of *'adam*, so the Church, the bride of Christ and mother of believers,[28] is born from Christ, the side of the new *'adam*. The woman comes from *'adam*, and human nature is a gift before the man, led by God Himself. The verbs used in Gen 22:22-23 recall those of a wedding in which the Lord assumes the image of the father who leads his daughter as a bride to the groom. God gives Himself to man through the woman. Just as *'adam* is for *'adam*â, so *išâ* is for *iš* a manifestation of God's presence. It is no coincidence that before forming her, God defines her as help suitable for him *'ezer kenegdô*.[29] She stands before the man, stable, energetic and in a condition of equality and dignity. In the Bible the term *'ezer* or help

---

[25] Once again, we should notice that the intervention of the calling changes the patriarch's name, and its theological meaning given above.

[26] See Jn 2:13-22, where Jesus defines his body as *naòn* (temple) and predicts his glorious resurrection in the expulsion of the merchants from the Jerusalem Temple. This episode is repeated in other moments in the NT. In fact, it also appears in the trial of Jesus in the Gospel of Matthew (Mt 26:61), where the verb used by the false witnesses is a more accurate verb, one related to construction and edification. The semantic shift of the Jewish lemma *banâ* is maintained, with deep meanings in other contexts. As for the generative function of Christ's sacrifice, from which the Church is born, see the reference to the flow of blood and water from Christ's side, who, already dead upon the cross, is pierced by a soldier in Jn 19:33-34.

[27] Once again, the value of the verb *banâ* is examined as was done above. Consider the calling of Peter as well, called to be the foundation of Christ's Church, mother of believers (Mt 16:18-19), where the verbs used are highly specific and related to the topic of material construction, equivalent to those mentioned above in Mt 26:61. The two values of generation and construction continuously intertwine in theological reflection.

[28] The spousal imagery central to the biblical texts, and frequently used to define the relationship between God and the people of Israel, remains active in the New Testament, and especially in the Pauline writings about the relationship between Christ and the Church. In the context of the New Testament, through reference to the woman's offspring in Gen 3 and the figure of Mary, Mother and bride of the Word, the spousal imagery is rich with uniquely maternal symbolism.

[29] Gen 2:18.

is often used to designate God himself.[30] This linguistic symbol expresses once more the theological significance of the woman's formation, leading the man to be the sacrament of God's love.

For this reason, marriage is the symbol of monotheism very early in the Bible,[31] which is sacred and holy.[32] Not surprisingly, in the subsequent verses, we read that "a man will leave his father and mother and be joined to his wife, and they become one flesh" (Gen 2:24).[33]

5. "Flesh of my flesh, bone of my bones": the love song and symbolism of sexuality, breaking with sin.

The beauty of sexual difference is recognized by *'adam*, who breaks out into an exclamation of surprise when he meets the woman, "This is flesh of my flesh and bone of my bones."

These are the first words in the history of salvation. Until now only God's voice, the voice of the One who loves, is heard by his beloved creatures and resounds in the book of Genesis. The moment the woman appears, a sea

[30] There are multiple recurrences, see, e.g., Gen 49:25; Ex 18:4; Deut 33:7, 26, 29; 1 Sam 7:12; 1Chr 15:26; see in particular the passages in the Psalms: Ps 20 (19):2-3, 28 (27):7, 30 (29):11, 33 (32):20, 37 (36):40, 46 (45):6, 54 (53):6, 115 (113B):9-11, 121 (120):1-2. "A Song of Ascents. I look up to the mountains, from where will my help come? Our help is in the name of the Lord, the Maker of heaven and earth," Ps 124 (123):8.

[31] L.C. Paladino, *Tutelare l'identità…*

[32] The Hebrew word for marriage is *Qiddušin* (*Qodešim*), the plural of the root *qodeš* (holy), which possesses a formidable theological value. (*Qodešim* means holy, sacred things and in Greek is often expressed by an adjective with a similar meaning: àgion. Hence the philological and theological reflection, which leads one to locate a possible condemnation of adultery and divorce in the obscure reference to *tò àgion* contained in Mt 7:6. They take into account the direct derivation of Matthew's Gospel, as today we possess it in Greek today, from an original Hebrew or Aramaic text now lost. "Do not give to dogs what is sacred (*tò àgion*); do not throw your pearls before swine. If you do, they may trample them underfoot and turn and tear you to pieces." (Mt 7:6).

[33] I have noticed the rhetorical construction of the verse, which posits man and woman as contrasting terms and father and mother as middle terms of a proposition. This structure is an attempt to point out the centrality of the terms *iš* and *išâ* by their stylistic position, terms that here as elsewhere in the Bible assume the dual role of man and husband, woman and wife. The whole mystery of existence, the couple and the family is condensed and even rhetorically structured in the short proposition of Gen 2:24. This verse involves and includes both the differences that are enhanced and protected in marriage and the family; i.e., the sexual and generational differences. For more information on the meaning and rules of Semitic and biblical rhetoric differing from the Western languages, see R. Meynet, "Rhetorical Analysis: Introduction to Biblical Rhetoric," *Journal for the Study of the Old Testament Supplement*, Sheffield Academic Press, 1998.

change occurs in the Garden of Eden. For the first time, the man's voice resounds, and that woman who is a beloved creation hears the voice of one who loves. As God beholds his creatures, recognizing their goodness and beauty, the man beholds the woman, also recognizing her goodness and beauty. He speaks both of her and of himself, both to her and to himself, about this extraordinary and original beauty.

He recognizes the identity of human nature characterized by sexual difference.[34] In the brief passage of Gen 2:23, the man reveals himself to the woman through words, to which she listens, and she reveals herself to him through her image, which he beholds. The dynamic God-creature relationship, especially the dynamic of love and election established between God and his people, repeats and manifests itself in all creation through the dynamics between men and women. It is a metaphor wherein the senses of sight and hearing imply deep and precise theological meanings. It is for this obvious analogy that from the very beginning, spousal symbolism becomes a sacred symbol that describes that relationship of profound love that binds God as a spouse to the chosen people, the people of Israel whom God contemplated, loved and treasured as a bride.[35]

The sentence that the man pronounces, describing the absolute wonder of both humanity and the woman's femininity, is one of deep emotion. None-

[34] The recognition of the identity of human nature occurs in the first part of v. 23: "This is now flesh of my flesh and bone of my bones." The specific reference to sexual difference is located in the second part of the verse: "she shall be called *išâ* for she was taken from *iš*." Here the two assume two names, different in kind but identical as to the root that is the same and evokes once more the unity of nature.

[35] The reader will recall the spousal symbolism in the books of the prophets: see Isaiah, in particular Isa 62; see also Ezekiel and Hosea, which have extreme accents, as they operate within the *topos* of the beloved, a restored yet unfaithful prostitute; see in particular Ezek 16, and Hos 1-3. See the prophet Malachi's position on marriage, which establishes a specific continuity between the prescription in Gen 2:24 and the prohibition of repudiation. He remembers that "God made them one" and urges the Israelites, because of this original truth, to "be on (your) guard, and do not be unfaithful to the wife of (your) youth" (Mal 2:14-16). On the topic, see L.C. Paladino "Il ta'am e il profetismo femminile: approfondimenti lessicali sulla sapienza delle donne e casi di donne sapienti nell'Israele Biblico," in *SEL Studi Epigrafici e Linguistici* su *vicino Oriente Antico*, 31, 2014, 139-169. The spousal imagery remains strong in the New Testament, where Christ is often the groom explicitly or through parables. He defines himself as such: Mt 9:15, 25:1-13; Mk 2:19-20; and Lk 4:34-35. See also the juxtaposition between the kingdom of heaven and the wedding in Mt 22:1-14; Rev 19:7, 21:2, 10. The new Jerusalem appears as a bride adorned for her husband, the same Jerusalem that Paul, in Gal 4:26, defines as "our mother," in a welding of nuptial and maternal symbolism. We will return to this below.

theless, the woman is silent, listening to the man's words, as she experiences wonderment within a different sensitivity. Staying silent and listening is specifically feminine, precisely how the creatures embrace the creative word of God at the dawn of time. It is as believers that they embrace salvation in silence and awe. It is the first commandment of Israel—šemâ—which involves the faithful act of listening.[36]

The spousal imagery is, therefore, sacramental. It reveals a transcendent truth directly connected to the theological dimension. Man, driven by love, reveals himself to the woman. The woman meanwhile lovingly accepts the man's revelation. She offers him her acceptance, hearing and presumably embracing his words.[37] John Paul II emphasizes that the Song of Songs, a real song to human love in biblical literature,[38] demonstrates the same dynamic.[39]

We must interpret the Pauline exegesis of Genesis in the Letter to the Ephesians in this sense.[40] These verses call husbands to love their wives with the very love of Christ,[41] who unreservedly reveals himself to the Church by giving up his life. Paul invites wives to "obey" their husbands as they would the Lord, recovering the etymological sense of the Latin verb *obaudire*, which properly means "to listen," and reiterating the female vocation of listening and acceptance. This verb does not imply humiliation but is instead a sublime expression of difference and specificity. In this way, believing entails an aspect of the feminine since everyone is called to listen, to accept and to re-

---

[36] Deut 6:4 and above. For more information on the value of the šemâ, see L.C. PALADINO, "La Sapienza nei testi biblici," in A. ERCOLANI, P. XELLA (eds.), *La Sapienza nel Vicino Oriente e nel Mediterraneo Antichi*, Carocci, Rome 2013, p.197-249.

[37] This hosting dimension finds a sublime model in the New Testament and Christian context, i.e., in Mary. She fulfills the Word of God and shelters it within the flesh of her womb (Lk 1:38). She ponders the mystery of words (*tà rèmata*) and treasures these in her heart (Lk 2:19).

[38] See the bride's female response to the groom's ample praise, with male initiative guiding her. He sings and speaks, and she responds, expressing her desire to listen: "Let me hear your voice, for your voice is sweet" (Song 2:4).

[39] *JOHN PAUL II, Man and Woman He Created Them: A Theology of the Body, Pauline Books & Media, Boston, MA (2006) [1986].*

[40] Eph 5:21-33.

[41] The love of Christ for the Church, mentioned by Paul in Eph 5:25 as a model for husbands to love their wives, is the same love of God for the people that appears in Old Testament symbolism. The verses recover the bodily dimension in the spousal metaphor of the Old Testament referenced above. In particular, Paul's invitation is to cherish one's wife as one's flesh: once again the "guardianship" symbolism returns, a wonderful symbolism in the story of creation, confirmed by the prophet Malachi in his exegesis in Gen 2:24, concerning the prohibition of repudiation, as mentioned above.

ceive salvation. God's role is masculine as He gives and speaks to believers, calling them into existence through his voice. There is a beautiful symbolism of sexuality underlying the Genesis texts. It reveals how the warping of roles and unilateral domination are, by contrast, the result of temptation and sin.

In this way, we can better appreciate the dynamics in the third chapter of Genesis. It presents symbolically many anomalies in the first two chapters of Genesis. In Gen 3, the woman listens to the words of another creature, the most cunning of all, and not to the man who is her husband and guardian. The man is not physically present on the scene and, therefore, fails in his duty to protect the woman. In his absence, the woman "saw that the tree was good for food, pleasant to the eyes and a tree to be desired to make one wise."[42] The tempter seduces the woman through hearing, which is the sense that distinctively characterizes her. She succumbs to the temptation of sight. She sees and recognizes beauty outside instead of the beauty inside her. She speaks for the first time and does not simply listen but takes the initiative to give something to the man.[43] Instead of welcoming, she initiates. Here we witness a reversal of the masculine and feminine roles symbolically described in Gen 2. This image is taken up anew by Paul, in a spousal metaphor for the relationship between Christ and his Church.

In Gen 3, all the original boundaries, the communion within, are broken. There is a rupture in the communion between man and God, as the creatures hide from their Creator. There is a break in the communion between man and woman. Ashamed, they cover themselves to defend from one another.[44] There is a break in the communion between man and nature—the moment the fruit is plucked and eaten, the relationship between *'adam* and *'adamâ* changes from one of mutual preservation to one of exploitation. Among all these ruptures, the man-woman couple suffers most, obscuring their former

---

[42] It is noteworthy that here the woman is guilty, specifically, of all three lusts outlined by John the Evangelist in one of the Catholic Epistles—lust of the flesh (good for food), lust of the eyes (good for the eyes), and pride of life (a craving for success). These things do not come from God but the world, as John warns and glosses in 1Jn 2:16.

[43] The tempter uses a woman's dowry, that of hearing and welcome, to induce her to disobedience. The passage from Gen 3:1-6 describes the dynamics of temptation, in which the dialogue between the woman and the serpent concerns a confusion regarding the forbidden tree.

[44] Gen 3:7. It is the second reference to the nudity of the pair; the first is in Gen 2:25 and is placed immediately after the verse about the meaning of marriage. There, before sin, the nudity of the two symbolizes openness, intimacy, sharing, a willingness to encounter each other, a full expression of being one and of the same vocation; here, after the fall, nudity now becomes a vulnerability, while each becomes a potential attacker.

complementarity and reciprocity. Now there is a dominion of one over the other, scarring sexuality and motherhood. Man now exploits and subdues woman like any other creature of the earth. He is oblivious to the fact that the woman is different from all other living beings, taken from his rib as the only suitable helper who can reveal man to himself.[45] The sign of this new phase—characterized by an asymmetry of domination between man and woman, the fruit of sin and the rupture of communion—is birth pains and the woman's new name Eve.

The name Eve is different from the first one, *išâ*. The original name implies a recognition of beauty, of perfection, of giving. It describes a truth about mutual complementarity and highlights the revelation that her name and presence holds for the man.

Motherhood now becomes a symbol of subordination. The name Eve directly refers to her generative role. The name *išâ* is, therefore, more significant than Eve, which *'adam* imposes in a way not much different from the way he has given names to all the animals as a sign of the dominion over creation he was granted by God.[46] Sin has affected motherhood, which in human history will be used to dominate the other, man or woman alike. It has become a source of pride for the female, who thinks she can do without the male.[47] It is a dynamic that has nothing to do with marital life. For this reason, the prophecy of redemption in Gen 3:15-16 explicitly mentions that from the woman's seed a child will save us from sin and defeat the author of temptation.[48] It is only fair that a woman, a mother, will defeat the serpent and the evil it symbolizes. It will be a maternity that no longer condemns but completes her femininity, restoring all the woman's and the man's original beauty.

---

[45] Gen 3:16.

[46] God now establishes such domination of women in Genesis 3:16 as to assign them a new name, in Gen 3:20.

[47] Read Eve's exclamation in Gen 4:1, during Cain's birth: "With the help of the Lord I have acquired a man." The etymological issues obviously lead back through the name of Cain (*Qain*) to the verb for "to acquire" (*qanâ*), recovering a powerful metaphor in several languages and dialects. In the experience of motherhood, the woman can experience the pride of having given birth to a man (that pride of life warned of 1Jn 2:16), as well as experience the temptation to exclude the man from this joy, ignoring, paradoxically, the father's contribution.

[48] This prophecy, in itself formidable, will be enriched and reiterated in Isaiah's text and will always be powerfully connected with the mystery of motherhood in Isa 7:14.

6. The sleep of 'adam, among corporeity, transcendence, and conjugality: "And the two shall become one flesh."

According to the account in Gen 1, the creation of the world takes place in the absence of *'adam*. He came to life at the end and culmination of God's work, to live and preserve the already existent creation.

This diachrony implies a wise theological truth. Since the man was not present at the creation of the world, he cannot demand to know its mysteries and subvert its structures. Such are God's words to Job, in one of the most significant texts of Jewish tradition, where Job questions God on what men do not understand: "Where were you when I laid the foundations of the earth?" This answer echoes and takes on its full meaning in this reflection. During the formation of *išâ, 'adam* is asleep. It is no accident that the biblical texts emphasize the sleep that God sends upon *'adam* before making the woman.[49] The message emphasizes that it is God's creative act. While human nature participates in and collaborates with the substance that makes the woman, neither the man nor the woman, being creatures, knows the origin and the ultimate laws.

The message in Genesis emphasizes the behavior required of *'adam* vis-à-vis the world and himself—he must listen to the creation and others as God's gifts. As such, these gifts do not belong to man, who has not created life nor the world but belongs only to the Creator who has called them into existence. If creatures do not participate in the creation of the natural order, they do not have the right to modify it but instead are called to guard and cultivate it, to make it fruitful.[50] The sleep of *'adam* evokes an ulterior truth undeniable at an anthropological level. Man and woman can never entirely and mutually possess each other.

Human love and the relationship between male and female do not initially lead to possession or dominion and do not permit either one to sum up all of humanity.[51] They do not eliminate the constitutive difference between man and woman but instead produce a mutual complementarity. The person always remains a mystery, *alteri incommunicabilis*. This mystery happens because man and woman are different, never exhausting all the humanity in one

---

[49] Job 38:4.

[50] In the Romance languages, the profound semantic value of the term "nature," from the deponent verb *nascor*, describes an action by the person who does not generate the result but requires something from outside the actor.

[51] Disparity and domination come into man's life with the original sin, according to Gen 3 and particularly in Gen 3:16, as was already seen.

or the other but representing only one of two possible incarnations as male or female. There is an initial inaccessibility that the union of the sexes cannot transcend and that allows one to contemplate in wonder, moving toward the unknown without dominating it.

Prov 30:18-19 reads, "There be three things which are too wonderful for me, yes, four which I know not: The way of an eagle in the air; the way of a serpent on a rock; the way of a ship in the middle of the sea; and the way of a man with a maid." Precisely because of its inaccessibility, the relationship between men and women stands as a metaphor for the relationship between God and man, between the Creator and the creature.

The exegesis of Gen 2:24 in the Gospels, attributed to Jesus himself in Mk 10:1 and Mt 19:1-9, adds to Genesis the explicit unlawfulness of the breach of marriage, permitted by the law of Moses due to the hardness of the human heart.[52] "Therefore, what God has joined together, let man not separate," the Gospel commands.

The whole passage uses significant verbs transparently traceable to the vocabulary used in the Greek version of the Torah.[53] It recovers, by contrast, the concepts of difference, distinction and separation that constitute God's action in Genesis. The human creature cannot arbitrarily construct his evident salvific significance except by distorting the original order and destroying God's image in the world. The spouses express this significance both in their indis-

---

[52] Mt 19:9 and Mk 10:5. There is an echo of Malachi's prophecies condemning repudiation, as aforementioned.

[53] In the quotation from Gen 2:24, cited in Mk 10:7, Jesus uses the verb *proskollàein*, the Septuagint version for the Hebrew verb *dabaq* in the Masoretic text of Genesis. It is a macroscopic anomaly since these verbs are usually not used to indicate sexual union in the Bible—verbs such as *yada* in Hebrew, *gignòskein* in Greek, are preferred. It is significant that before sin, i.e., before the fatal fall that is firmly connected with life and knowledge, as I have emphasized elsewhere (L.C. Paladino, *Dio non è dei morti, ma dei viventi...*). God uses the sexual union verbs at the foundation of the first indissoluble marriage in what John Paul II calls "theological prehistory." These imply a total and complete sharing: *dabaq* and *proskolàein* indicate "to adhere inextricably" entirely. It is important to recall that these are the same verbs that in the Bible indicate a deep love and are used to announce adherence to God and the monotheistic faith codified in the Torah (e.g., Deut 4:4, 10:20, 11:22,13:5). They indicate a firm, steady faith, as demonstrated by the use of tenses that, in Gen 2:24, in Hebrew, unlike in Greek, are not in the future tense but the perfect tense. Again, through lexicon and language, the Bible indicates that a single marriage is a representation of faith in one God and is a sacrament of the love, proper to Him, that He has for man.

soluble unity[54] and as a sacrament.[55] While human love allows the meeting of the two separately, it also makes them one flesh. As the text of Genesis affirms, unity, which remains dual, is the manifestation of the Creator, as it renders visible the relationality of the God of Israel. The word flesh (*basar*) also means "manifestation" in Hebrew.[56] The unity of the two in marriage is, therefore, an expression of the divine, revealing God's love for the world as well as its intimate relational dimension. That is why it is also a sacrament.

The uniqueness of this flesh and manifestation reflects and mirrors God's originality. It is "One alone," *'ehad* according to the most genuine professions of faith in the Biblical texts.[57] This oneness confirms the necessity for marriage to be indissoluble, a necessity highlighted by the prophets and confirmed by Christ.

---

[54] The verb used in Greek to indicate this communion is *sunzeugnumi*, which bears within it the root of the "yoke," the bond that leads together two different living beings, leads them together and induces them to advance. By contrast, the verb of separating is *chorizomai*, which closely follows the Greek version of Gen 1, where exactly this word is used to translate *badal*. For more on the image of the yoke and other issues related to marriage, see J. GRANADOS, *Una sola carne en un solo Espíritu. Teología del Matrimonio*, Palabra, Madrid 2014, trad. It. Cantagalli, Siena 2014.

[55] In the New Testament and Christian tradition, marriage assumes an additional sacramental symbolism, as it becomes an image of Christ's incarnation, an encounter between the divine and human nature that indissolubly takes place in Him, and is repeated every day in the Eucharist. The indissolubility of marriage acquires its importance in Christianity, specifically in the mystery of Christ, guarded by the Church. The Incarnation and the Eucharist, the sacrament of Christ's flesh, are both symbolized in the indissoluble marriage, a sign of the unity between God and man. That is the man whom God has wanted to restore by sending His Son into the world, to redeem the ancient fault, not by chance defined as "felix culpa" in the Easter Sequence hymn Exsultet. A wedding is an ultimate symbol, evoked when referring to the Lamb as mentioned earlier in Revelation. For more on the theological relationship between sacramental marriage and Holy Communion, read E. ANTONELLI, *Crisi del matrimonio ed Eucaristia*, Ares, Milan 2015, with a preface by E. Sgreccia.

[56] It is the root used in Hebrew to describe the living body, which in Greek is typically expressed with the word *sarx*. By contrast, a different noun describes the corpse and is preferably translated by the word *soma* in Greek, not without a semantic shift. It is *geviâ*, correlative to *goi*, which distinguishes the different peoples, often polytheistic and dangerous for the faith of Israel, from the one elected, as I have emphasized elsewhere (LC PALADINO, *Tutelare l'identità* ...). The root is, therefore, deliberately ambivalent, as it also seeks to evoke the danger of idolatrous corruption; basically, it is an invitation to meditation upon how the body can become an utterly hostile witness to God's plans if it does not manifest the presence of God and fails to be a *basar*, a revelation. For the noun *geviâ*, e.g., see Deut 10:6; Judg 14:8; Neh 9:37.

[57] Deut 6:4: "Listen, Israel: Yahweh our God is the one, the only (*'eḥad*) Yahweh".

7. Procreation and unity within distinction: family, fatherhood and motherhood in the biblical texts.

The unity of two people consecrated in marriage opens the way to the generation of new life. Through generation, the difference perpetuated in a male or female child makes God's love visible, as paternal and maternal love in the Bible. In the Sacred Scriptures, numerous passages confer a paternal role upon the Lord as one who leads his people, as a father who leads his son beyond the secure perimeters of his birthplace, beyond the experience of the family into the chaos of the world. [58] At the same time, the Bible portrays the Lord with the sensitivity of a mother who feeds her infant with love and who tirelessly welcomes and protects the child.[59]

The fact remains that the paternal dimension attributed to God is most predominant and distinctive in all the biblical texts. Scriptures unreservedly attribute paternal roles to God, with His creative activity, of which the perfect creature is *'adam*. The male and female pair carries on the task of naming creation from generation to generation. The man-father specifically has this task due to the symbolic meanings we have already examined, whereas the mother embodies closeness and warmth. Paternal responsibility consists in setting a standard indispensable for the child to achieve autonomy. This distance also contributes to giving thanks to God the Father "who is in heaven."[60] It manifests the father's prototypical authority, who with his strong voice passes on the code of the Covenant and the laws of the Decalogue.[61]

Thus, the father embodies the ultimate authority in the family, even when he is physically distant for different reasons, and is the one we wait for. This dimension of God is evident in the biblical texts when the authority and distance increase.[62] It is part of the vocation as a father who is sometimes looked upon as ungrateful because he rigorously imposes "no" on his children. While this negative is functional and necessary for their psychological development, it can also produce major recriminations. The father is often the one who, after a week of hard work, painfully experiences the frequent ingratitude of

---

[58] Just think of Abraham's experience or the great epic of the Exodus.

[59] Isa 49:14-15, 66:13; Ps 131:2-3.

[60] 2Chr 20:6; Jb 16:19; Ps 2:4, 8:3.

[61] Ezek 20:1-21; Deut 5:1-22.

[62] Numerous are the Psalms of waiting, which also insist on God's silence. E.g., see Ps 6, 13 (12), 42 (41), 85 (84). God seems absent at times, and man invokes him in order not to be abandoned: Ps 22 (21). It is interesting to notice that the very opening words of this Psalm are uttered by Christ, the Son, on the cross, to invoke the Father in times of trial.

his children. Similarly, the Bible depicts God as a loving father whom his ungrateful people repeatedly reject in calling upon other gods.[63]

The Lord's multifaceted paternal dimension is so pervasive in the Old Testament that Paul of Tarsus labels God as the one "from whom every family in heaven and on earth takes its name."[64] Christianity further emphasizes this with the Father as the first person of the Holy Trinity, who resolutely decides to send his Son to incarnate as a man for the salvation of the world.[65]

In anthropological terms, reaffirmed in the theological language of the Bible, the man-father's role in the family is impartial. He is called to separate the child from his mother in imitation of God the Father and Creator, who separates, divides and distinguishes reality, extracting order and differentiation from chaos. This takes place from the first instant until the supreme moment of the woman's formation, distinct from man.

Similarly, the man-father is called to raise his child, on the model of God, for autonomy and maturity. God is the Father who chooses and blesses humans, sending them to fill the earth and subdue it in his name. He calls Abraham to set his eyes on the future and sends him to a new land. "Go," exhorts the Father. "Go from your country," your kindred and your father's house, "and leave."[66] It is the father, not the mother, who guides the child to autonomy and spurs him to gaze beyond what he currently sees.[67]

It is the father who tests his son while the mother would like to spare him from suffering. The episode of Jacob wrestling with the angel, which symbolizes the sacredness of God's presence in history, is also an expression of God's fatherhood. It manifests the male's resoluteness, strength and firmness, like

---

[63] This situation is recurrent in the Book of Judges: e.g., Judg 2:11, 13, 3:7, 10:6. Cf. also in 1Sam 12:10, 1Kings 16:31-32; 18:18ff. For more on this theme, see Psalm 106 (105) on the people's true confession for their sins of idolatry.

[64] Eph 3:14-15.

[65] The "Parable of the Vineyard" contained in the three Synoptic Gospels foreshadows the Father's decision: Mt 21:33-46; Mk 12:1-12; Lk 20:9-19. God's paternal dimension is powerful in the New Testament: see the parable of the merciful father (Lk 15:11-31) and Christ's habit of calling God "Father," which culminates in the prayer "Our Father."

[66] Gen 12:1.

[67] The notation contained in a gloss of the first verse of Gen 12, immediately after God's call to Abraham to leave his country, is not of secondary importance. The biblical text adds "go to the land that I will show you." God's vision of the future is powerful, dependable, and unfurls into the full blessing of Gen 12:2-3. Once again, the symbolism of life and hearing returns, and Abraham immediately assumes an attitude of attentive listening typical of the chosen creature and goes forth "as the Lord commanded him" (Gen 2:4).

a rock upon which the child and the mother can rest.[68] At the same time, the Bible describes how he maintained his strength flawlessly and tenderly.[69]

If the woman marks the sexual difference in the couple and, in the Garden of Eden, manifests and reveals to the man who he is, then the man characterizes the procreative difference in the family and gives his child a name.[70] He invites the child to explore beyond the family's boundaries and consciously forms his or her conscience.

At the same time, the generative dimension belongs to God the Father. He allows for the possibility of both fatherhood and motherhood in the couple's generativity, in the unity of that pair. The couple reveals the image and likeness of God, an analogy with the divine "generation"[71] that never leaves us "orphans."[72]

The meaning of the verb *bana*, examined in Gen 2 concerning the woman's formation, allows procreation to take on an extraordinarily sacred value. It prompts the couple to assume the task the Creator assigns them—to continue human life in the image and likeness of God. It is the task to "build" the city of the living, the home of the Lord and his people because "the glory of God is man fully alive."[73]

---

[68] The symbolism of the rock is most present in the context of the Old Testament and, once again, describes God's reliability as the Rock of Salvation: e.g., Deut 32; Ps 18:2-3; 42:10; 78:35.

[69] See the prophetic passages in Jer 3:19 and Hos 11:1-4.

[70] The icon of the father in the Christian context is Joseph, Mary's husband: he embodies all the complexity of the paternal figure as it has been outlined above, presupposing the multiple and sometimes contrasting attitudes a father must display to a child for him or her to mature and confront life with confidence.

[71] See specifically Ps 2:7: "He said to me, You are my son, today have I fathered you."

[72] Jn 14:18.

[73] Irenaeus of Lyons, *Adversus Haereses*, IV, 20, 7.

SUSY ZANARDO*

THE FUNDAMENTALS OF SEXUAL DIFFERENCE: ARE "MASCULINE" AND "FEMININE" MEANINGFUL TERMS?

1. Identifying the issue

We are increasingly witnessing either an indifference towards or an acceptance of the interchangeability of masculine and feminine roles and identities. In fact, many in society contest the idea of a male and female specificity today. This character has been reinterpreted as a historical and conventional construction, an imaginary projection we produced. Does being male or female not have any identifiable features?[1]

Today's culture addresses the issue from at least two paradigms. The gender theories prevalent today represent the first, which ignores corporeity. They reject sexual dualism in favor of an indefinite production of variations. They assume gender to consist of practices, representations and institutions that produce male and female identity and roles culturally.[2]

The second paradigm emphasizes sexual difference as a principle in various ways. We will distinguish three models. The first is the biblical model, according to which God's desire for creation culminates in the relationship between the two sexes. Biblical anthropology reveals not only that man and

---

* Associate Professor of Moral Philosophy at the University of Europe in Rome and member of the Governing Council of the Italian Society of Moral Philosophy

[1] See J. Butler, *Gender Trouble: Feminism and the Subversion of Identity*, Routledge, New York 1989. Catholic theologian Benedetta Selene Zorzi explains the difficulty of specifying identifiable contents for masculinity and femininity. In fact, she claims that, if we proceed inductively, by comparing the characteristics of a statistically significant number of women from a variety of cultures, we risk producing ever-changing contents or else limit ourselves to a perspective that is either parochial or trivial. If instead we seek to use a deductive method, we either fall back into an undue naturalism (from which, given a woman's body, we can draw some indications); or else hypostatize a feminine essence or nature, of which every woman would be a "defective" instantiation. In this case, the risk lies in the prescription of normative contents to the detriment of those who do not fit into a category.

[2] For an introduction, see S. Zanardo, "Genere e differenza sessuale. Un dibattito in corso," in *Aggiornamenti sociali*, 65, 5, 2014, p.379-391. See also L. Palazzani, *Sex/gender. Gli equivoci dell'uguaglianza*, Giappichelli, Turin 2011.

woman are made in God's image but that the Creator's face shines on the couple's difference as mutual desire and self-donation.[3]

The second model refers to sexual difference as a simple biological fact, an "empirical state."[4] The sexual difference is merely the result of evolution, which results in material and social organization but does not have any symbolic significance. There is a risk of reifying male and female identity by hypostasizing them as ahistorical essences. The factuality of this difference in the division of labor and the relationship between the sexes constitutes the principle of political exchange and thought production, which change and evolve with time.

A third model in the current thinking of sexual difference insists on developing an autonomous female subjectivity and offers symbolic expression as evidence of a clear sense of difference. This model has been introduced by Second Wave feminism with Luce Irigaray in France, *Libreria delle donne* of Milan and the *Comunità filosofica femminile Diotima* in Italy.[5]

2. Sexual difference

How can we think of sexual difference today without falling into stereotypes (as gender culture warns)? How do we do this without vapid, abstract terms lacking any real meaning (as the thinking on sexual complementarity warns)? Can we locate any fundamental difference? Can we find words in which we see ourselves, words that resonate with some portions of our experience? To answer these questions, we will analyze the current debate on sexual difference which are theoretically stimulating and pragmatically efficient. We can draw on two significant points from this line of thinking.

1. Sexual difference is a personal, contextual and original bond of the body and the word. It is an endless trade-off among biological, symbolic, relational and social dimensions. There are three levels involved:
   a. The living and sexed body;

---

[3] John Paul II, *The Original Unity of Man and Women*, Pauline Books and Media, Boston 1981. See also the current volume the contribution of Laura Paladino.

[4] G. Fraisse, *La differenza tra i sessi* Bollati Boringhieri, Turin 1996, p.46.

[5] See L. Irigaray, *Speculum. L'altra donna* (1974), Feltrinelli, Milan 2010; Id., *Etica della differenza sessuale* Feltrinelli, Milan 1985; Libreria delle donne di Milano, *Non credere di avere dei diritti. La generazione della libertà femminile nell'idea e nelle vicende di un gruppo di donne*, Rosenberg & Sellier, Turin 1987; Diotima, *Il pensiero della differenza sessuale* La Tartaruga, Milan 1987; L. Muraro, *Tre lezioni sulla differenza sessuale e altri scritti*, Orthotes, Naples 2011.

b. The symbolism arising out the body within the cultural context, or else the processing of a new symbolic order (we are always part of a society that influences our way of being in the world);
c. The singularity or biographical data (which ties each one of us to a body, culture and desires, conferring meaning on being a woman or a man). The weaving together of these analytical levels makes the sexual difference an inclusive category.

2. The second insight on sexual difference is the impossibility of bypassing matter. We cannot ignore the issue. It forces us to seek cultural and symbolic mediation to signify our embodiment (conferring meaning upon its expression, recognition of our bodily experience and its relational modalities). In other words, the body is not confined to its immediacy but is also symbolic. It is necessary to answer the "passion" of the difference, conceived as something that one experiences "passively," with a reflection upon concepts and the speech order that must be mediated precisely through the person (in this case, the thought of a woman who is writing this). This point seems particularly necessary, above all in contemporary culture, which accelerates towards an experience of instantaneity—concentrating on the intensity of the moment seems the most promising way forward for a critical and constructive approach to this issue.

Which flashpoints provide the best position for dialogue?

1. Sexual difference is a signifier with no identifiable signified, or else it finds itself within the most varied contents and inevitably turns into a paradox. We have not offered a definitive answer to the question of sexual difference because its contents are elusive and mobile within time. In what way is sexual difference distinct from any individual difference that one cannot identify, even circumspectly or in an analogical or symbolic way, some "constant" or female form that resists historicity and the individuality of all the responses? In what sense is sexual difference a horizon between the human race and individual differences?[6] We positively need to avoid any oversimplification. One objection says: If I, for instance, attribute to women the "inclination" to care for,[7] the privileged contact with the body, an emotional depth

[6] For the formulation of this question, see G. Salmeri, *Determinazioni dell'affetto*, Aracne, Rome 2013.

[7] I take this term from A. Cavarero, *Inclinazioni. Critica della rettitudine*, Raffaello Cortina, Milan 2013.

and a rich interpersonal syntax (which concerns "women more than men"),[8] might I not risk marshaling responses that bind women to a normative ideal which—even if it corresponds to the experience of many —causes discomfort to others who feel they do not fit such categories? If we propose substantive content for sexual distinction, might we not risk rigidifying feminine qualities, impeding one's self-definition?

Leaving the debate open so that everyone can begin with herself, listen to herself, and question herself constitutes a significant formative function. It is essential especially at a time when everyone is accustomed to inserting queries into an internet search engine from which a bewildering number of replies (ready for use and selected via automated filtering) tumble out.

On the one hand, such caution may dovetail with the idea of the human being as a mystery, and sexual difference an inaccessible threshold precisely *because* it is human, bearing the imprint of a being open to infinity. Sex variance, in the human form, transcends any single determination of experience as well as any sum of them because none of them can exhaust it all. It is impossible to say everything about sexual difference, not even one's own, just as it impossible to say everything on the subject of human beings because it remains something "beyond," something we cannot reduce to a formula.

On the other hand, if we do not seek any interaction or synergy between the signifier (at the origin of the signification process) and the signified content, are we not depriving ourselves of the chance to say something about what it means to be a woman? Would we not risk sitting down at a lavish banquet without tasting the food? Would we not get lost setting sail on an open sea and not finding any points of reference? It may be necessary to identify further mediations between an indefinitely open horizon of meanings and the lived body. It will be good to trace the slender and ineffable threads that support becoming a woman (or a man), without which the process of sexualization becomes either biologically determined or reduced to a mere mirror of the age.

2. A second point consists of the fact that sexual difference is "earned" within a process of self-signification. It is developed not just relation-

[8] I take this espression from *Libreria delle donne di Milano, Sottosopra verde. Più uomini che donne,* Milan 1983.

ally but also subjectively. For example, it manifests via feminine mediations within peer relationships. In fact, the difference is not just between me (a woman) and the *other*, but within me, inside of me.[9] It is a sign of our incompleteness. This incompleteness does not just find its fulfillment in complementarity. If it did—we are obliged to add—we would be forced to seek ourselves in another endlessly and find ourselves in a pre-existing totality that we can never reach.

The following reflection seeks to avoid two tendencies. On the one hand, the fallacy of defining one sex according to another model. Historically this happened to women when they were expected to conform to a male paradigm, either in a denigrating or an idealized way, leaving women no symbolic order of their own. On the other, an ambiguous and merely functionalist account of complementarity, like two pieces of a ripped card that match each other, leaves us unsatisfied. While we understand these concerns, what is missing in such claims is the reference to a human couple. This absence constitutes as great a lacuna in gender theory as in any speculation on sexual difference. We shall return to this issue further on.

3. The body at the origin of the difference

If we can neither accept the ideal of a woman as an incomplete and deficient incarnation nor give up on female difference altogether, then we must think this through. More fundamentally, what is the root of this variance? To answer this question, we must look at the sexed body. We are not referring to the organic matter, but to the living body or lived experience.

The objection addressed to those who draw attention to the difference in the body is the following: Isn't there a risk of falling into reductionism? Aren't we condemning the human being to mere animality? Wouldn't we end up living sexual difference merely as animals? At this point, it is appropriate to interrogate the human quality of sexual difference. As one might expect, it lies upon the fault-line of body and thought. Everything within the human being is the body and thought already transformed within the flesh. Body and *logos* are two dimensions that explain the human condition in its entirety. Together they include all human experience, but neither of them alone can say it "all." They say it together. This duality is not, however, the sum of one plus one. We might instead say that one dimension is wholly wrapped up within the other,

[9] See L. Muraro, "La differenza sessuale c'e," conference, Milan, March 29, 2015, www.youtube.com/watch?v=aaKcqXcC6gI&t=4s [accessed October 31, 2017]

to the point of one altering the other's meaning and expression. In this way, there is an asymmetrical reciprocity that the *logos* directs.

The *logos*, in fact, knows all about the body. It measures the urgency of the body's instinctual impulses and extracts meaning from its experiences, all within a process of labeling and signifying. The body also exerts action upon thought and human desire. As a lived body, the *logos* imprints the soul, colors the horizon of experience and leaves behind symbolic impressions for decoding. *Logos* itself is the opening of a world, as it modulates one's understanding of reality while mediating one's relation to it.

What do a woman's and a man's body "evoke"? A woman can do anything a man can do (if not in the same way), and a man can do anything a woman can do (though not in the way she does it). The sphere within which *neither* of the two can do what the other does is in the exercise of sexual procreation (which, naturally, should not be reduced to merely mechanical or biological data, but should rather be regarded as an interweaving of all human dimensions).

We appropriately interpret sexual difference as a relational difference, as a different way of relating with oneself and with the *other*, in love and within procreation. Now with these two relational modalities, we will dwell on the second, which is more radical. In the temporal order, sexuality precedes the process of generation. But it is also true that procreation precedes sexuality as the former confers intelligibility upon the latter. In fact, sex is ordered to reproduction (as well as the regeneration of the couple), and not the other way around.[10]

At present, the experience of procreation expresses the highest and most specific way of "living" the body. We say "at present," because the dominant technological instrumentalization and visionary designs of a post-human order—which intends to manipulate genetic material and interrupt the order of procreation—could alter this scenario.[11] Still, it is an illusion to believe that we

[10] This point is illustrated efficiently by C. VIGNA, "Antropologia trascendentale e differenza sessuale" in R. FANCIULLACCI and S. ZANARDO (eds.), *Donne, uomini. Il significare della differenza*, V&P, Milano 2010, p.218.

[11] It can occur in several ways: 1) through the selection of embryos or gamete donors offering characteristics deemed desirable in a child according to the whim of the one giving birth. 2) through an alteration of the symbolic order of procreation, according to which a woman may carry her daughter's ovum in her womb (fertilized by her son-in-law), becoming grandmother and mother of the same infant. Likewise, a transsexual person could, after completing the transition, carry his partner's ovum in his womb (fertilized by an anonymous donor), simultaneously becoming mother and father. 3) Finally, by the violation of the incest taboo upon which human civilization is built (as in the case of a woman who carries the oo-

can change the relational style of the sexed body, from sentient life to the innermost layers of our being, without eliciting a profound agitation of violent passions, uncontrollable fears and rampant depersonalization.

4. Woman as body-word

I will dwell primarily on the symbolism of the female body because of my experience, as I have no immediate access to a man's unique experience.

How to decipher this body? It is the most delicate of topics, and we must avoid two extremes. On the one hand, we must not rush to assign a clear and distinct content, because being a woman, just as being a man, in the depth of one's humanity, is ultimately a mystery. If we inscribe femininity within biological matter alone, we may curtail her freedom and original significance.

On the other hand, if we renounce any differential content, it becomes such an abstract and empty figure as to be sterile and meaningless. How to confront this dilemma? We believe a woman's body is a sign and a reminder (including for men) of her "capacity for the other"[12] inscribed within her corporeality.

In love, and even more in gestation, her body prepares for the other as the womb of an alliance open to life. Her body becomes that space which contains the longings of a small infant. Even more, the space (and time) of a triangle of desire is present. It is present in her yearning, as well as in that of the tiny baby fiercely attached to the mother's womb. And it is present in the father who entrusts the infant to her and coats her flesh in a language of love pronounced by them all.[13]

Within this triangle likewise converge a family, its ancestries and its cultural expectations. This amalgam of desires, hopes and fears can be explosive due to a mother's overexposure at this point. When we assume she "lives" her body and gestation with immediacy and instinct, we neglect all the whirling and symbolic strands she must unravel in a tangled web of desire without falling into the dark, sensorial, archaic power of the maternal *imago*. This interweaving of flesh can demand a sudden transformation of the body, a donation

---

cyte of a donor fertilized from her brother's gamete). The examples are from E. Roudinesco, *La famiglia in disordine*, 2002, Meltemi, Rome 2006.

[12] See J. Ratzinger, *Letter to the Bishops of the Catholic Church on the Collaboration of Men and Women in the Church and in the World*, no.13, in www.vatican.va/roman_curia/congregations/faith/documents/rc_con_cfaith_doc_20040731_collaboration_en.html

[13] See F. Dolto, *L'immagine inconscia del corpo. Come il bambino costruisce la propria immagine corporea* (1984), Bompiani, Milan 2002.

of meaning, a relationship to a baby's father, the relational web to inhabit, and the reorganization of her time and way of life. The tendency to churn thoughts, fantasies and desires, as well as dealing with the regressive specter of gestation's darker side, begins very early in a woman's life.

Psychoanalyst Silvia Finzi Vegetti claims that a girl withdraws into herself to process the changes of her body, as well as both the idealization of motherhood and the fear of infertility from her early youth.[14] We could probably say that the girl's dreams represent a sure way to draw another to her, even when he is absent. In her dreams and imagination, she is open to a fantasy encounter with the *other*, still before this meeting is real. In this intermediate zone, she experiences the appearance of desire, which sketches out a plot within which she rehearses this encounter. Often, though, the boy struggles to follow her in this area and to keep pace with the acceleration of her longing, which remains within a transition zone wherein they first learn more about each other.

Some may argue that the experience of pregnancy described above may be too anatomical and excludes women who do not wish to or cannot procreate. This objection is interesting as it implies two risks. On the one hand, there is the risk of ending the discussion by founding everything upon a merely physical motherhood, one reduced to blind organic production. On the other side, there is the risk of bending motherhood too quickly towards a merely symbolic and spiritual one, detached from the body. If spiritual motherhood does not contain the token mediation of flesh (without dealing with a living organism), it can acquire a sour taste. It is as if before the majesty of a pregnant body, any other form of maternity loses its power.

To this objection, we answer that the difference lies not in pregnancy itself, but in its physical and symbolic process. (A woman can become a mother without understanding its deeper meaning.) Another objection is that, without physically being a mother, one can become a mother to all humanity. Alternatively, as in the experience of adoption or child custody, she can find love that transcends blood ties and love the other person beyond her dreams of gestation. When the child becomes a son or daughter, the boundary between generated flesh and beloved flesh disappears. The two mental categories fuse while remaining distinct. She still needs to work out the stories of love and absence, attentive that the two categories do not lose their identity. Procreation

---

[14] S. VEGETTI FINZI, *Il bambino della notte. Divenire donna, divenire madre*, Mondadori, Milan 1996, p.83.

is not only about bodies, as there is an ulterior sense that no merely corporeal form can fully capture.

To avoid possible splitting of the self, we cannot overlook the carnal dimension. The body calls forth, but is not exhausted by, the experience of pregnancy. It introduces pregnancy while leaving space for other lessons. There is an imprint of the body—both evident and unconscious, superficial and internal, transparent and secret, wanted and suffered. The impression does not have a physical meaning alone. Every woman must confront it, even if she decides to extend her body in the form of surrogate motherhood.

We have talked about the mother's body as a woman who becomes a mother. We will now address a daughter's point of view. This observation is not secondary. While not every woman is a mother, every woman is always a daughter—apparently the daughter of a couple. Yet the daughter's identification with the mother's body is a particularly complex issue. In fact, there is no symmetry between the two sexes with regard to adhesion and contiguity with the mother's body. A daughter enjoys the relational advantage of being like the mother, identifying herself with the fantasy of an internal, primitive and generative body. Being like the mother is being able to become a mother, or to enlist generation within her body image. This identification can accentuate experiences of closeness to, and contact and intimacy with, the origin of life.

Nonetheless, it can be morbid if the daughter falls into the body's silent vortex and becomes paralyzed.[15] In comparison to the mother's procreative body, the child experiences an insurmountable disproportion because her generative power exists in dreams. It is about imagination but also absence, inadequacy and fear. Being born with the same sex of the mother, according to Luisa Muraro, "is a great but onerous privilege, because it impresses the opportunity to be a mother upon the body and the mind. This opportunity is an advantage, yet in its impression it can also be a 'minus,' a deficiency."[16]

Due to the extent of a non-differentiation from the mother's body, "the little girl remains 'absorbed' with the mother alone for much longer, reinforcing a mutual ambivalence and confusion."[17] According to Muraro, this absorption makes a woman more intimate with the maternal language, that matrix of knowledge "made up of loving dependence, pleasures without meas-

[15] G. Buzzati, A. Salvo, *Il corpo-parola delle donne. I legami nascosti tra il corpo e gli affetti,* Raffaello Cortina, Milan 1998, p.38-68.

[16] L. Muraro, *Il Dio delle donne*, Mondadori, Milan 2003, p.130.

[17] G. Buzzati, A. Salvo, *Il corpo-parola delle donne...*, p.61.

ure, needs with no response, and arbitrary excesses."[18] In maternal language, thinking occurs in the presence of things, in contact with their dense and opaque materiality. Here, words become animated, tactile, sensitive. They relate to each other like beads on an endless string or a woven mesh under the hands of an expert who focuses on each point of the fabric, embroidering stories, starting with one's own.

On the one hand, such a language highlights the most basic and minute things in everyday life. On the other, it is traversed by suspensions, hesitations and roundabouts in an involved and enveloping proximity (with ideas and experiences). In fact, in maternal language words and things search each other out, play together, agree, elude each other and multiply. A woman's body is the privileged point of observation to understand sexual difference as a call to the other.

How might a male body experience the absence of all this? A man generates out of himself. He utters a word of love, respectful and heartfelt, that awaits a response. Of course, he can second a mother's work, but he must pervade a woman's body since, without her who bears the flesh of his child, the power of his fertility dissipates into a barren waste. Otherwise, it turns to violence and domination. Every man, whether he becomes a father or not, must lay his desire before her. To do this, he must place it within a space that is hers alone. For this reason, he must discipline himself to transcend both himself and his peers, becoming attuned to a broader and richer relational syntax. To embrace sexual difference, rather than just put up with it, means being able to provide the conditions needed for communication. It is a fact that the use of different emotional syntaxes can lead to continuous misunderstanding and painful conflicts.

It happens, for example, during adolescence. A girl tends to project her specific relational disposition onto a boy, imagining that her counterpart shares her dynamics and emotional modulations. She expects a response that is not just reciprocal but symmetrical. The love she requests, as Lacan puts it,[19] is a love for something indeterminate, a demand for the whole space of another's desire. Such a request is often frustrating for the male because even if he corresponds, he does so from within a different emotional syntax. "She offers the boy a relationship between individuals that lack any specified goal,

---

[18] L. Muraro, *La maestra di Socrate e mia, in Diotima, Approfittare dell'assenza. Punti di avvistamento sulla tradizione* Liguori, Naples 2002, p.33.

[19] J. Lacan, *Encore: Le séminaire, livre* XX. (1972-1973), Seuil, Paris 1999.

which he cannot stand, and of which he is not capable. She tries to attract the boy into a relationship that he fears, rejects and flees."[20]

For a woman, the disparity is likely to result in a charming game of being in demand. For the male, it issues either in withdrawal from the relationship or else in a temptation to dominate. This dynamic reinforces a relapse into gender stereotypes, which intensifies when a relation based on difference is absent. On the contrary, a consideration of sexual difference as an unavailable threshold may prevent one from seeing his or her symbolic framework as the only one possible. Nevertheless, in an era of non-differentiation models ending in a unisex vision, the loss of disparity risks taking boys and girls out of themselves, out of the experience of their bodies. It risks exposing them to the loss of a desire for the other and constructing social bonds that are ever more tenuous.

5. The human couple and the gift of the difference.

The disquieting aspect is that today couples seem vacuous in their ideation and creativity, as if there were no longing between them. Children are not orphans of one father or one mother only but sometimes find themselves in alien family constellations. They may have "too many" mothers and fathers. The problem is not having an experience of the couple's generative relationship, or of longing and its symbolic extension. They lack that emotional nourishment that proceeds from a flowing gift of self-donation.[21]

We are dealing with double bonds, along with their sequential multiplications, in which the problem lies in the passage to a third person—the offspring who is the *other*. The child should not be viewed merely as an instrument for the transmission of desire. On this apparent inconsistency of the couple, the third person struggles to find his or her place. However, if there is no room for this third person, there is no closure for the family. If the family unit does not hold, then the entire society suffers. If there is no bond between the parents as a married couple, the child confronts an experience of emptiness (of meaning and love).

Nothing is more painful for a child than to think that she is the result of chance, rather than a rely to love which elicits a shared "word." When this word transcends speech, it becomes flesh.

---

[20] L. Irigaray, *Oltre i propri confini*, Baldini Castoldi Dalai, Milano 2007, p.50.

[21] See M. Francesconi, "Tra-mutazioni antropologiche", in *Psiche* 2, 2008, p.118-119. See also T.H. Ogden, *Rêverie e interpretazione*, Astrolabio, Roma 1999, p.57. [English original: *Reverie and Interpretation*, Jason Aronson, 1997]

The only path left is to re-enchant the world with the gift of difference. To donate difference means to offer my partiality and insufficiency. This insufficiency is the most precious thing I have because it is a space for the *other*.[22] To donate my incompleteness is to grant my desire for the *other*, offering space and time to the horizon of his meaning. Here, he may find in the area I have preserved that path through which he seeks, builds up and expands his longing.

Difference—becoming a place for the *other*, in reciprocity—can then nourish the infinite. It always generates beyond itself a world, children, meaning, civilization, the future.

[22] On this, Laura Muraro has written passionate pages in the above *Il Dio delle donne*.

CHIARA ATZORI*

SEXUAL DIFFERENCES: SCIENTIFIC ASPECTS

Since time immemorial, the family has consisted of a man and a woman who, united by a stable and public bond, took responsibility for the fruit of their carnal relationship—the children born from their marriage. The two fundamental axes of every human experience are present in this triangle. The horizontal axis of the sexual difference, and the vertical-generational axis, which connects origin with a child's vocation that fully blossoms into maturity.

Thanks to this triangle, every child can verify the existence of differences in humans without any scientific or anthropological knowledge. Every child can ascertain that the sexual difference is fertile and that his or her identity originates from it. This identification is not vague or optional and is limited to membership in one of the two sexes. It is both a received gift and an entrusted task.

Within the family, the couple is the first model of a relationship between sexually diverse entities. We recognize without elaborate explanation the spouses' ability to unite, interact naturally and complementarily at a physical level, transmitting life through mutual care.

This model can exist in an atmosphere of harmony, affection and mutual esteem or, conversely, can be unbalanced, manipulative, oppressive and violent. The parents' behavior towards each other and their children—the fundamental triad of relations—influence their sexual identity for better or for worse. Through this attachment, the children's identification or non-identification, body comparison and internalization—initially linked to sensorial, emotional and affective contents—progress with the development of their cognitive and rational faculties.

Today, society tells us that there are several types of "families" or "parental forms." New forms of unions have taken over the "traditional" family. These new unions have rights irrespective of their sexual orientation to produce the baby they desire technologically.

The images of Foster, spread globally and provocatively renamed as "Gay Nativity" by the media, is illustrative. Attached to the photos was the fol-

* Medical director of the L. Sacco-Azienda Ospedaliera-Polo Universitario hospital and member of *Scienza & Vita* in Milan.

lowing note: "Milo was born on June 27 [2014] via an unrelated surrogate who did not use her own eggs. The two fathers, BJ and Frankie, were bare-chested when they hugged their son for the first time since direct skin contact has a calming effect on infants."[1] With these words, the first pictures of the baby, born from a surrogate mother and handed over to two gay men, were launched worldwide.

The surrogate mother's non-involvement from a genetic point of view further emphasizes the techno-scientific method of the birth. It presents an icon of the anthropological revolution that we are witnessing. We live in a society where sexual activity has been separated from procreation thanks to the birth control pills. Subsequently, reproduction is severed from sex through IVF, making it possible to freeze embryos. "Sperm banks," "ova banks," "wombs for rent" and the development of artificial wombs are some of the consequences.

The photos of a baby's birth are emotionally captivating. Nonetheless, the act of separating a baby from the female body that for nine months has given him nourishment, warmth, delight and a wide range of reassuring sensorial experiences, and catapulting him onto a man/customer's chest is particularly troubling. Milo is one of many "desired" children whose conception violates the anthropological, biological and psychological facts that form our natural, cultural and scientific heritage.

Apart from economic considerations and the "objectification" of the child (also applicable to different forms of ART), this anthropological distortion requires careful consideration:

1) In what way is sex difference relevant in biological, psychological and symbolic terms? These three perspectives are related since psychical sexuality is emanation, extension, internalization and integration of corporeality in the psychic life through symbolic codes.
2) Will this deconstruct male and female roles at will within the family and education?

Looking at the first point, we may consider a simple logical-mathematical formula: if A (woman) and B (man) are different, can A+A or B+B be equal to A+B? We live in an age of widespread social irrationality, where emotion and impulsiveness trump logic. Pseudoscientific subordination requires us to provide "scientific" or "evidence-based" arguments even for issues of common sense.

---

[1] See http://www.ilfoglio.it/articoli/2014/07/05/la-lacrimosa-nativit-gay-e-post-moderna-che-emoziona-il-mondo___1-v-118863-rubriche_c414.htm, [accessed 30/5/2015].

The question of "roles" carries within it the insuperable dichotomy of male and female. In fact, deeply rooted in the human being is an aptitude for symbolism. We cannot deny the universally recognizable "symbolic" or "archetypical" nature of male and female roles, regardless of the varied and culturally diverse expressions of these roles in different geographical areas and historical periods. "Pointed" and "perforated," penetrating and enveloping, linear and circular are all expressions attributable to the symbolic world of sexual differences. Men and women are different in their biology, psychology and behavior. Regardless of the different cultures and educational approaches, they evoke through their very existence as sexual bodies a symbolic role that cannot be denied or obscured by any theory or ideology that separates sex and gender. Men and women are human beings with the same dignity, yet they are different in many ways, from the shapes of their bodies (the biological phenotype) to their psychological traits, attitudes, activities and specific characteristics such as stereo-spatial skills, memory, language and response to stress.[2]

When speaking of "roles" in the family—role understood as a manifestation of identity—we must remember that from the first cell to the whole organism, one's identity is shaped by sexuality. We cannot deny the importance of the biological differences between the two sexes without introducing a fundamental error into any consideration of the cultural effects on the manifestations of identity. Male and female roles are not reducible to abstract cultural constructions, which are amorphous, deconstructible, and reconstructible as if the human being were only inert or "sexless" material.

The relational dimension is connected to the biological component. Relation presumes a difference, an encounter, a dialogue. It is what happens on the ultramicroscopic level in each cell and on the social scale in every human being.

Each characteristic of the body is affected by a modulation that, for the sake of simplicity, we define as the "environment," or to use a more scientific term, "epigenetics." We are "relational" in our very structure as living matter.

An American author with degrees in physics, medicine and Jungian psychoanalysis wrote, in a fascinating way and with broad scientific support, that we humans have a "quantum" mind. Quantum physics confirms the untenability of previous perspectives and shows the seemingly stunning but increasingly convincing evidence that matter itself is made up of relationship, inter-

---

[2] See E. Luders, C. Gaser, K.L. Narr, A.W. Toga, "Why Sex Matters: Brain Size Independent Differences in Gray Matter Distributions Between Men and Women," in *The Journal of Neuroscience*, 29, 2009, p.14265-14270.

action and dynamism.[3] Without going into disciplines beyond the subject of this chapter, and focusing on the issue of sexual identity and differences, we can summarize the question in the following way. The essential core of who we are at an individual level lies within the genome. Far from being a static structure, the gene pool or DNA (of which X and Y chromosomes determine its sex) is subject to an on/off gene expression (corresponding to whether the individual genes are active or not) that is in continuous dialogue with the surrounding environment. Using a symbolic image, we can visualize the DNA as material immersed in a "soup" of expanding concentric circles. The nuclear and cellular matrix not only affect it but, in turn, are subject to the continuous modulation taking place in the tissue matrix that contains the cells. As for the tissues, there is a "dialogue" between the different organs and systems, as well as between these (which together constitute the body) and the "control unit" of the brain. This setup leads us finally to consider the influence of the external and internal environments on the body through the senses and receptors of the body itself.

We can scientifically agree that every individual, despite her uniqueness and individuality, is not a thing—an isolated and self-sufficient monad—but rather a distinct substance who lives owing to a continuous relation between her inner, biologically constituted world and her outer world. The self is "self-in-relation." There is still no scientific explanation for the self-awareness of existence perceived as a unified and unifying experience (the self) that naturally tends toward communication through language, poetry and music—all "higher" faculties than the pure instinct of self-preservation. Above all, there is the typical human possibility to exercise the freedom to act or not. This choice occurs according to ideal, ethical or moral motivations in response to the emergence of spontaneous impulses or as resistance to forms of coercive conditioning.

From the macro-observation of any man or woman to the ultramicroscopic evidence of the epigenetic-DNA dynamism, without which there would be no life, the human being is relational, originating in an encounter with something different. It is very significant that the zygote, the first cell of every individual, forms from the meeting between gametes (egg and sperm) that come from people of different sexes. ART clinics that offer their services to those who want a child are well aware of this fact.

Thus, there are fundamental differences between the sexes rooted in biology, yet continuously modified by the environment. Concerning sexual iden-

[3] See J. Satinover, *The Quantum Brain: Freedom and the Next Generation of Man*, Wiley, New York 2002.

tity, it is not scientifically defensible to consider the link between "nature" (not in its ontological but rather in its biological meaning) and "nurture" (the relational factors, together with the internal and external environments) as either-or, contradictory or outright absent. In place of a static or purely material concept of the brain as a network of cells, there is evidence today for the plasticity of organs mediated by chemical and sensory stimuli that modify, create and eliminate cell connections in the synapses. Aggregates of cells (nuclei or brain areas) react to the connections between them in a widespread network of communication, including both sensory inputs coming from the "periphery" of the body and the chemical composition of the body. This "soup" tends toward self-preservation through continuous responses to perceived changes in an innate model (homeostasis).

The unconscious impulses of regulation and self-preservation (e.g., temperature, nutrition, energy) depend strictly on sensory receptors. The receptors are arranged in various ways in the body and rely anatomically and functionally on the person's sex. Therefore, there is a sexual neuro-sensory map of the body's boundaries, or what we call personal identity (who I am and who I am not), of which we are cognitively and consciously unaware. Nevertheless, our brains are continually comparing this map with the surrounding world to maintain a balanced homeostasis. A simple example of the different modes of distribution and processing of the sensory receptors is the perception of heat and cold in men and women under the same ambient condition. Another example of the variation felt by the sexed body is the man's inability to have a subjective sensory awareness of vaginal lubrication and conversely the woman's failure to experience penis erection. It is true, nonetheless, that these feelings can be indirectly felt by touch in the moment of intimate relations between the two sexed bodies. It is an awareness of the existence of personal identities, desirous of a relationship, that meet in an irreducible otherness.

Antonio Damasio offers detailed information on the integration of one's substantial cognitive unawareness of the inner world and body boundaries, on the one hand, with the mysterious origins of consciousness and full self-awareness on the other. It is a process typical of every human being, whether man or woman, but naturally dependent on the body phenotype through which the person manifests.[4] The sexual differences in the masculine and feminine brains have significant implications. They uniquely influence biochemical processes and contribute to one's susceptibility to diseases and specific behavior.

---

[4] See A. DAMASIO, *Il sè viene alla mente*, Adelphi, Torino 2012.

These differences between the male and female brains do not refer to superiority or inferiority in a possible discriminatory confrontation. They are merely scientific facts. Knowing these variations enables us to understand the complexity of men and women, differences that sometimes generate conflict. Such complexity is the object of study for researchers and physicians today who are more attuned to the existence of "gender medicine."

By considering these natural differences, we can address critical issues of how genetic sex differentiates the etiology and progression of diseases, drug metabolism, neuronal maturation linked to cognitive activities, and finally behaviors with evident influences on roles. "Brain sex" and the resulting behavior are not genetically determined solely by the mediation of hormones secreted physiologically by the gonads (testes in 46XY or ovaries in 46XX) from the first moments of embryonic development. Although this mechanism is prevalent, sexuality is also a result of the direct effects of genetic expression in non-gonad cells, which function according to sexual differences.[5]

In today's era of gender ideology, we tend to disregard the many biological variances between males and females. It is most apparent at the macroscopic level, where differences are noticeable without unique biomedical skills or knowledge of the statistical distribution of height, weight and external genitalia. Less obvious are physiological differences that are nonetheless critical, such as susceptibility to various diseases and the ability to metabolize drugs and nutrients. There are also forms of adipose buildup that separate men from women, as well as the varying frequencies of disorders like anorexia-bulimia.

Without neglecting these biological and physiological disparities and their impact on male and female roles, it is worth documenting disparities in the brain anatomy and chemistry, such as the prevalence and functions of neurotransmitters. The two sexes have similar but not identical brains according to the popular classical explanation of neuroscientist Brizendine.[6]

Studies on the contrast between male and female brains initially focused on "measurable" data, such as the size of specific brain regions. Today, dynamic methods of functional neuroimaging unexpectedly confirm that the on/off modalities and the dialogue between distinct areas are dimorphic in the sexes when stimulated in real time.

Damasio presents a convincing scientific synthesis on the unity between the body and the brain and the continuous relation between the body and the en-

---

[5] See T.C. Ngun, N. Ghahramani, F.J. Sánchez, S. Bocklandt, E. Vilain, "The Genetics of Sex Differences in Brain and Behavior Frontiers," in *Neuroendocrinology*, 32, 2011, p.227-246.

[6] See L. Brizendine, *The Female Brain*, Bantam Press, Great Britain 2007.

vironment. One perceives himself according to various levels of self-consciousness, from the most primitive (the "proto-self") to the highest (extended consciousness). Damasio's works explore the intricate interrelationships among body, brain, mind and thought. We in the West are heirs of a philosophical Platonic dualism, who also suffer from a cyclic recurrence of Gnostic dualism that tends to separate the body from the mind. This heritage is evident in the current field of science in thoughts about gender, with recognizable cultural and political influences.[7] Scientific studies by the likes of Damasio are particularly significant because they cautiously recognize the interdependence and limits of a biochemical-genetic-biological substrate. Damasio does not linger on the question of human sexual dimorphism, which is a biological fact since the discovery of chromosomes and DNA. Every human cell, whether somatic (diploid cells with 46XX in the female or and 46XY in the male) or germ (haploid sperm cells with 23X or 23Y and haploid ova cells with 23X), is unmistakably marked by this dichotomy, whether physiological or pathological.

A binary system characterizes a similar "separation." The choice of symbols used in the binary system—0 (zero) and 1 (one)—already carries in itself an interesting symbolic reference. The former sign is concave and circular while the latter is a vertical line that psychoanalysts would probably call "phallic." Thus, even the binary system can represent "sexual" signs.

In biology, this orderly system, based on a parallel harmonious program including the gonadal, hormonal, genetic and phenotypic modes of sexuality, is recognizable in physiology. It is possible both to identify deviations (pathology) and to propose potential remedies (therapy). If we drop the first distinction between what is physiological and pathological, any question about sexuality becomes unclear, ambiguous, confused and incomprehensible. This chapter will not deal with topics of diseased states or make a value judgment about those with genetic, gonadal, hormonal or phenotypic defects.

Brain sex differences are found not only in neuronal morphology but at a subtler level as well. The protrusions that connect and dialogue with the nerve cells (synapses) are affected by hormones that are both sexually conditioned and conditioning. Hormones influence not just the synaptic connections, but also neuron density, cell lifespan and the mode of programmed cell death (apoptosis)[8].

---

[7] See E.S. Lodovici, *Metamorfosi della gnosi*, Ares, Milano 1991.

[8] See C.D. Good, I. Johnsrude, J. Ashburner, R.N.A. Henson, K.J. Friston, R.S.J. Frackowiak, "Cerebral Asymmetry and the Effects of Sex and Handedness on Brain Structure: a Voxel-Based Morphometric Analysis of 465 Normal Adult Human Brains," in *NeuroImage*, 14, 2001, p.685-700. For further study, see M. Hines, *Brain Gender*, Oxford University

Men and women have unequal patterns of secretion, transmission, regulation and processing of biomolecules called neurotransmitters, chemical messengers between neurons.

Studies carried out on animals, and especially on rodents, have identified many of the neurochemical sex differences. When we extrapolate the results to humans, they should be interpreted cautiously. Despite the claims to overcome "speciesism" by researchers and gender theorists like Haraway and others, scientists are aware of the differences between humans and the animals.[9] We cannot apply animal and even mammalian models to humans crudely and uncritically, especially when it comes to sexual identity. All the same, we would not have developed effective drugs for mood disorders (anxiety and depression) and insomnia, or major psychiatric diseases (antipsychotics), if there was not a reasonably reliable correspondence in experiments with the differences observed between males and females. An example of neurotransmitter sexual dimorphism is the monoaminergic system involved in neurological diseases and various psychiatric disorders that affect men and women differently. Monoamine neurotransmitters are small molecules that help control multiple processes, including sexual behavior, breathing and stress response.[10] There are also divergences between the sexes in some mental disorders, such as the affective and autistic pathologies, in terms of frequency and manifestation.[11]

The significant catecholamines, commonly known as "stress agents," are dopamine, norepinephrine and epinephrine, all synthesized from an amino acid called tyrosine. The dopamine regulation affects the level of the other catecholamines, as they derive from dopamine itself (the cascade effect). There are common clichés about them. "You have high-dopa" refers to a state of hyperexcitability, including sexual one. "I am pure adrenaline" is a response to a stressful environmental or relational situation. Besides the apparent varia-

---

Press, Oxford-New York 2004, p.191-197; G. Einstein, *Sex and the Brain*, MIT Press, Mass, Cambridge 2007; J.B. Becker, *Sex Differences in the Brain: From Genes to Behavior*, Oxford University Press, Oxford-New York 2008.

[9] See D. Haraway, *Simians, Cyborgs and Women: the Reinvention of Nature*, Routledge, New York 1990. See http://www.antispecismo.net, https://restiamoanimali.wordpress.com, https://musiemuse.wordpress.com.

[10] See L.H. Gargaglioni, K.C. Bícego, L.G.S. Branco, "Brain Monoaminergic Neurons and Ventilatory Control in Vertebrates", in *Respiratory Physiology & Neurobiology*, 164, 2008, p.112-122; C. Kordon, J. Glowinski, "Role of Hypothalamic Monoaminergic Neurons in the Gonadotrophin Release-Regulating Mechanisms," in *Neuropharmacology*, 11, 1972, p.153-162.

[11] See M.V. Seeman, "Psychopathology in Women and Men: Focus on Female Hormones," in *The American Journal of Psychiatry*, 154, 1997, p.1641-1647.

tions in individual response to stress, there are pronounced variations of neurochemistry in males and females in response to same experimental stimuli.

The organization of the response to stress differs in males and females before birth. It is therefore not the result of cultural or educational pressures but the expression of a pre-genetically coded mechanism. Emotional and behavioral effects, the ability to react to adversities (resilience), occur through hormonal and neurotransmitter mediation. Curiously, and contrary to the collective imagination, males are more vulnerable to stress. This weakness manifests itself in a higher frequency of male than female embryos at conception, with a corresponding higher incidence of disease and overall mortality.

During pregnancy, when development proceeds at a pace that is unequal to any other stage of life, the human embryo—due to the peculiarities of "performance" in the brain structure—is particularly sensitive to chemical disturbances. Studies focused on exposure to prenatal adversities have discovered chemically-mediated neurological changes, the basis of an increased risk of mental illnesses. Since conception, males and females show different trajectories of development and stress response. It is likely that the organization of sex-dependent neuronal circuits can explain the differentiated vulnerability of mental health during the fetal period. Scientists have examined the relation between prenatal sexual dimorphism and stress exposure in early life, and the link with two developmental disorders—emotional problems (higher prevalence in women) and autism spectrum disorders (more male-dominated).[12] The differences in some attitudes and sexual behaviors between the two sexes may have a biological basis. Without forgetting the caution in extrapolating data on humans, we find in the rat neuro-anatomic selective differences in the sexually dimorphic nucleus of the pre-optic area (SDN-POA), which is involved in the regulation of male copulative behavior. Select injuries of the SDN-POA result in a slowdown of response (regardless of testosterone levels linked to sexual desire par excellence). The equivalent of SDN-POA in the human brain is the INAH-3 nucleus, which is on average 2.6 times larger in males than in females.[13]

Another example of a significant divergence is the Anteroventral Periventricular Nucleus (AVPV) responsible for the regulation of the female luteinizing hormone (LH). AVPV also affects the male sexual behavior. It is 2.2 times

[12] See E.P. Davis, D. Pfaff, "Sexually Dimorphic Responses to Early Adversity: Implications for Affective Problems and Autism Spectrum Disorder," in *Psychoneuroendocrinology*, 49, 2014, p.11-25.

[13] See L.S. Allen, M. Hines, J.E. Shryne, R.A. Gorski, "Two Sexually Dimorphic Cell Groups in the Human Brain," in *Journal of Neuroscience*, 9, 1989, p.497-506.

larger in females and equipped with a higher cell density. Another nucleus that monitors male sexual behavior is the bed nucleus of the stria terminalis (BNST), involved in the release of gonadotropins (that regulate the hormonal fluctuations in the testes and ovaries) and the modulation of stress.[14] The primary nucleus (BNSTp) has a higher volume in males. There is a constant feedback between the cerebral peduncle involved in the release of hormones and the effects exerted on the brain by the differentiated "male" and "female" hormones. There is a different rate of programmed cell death related to the exposure to sex hormones.

The latter are qualitatively present in both sexes but selectively linked in quantity and temporal variations to genetic sex and different stages of life. As a symbol, the female menstrual cycle and masculine linearity are related to the influence of the neuroendocrine brain stem called the hypothalamus. The latter is influenced by a complex web of connections that form the brain surface, called "cerebral cortex." Regarding sexual dimorphism we can also mention the bridge structure called corpus callosum, which connects the two hemispheres of the brain, enabling the exchange of information.[15] Even if corpus callosum is fuller in male babies, there are more interconnections in women, which means less lateralization of functions to the right or the left. It is particularly true for a feature in which the female brain seems to excel, that of spoken language. That is why we sometimes jokingly call the female brain "a chatterbox" for its richness of expression and emotional content due to a wide exchange between the left and the right brain. The greater lateralization to the left of the male's language skills can anecdotally explain the inability to "silence" a woman with a well-aimed pat on the left side of her head, which otherwise is probably enough to shut a man up!

The cerebral cortex has a wide range of processes, from memory[16] and language[17] to emotional processing,[18] and it maintains a constant dialogue be-

[14] See D.L. Walker, D.J. Toufexis, M. Davis, "Role of the Bed Nucleus of the Stria Terminalis Versus the Amygdala in Fear, Stress, and Anxiety," in *European Journal Pharmacologist*, 463, 2003, p.199-216.

[15] See R. Sperry, "Some Effects of Disconnecting the Cerebral Hemispheres," in *Science*, 217, 1982, p.1223-1226.

[16] See D. Badre, A.D. Wagner, "Semantic retrieval, mnemonic control, and prefrontal cortex," in *Behavioral Cognitive Neuroscience Review*, 1, 2002, p.206-218.

[17] B. Shalom, D. Poeppel, "Functional Anatomic Models of Language: Assembling the Pieces," in *Neuroscientist*, 14, 2008, p.119-127.

[18] K.N. Ochsner, "The Social-Emotional Processing Stream: Five Core Constructs and Their Translational Potential for Schizophrenia and Beyond," in *Biological Psychiatry*, 64, 2008, p.48-61.

tween the right and left hemispheres (known to neurosurgeons). However, all this occurs in different ways in the male and the female brain. The posterior cortex is thicker on the left only in males and, in fact, gonadal hormones play an important role in maintaining sexual difference (as shown from oophorectomy, which "masculinizes" the female cortex). No hormonal intervention can radically transform a male brain into a female brain or vice versa.[19] The female brain's sexualization seems to depend on estrogen, and reduced prenatal exposure to testosterone strongly influences it. In the complete form of Morris syndrome (complete androgen insensitivity syndrome, CAIS), the genetic male with 46XY karyotype is incapable of responding to androgens and prevents the development of male secondary sexual characteristics. They also have structural and functional features of an apparently "female" brain.[20]

Other dimorphisms involve the arcuate nucleus (ARC), which helps to regulate the estrogenic hormonal cycle, appetite and body weight; and the amygdala, which strongly influences emotions and decision-making. The medial amygdala is more extensive in males due to circulating androgens, so females have fewer synapses than men. The organizational effects exerted by testosterone, when detected adequately by the receptors in the fetus, are crucial to the development of the male brain and its maturation during adolescence. They are present especially in those areas almost entirely formed by dopaminergic neurons.

Dopamine is involved in the control of motor activity, and females have 20% fewer dopaminergic neurons. It does not mean that women have an inferior motor ability but are merely different from men. In sum, one cannot deny the evidence that neuronal organization, neurotransmitter compositions and structures controlling emotions and actions affected by hormonal modulation are different between the sexes.

Even the so-called psyche can be differentiated since the structure dealing with complex emotional, motor and behavioral processing is established and structured in a dimorphic way. Men and women have equal dignity but distinct organizations, in which the environment influences neuro-sensorial "receptivity" from the beginning. Unable to escape from biological differences, men and women consequently differ in many psychological and behavioral aspects. For example, men statistically perform better in specific visual-

[19] M.C. Diamond, G.A. Dowling, R.E. Johnson, "Morphologic Cerebral Cortical Asymmetry in Male and Female Rats," in *Experimental Neurology*, 71, 1981, p.261-268.

[20] See D.G. Zuloaga, D.A. Puts, C.L. Jordan, S.M. Breedlove, "The Role of Androgen Receptors in The Masculinization of Brain and Behavior: What We've Learned from the Testicular Feminization Mutation," in *Hormones and Behavior*, 53, 2008, p.613-626.

spatial tasks (e.g., mental rotation) compared to women. Women generally show better performance in language skills than men[21] (e.g., verbal fluency). Besides, there is a big difference in the interests and sexual behaviors between the sexes, in random sex, multiple sexual partners and sexual visual stimuli (e.g., pornography).[22]

Some may argue that these differences are due to social and gender socialization; however, biological traits are at the basis of many role differences.[23] By and large, understanding the biological factors involved in male and female expressions can explain the relationship between the body and the sexed brain, environment and behavior, and the emergence of symbols. It can clarify how biological sex influences different modalities of relation and learning. Social or cultural factors alone do not explain the diversity in behaviors and roles of different eras, cultures and geography. They are therefore not attributable to "sexist" cultural stereotypes and cannot be deconstructed arbitrarily.[24] Biological sex and gender as a culturally stratified layer of behaviors identifying one as male or female, therefore, cannot be separated except ideologically or abstractly.

Life sciences have demonstrated that sexual differences owe primarily to genes and sex hormones, which assist phenotypic dimorphism and brain sexualization after the gonad differentiation. Another issue regards abnormalities caused by endocrinological genetic defects affecting the adrenal hormones or otherwise linked to sexual development disorders (called the intersex states).

Science once thought that the gonadal hormone under the influence of sex chromosomes is the only determining factor in the physiological development of humans with a harmonious sexual identity. Evidence now suggests that other genetic abnormalities may also have direct effects. Sexual *determination* (46 XY, 46 XX) and sexual *differentiation* may not precisely coincide. Determination is the process by which the bipotent gonad develops into a testis or an ovary. Differentiation of reproductive structures, the external genitalia and other non-gonadal differences are affected not only by gonadal

---

[21] See J.S. Hyde, "The Gender Similarities Hypothesis," in *American Psychologist*, 60, 2005, p.581-592.

[22] See R.A. Lippa, "Sex Differences in Sex Drive, Sociosexuality, and Height Across 53 Nations: Testing Evolutionary and Social Structural Theories," in *Archives of Sexual Behaviour*, 38, 2009, p.631-651.

[23] See M. Sylvester, S.C. Hayes, "Unpacking Masculinity as a Construct: Ontology, Pragmatism, and an Analysis of Language," in *Psychology of Men and Masculinity*, 11, 2010, p.91-97.

[24] See C. Atzori, *Il binario indifferente*, Sugarco, Milano 2010.

hormones (whether physiologically or pathologically transposed in CAIS) but maternal environmental influences as well. Gestation is the relational modality par excellence. The *other*, despite its radical dissimilarity, is hosted and immunologically "tolerated" in the body through a continuous and dynamic chemical mediation until birth, marking the physical "detachment" of the mother-child dyad.

Decades of research has demonstrated that these organizational effects depend on hormones and gonadal synthesis of the child and her sex. The results consist of cell proliferation, migration and organization, which lead to a recognizable and irreversible morphological structure produced during embryogenesis and fetal maturation. The body and brain organize in a harmonic and physiological male or female pattern or else develop pathologically (e.g., intersex states). It all happens within a hosting body that is biologically female.

This itinerary is subject to possible "environmental" disturbances. The embryo-genetic program is subject to factors related to the circumstances of the mother, who is a living person affected by her environment. Maternal stress can produce chemical substances and circulating hormones (prolactin, oxytocin, catecholamines, etc.) with effects on the placenta, which metabolizes them in different ways depending on the genome and sex of the child, as the placenta is also a sexed structure of somebody different from the mother. These effects are short-term changes that occur in the body. Depending on the presence or absence of hormones or biologically active substances, they can influence the child's "genetic" program in continuous dialogue with the environment. These direct epigenetic modulations are extensive and may include the effects of locally produced hormones (from the metabolism of the placenta) or other non-hormonal but metabolically active messengers (e.g., smoking, drugs, substance abuse).

There are examples of brain sexualization differences, known for their role in brain structuring, that predispose male and female behavior. With the discovery of hormones and DNA, these differences are first attributed solely to "static" biological factors. The emerging research now shows that the interaction between subject and environment, as well as between individuals, has a direct effect on "biological" mechanisms. Environmental influences can modulate expression of the genes (epigenetics).

We now analyze how biology is related to the topic of "roles." For those who consider parenthood only from an ethnologic point of view (and consider the human being as an "animal"), parenting is a set of social behaviors regarding care that evolution has conserved with a predictable trajectory and exclusive contents. However, the relationship of each parent to a child and the motivation to provide parental care offers a wide margin of variability and a unique spectrum of possibilities. It is because the exercise of freedom is an exclusive prerogative of the human being (for better or worse) even in that most "binding" of biological relationships between parents and their children. Animal behavior is aimed primarily at preserving life and conserving the species through instincts that are rigidly constrained, repetitive and possibly trainable through punishment or gratification but otherwise mainly determined by the genome. Alternatively, there is an impulsive behavior in humans. Impulse differs from instinct as it is adaptable, plastic, easily influenced, educable and free.

From a historical and anthropological point of view, there is a spectrum of diversified possibilities in which parental care or roles express themselves through time and the specific cultures of people and traditions. But in every culture and time, a fundamental dichotomy linked to sexual difference is recognizable. There are many varied and diverse expressions of the parental role in different ages and cultures. However, there is a symbolic role based on the sexual difference that could be called "archetypal." We find this from the beginnings of "civilizations," regardless of the geographic coordinates, with global ethnic echoes linked to the myth of "mother earth" and "father sky."

This primitive symbol, attributable to the sexual difference in its repetitiveness and persistence, supports its anthropological importance as more than a simple cultural "construct," a Greek-Judeo-Christian heritage, obscurantist and now freely surmountable. This symbolism holds even in the difference detectable in relationships between parents and children. Quite apart from PC language, "Parent 1" or "Parent 2" does not exist. While in gender (etymological root: *genus*, common to generate, genital, etc.), there are male and female, man and woman, father and mother. In parenting, the symbolic role is inscribed within a matrix that has specific natural maternal and paternal connotations and that emerges particularly in the early stages of life, in what is called the primary caregiver.

Bearing in mind the definition of a person (individual substance of a rational nature, relational, sexed and possessing language), the theme of "roles" in the family is dimorphic, not "stereotypical" but realistic. It is not crystallized within a "biologically determined" behavioral modality but rather is based on a difference that is biologically incontrovertible and so necessarily symbolically insurmountable. There is an intrinsic "symbolic" value, precisely because sexual difference, in itself, indicates a rupture and an impassable limit, called sex. The typical human characteristic of symbolization, present from birth, appears inextricably linked to "primitive" sensory experiences like the satisfaction of basic needs. To be fed through oral suction in a mouth without teeth, to be dressed and to be kept clean in both the anal areas, the same for males and females, and the genital areas, different in males and females. From Freud onwards, we can say that the symbolic importance of the "holes" and "bumps" of the body, different in males and females, appears to be an accepted fact true for all ages, even if today there is an ideological will to obscure these elements of psychoanalytic contribution.

The symbolic meaning of sexual difference is transmitted, regardless of "culturally modified" actions, through language, even a simple "sound." Human beings, gifted with the word, are provided with a linguistic "instinct." The center of language and its organization (in addition to timbre and the voice box) appear differentiated and recognizable in the two sexes. The simple way of talking to a baby already "transmits" a symbolically different auditory binary code, which is certainly captured in a pre-rational, but not for this reason less important, way in the different sexes. It happens without taking into consideration the feminine rather than the masculine way of transmitting thoughts and sentences or approaching the child with a special tone of voice. For this reason, psychoanalyst Simona Argentieri's recent reflections appear confusing. In an essay entitled "The Maternal Father," she seems to minimize, if not deny, the psychological and symbolic results of the physical mediation of early male nurturing. In other words, the effects of what the author simplifies as a "maternalization" of paternal roles. In the oxymoron title of "the maternal father," this proposal (perhaps ironic, certainly semantically questionable) cannot ignore the sexual difference contained in the noun (what is "father"?) and the adjective (what is "maternal"?).[25]

An easily accessible and valid contribution to rediscovering the symbolic difference between father and mother is by Francoise Dolto, a Lacanian psychoanalyst, doctor and mother who believes that children do not experience sex but the sexes—those of their parents. Sex does not exist for them if the adults around them do not represent it. Therefore, it is not possible to distinguish sociocultural factors from biological ones. It is impossible even regarding each family's style, every triangle of father-mother-child. All family structures, traditional or not, are favorable to the development of the child as one who is led in the dynamic of becoming male or female in a future act of procreation within the complementary encounter of the sexes.[26] Returning to the famous image of

[25] S. Argentieri, *Il padre materno*, Einaudi, Torino 2014.

[26] F. Dolto, *I problemi dei bambini*, Mondadori, Milano 2003.

"gay nativity," it is clear now that gender vision has distorted the neurophysiological and neurobiological bases of the mother-child and father-child relations. Gender theories demand the painless replacement with the sterile term "parenting" in a relationship in which all the involved parties are asexual. But this relationship is "ontologically" sexed, in every constitutive cell, body shape, brain and mode of interaction, through an inescapable symbolic binary code.

Among the various theoretical frameworks regarding the child's needs within the parent-child relationship, attachment theory seems to have the most significant scientific validity. Today we know that this argument has a neurobiological basis.[27] It originates in a study of the association between maternal deprivation and juvenile delinquency. One of the points of reference in contemporary evolutionary psychology is psychotherapist John Bowlby. He postulates the universal human need to form a primary psycho-affective proximity as a newborn, upon which depend personal balance, responsibility and commitment as an adult. This form of attachment is based on the fundamental relationship between mother and child. Bowlby strongly affirms that this attachment is an innate biological system that promotes closeness between the child and a specific caregiver. All newborns attribute the bedrock of their security to those who take care of them, even if it has been rough or negligent. There are various models of attachment. If the child had sensitive figures for their physical and emotional needs, they tend to show patterns of "secure" attachment. However, if the primary caregiving is chaotic, unpredictable, rejecting, negligent or inadequate, the child can develop anxious, insecure, disorganized or aggressive behaviors. An initial stage of secure attachment is crucial for the child's life. It provides the relational environment for modeling identity, temperament and future behavior.

Much research has explored the neural basis of attachment at molecular, cellular and behavioral levels. The studies have found many parallels between Bowlby's original thesis and the biological systems that form the basis of attachment and the ability to respond to stress. Rodent cubs are dependent on a specific set of maternal postpartum behaviors for survival—maintaining the nest, taking care of cubs, defending them from predators. These behaviors are attuned to the progeny's needs expressed through vocalization, the rooting reflex, lactation permission and the experience of aromas and flavors. Let us consider the baby in the "gay nativity" scene, placed on his fathers' bare chests.

---

[27] J.E. Swain, J.P. Lorberbaum, S. Kose, L. Strathearn, "Brain Basis of Early Parent-Infant Interactions: Psychology, Physiology, and in Vivo Functional Neuroimaging Studies," in *Journal of Child Psychology and Psychiatry*, 48, 2007, p.262-287.

Body care and feeding are parental behaviors best associated with the newborn care. Women describe breastfeeding as a unique, intimate, very physical, sometimes sensuous experience that creates an extraordinary union between the mother and her baby. Also, cleaning, dressing, playing with the baby and other gestures create a lasting significance as they allow proximity between parent and child, and allow for frequent inspection and manipulation of the child's body by an adult. The presence of fixed behavioral patterns in parents may seem minimal, suppressed or perhaps insignificant in humans compared to other animals. However, detailed analysis of filmed parent-child interaction is leading us to appreciate its biological importance as being regulated by critical hormones and neurotransmitters. In particular, maternal behaviors are influenced by child stimuli and have a direct sensory impact (auditory, visual) that activates certain sexually dimorphic neurotransmitters, including oxytocin, prolactin, vasopressin and dopamine. The oxytocinergic system is vital for the formation of social and spatial memory, affiliative behavior and emotions. The oxytocin receptors are related to a mother's demeanor and are notably present in the brain areas and in many cognitive and emotive activities, including the management of social stress and establishment of trust.

Joyfully expressed love and a balanced concern for the child's safety and well-being, rather than an anxious tension between joyful fantasies and worries that something terrible might happen to compromise the relationship, will produce different emotional states in the child.

Due to dimorphism in their brains, stress and reactivity are different for men and women. We know by now that a parent's frequency and intensity of joy and worry, anxiety and depression, as well as their substance abuse, reverberate in their children, causing obsessions, compulsions, addictions, attitudes toward life and the insurgence of subsequent romantic inclinations.

The frequency of psychiatric disorders and substance abuse (from alcohol to drugs) is statistically different in people with different sexual orientations, with higher prevalence in persons with SSA and in men who have sex with men (MSM).[28] The claim of "equal parenting" for same-sex couples—leaving aside the lack of sexual difference according to the neurobiology and neurophysiology of caregiving—should be prudently viewed through the lens of epidemiological analysis. "Same-sex parents" statistically tend to have higher

[28] M.G. Flores, S. Koblin, B. Hudson, S. McKirnan, D. Colfax, "Alcohol and Drug Use in the Context of Anal Sex and Other Factors Associated with Sexually Transmitted Infections: Results from a Multi-City Study of High-Risk Men Who Have Sex with Men in the USA," in *Sexually Transmitted Infections*, 84, 2008, p.509-511.

exposure to recreational substances (alcohol for women and drugs for males), which can impact the child's mental health. Parental behaviors crucially affect the neonate through that first imprint, which will later influence the future actions of the child, adolescent and adult. The parent-child relationship offers children their early social experience, forming paradigms of what to expect from others and how to meet the other's expectations.

In a study by Swain, the author focuses on the neurobiology of parental behavior, including data from experiments using functional neuroimaging (fMRI). The psychological aspects of parenting based on neuroscience reveal brain differences between the sexes. Without falling into "biologism," the study supports the importance of the biological bond of early attachment. Looking at the neuro-hormones essential for the regulation of social bonds, and their complete deregulation of the normal parenting mode in cocaine abuse, the study highlights the fragility and sensitivity of these biological bonds under the influence of substance abuse. The most interesting part concerns the description of the brain circuitry underlying the interaction between child and parents. From an animal model (rodent) with a species "approach" through studies of non-human primates, one can arrive at the human experience. These conclusions must be calibrated in view of the difference between animal instincts and human impulses. Through the review of functional neuroimaging studies in humans, research suggests that the neural networks, called the hypothalamic-midbrain-limbic-paralimbic-cortical, act jointly to support the parental response to children. These processes include emotion, attention, motivation, empathy and decision-making. All these brain features, as we have mentioned before, are strongly influenced by processes of brain sexualization, distinctly experienced by men and women. They inextricably bind the response of "parental role" to sexual difference.

AN INTERVIEW WITH CARLO ROCCHETTA*

Today we witness a real abuse of the word "love." The current view perceives love as primarily attributable to the truth of "feelings." However, what is its deeper meaning—instinct, spontaneity, reason, will or sacrifice?

The word "love" is probably the most commonly used in everyday language, and the most abused and misunderstood. The neo-Latin verb "to love" originally derives from the verb *kamare*, where the preposition ka/kam indicates an impetus towards, a desire for, and an encounter oriented towards another. The etymology already reveals a potentiality, a dynamic force within the spiritual-corporeal human identity (of a man or woman) that tends toward giving, acceptance, and sharing. There can be no real love in an individual who is withdrawn. Love means an opening-up, an interpersonal communication in two directions. It applies to all forms of love. It is as valid for the love of a young couple as for spouses, for the love of parents toward their children and of children toward their parents. It is true for every real friendship and love toward the *other*.

The first step in every education to love, therefore, is educating someone to pass from childish selfishness to a mature, self-sacrificing choice, from narcissism to a spousal relationship. As such, love goes beyond a mere emotion or epidermal feeling. It implies a decision involving the whole person, his relational vocation and his life project. The second step in every education in love requires being able to ensure that the spiritual self guides the orientation to love and be loved. When this does not happen, when the only logic of "Go where your heart takes you" prevails, then love's potential turns into a form of arbitrary spontaneity having no direction. It is like a wild horse out of control, unable to carry one beyond a chosen life project. The vocation to love needs to be guided by the person's deeper self and by the higher faculties that distinguish her—reason, will and moral conscience. Only then does it take place as a complete, fully human and humanizing experience. Love's potential in us knows a variety of applications.

The Greek language offers three particular words: *philía*, éros, and *agápē*. The first word, *philía*, indicates love-friendship as an interpersonal relationship characterized by the elective correspondence between two or more peo-

---

* Professor of Theology, and director of Perugia's Centro Familiare Casa Della Tenerezza in Italy.

ple. The second category, éros, refers to falling in love as the attraction to the opposite sex and implies a powerful sensory, emotional and passionate experience. The third category, *agápē*, indicates love as gratuity, including a profoundly spiritual dimension. It is selfless love, the giving of oneself to the point, if necessary, of offering up one's life for the other. The Christian vision captures these three meanings together, in profound correlation among themselves and with God. The consequence is clear. Those who wish to learn to love must grow within all three horizons and accept the hardships of the art of controlling one's selfishness and instinctual impulses. This implies self-determination within a chosen perspective of giving, acceptance and sharing. Love in all its forms requires a choice, and implies an attitude, that cannot be improvised but is only learned by actually living it out.

In relation to the couple, then, the most important moment is to know how to pass from an initial stage of falling in love over to true love. Only love makes it possible to build lasting and strong relationships and can build a relationship able to resist through thick and thin. As for young couples and spouses, the question is whether falling in love, at a nascent state, manages to evolve into a relationship of conscious love. Love is a conscious ability to accept the other, for what he/she is, and not for what we idealistically would have liked. It means accepting his/her limitations, and to work to draw out his/her best qualities. Conscious love is the ability to promote the other person and to create an equal exchange (symmetric and asymmetric at times), whereby one feels loved and appreciated in each other's respective experience, without being flattened or canceled out. Conscious love is an exchange and a profound communication, heart to heart, soul to soul, in which both learn to support each other in their weakness and to grow together, with an ever newly effective and affective encounter, full of beauty and enchantment.

Falling in love is essential at the beginning of the relationship. But only a conscious and mature love allows one to put up with "everything" and the "forever" of spousal existence. A conscious and mature love is one in which each perceives the other as a welcoming gift, in joy and sorrow, in sickness and in health, just as the spouses promise on their wedding day. The story of so many couples who after twenty, thirty, fifty years of marriage say they are more in love than when they were very young testifies to how this goal is possible, and is not an unattainable mirage at all. What is required is to learn the grammar of an adult and responsible love.

At this point it is essential to take one further step. What has been said so far is true for everyone, even for those who do not believe in God. Yet those who marry "in the Lord" welcome a newness in themselves that comes from above as an added value. It is a newness that springs from the transfiguring Love of the Triune God and from the gift of the Spirit to newlyweds with the marital sacrament. The sacrament of marriage, in fact, is an event of grace embracing the male-female relationship and determining a new way of being for two baptized persons in the Church and in the world. The entire journey of the couple's life will be forever marked by the presence of Christ the Bridegroom. Nothing will any longer be unknown to His presence. The spouses can always appeal to the gifts of the sacrament—permanent union and sanctifying grace—to fulfill the deeper meaning of their nuptial relationship and intimacy.

If, on an anthropological level, love stands as an "ascending love," a love that reaches to heaven, on a sacramental level it meets with the "descending Love" of God, who has given himself to humanity and has redeemed it in his Son, Jesus of Nazareth. These are two dimensions of love inseparable from one another, just as Pope Benedict XVI explained perfectly: "*Eros* and *agápē*—ascending love and descending love—can never be completely separated. The more the two, in their different aspects, find a proper unity in the one reality of love, the more the true nature of love in general is realized."[1] In the New Testament the category of *agape* corresponds to the Love of God ("God is *agápē*," 1 Jn 4:8,16), which can transform the spouses' human love and their conjugal sexuality, elevating it.

Agápē does not represent the ascending human love reaching God that is éros, but rather God's Love descending to man to the point of the madness/scandal of the cross. It is a love that made *charis*, grace, within a Trinitarian ontology, spread out in the heart of the baptized by virtue of the Spirit's gift: "the love of God has been poured into our hearts through the Holy Spirit that has been given to us" (Rom 5:5). On this matter the Catholic vision differs radically from the conception of Lutheran theologian A. Nygren, who, in a famous study, concluded an absolute irreducibility *between* éros and *agápē*: éros is a possessive love centered on the satisfaction of ego, a material love, whereas *agápē*, is gift-love, oblation, spiritual love.[2]

Nygren's position reflects a Protestant tradition extending from Luther to K. Barth, according to which in human nature—and therefore in the natural love between men and women—there cannot be anything positive, as

---

[1] BENEDETTO XVI, *Deus caritas est*, Vatican City 2005 n. 7.

[2] See A. NYGREN, *Agape and Eros: The Christian Idea of Love*, trans Philip S Watson, University of Chicago Press, Chicago 1982.

it has been radically corrupted by original sin. Only *agápē* love would have value and deserves consideration. The question is whether a dualism of this kind truly reflects the teaching of Revelation and is consistent with both the original idea of éros and the same biblical concept of *agápē*. Undoubtedly the Christian idea of *agápē* differs from the Greek idea of éros, but this does not mean that the two forms of love are incompatible with each other or even opposed. There is no opposition, but reciprocity between the love of man who seeks God and the love of God who comes to meet man. Once éros indicates a love tending upwards as Poverty (*Penia*) seeking a greater perfection (*Póros*), what impedes receiving this love descending from above as an announcement of the newness of God's *agápē* manifested in Jesus the Bridegroom and the effusion of his Spirit?

In fact, this is not only possible but necessary, because without the powerful support of grace proceeding from the Redeemer, "human nature" would be left to its own devices. What is true for love in general is also true for the intimacy of a couple. In virtue of the sacrament of marriage, grace springs from Christ's marriage to the Church and the gift of his Spirit configuring the entire loving relationship of spouses, making it a sacrament. The sacramental gifts model marriage on the nuptial Christ-Church relationship rendering it a sign of grace. The human love of the spouses is purified, assumed, elevated by the divine love of Christ the Bridegroom for the Church his Bride. It is transformed into grace, just as at the Cana wedding when water became fine wine.

Can we still talk about marriage? Or, given the legal but especially anthropological-cultural tendency to legitimate various forms of unions, such as those which ignore sexual complementarity or even exceed the bounds of monogamy, should we use the word "marriages" in plural?

We absolutely must continue to speak only of "marriage," not of "marriages." The forms of unions that are propagated with so much emphasis today may possibly be qualified as "civil unions," but marriage is that only between a man and a woman. It is not only demanded by Christian revelation, but by the anthropological statute of sexual duality. Only a man and a woman can welcome each other and give themselves respecting their deepest identity and their own body structure. The woman is a being that welcomes man, and the man is a being that gives himself to his woman. Both are beings capable of sharing not something but their very selves and are dutifully open to life.

Behind the denial of the uniqueness of marriage, there are—as you know—"gender theories". Already the use of the word "theory" is incorrect, as it seems to give a scientific rigor that it absolutely does not have. It is more correct to call it well-oriented gender ideology that offers serious philosophical or biomedical reflections. Intended to pursue the equality of roles between men and women, this ideology asserts the irrelevance of biological sex in defining the masculine and the feminine and supports the rights of everyone to identify themselves as male or female based on how they feel or want to be. Sexuality does not belong to the corporeal-natural dimension of the person, but only to the dimension of individual choice. The "subjective feeling" is ontologized and the ontic and objective foundation of nature is denied. Behind this ideology there are strong powers that propagate and finance it, with the aim to destroy the family and to manipulate individual at will. The American Secretary of State, in October 2013, expressly stated that the United States (through the Global Equality Fund) financed the LGBT projects in more than 50 countries in the world.

The Church's position is clear: no to homophobia; yes to the natural family based on marriage between a man and a woman; no to gender ideology and its attempt to colonize humanity. No to homophobia, as each person must be respected and attitudes of contempt are not acceptable. As it is stated in the Catechism of the Catholic Church (CCC 2357 to 2358), same-sex persons "must be accepted with respect, compassion and sensitivity. Every sign of unjust discrimination in their regard should be avoided." Of course, people are one thing, behaviors are another. It is the latter that is ethically unacceptable, not people. Yes, to the family founded on the encounter between men and women and their openness to another third born from them, their child. The family community is the icon of God the Trinity-of-Love. According to the stories of the Genesis, the male-female couple is manifestation of the person's unique subjectivity, male or female (Gen 1-2), and is the historical expression of the eternal intra-Trinitarian communion. We have to remember that the Christian monotheism is radically different from Jewish or Islamic monotheism in this regard. The one God in whom we believe in is not an I-Solitude, but an I-Com/union—Three-in-One[3]. At the beginning there isn't the loneliness of the One, eternal, isolated Being. At the beginning there is the communion of the Triune.[4] The one God is not an I-Solitude, but an I-We, a God-communion, the one God as Father, Son, and Holy Spirit. According to the theological concept of Trinitarian *perichoresis* the divine persons are not closed in upon themselves, but exist in an eternal self-giving relationship to the point that none of them could exist without the other. It is an interre-

---

3 L. Boff, *Trinità: la migliore comunità*, Citadella, Assisi 1990, p.12.

4 *Ibid.* p.21.

latedness that says the God of faith is the One-God-Communion of Love (1 Jn 4:8,16). And it is crucial that it is so. If there were One Solitude, loneliness would exist. Behind the Universe, so different and harmonious, there would be no communion, but only loneliness. Everything would end as the tip of a pyramid. If there were Two Singles, the Father and the Son, there would primarily be separation. One would be other from the other and exclusion would dominate, since one wouldn't be the other and there won't be communion. Instead perfection is reached with the Trinity because there is unity and inclusion. It avoids the loneliness of the One and exceeds the separation of the two, going beyond the exclusion of one from the other. Trinity allows communion and inclusion. The Trinitarian figure reveals the openness and union of opposites. It is therefore not arbitrary that God is a communion of the Triune. The Trinity shows that a dynamic communion inhabits in everything that exists and moves.[5] To believe in the Triune God is to believe that at the root of all that exists arises an eternal communion of the Three in the unity of the One.

The male-female couple which opens to the other third is the greatest manifestation in act of the mystery of God-One-Trinity-of-Love. In fact, the male-female duality alone offers an incomplete picture of the Triune God. Once established, this duality needs to open up to the dimension of the third. The vocation of being man and being woman reaches its perfection becoming "one flesh" only in the child. In the child, father and mother are united under a new self-relationship that exists in itself and for itself at the same time that it fulfills and manifests their indissoluble unity. Man's and woman's I-you reciprocity is directed towards an "us." The vocation of the "two" in "one" leads to becoming "three," as Maurice Blondel noted with a direct but effective language, "In marriage, two beings are only one, and that is when their one becomes three."[6] It is not an exaggeration to connect parenthood to the Trinitarian communion and its eternal fecundity. Read theologically, procreation supposes at least two fundamental contents. It has its roots in the eternal fecundity of God-Trinity of which marriage / family is a revelation and historical implementation. And it is formed on the model of that fecundity from which it recovers the dynamics of acceptance, donation and sharing[7].

[5] *Ibid.* p.23-24

[6] M. Blondel, *L'Action II, L'action humaine et les conditions de son aboutissement,* Alcan, Paris 1949, p.264. "Dans le mariage, deux êtres ne sont plus qu'un, et c'est quand ils sont un qu'ils deviennent trois."

[7] For more information on the family as an icon of the Holy Trinity, see C. Rocchetta, *Teologia della famiglia, Fondamenti e prospettive,* EDB, Bologna 2011, p.133-222.

An inseparable reciprocity must be affirmed on the basis of this Trinitarian foundation. This Trinitarian foundation affirms an inseparable reciprocity—between the unitive and procreative meaning of the conjugal act, between conjugality and parenting, and between parenting and filiation. It is a unitary indissoluble path. Unity and Trinity are inseparable in God—one does not exist without the other. God is communion of Three in One; and only because the basis of God's being is communion that unity is possible, and vice versa. Is it not the same for parental fertility? Becoming fathers and mothers is an act that manifests the communion in unity and unity in communion. In the logic of the nuptial mystery, becoming spouses and becoming parents is part of a continuum. From the perspective of faith, it is therefore not acceptable to undo what belongs to the unified plan of the Creator and is confirmed by the revelation of the Begotten and the gift of his Spirit to the Church. As *Familiaris Consortio* (FC) 14 beautifully evokes, the reality of the son is a living reflection of the spouses' love, permanent sign of their unity, living and inseparable synthesis of their becoming father and mother. The three separations in act today, made possible by biotechnology, cannot be considered an advancement, but rather a regression and a serious threat for the future of humanity, a manifestation of a true "delirium of omnipotence".

As a popular saying goes, "God forgives, but nature never forgives." To go against nature is never without consequences, as it always brings about uncontrollable chain reactions. Not everything that is technically possible is also ethically acceptable. The final criterion to look at is what is good for the human person, is to start with the weakest. Just think, by way of example, of the child's right to tenderness—the right of every child who comes into the world to have a male figure and a female figure who welcome her and make her feel loved, who protect and help her discover the world. An inborn and inalienable right totally unacknowledged today, both in the laws of the various States and in the Charter on the rights of the child. The paradox is that we continually debate on the civil rights of the same-sex persons, but no one talks about the civil rights of the child, the weakest being, to have a father and a mother who hold him in their arms, and make him feel like a person. Is this not the first right that society must protect? In fact, it is on the foundation of this right that Christian vision rejects as normal or natural child adoption by a single person or same sex couples. Nobody can prevent civil societies to move in the other direction, but they do so taking on the full responsibility towards future generations and their good. The absence of one of the two parental figures will impede the child's identification/differentiation essential in the development of sexual identity. Similar considerations can be applied to overthrowing monogamy and permitting polygamy. Choices of this sort do not only concern the individuals and their free will, but the common good of humanity.

Is it outdated to talk about conjugal chastity today, in a society where sex is reduced to consumption? What aspects of beauty can tenderness bring to the life of a couple?

It is not at all obsolete, but it is indeed indispensable. It is known that the problem we face today is a troubling affective analphabetism. It is an analphabetism that dominates the horizon and affects every private and public sector, every age group and the couples themselves. Arturo Paoli is right when he observes, "Most human beings have experienced sexuality before true love. They ignore affectivity and its tender forms. They ignore the emotional needs dominating the person and their ability to turn into tenderness."[8] Tenderness is relegated as part of the indefinite, the unsaid, useless or irrelevant. We have discovered the Human Genome and we are in the process of identifying the genetic map of every individual. Yet very few worry about their affective world and are prepared to choose tenderness as a life project and lifestyle. Now, many psychologists affirm that neurosis and psychosis are caused by the lack of tenderness, leading to not-feeling-loved and not being able to love. This induces in the depths of the person, man or woman, a permanent desire for revenge or vindication. Personality disorders are usually the result of an unfulfilled life in terms of affective integration, and thus about tenderness offered and received. Affective education is therefore not only a problem of psychology or family pedagogy. It is an anthropological matter since people's or a couple's state of happiness or misery depend greatly on it. From the moment we are born, when we open ourselves to the smile, we are already relational beings manifesting a desire for tenderness. Our first groan is not the beginning of a "life of tears", as G. Leopardi thought, but an appeal to be recognized as persons who need affection, to love and feel loved. The problem today regards what is the best way to arrive at an appropriate understanding of tenderness, without ambiguities particularly common in this field.

Unfortunately, romantic novels have reduced the sentiment of tenderness to sentimentalism. We must reject this reduction and seek the most adequate

[8] See A. Paoli, *Della mistica discorde*, La meridiana, Molfetta 2002, p.14-15.

answer possible.[9] Dictionaries define "tenderness" as a feeling of "sweet emotion," a "sweet and gentle affection" of "loving attention." However, they qualify "sentimentalism of tenderness" as a "mushy" attitude, an "excess of sentimentality", "fluff" or "false tenderness." The difference jumps out, and this is essential. Tenderness belongs to the radical experience of being a person and fulfills itself in the openness to the other, in a dimension of loving acceptance, gift, and sharing. On the contrary, the sentimentalism of tenderness is the retreat on oneself and is predominantly captive. It searches the other for selfish benefit. One considers tenderness as "being"; another considers tenderness as "having." The former is combined with fortitude and creativity; the latter is synonymous with weakness and passivity.[10] In the former, the ethics of responsibility dominates; in the latter, superficiality. Tenderness is a strong sentiment that touches the deepest chords of the person and involves his whole being and put him in "relation with" and in "relation for" positive, free and liberating exchanges. On the other hand, sentimentalism is a fleeting emotion, a "faint feeling" oriented to create dependencies or dominion on both parties. The difference is critical, but not always adequately understood or taken into account. Hence, there are so many misunderstandings like those regarding emotions and feelings, infatuation and love.

Sexuality is inseparably combined with the human person's vocation to tenderness. What the soul is to the body, tenderness is to sexuality and its exercise. E. Fuchs writes, "Between desire and sexuality there is a way of humanization by way of tenderness, which is a wondrous recognition of the other's otherness. It gives meaning to desire, and desire itself—strength of life and gift of joy—becomes the source of all possible tenderness."[11] Tenderness offers what sexuality alone is not able to guarantee—the sense of giftedness, the joyful wonder of encounter, the generous and creative liberality. It allows the sexual gesture to remain at the aurora and always growing. The ability

---

[9] On the theology of tenderness, see C. ROCCHETTA, *Teologia della tenerezza. Un "vangelo" da riscoprire*, EDB, Bologna 2000 (con bibliografia, p.439-440); Id., "Tenerezza", in AA.VV, *Temi teologici della Bibbia*, Cinisello Balsamo 2010, 1371-1376; C. ROCCHETTA, R. MANES, *La tenerezza grembo di Dio Amore. Saggio di teologia biblica*, EDB, Bologna 2015. On the spirituality of tenderness, see C. ROCCHETTA, *Viaggio nella tenerezza nuziale. Per ri-innamorarsi ogni giorno*, EDB, Bologna 2004; Id., *Elogio del litigio di coppia. Per una tenerezza che perdona*, EDB, Bologna 2004; Id., *Gesù medico degli sposi. La tenerezza che guarisce*, EDB, Bologna 2008; Id., *Le stagioni dell'amore. In cammino con il Cantico dei cantici*, Bologna 2009.

[10] For more information on the difference between "being" tender and "having" tenderness, see: C. ROCCHETTA, *Teologia della tenerezza...*, second chapter.

[11] E. FUCHS, *Desiderio e tenerezza*, Claudiana, Torino 1988, p.7.

to be tender is not of lesser importance and is neither optional nor secondary to sexual intimacy. On the contrary, it is constitutive for the realization of its highest meaning. Only in this way, conjugal sexuality does not lose its profound meaning and is not reduced to a mere satisfaction of instincts or mechanical routines, but is implemented as an interpersonal occasion of gift and acceptance, the fruit of Love and growth in Love. Conjugal chastity must be understood in this context.

One point must be made clear beforehand—chastity is not a virtue reserved only to those who are consecrated to God. All Christians are called to chastity in relation to their state in life or vocation. For the baptized, chastity is the moral virtue that regulates—according to right reason enlightened by faith—the sense of sexuality and its exercise. It is a virtue that concerns every Christian both outside and within marriage. It affects the spouses' life in the same measure it channels their sexuality in direction of their love. In this sense, conjugal chastity is an ethical imperative and corresponds to the Pauline discourse on the use of the body for the sanctification and glorification of God, and not for immorality (1 Cor 6:12-20; 1 Thes 4:4-5; Rom 6:19). *Familiaris Consortio* 37 is right when it says that, "In this context education for chastity is absolutely essential, for it is a virtue that develops a person's authentic maturity and makes him or her capable of respecting and fostering the 'nuptial meaning' of the body." Chastity in marriage arises in this direction and represents an expression of intimate love for the spouses as significant and real as marital intimacy. The same dynamics of the bodies and of conjugal love involves renunciation and waiting. Of course, these times must be experienced as an expression of a consensual, free and responsible choice, and must harmonize with their path of growth, avoiding any form of abuse.

In 1 Cor 7:2-5, Paul offers a fundamental point of reference. According to the Apostle, spouses have an equal and mutually exclusive "right" to each other, in relation to their acts of marriage. Equality is established in opposition to each state of inferiority of women with men, as it was for the Jewish and pagan law. The spouses can renounce to this right, but they must do so based on a "mutual and temporarily agreement" avoiding the danger of "incontinence" they could encounter (v. 5). Paul wants to offer the principles of balance that curb the untimely zeal of one or both spouses, but at the same time reveal the merits of conjugal chastity that can harmonize with the demands of marriage, granting a specific space to "encounter with God" ("for your prayers," v. 5). The choice to abstain from marital relations, in this case, has nothing negative or phobic. On the contrary, it is an option designed to grow in mutual love and grace of the sacrament. The choice of conjugal chastity is in this case the ability to love each other more, with the effect of freeing the couple from the danger of narcissism and elevate the joys of an intimate oblation of a spiritual love that goes from person to person, and not just from body to body. It should of course be balanced with the effective enhancement of the spousal body language, beginning with the language of tenderness and multiple affective manifestations typical of conjugal love.

How can the Church, faithful to the truth of marriage, respond to the civilly divorced and remarried?

It is not a cold, aseptic or neutral fact for the Christian community to meet with many separate and "wounded families." Rather it must rethink itself as a community capable of acceptance similar to Christ's acceptance. The Magna Charta enunciated by Paul in Romans 14-15, is a clear imperative, "Welcome one another as Christ has welcomed you for the glory of God" (Rom 15: 7). No one should feel excluded. Each and one of us, in our own way, is part of Christ's body which is the Church. Who is stronger in faith must indeed know how to draw near to the weaker, without judging their hearts (Rom 14:1), "Why then do you judge your brother? Or you, why do you look down on your brother? For we shall all stand before the judgment seat of God... So [then] each of us shall give an account of himself [to God]. Then let us no longer judge one another, but rather resolve never to put a stumbling block or hindrance in the way of a brother" (Rom 14:10-13). Meeting with the separated and "wounded families" provokes our communities to come out from their false security or a state of inactivity. It is a call to rediscover itself as the people of God on its journey in history, including within her womb saints and sinners who are on the path of penance and renewal (LG 8). Before all this, ecclesial communities cannot close their eyes or sit back and watch as if nothing was happening. Much less should they limit to generic speeches about today's family crisis and the need to rediscover its value. It requires a precise and concrete answer that gives shape to charity and organizes hope at the service of those brothers and sisters living in a situation of marginalization and loneliness. It is not exaggerated to speak of a class of the "new poor." The separated and divided families represent the "new poor" because—although economically well off—they experience years of suffering. They are unable to extricate themselves from it, with endless conflicts, even from a legal viewpoint, violence and retaliation of all types. They are the "new poor" because if they are not helped in a real and effective way, they continue to harm and massacre their children even after the separation. They are the "new poor" because they experience suffering, humiliation and are wounded without end. They arrive to exploit their children for their own purposes, making them "elements of contention in a battle without boundaries." Before these brothers and sisters, we can paraphrase the Gospel of Mt 25:31-46 addressed to each one of us, "I was separated and you left me alone! I lived the suffering of a divided family, and you did not come to see me! I was the son of the separated and you did not show any affection! You could have prevented the separation of my parents and the suffering it implicates but you have done nothing to be close to me, nor have you put in place adequate structures! You could have helped me when I lost my way, but you crossed the other side of the street!"

What kind of pastoral plans are we implementing as pastors and family counselors? Faced with this question, we must recognize that we are quite deficient. We must seek a creative imagination that makes the Church more welcoming, the same way Christ's heart is. As the Italian Episcopal Conference (CEI) Family Pastoral Directory (DPF 96) states, "Every family and all families are entitled to the Church's loving and maternal care. For this reason, the Church's concern will not be limited only to the closest Christian families, but broadening its horizons similar to Christ's heart, it will be even closer to all the families and in particular to those who find themselves in difficult or irregular situations."

The Directory's text offers what represents the underlying directive of the whole family pastoral plan, the heart of Christ—broadening its horizons in the same measure of Christ's heart. And this is the paradigm of all pastoral activities—the compassionate tenderness of the Begotten Incarnate who died and rose for all. There can be no other horizon. The text speaks of "difficult or irregular situations," meaning by difficult all critical situations where it is still possible to prevent the separation, and meaning by the irregular situations the divorced, the divorced with new partners (DPF 210-212), the remarried, the civilly married, and cohabitants (DPF 213-230).

The text also assumes those who have experienced separation or divorce without having desired it, and therefore are not responsible for their situation, "to not get involved in a new union and engage in fulfilling their family duties and Christian responsibilities" (DPF 211). In this case, "there is no obstacle in itself for the admission to the sacraments" (DPF 209). Different is the situation of those who are in a new union or have remarried. These two situations are in fact objectively different both existentially and ecclesial-spiritually speaking.

Regarding sacraments for the faithful who have been separated, the documents of the Church offer them closeness, welcome and support. The CEI invites priests and deacons, sensitive couples and Christian communities to draw these separated faithful close to the sacrament "with care, discretion and solidarity." With care: to recognize "the value of the testimony of fidelity when the innocent party bears and accepts the suffering and loneliness of the new condition." With discretion: to share their reality and invite them "to participate in the life of the community with charity and prudence," avoiding the possible risk of self-withdrawal. With solidarity: to lavish esteem, understanding, kindness and practical help, especially at times when the loneliness is so strong that they will be tempted to not attend the liturgy (DPF 208). The underlying task remains to help these brothers and sisters to "help them to cultivate the need to forgive which is inherent in Christian love and to be ready perhaps to return to their former married life" (FC 83).

The issue of those separated or divorced with new partners or remarried is more complex, also because of the many variations they present. "We see before us in our daily experience quite a number of people who after divorce, move on to new unions, obviously civilly. Some of them are totally detached from the Church and live almost in a general religious indifference. Others are not fully aware of the fact that their new union is against God's will. Others, even though they are aware of not living in accord with the Gospel, continue their Christian life in their own way, manifesting sometimes the desire for greater participation in the life of the Church and its means of grace." (DPF 213)

Weighted discernment. Not all situations are equal and have the same ethical weight. Pastors and family counselors must be alert to these differences and the causes that led them to the new life choices.

Leave every sterile confrontation. One path is chosen to overcome the sterile contraposition of the dialectic "yes / no sacraments" which contains this type of reasoning: since the sacraments cannot be granted to the divorced with new partner or remarried, there is nothing to do than to await a change in doctrine. In the meantime, one can only stand still, leaving these brothers and sisters in a kind of limbo as in a dead-end alley. In this regard, we want to strongly reiterate three key points: 1) The failure of a marriage does not break one's relationship with God, and does not exclude those affected from his infinite tenderness. 2) The failure of a marriage does not erase faith. To believe and to love God and respond to His love with our love is not deleted from the event of separation and/or a second marriage. 3) The failure of a marriage and the consequent new bond does not cancel the baptismal communion with the Church, even if it injures it. It does not destroy the participation of the baptized to its life and mission. The baptismal font is indelible, "Once a Christian, always a Christian."

The post-conciliar documents and the New Code of Canon Law (1983) have started a new path, stating that they remain part of the Church and are subject to its life and edification, although they are not in full communion with the ecclesial community.

Benedict XVI, after reaffirming the ineligibility to the Eucharistic communion of the divorced remarried, goes on to say, "Yet the divorced and remarried continue to belong to the Church, which accompanies them with special concern and encourages them to live as fully as possible the Christian life through regular participation at Mass, albeit without receiving communion, listening to the word of God, eucharistic adoration, prayer, participation in the life of the community, honest dialogue with a priest or spiritual director, dedication to the life of charity, works of penance, and commitment to the education of their children."[12] The effort of pastoral workers should be oriented in this direction and must welcome these spouses with God's heart.

---

[12] Benedict XVI, *Sacramentum caritatis*, n. 29. Also see, Congregation for the Doctrine of the Faith, *Pastoral Care of the Divorced and Remarried*, LEV, Vatican City 1998.

PART III

THE GENDER QUESTION: PHILOSOPHICAL AND CULTURAL ASPECTS

PIERLUIGI PAVONE*

THE PHILOSOPHICAL ORIGINS OF GENDER IDEOLOGY

Logic is no mere technique of reason. It can also be a *habitus*.

It is a mindset that spurs one to seek the first cause of things, that favors straightforward discourse over ambiguity, and that always strives to develop an overarching view of things. In "Perfect Information" Game Theory, it is "Game Screening." Only those who have a skill for interpretation may understand how something works. Otherwise one learns, or even just repeats complicated concepts, while understanding nothing.

With respect to nothing, to "understand nothing" has a relative meaning. It means understanding "nothing" *about* that thing, that lesson, that discourse, that rule, etc. It means that "nothing" is not *always* relative, it could also be absolute. For example, scientists claim the universe expands not in space, but in nothingness, because it creates time and space precisely through the mutual estrangement of the galaxies, starting from their initial singularity. This phenomenon, at least, according to the Big Bang theory, does not exclude a "Big Crunch" or a ceasing of expansion and the start of an inverse process of cosmic contraction. This hypothesis comes from the Theory of General Relativity.[1]

One could also create—with due prudence—a comparison between these theories of singularity, gravitational concentration, anti-gravitational force, expansion-contraction, space-time continuum and determination of light, on the one hand, and, say, Kabalistic mysticism, on the other. The latter focuses on the *ad intra* becoming of a God of indeterminacy. It is a divine infinite principle that contracts within itself (in a self-alienating movement), to then become an explosion of light, radiant, with gradual enactment of the ten di-

---

* Doctor of Philosophy, Visiting Professor at the Pontifical Athenaeum Regina Apostolorum, and Professor of History and Philosophy at the Pontifical Institute St. Apollinaris.

[1] These are complex and debated issues, which proceed by groping and hypothesis to be confirmed over the long run, even for the scientists at CERN in Geneva. The charm of a "Theory of Everything" persists for some, to offer a valid unified law for any cosmic phenomenon, the secrets of God's Mind. For one approach, see S.W. HAWKING, *A Brief History of Time: From the Big Bang to Black Holes*, Bantam, New York 1998; M. Gasperini, *Lezioni di relatività generale e teoria della gravitazione*, Springer Verlag, Milan 2010.

vine powers. This process is retraceable backwards from man, to elevate him from the material to the spiritual level.[2] All with the goal of self-deification.

It is the alternative, mystical method, that of substituting the traditional biblical concept of the creation of the world, according to which God created everything ("the heavens and the earth" in the Semitic expression) from nothing. In fact, the universe was not shapeless matter to be molded, as Plato plausibly narrates in his *Timaeus*. It is true that this is not an easy concept. In *Genesis*, it is not expressed directly in this way, and the book of *Wisdom*, written in Greek in Alexandria, Egypt, is influenced by Platonic tradition. It is *2 Maccabees* 7:28 that is the explicit landmark which presents us with the possibility of creation's not proceeding from already existing things. This expression likewise appears in the *Shepherd of Hermas* and in Theophilus of Antioch in his three books *To Autolycus*—which supports the originality of Christian thought regarding belief in *creatio ex nihilo*. On the other hand, we owe to Tertullian in his *Apologeticum* the first use of the term *de nihilo*, to indicate precisely "from nothing." Moreover, for the Christian faith, it is appropriate to bear in mind that only the Fourth Lateran Council in 1215 defended, for the first time in a magisterial document, *creatio ex nihilo* against the hypothesis of pre-existing matter. In any case, when one speaks of creation from nothing, it does not intend to mean the "nothing" of God or a "nothing" that is God.

Now in hindsight, even the self-alienation of God is not an easy concept. It opens up a type of mystical pantheism. If you care to become acquainted with the heterodox texts of a medieval exegete, then the Calabrian monk Joachim of Fiore, offers you all elements needed for your conversion to New Age thought. He is convinced of a concord between the Old and New Testament with a historical order based on the Trinity and punctuated by three ages (those of the Father, Son and Holy Spirit).

You need, besides, the following noteworthy supplements. First, you must reassume the denial of Original Sin, as Pelagius proposed. You must make sure that you are no longer interested in salvation in the heavenly realm but instead you must concentrate here on earth. Finally, you must make sure this impending earthly salvation can be reached through an inner process of consciousness-raising (for this dear Hegel is the master) and—*presto!*

If you struggle to believe that the entire universe can be a living being, because in high school your teacher made you skip the physics of the Stoics,

---

[2] See G. Busi, E. Loewenthal (eds.), *Mistica ebraica: Testi della tradizione segreta del giudaismo dal III al XVIII secolo*, Einaudi, Turin 1995; G. Sholem, *Le origini della Kabbalà*, Dehoniane, Bologna 2013, and *I segreti della creazione*, Adelphi, Milan 2003.

you are welcome to watch that fantastic film *Avatar*, and apply the creed of synapses among the roots of the trees of Pandora to planet Earth, according to the noble perspective of Deep Ecology.

If you manage to navigate the collateral effects of considering man just as part of a divine totality (and perhaps as the cancer on the planetary organism, a lethal virus within the Great Mother), maybe then you too can attain the mystic condition of a Cosmic Self, inaugurating a spiritual era, a new spring for Humanity.[3]

Let me be clear. Even the Catholic Church sixty years ago thought that with Modernism it would have found a "new springtime." Instead, it found "the smoke of Satan" as Paul VI declared and a "silent apostasy" as John Paul II noted. But maybe the "Age of Aquarius" will be different! Maybe there will be no need to guillotine anyone as the Jacobins did (as always, of course, to bring to fruition the era of Peace, Brotherhood and Freedom).

It is not an easy concept, that of the self-alienation of God.

Hans Jonas proposed this too, to offer the Hebrew God a second chance after the Shoah. Because the apparent silence and absence of God either conducts Hebraic thought toward the direct negation of God (He cannot exist) or renders God immanent within the historical process, itself abandoned to the tragic responsibility of man.[4]

Here, the Christian must always bear in mind how the sacrifice of Christ has had the triple value of redemption from sin, the defeat of the works and reign of Satan, and the bearing of all pain, innocence, injustice and scandal. It pains one to find an immense number of Christians who consider themselves to be such while *denying* sin, the personal reality of the devil and, ultimately, the very sacrifice of Christ itself. Or perhaps denying even Christ himself. If the allegedly "Catholic" theologian *Hans Küng* can allow himself to say that to believe in the Son means to "believe in the revelation of the one God in the man Jesus of Nazareth."[5] Has the fact escaped him that this very man—at least according to *Christians*—is the incarnation of God?

---

[3] See G. Filoramo, "Antica e nuova gnosi: proposte per un confronto", in I. Tolomio, *Ritorno della Gnosi?*, Gregoriana Libreria Editrice, Padua 2002.

[4] See H. Jonas, "The Concept of God after Auschwitz: A Jewish Voice", published in *The Journal of Religion*, Vol. 67, No. 1, Jan. 1987, p.1-13.

[5] H. Kung, H. Von Stietencron, J. Van Ess, *Christianity and World Religions: Paths to Dialogue*, Maryknoll Orbis books, New York 1993.

In any case, this same idea of self-alienation constitutes the very essence of the Modern Era. I am, in fact, convinced that all modernity has been forged by an interpretation of itself as a New Era. Joachim of Fiore was convinced that, in the immediate future, those same Catholics who would have suffered the persecution of the Antichrist, stayed loyal to the Church, and persevered in the faith, would await a brief period of pause before the ultimate battle, the Final Judgement, the end of time. It is a spiritual order that would have been formed in an age marked by the living presence of the Holy Spirit. It is a period following the Antichrist but preceding the last persecution and Final Judgement, an impressive detonator for every heretic, schismatic and opponent of the pope or the papacy. It is easy for many, from the "Spiritualist" wing of the Franciscans to the Pilgrim Fathers in the English colonies of America, to see in themselves that "new" spiritual order, and to find traces of Antichrist in the older structure, in the opposing power.[6]

It also reveals how the idea was secularized—by renouncing the Holy Spirit, the universal Judgement and the Kingdom of Heaven. It humanizes and renders worldly the earthly kingdom, reinterpreting a naturalized Christianity as the vital energy of historical order (similar to what was re-proposed by Maritain). It overlooks the action of Satan, who (according to Scripture) is the prince of this world. It focuses on the present age as one to be overcome, bent upon building a future *etsi Deus non daretur*.

Marxists and fellow travelers (Liberation Theologians—our revolution with a human façade) would apply this logic most thoroughly. For instance, in the Mexican Revolution amid the ruins of the old order, they offered to build a new, just and immaculate modern society directed against God. "Communist" Catholics tried doing this against God in the name of Marx and God alike. In fact, this is done in the name of an anarchic revolutionary carpenter, Jesus of Nazareth, the alleged forefather of Che Guevara.[7]

Today globalized capitalism chases the same ends using the far more hidden power of monetary control by some central banks (the system's heart is money, not the means of production as Marx envisioned it). It relies on the seemingly harmless ideas of progress and the education of human beings, as Lessing proposed during the age of Enlightenment.[8] Today this education is

---

[6] For the classic statement of this, see H. de Lubac, *La postérité spirituelle de Joachim de Flor: De Joachim à nos jours* (Oeuvres d'Henri de Lubac) Cerf, Paris 2014.

[7] A beautiful text that offers an analysis of the age is G. Morra, *Marxismo e religione*, Rusconi, Milan 1976.

[8] See E. Voegelin, *The New Science of Politics*, University of Chicago Press, USA 1987.

called "family planning," sex ed, gender theory, rights to eugenics, abortion and euthanasia, and the application of social Darwinism.[9]

But Joachim of Fiore and his legacy have not been enough. There is still a need for an ancient idea of man, for an anti-Christian anthropocentrism. It is found in the classical doctrine of Gnosticism.[10]

This doctrine teaches that this world is a cosmic prison, analogously to the way Buddhists interpret the world as an illusion from which one must escape, over and against the Christian creed of a benevolent cosmos created by God with infinite love. It is a doctrine that viewed the God of *Genesis* as a fallen creator, a demiurge who along with his archons dominate the cosmic prison of matter. They see body and soul as distinct layers of imprisonment against which a spiritual person must rebel. It is a doctrine in which a religious man should affirm his dominion, his victory, his antinomian and anti-cosmic action. He is indifferent to political laws, condemns marriage, is confident when performing any perversion in this worldly prison thanks to the spirit's immunity to matter, and is convinced of the individual's self-determination as the resolution of power.

Gender ideology today trusts this self-determination as the absolutizing of a perception of the Self against any objectivity. And objectivity is traced back to a subjective impression that is always momentary, experiential, continuous and fluid. In the modern era, Descartes first relativizes being for human thought, then Luther relativizes God's subsistence within the experience of individual conscience, inaugurating a standard principle of Anthropocentric Immanence.

But there is more. Ancient Gnosticism teaches that the words of the devil in the temptation of the Garden of Eden were real, that God was an executioner against whom one must rebel, offering one's law against nature. It was to become a rainbow of reversed colors, like the one the satanic Theosophical Society conjured up and from which stems the current flag of "peace." It is a doctrine that teaches one to despise God and to consider oneself "god" (as in Augustine's "earthly" city of man). It teaches that the ultimate truth of man is the creed of Lucifer and can be summarised in *non serviam*, I will not serve.[11]

Nonetheless, this doctrine of European humanism is in need of a final decisive ingredient. For ancient Gnostics, the world coincides with evil. That

---

[9] See E. ROCCELLA, L. SCARAFFIA, *Contro il Cristianesimo*, Piemme, Casale Monferrato 2005.

[10] See H. JONAS, *The Gnostic Religion*, Beacon Press, Boston 2001.

[11] Giorello acknowledges with intellectual honesty that such is the ultimate, militant truth of true atheism. See G. GIORELLO, *Senza Dio. Del buon uso dell'ateismo*, Longanesi, Milan 2010.

same evil Luther imputes to man in order to save the Creator, thus founding the atheist and nihilistic heritage of modern thought.

Until one achieves the utopian future upon Earth, a correction and condemnation are needed.[12] The condemnation is that of medieval Christianity as a forgery of original Christianity. Such is the Gnostic turn, with every philosophy and religion of ancient arcane knowledge and their offspring. Consequently, in humanist Florence, the *Corpus Hermeticum* was translated, and this idea is legitimised by the erroneous dating of these books. This knowledge is the Kabbalah, which constitutes a transformation of the ancient Gnosticism.[13]

The Kabbalistic doctrine (from which also stem Jonas's proposals we hinted at above) replaces belief in creation with that of God's "self-contraction." It renders the divine spirit immanent and relocates God and man within a relationship of descent and ascent that ultimately makes man divine, placing him within the sphere of the divine—that root from which all Modernism stems (Catholic Modernism included).

It renders the world a divine-human process, as in Teilhard de Chardin. It makes the world not a prison anymore, but the very abode of God.[14]

Pico della Mirandola is convinced of this, asserting that Kabbalah is the ancient and the only knowledge from which all philosophies and religions derive in accord with a perfect universal syncretism. He thereby shows dissatisfaction with accounts of human dignity by offering his idea in line with principles of self-generation.

In his work *De Dignitate Hominis* Pico attributes to God an explicit intention of creating man with an indeterminate nature, leaving him with the will and capacity to define his role, his own home, his private law, his essence. In this way, man would affirm his superiority over the beasts in his autogenetic freedom, with the potential to achieve self-awareness and reach ultimate truth—his divinity (from which we get Hegel).

Here we must consider something carefully.

Luther would have condemned man to his evil, opposing man to the distant justice of God, an anarchic God whose benevolence and decision-making possess nothing analogous to human rationality.

---

[12] See F. A. Yates, *Giordano Bruno e la tradizione ermetica*, trad. It., Laterza, Roma-Bari 1992.

[13] See his important contributions in P. Pini (eds.), *Il Neoplatonismo nel Rinascimento*, Istituto della Enciclopedia Italiana founded by G. Treccani, Rome 1993; and C. Vasoli, *Le filosofie del Rinascimento*, Bruno Mondadori Editori, Milan 2002.

[14] T. de Chardin, *Writings in a Time of War*, Harper Perennial, New York 1965.

As a follower of Ockham, Luther embraces that late medieval ideal according to which God's free will must be preserved from any logic. Accordingly, the order of God is opposed to the world as much as the anarchy of saving grace is contrary to reason. Just as the search of reason, good intentions, the capacity to know and love God—despite original sin and its permanent wound—are in themselves obstacles, satanic deceits, actions reduced to the guilt of arrogance, vainglory and pride.

Such a faith is opposed to reason because reason as such—and not just the geometric and abstract reason of Descartes condemned by Pascal—is a slave to the devil. For this reason, works are pointless. Not only the works of the Law but even those of Grace described by Saint James in his Epistle admonishing the sterility of a "faith" not manifested and vivified by Christian works. According to Luther, when God justifies He does not make one just. He limits Himself—the way a human judge stands before a defendant—to considering the sinner justified and predestined for salvation. A human judge, in fact, cannot transform an offender into an innocent man. He is limited to merely considering him as such.

The God of Luther and Melanchthon behaves the same way, contrary to the ancient Augustinian teaching on the efficacy of the sacraments.[15] Grace for Catholics vivifies and renders one just, in virtue of the Holy Spirit. Communion is the Body and Blood of Christ, whose sacrifice on the cross is represented on the altar at every Eucharist. Luther, on the other hand, creates such a radical incompatibility between man and God that Marx—as we must admit, with Lutheran coherence—had to destroy God if there was to be any systematic ethics for man.[16]

On another front, Gnostic humanism—a humanism that is not Christian in the least—naturalizes this same human evil until it empowers the Idealists (e.g., Schelling) in a newly foundational theology to speak of evil in God.[17] For them, God is derived from the free, benevolent self-creation of an infinite, indeterminate principle, a purely anarchic free will.

Alternatively, Gnostic humanism will relegate to historicism a present fraught with the future, as Leibniz wished, with the effect of absolutely denying the overcoming of the structure and current order.[18] It is the "future," "progress," the optimistic terrestrial view of a world self-redeemed to become

[15] See A.E. McGrath, *Reformation Thought: An Introduction*, Wiley-Blackwell, UK 2012.

[16] See G. Girardi, *Marxism and Christianity*, Gill and Son, Dublin 1968.

[17] F.W.J. Schelling, *Mythologie: Zur Auslegung der Philosophie der Mythologie und der Offenbarung* (Spekulation und Erfahrung) Vol. 31, Fromman-Holzboog, Stuttgart 1993.

[18] See È. Gilson, *Les Métamorphoses de la Cité de Dieu*, Université de Louvain, Louvain 1952.

a place for the new man, the superman, the man-god. He has passed through the nihilistic phases of slave and rebel to identify himself with his own destiny—the camel, the lion and the child in the renowned Nietzschean image. In two centuries nature exhausted its effects, only to come back into vogue in the contemporary era with the New Age movement, environmentalism and mystic neo-pantheism.[19]

When nature's effects disappeared between the 1700s and 1800s, Masonic lodges fused Gnostic and anti-Christian doctrine with politics. Self-divinization finds its ideal dwelling within the State, and in a revolution, in the direction of a New World Order. The same phenomenon imposes itself today—lurking behind economic blackmail—in the culture of gender ideology, using a Soviet and Jacobin modality, while preserving the appearance of democracy and succeeding in presenting itself with the rhetoric of the "everyday man" as *the* quintessential tolerance of human rights.

Whoever resists is a homophobe, intolerant, a neo-Nazi, obtuse, medieval, retrograde, a traditionalist. He is to be silenced in the media as an "enemy of the people," a classic nomenclature French revolutionaries used for their genocide in the Vendée. The Freemasons of the *Risorgimento* used it against the Bourbon patriots, transformed indiscriminately into "outlaws"; and the Bolsheviks used it in 1956 against "fascist and reactionary" Hungarians.

There is one evolutionary novelty. The Soviet System and, in part, the Chinese Communist dictatorship have demonstrated that a New Order cannot be imposed explicitly from above. It generates too much resistance, perhaps thanks to a natural instinct for self-preservation. So it is necessary to devise a brilliant plan, to find a way for people *democratically* to seek a New Order. Satan's master game plan, according to Christian eschatology, at least a version that does not renounce the revelation of the Antichrist in a general apostasy as a truth of the faith (cf., 2Thes 2:3, 1Jn 2:18, and Rev 13, 16, 19-20), is to inculcate the Gnostic doctrine as if it were Catholic. It is to guide humanity toward rebellion against God in the name of goodness, brotherhood, and peace among nations. For the New Order, it is essential, after centuries of an occult and patient preparation, to forge a new mythological culture of the masses.

It was Nietzsche who contrasted Apollo to a nihilistic dominion over reason and its betrayal by a primal orgiastic vitalism uncontrolled by laws or the

[19] See J.D. Barrow, *New Theories of Everything* (Gifford Lectures) 2nd Ed., by John D. Barrow, Oxford University Press, UK 2007; F. Capra, *The Tao of Physics: An Exploration of the Parallels Between Modern Physics and Eastern Mysticism*, Shambhala, Boston 2010; E.O. Wilson, *Consilience: The Unity of Knowledge* Reprint Edition, Vintage, New York 1999.

harmony of form. Today many followers of the Heideggerian deconstruction of western metaphysics (e.g., Colli) burrow to the ancient roots of pre-Socratic philosophy, proposing Socrates and Plato as the inventors of man as a rational animal.[20] Dionysus, after all, allows himself to be found—not even reason can always dominate lust. In the Christian sense, free will can decide against vices, but the help of saving Grace is needed. The Nietzschean superman, the rebel of '68, is not only he who refuses Grace but also he who condemns any rational order. 1968 marks not merely a cultural revolution, an emancipation from those retrograde schemes of a generation all too different from the one born during the post-war economic boom, with the creation of a piece of music that breaks away from all the old rules. It is a very real mystical conjuring of the Dionysian spirit: the use of drugs is not merely for transgression. It is also, or above all, a canonical pathway, a method to access hyper-rational levels, spiritual levels that mark the ultimate goal of human development.

Even the invention of extra-terrestrial figures falls into this scheme and is created for these purposes. The alien of space technology plays a part destined for the masses as propaedeutic. The real creed of belief in extra-terrestrials describes them as messengers of light, as spiritual essences, as prophets of a new mystic era both post- and even anti-Christian.[21] The Europe of the seventeenth century knew of the figure of the Jewish messiah Sabbatai Zevi who declared his status as a messiah before the Sultan, apostatizing from his faith and identifying in this way for some of his most devoted followers even before there was any evidence. His apostasy is a form of redemption—sin as a form of mystic sublimation, the dissolution of all things as a form of initiation, the destruction of all order as a pathway to the divine.[22]

Now, two centuries later, we still proceed in the name of Dionysian pulsations of the non-form, the dissolution of all values, the androgynous god and the liberation of the unconscious of Gnostic esotericism. There is a new and efficient combination—the anarchy of Freud's instincts amalgamated with the Marxist ideal of a hegemonic structure as obstacle and oppression.[23]

---

[20] G. Colli, *La nascita della filosofia*, Adelphi, Milan 1975.

[21] See G. Marletta, E. Pennetta, *Extraterrestri. Le origini occulte di un mito moderno*, Rubbettino, Italy 2011.

[22] See M. Blondet, *Gli Adelphi della dissoluzione. Strategie culturali del potere iniziatico*, Ares, Milano 1994.

[23] See H. Marcuse, *Eros and Civilization: A Philosophical Inquiry into Freud*, Vintage, New York 1961.

Religion becomes the narcotic instrument of neurotic cultures and societies, the identity of a person in chains. Let us ponder these hypotheses deeply. The question remains the same. What do we need to assume to make these proposals valid?

Religion, in fact, would be a collective neurosis with precise conditions, according to valid psychoanalytical reconstructions, provided we accept the following Freudian scheme: 1) a tribe enslaved by a hegemonic father and master who satisfies his sexual impulses with all the females, including wife, mother and daughters; 2) a coalition of male sons, brothers among themselves, emasculated or banished from the tribe as enemies and antagonists of the father (without counting those killed), succeed in killing the father, eating the body and restoring, with the strongest brother, the previous situation of the absolute hegemonic alpha male; 3) the reiteration of these relationships occurs for centuries culminating finally in the decision to enter into society, following the collective renunciation of anarchic pulsations, to be handled only by the family (apart from its mere preservation for the hegemonic, aristocratic and regal class in its ancient right of parental coupling); 4) the development of the totemic cult, until Hebraic monotheism, as the return of the withdrawn. Therefore, the birth of religion is the unconscious guilt for parricide, and the reverential cult of the father symbolised in the phallic object reaches the most abstract and transcendental forms.

Morality, law-like and Hebraic, is nothing other than the structured realization of this sense of guilt. It is the expiation of the ancient debt of freedom conquered through homicidal and cannibalistic practice.[24]

It makes one smile to realize that whoever believes in what I have just summarized is an educator and a teacher, while anyone who believes in the terrestrial paradise or original sin is a naive dupe. I ask myself: who has constructed his myths? In any case, let us welcome the lectures of the masters of suspicion. Man, educated to rebellion by the serpent and self-generation in the erotic game, free with his instincts as the Marxist Marcuse desired, is not always capable of sustaining the weight of freedom. Nor, as Nietzsche taught, has he the strength to affirm himself, to impose his own will of power, to resist the morality of priests, the mediocrity of the masses and the fear of the herd. For this reason, man must be liberated again, outdo himself again, reorient himself, as always, to reach his ultimate goal. He must kill God, that sophisticated, alienated image of the paternal tyrant. This freedom is Eros, the path for an identity ever in a state of becoming, because the order of reason

[24] See S. Freud, *Moses and Monotheism*, Vintage Books, New York 1939.

is a nihilistic deception. Law is not a path or condition for freedom (when a precise road is the precondition for reaching the goal) but rather an obstacle to self-expression and life. The body is a prison (coinciding with the ancient Gnostics). Sexual identity is denied as self-evident and traced back, against the sanest realism, to hegemonic, slavish cultural construction.

For Saint Thomas, life in community is the product of man's relational nature as a social animal by definition, a part of the order of his creation even before the Fall. Now living in the polity creates structures of oppression. In fact, it is the very structure of abuse. Here we find an essential development with both Marx and Hegel. For the former, in fact, all of history is viewed a struggle between classes within a capitalist society. So the State is the structure of oppression *par excellence* as it is the only system where the worker, instead of having his humanity affirmed, always has it denied by alienating himself in a factory. It has been claimed that Marx had a negative view of work in general: a profound error. Marx inherits from Hegel (exponent of the master-slave dialectic of the *Phenomenology of the Spirit*) the idea of the humanization of man through work and thus has an ultra-positive view of work as such. What he condemns is capitalist work, because it is capitalism that denaturalizes the "genetic efficacy" of work. In this way, a Hegelian slave reaches a higher level of freedom-consciousness of her humanity. It is not because she rebels against the master, but because by working, even as a slave, she objectifies herself, she self-affirms and self-creates herself as a person. She manifests and, therefore, determines her essence. However, Hegel adds, this determination will not be able to become concrete except within the State, a living organic totality, the whole within which free self-awarenesses affirm themselves and recognize one other. Otherwise it will not be able to implement itself either in the solipsistic name of freedom as the apathetic detachment from things, or as a suspension of the judgement of truth (Stoicism and Skepticism). It will not be in the individualistic claims of possession (Locke and the bourgeois Right) nor in the formal elevation to abstract moral imperatives (Kant).

Now in this regard economic structures, with their endemic relationship of force between property and productive forces, are replaced by a cultural fabric. While, at the same time, the liberation occurs according to a perspective that is on its face anarchic, ecological, pantheist, globalist, without a heaven or a hell, without properties or limits, like John Lennon's song *Imagine*. A father and mother are reduced to Parent 1 and Parent 2, proximate sources of a child's genetic material. They are likely the first to foster intolerance because if they consider their son John, an anatomical male, to be a boy, they, in reality, are imposing a cultural scheme on him and are not respecting his freedom of expression and self-determination. In fact, their son is not a male. He is nothing. He is an indeterminate origin who should affirm himself freely, and infinitely reinvent himself. What used to work is now substituted by sexual orientation through the ideology of the "gay lobby," an instinctual tendency of an erotic foundation, a momentary perception stripped of every realism. Now the tendency of the moment is oriented toward what "one feels like," wherever the heart takes him, understood as an unconscious pulse, spontaneous because anarchic, therefore free to determine and define one's own identity.

That is to say, sexual orientation, the tendency of the erotic instinct, pursued for itself, is the source of sexual orientation of the individual. It means you who are reading these lines, in truth, don't have a given sexual identity. It is not true that your body is a sexed body. It is not true that your psyche will read reality through feminine or masculine categories because of the simple and evident fact that you are neither a man nor a woman. It would be a mental or cultural construction to maintain an approach to reality based on logical, deductive and linear de-codification according to a problem-solution schema. That is an aggressive and competitive instinct; an egocentric perspective; an infantile fascination with a movement that meticulously constructs a masculine way of understanding the world. This is opposed to a feminine approach based on the allocentric, the affective-emotional, the intuitive, upon a high development of the linguistic axis and upon a searching of faces and their expressions.

It may be a shame, but neuroscientific research confirms that these different approaches are not learned by way of a primal amorphous structure but are determined by the brain. That elementary difference of 1% between the masculine and feminine genetic codes influences every last cell. Men and women use different cerebral areas to complete the same tasks. External stimuli are processed in different ways, from activated areas of the brain region (for example, a baby who cries in the cradle) to stress reaction. "The starting point of the cerebral structure is not unique; the masculine and feminine brains are different by nature."[25]

Child pedagogy researchers today continue to promote what was done in the past, before feminism, before the ideological masculinization of women, on the one hand, and the loss of masculinity's natural virility on the other. They do so with a view to providing answers to the needs of male and female brains, which are structurally different, in their vision of reality, their intuitive

---

[25] L. Brizendine, *The Female Brain*, Harmony, New York 2007.

and emotional or deductive and scanning capacities, their communicative abilities or in men's constant search for competition, combat and physical supremacy. Even the ability to listen is entirely different. A little boy listens to far fewer words than a little girl and decodes still fewer. It is a question of hearing and the brain. The bare positioning of a boy in the last row in the classroom causes him to lose a good part of the lesson.[26]

We can act out all the parts required by the gay lobby. We can mask what we think and lie to ourselves in an eternal carnival. We can also turn to surgery. The truth is that a man will always see things as a man, through ineluctable categories, though, if he wishes, he can come to master his endemic egoism, egocentricity and resolutely ironclad but arid logic. The truth is that a woman will continue to have a limitless need for verbal communication, nurture, a desire to feel cherished and listened to, and empathized with. She may harbor tendencies to verbosity and anxiety. A beautiful complementarity emerges from these very differences.

What happens if we locate the Oedipus complex between the boy and his mother, or between the girl and her father? Let us imagine some alternate history of philosophy. If Hegel were a woman, would "she" have developed the master-slave dialectic along with the doctrine of a struggle for recognition? I don't think so. She might have proposed a theory of hospitality and listening, or of the emotional relationships between faces. Men developed Christian theology. They could only suggest that God is reason, *logos*, much as Aristotle conceived God as thinking about thought, based on the mere strength of the principle of non-contradiction. The fact that God is Love necessarily had to arrive at the scheme of providence—beyond the wound of original sin.

If Hobbes had been a woman, "she" would never have reduced the need for a social contract to the hostile aggression among men, constrained merely by a need to escape violent death. Hobbes could write this only as a man. A boy plays alone a lot more than a girl and is interested in how things work. A little girl would be capable of rocking a toy police van to sleep!

Catholic tradition owes to Saint Catherine of Siena the elevation of the mystic to the sublimity of Christian love as spiritual "maternity," a love of sacrifice and self-denial that women alone can conceptualize and live out. Even from the Satanic perspective, the devil chose to address the woman, establishing a communicative relationship with Eve! One must reflect upon this fact, also on the grounds of sexual differences.

---

[26] See T. CANTELMI, M. SCICCHITANO, *Educare al femminile e al maschile*, Paoline, Cinisello Balsamo 2013.

What has been happening in the last few years does not come from nothing, nor is it a "trend." It is a result of the precise, patient plowing of a field—the field of the average person—rendered more and more unfit for knowledge, reason and the use of logic. Today he is told to say the sky is blue reveals a severe intolerance for those who maintain that it is also yellow with violet dots. Still, he allows himself to be convinced—in the name of justice. Of course, there is a theoretical and philosophical root underlying same-sex attraction, as well as underlying gender ideology. Who among us studied ancient Gnosticism and optimist Gnosticism in high school? Who among us has been educated to think, as opposed to being pestered by vacuous, sterile, sophistic do-gooder rhetoric?

Today a cultural battle is being fought by the LGBT lobby proposing gender theory and censuring homophobia. But this is a linguistic strategy. All dictatorships have controlled history, education and language. Often language has become the most effective weapon—to create slogans, create words and immunize the mind. The incredibly subtle game of opposing "homophobia" to gender ideology has been a successful operation, and—it saddens me to admit—even Catholics refuse to confront this problem at its root. Sexual education in schools taught according to the principles of gender theory cannot be separated from the question of same-sex attraction. Today this is done by imposing the subject from a social stance or in the name of tolerance toward persons with these tendencies. This is done while refusing to consider its roots. For example, regarding male SSA, one would have to tackle the questions of narcissism; of a (lost or defective) identification with one's father; of issues regarding differentiation from the mother; and of the eroticization of that which one unconsciously longs to be—a man.

But gender ideology is not something separate just because of the ideological modality in which it presents itself. The philosophical root is, in fact, the same. It is based on an alleged truth—that one's tendencies, that one's erotic orientation, whatever it may be, are the source of one's identity. This "truth" is based on a premise, namely, that sexual status is not a given but is self-determined. I am the cause of myself in regard to my essence, to my identity. This thesis, in turn, can hold together only if I accept that a person at the beginning is but nothing, indeterminate, and altogether undifferentiated.

This theory is, in effect, maintained by Hegelian anthropology and theology. It is based on the idea of self-creation. For Hegel, to be, to exist, means to know oneself, to have self-consciousness. *God is God only when He knows that He is God*. When He knows Himself to be God, He knows Himself as such just at the end of a rational process that is necessary, progressive, historical and dialectical (the famous thesis-antithesis-synthesis). Hegel thinks that before the world's creation, God had an empty conception of Himself, and He must therefore "negate" Himself, in nature, to then reaffirm Himself through His Word—this is the history of philosophy as the philosophy of history. It also applies to man. Even man in his ultimate truth is thinking about thought. Being, simple existence, does not coincide with his essence. One *becomes* a man. Man must bring his own life into play, must overcome the fear of death, must outdo himself as an animal, must work to become his object, must fight for recognition and must reach the fullest level of reason. He is a rational animal, and a man only when he "knows" himself to be one. In the family he is recognized merely as a son, he denies himself within the anonymity of civil society to overcome his abstract self-knowledge, and he reaffirms himself in the State which is God's embodiment in the world.

The Hegelian level of interpenetration between the human and divine spirit, between a theological spirit and a worldly one, is such that Feuerbach will read Hegelian philosophy as *the* last refuge of theology, proposing anthropology as its ultimate fulfilment. Today Protestant and Catholic Modernism tend to come to the same conclusion, albeit subtly, in the name of "opening up to the world." Environmentalist ideology is analogous, preferring to substitute God with the Universe of planetary mysticism, with Great Mother Nature and similar pantheistic paganism.

All these perspectives—which today encounter a renewed popularity thanks to their similarities with such oriental mysticisms as Hinduism and Buddhism—gather under the banner of the same Gnostic idea. Man coincides with his development of self-consciousness, of self-creation, of self-generation, and with the self-definition of his essence, of his humanity; in a word, with his self-divinization.

Even Buddhism, which structurally is irreducible to Christianity, shares this idea.[27] Buddhism, in fact, maintains that the world is an illusion (Gnosticism defines it as a material prison). It believes that the world comes from

[27] I distance myself entirely from the comparison made by R. Panikkar in *Intrareligious Dialogue,* Paulist Press 1978, according to which the conventional notion of fall-and-salvation would seem sufficient to have the two religions overlap. On the contrary the conceptualization of a monotheistic personal God is irreducible to the impersonal Unity or "Unconditioned" of Nirvana; the idea of creation as a good work is irreducible to the notion of reality as illusion; the concept of redemption in virtue of Christ's sacrifice is irreducible to mystical self-elevation, itself so very close to the Gnostic perspective on "self-deification." One may observe this total distance from Christianity in the essays of the Dalai Lama, e.g., *The Door*

a failure to control desire on the part of eternal sentient beings (Gnosticism speaks of evil demiurgic creation). It affirms that everything is suffering, and the only way forward is to overcome this state through the extinguishing of a reincarnation cycle determined by karma (Gnosticism claims everything is slavery and the only way forward is the spirit's liberation from soul and body). In Buddhism, the ultimate goal is a self-nullification in Nirvana (in ancient Gnosticism it is reunification with a primal *Pleroma*).

It is a process that, as regards personal identity, originates in the nothingness of the self and terminates in the oblivion of that person. The heart of Buddha's teaching is to view illusion as the cause of suffering and the root of illusion as a false belief in the self's subsistence. Christianity, meanwhile, affirms the subsistence of self, and that which Aristotle calls substance is good and true precisely because it exists independently of anyone's judgment.

Nor is original sin the rupture of a divine Unity corresponding in Hinduism to the All-Self. The goal of life is not the reabsorption of all things into a celestial ocean in which every drop loses its subsistence as a drop. God is not Spinoza's monistic divine Nature-substance.

Fallen man saves himself primarily not b self-elevation to the divine but by the sacrifice of Christ, God made flesh; and we will preserve our identity, as a male or a female, in an eternal life.

Modern Gnosticism, especially its pantheistic avatar, is even closer to Eastern sensibilities, albeit conserving, as we see in Pico della Mirandola, one basic idea—namely that man self-divinizes, self-humanizes and self-creates. Gender ideology does no more than develop these Gnostic theories. Today the evil demiurge is viewed as the hegemonic culture, and one's family as the new cradle of intolerance. Man in the main is an "ever-becoming" derived from nothing (regarding sexual identity) and proceeding toward nothing (regarding the same identity), since this character never "is" but instead morphs continuously.

In this, it is similar to that amorphous material that, according to the Platonic creationist idea, the Creator shapes and gives form to according to an eternal ideal model. Here, on the other hand, such amorphous material is a subject giving itself a form, all by itself, according to many erotic tendencies. So much so that transsexuality and bisexuality are now considered touchstones of the truth about gender.

---

of Liberation: Essential Teachings of the Tibetan Buddhist Tradition, Wisdom Publications, Boston 2016.

GIORGIA BRAMBILLA*

ANTHROPOLOGICAL ASPECTS OF SAME-SEX ATTRACTION: BETWEEN BIO-POLITICS AND UTOPIA

> A T for the males, a circle for the females and for those who were destined to become freemartins a question mark, black on a white ground... "Guaranteed sterile... out of the realm of mere slavish imitation of nature into the much more interesting world of human invention."
>
> —A. Huxley, *Brave New World*

Gender theory and "homosexualism"[1] anchor their arguments in an egalitarianism that considers sexual difference to be foundational for discrimination. This approach is transformed into a blockade, when not a strategy, rendering it impossible to enter a debate on same-sex attraction (SSA) with all its countless individual, cultural and social implications.[2] The whole subject is constantly brought back to rights, to a fight against discrimination and to a quest for equality.

The LGBT movement claims that any difference between men and women presupposes an injustice. They do so by deploying a syllogism. Namely, the difference between the sexes constitutes inequality, and inequality is an injustice; so sexual difference is an injustice.[3] The problem is that when we claim these two realities—male and female sexuality—as equal, we are denying their difference. But is it not discriminatory to say two different things are "equivalent"?[4] If we go deeper into the logic of advocating identity for purposes of abolishing difference, then sameness—the ability to name different things by the same name—prevails. The result is a standardized, self-referential knowledge that reflects back upon itself, recognizing itself as always identical to itself."[5]

* Doctor in Bioethics and Moral Theologian. Specialist in Family and Sexual Ethics. Adjunct Professor of the School of Bioethics, Pontifical Athenaeum Regina Apostolorum.

1 This term is used to indicate militant LGBT groups that seek the recognition of certain rights.

2 See G. Ricci, *Il padre dov'era*, Sugarco, Milan 2013, p.16.

3 See L. Palazzani, *Identità di genere? Dalla differenza alla in-differenza sessuale nel diritto*, San Paolo, Cinisello Balsamo 2008, p.60.

4 See M. Schneider, *Big Mother*, Odile Jacob, Paris 2002, p.221.

5 G. Ricci, *Il padre dov'era*, Sugarco, Milan 2013, p.17-18.

One wonders whether equality can really be achieved by eliminating diversity. This paper proposes not to consider SSA as such but rather to offer an analysis of anthropological contradictions within the LGBT view itself, especially regarding such concepts as freedom and equality. This chapter proposes that the sexual enhancement of otherness in marriage is a symbol of communion between people where difference implies not inequality, but rather a search for unity.[6]

1. Depriving heteros of eros: Uniformity between Egalitarianism and Control.

In compliance with that principle according to which diversity is synonymous with inequality, and so synonymous with an unacceptable source of discrimination and oppression, it is necessary to ensure that all human beings are no longer classified within intolerable classes based on sexual behavior but rather belong to new categories that promise a future of happiness and peace for everyone; one where all barriers and discriminations have finally fallen.[7]

John Money's definition of "gender identity" underlies a utopian ideal in imagining a new world formed by individuals without "classes of sex." It is a world that transcends genetic imprinting and genital configuration in which what matters is sharing a common humanity. Difference, specifically sexual difference, entails a lack of communication. Supposedly this lack leads to division, and division to conflict. Money's proposal was not to recognize that people have a "core," a nucleus serving as a basis for dialogue and respect for human dignity. Rather, his proposal endorses a kind of neutralization of sexual identity and, above all, an elimination of limits when it comes to sexuality. It is easy to see where this underlying vision of reality and of human beings is heading in its subsequent phase. Namely, what is proper to male and female—in a broader sense, difference as limitation—means a limit prohibiting me from exercising a freedom understood as absolute self-determination. It is worth pointing out that the determination to eliminate limits —which fails to reflect liberty properly understood as "freedom for"[8] —is not even a proper expression of *libertas a coactione* (in the sense of freedom from con-

[6] See S. Agacinski, *Parity of the Sexes,* (European Perspectives: A Series in Social Thought and Cultural Criticism) Columbia University Press, New York 2001.

[7] See D. Nerozzi, *L'uomo nuovo. Dallo scimpanzè al bonobo*, Rubbettino, Soveria Mannelli 2008.

[8] See F. Bergamino, *La struttura dell'essere umano. Elementi di antropologia filosofica*, Edusc, Rome 2007.

straints). Rather it is an uncontrolled exploration of one's own impulses in perfect conformity with that liberal vision according to which a consumer is a "producer" of her own satisfaction to the extent that she consumes.[9]

The problem is that from an anthropological point of view, to eliminate this particular "class" of the sex to which one belongs, first means giving lesser importance to the body in favor of an almost "spiritualist" view of the person. Second, it seeks to eliminate nature, which in the sexual sphere means achieving a desired gender called "neuter" to which all humanity should aspire for purposes of attaining the mirage of peaceful coexistence on Earth. According to this line of thinking, differences—even biological ones—are dangerous and must be sacrificed to cultural uniformity, understood not as the assertion of a self (expressed through action) but rather as an evacuation of the same.

It is easy to see how the same claims arising from so-called "gender studies" refer to an aspiration for "corrective" justice. It is as if natural sexual difference was itself a privation, and thus an injustice. Equality is obtained in a negative way by removing something—in this case sexual identity—rather than simply affirming and recognizing a person for who he or she is. We thus see how gender theory bears a political component, actually a bio-political one, and in two ways seemingly opposed to each other. On the one hand, since the concept of "difference" is joined to the concept of "authority" (viewed as a power system) liable to "deconstruction," first sex, and then nature, becomes a form of liberation. But this new freedom is a freedom that degenerates into having power over one's own (now objectified) body. On the other hand, the obsessive pursuit of uniformity is itself a form of "control." It is one that results in an increasing pervasiveness of politics within the realm of biology. I will seek to analyze both of these aspects briefly, highlighting their potential repercussions.

1.1 Freedom? Or "Power" Over the Body?

Judith Butler believes that any difference between men and women results from a heterosexual power matrix.[10] So by deconstructing sex, one can then view "gender" as a social construct, thereby empowering an individual to freely create his or her own identity. As noted above, this results in extreme consequences for the pursuit of a freedom univocally interpreted as self-determination. Following hot on the heels of this proposal are demands

---

[9] See M. Foucault, *The Birth of Biopolitics: Lectures at the Collège de France, 1978-1979, Lectures at the College de France*, Picador Palgrave-Macmillan, New York 2010.

[10] See J. Butler, *Undoing gender*, Routledge, New York 2004.

for a right to engage in all the consequences within a Rawlsian view of justice as equity. Even to the point that if technology can actualize what is desired, then this equity must absolutely be promoted.

Such is the man of the liberal system, the *homo faber ipsius fortunae*, whose privilege lies in forging himself and his destiny in the world.[11] Man is "free and sovereign." Of a malleable and indeterminate nature, he has the ability to make himself. Above all, he feels a need to build and carve out a place of his own in the world.[12] Human beings who hold their destiny in their own hands and need not accept any revealed truth that they cannot understand are, according to Locke, bearers of inalienable rights that no one may violate because no one holds such authority.[13] Since increasing freedom of choice naturally promotes an individual's private autonomy, it is easy to comprehend how science and technology have organically harmonized with the liberal idea to date. That is the idea that all citizens enjoy an equal opportunity to order their lives.[14] An individual may decide if what nature offers is the best option possible, or else seek ways to refashion this, "We can make our bodies objects of our judgment and manipulation. We can find ways in which we could have been better fashioned…"[15]

Beginning with bioethics, this debate highlights what happens when the body goes from being an unavailable good to a fully available one and, finally, is objectified. The body is objectified when it is detached from "me," flowing from a Platonic, Gnostic and Cartesian dualistic anthropology. It is clear that those who propose the idea of a "fluid," malleable—even surgically constructed—sexual identity strongly emphasize that the body (and, we repeat, a body clearly sexed from the very beginning in all its materiality) lacks any link to the interior life strong enough to influence human existence. Pruned of all limits, freedom degenerates into a delirium of omnipotence: sex changes, genetic manipulation, "parenting at all costs" (surrogacy, IVF, etc.)

Yet in fact the starting point for corporeality "is built upon an original self-understanding or pre-reflective experience: more precisely, upon an im-

---

[11] This term is attributed to Appius Claudius Caecus, a Roman politician and man of letters belonging to the Gens Claudia who lived between 350 and 271 BC. The term was used primarily during the Renaissance.

[12] See R. Esposito, C. Galli, "Liberalismo," in *Enciclopedia del pensiero politico*, Laterza, Rome, Bari 2000, p.384.

[13] See J. Locke, *A Letter Concerning Toleration*, Awnsham Churchill, London 1689.

[14] See J. Habermas, *The Future of Human Nature*, Polity Press, Cambridge 2004.

[15] H.T. Engelhardt, *The Foundations of Bioethics*, Oxford University Press, 2nd edition, New York 1996, p.413.

mediate perception of the body. It is the first reality that we encounter phenomenologically in the awareness of our own body."[16] The human person is a sexual being in her psychosomatic constitution, and this feature determines her being. Sexual duality is the specific way for us to live in the world and to relate to others. It is through an awareness of one's own corporeality that a man reveals a woman's femininity to her, and that a woman reveals a man's masculinity to him. In this way a body becomes the inevitable revealer of an identity, the mediator of a psychic identity, bringing the self to fulfillment via an encounter with diversity.

Just as the person is an "I" open to a "Thou," and is thus a being in relation, so too sexuality has an essentially relational dimension. It is a sign and locus for openness of encounter, of dialogue, of communication and of a unity of persons. An "I" exists only in relation to a "Thou," and sexuality is a reality that manifests the communion of an "us." The essence of human sexuality lies precisely in the relation of an "I" to a "Thou" having its foundation in the relational constitution of a personal ego. The metaphysics of the *actus essendi* reveals that a human being is not contracted into him or herself but rather opens outward in the direction of others, such that a mature identity passes through alterity (of the *other*) and is fulfilled in a communion of love.[17] Man understands himself as an *ego-ad* and as an *ego-cum*. The *other*, which is symmetrical with the "I," imposes itself without relying on the latter for its existence. An "I" who gratuitously approaches the *other* remains a *subject* precisely because she facilitates an enhancement of being in the *other*. A "Thou" remains a *subject* as well, to the extent that an "I" approaches a "Thou" with deep, formal and substantial respect. It is in this way that an "I" will not view a "Thou" through a manipulative lens but rather leaves the *other's* dignity intact, enhancing his own being while putting himself at the service of the *other's* subjectivity.

1.2. Uniformity and Control

To undermine, weaken, flatten or homologize sexual difference on the basis of an egalitarian principle implies a *loss* of sexuality.[18] Furthermore, when-

---

[16] S. Palumbieri, *L'uomo questa meraviglia*, Urbaniana University Press, Rome 2000, p.102.

[17] See R. Lucas Lucas, *L'uomo spirito incarnato*, San Paolo, Cinisello Balsamo 2014, and J. Villagrasa, *Fondazione metafisica di un'etica realista*, Athenaeum Regina Apostolorum, Rome 2017.

[18] See C. Ricci, *Il padre dov'era...* p.27.

ever one proposes any kind of "standardization," it goes without saying that one is obliged to think in terms of a "mold." Who decides which model is the right one?

In a previous work I wrote that liberal eugenics stipulates that parents are the child's designers via genetic manipulation.[19] Going further back in time to what some authors call "the old eugenics," the State invades citizens' lives and imposes policies for sexuality and reproduction.[20] The State's interference in a person's life is actually the "old-fashioned" way. It is enough to recall the Italian positivist eugenic utopia closely linked to educational reform, based on the introduction of a "scientific" education in schools favoring the development of a "realistic understanding" of sexual hygiene.[21] This "eugenic utopia" was formed in close relation to the establishment of a public health care bureaucracy erected by the Italian Francesco Crispi's Penal Code of 1888. Medicine became "political" because in this way it was able to translate the alleged collective interest into ideological-normative terms. The term "collective" soon became an emblem for socio-political activism and, in this way, for medical activism. The category of "collective responsibility" soon proved to be an effective legitimizing factor in underwriting reforms reflecting a collectivist paradigm. Since if the community had a duty to ensure the health of its members, it also had a duty to verify that an individual's behavior was biologically "responsible."

It is interesting to note that for a generation such as ours, socio-culturally obsessed with "privacy," we now are witnessing massive State intervention in the private sphere. It is precisely consistent with a collectivist vision armed with the apparent aim of the immunizing logic of self-preservation.[22]

Michel Foucault (1926-1984) defines "biopolitics" as the control of political power over biological life (biopolitics being the "politics of biological life"). Power thus becomes "biopower." From the seventeenth century on this has led to two main outcomes. First, a politicized anatomy of the human body

[19] See G. Brambilla, *Il mito dell'uomo perfetto*, IF Press, Morolo 2009; Id., "Luci e ombre del potere biotecnologico nel tempo prenatale e perinatale", in E. Larghero, M. Lombardi Ricci (eds.), *Venire al mondo tra opportunità e rischi. Per una bioetica della vita nascente*, Camilliane, Torino 2013, p.185-204.

[20] M.J. Sandel, *The Case Against Perfection: Ethics in the Age of Genetic Engineering*, Belknap Press of Harvard University, Cambridge 2007; F. Nicoletti, "La sfida dell'eugentica nell'orizzonte della biopolitica" in *Humanitas* 4 2004, p.725-736.

[21] See F. Cassata, *Molti, sani, e forti: La eugenetica in Italia*, Bollati Bolinghieri, Turin 2006 p.80.

[22] R. Eposito, C. Galli, entry "Liberalismo" in *Enciclopedia di pensiero politico*, LaTerza, Rome, Bari 2000, p.384.

for controlling, within a mechanistic horizon, the human body's functioning on the one hand. Second, a "population biopolitics" for controlling the body of the race and its mechanisms of reproduction on the other. This increasing pervasiveness of political dominance over the biological finds paradoxical sanction, and even incentives, in an affirmation of human rights as foundational for the rights regime of a revolutionary age. Such statements proclaim an overlap of human rights to natural human existence with the rights of the citizen, opening the door to a nationalization of the biological, as well as the regulation of increasingly broad swathes of human life by the nation.

> [T]he social whole has greater worth and significance than its individual parts, that inborn biological differences should be sacrificed to cultural uniformity... [Man] must sacrifice his inherited idiosyncrasies and pretend to be the kind of standardized good mixer that organizers of group activity regard as ideal for their purposes. This ideal man is the man who displays "dynamic conformity."[23]

A politicization of life that appears to "protect" and immunize a community through the uniformity of its members can only extend its control to areas of sexuality and procreation by beginning with younger generations. Sex education in schools (of which the LGBT community is such a huge promoter) is extremely significant.[24] Starting in early childhood, projects conforming to the standards of the World Health Organization (WHO) betray a specific anthropological vision, within which one is biologically male or female without this accounting for sexual identity. Thus a child should "experiment," perhaps dressing up as female if male, or vice versa. This leads to addressing genitalia at an earlier stage as well—under the pretext of "gender equality"—in light of a possible future "coming out" in homosexual terms.

Sexuality and reproduction are back in the public domain again—but it is a far cry from the Judeo-Christian tradition's consideration of the marriage bed (*thalamos*) as something intimate and sacred to the point of veneration.

Rather, control is implemented through a devaluation of the family as the only unit competent to deliberate on the number of children to have, as well as through the supervision of children's education, above all, children's affective and sexual education.[25] On the one hand, specifically, we have inter-

---

[23] A. Huxley, *Brave New World*, Harper, Vintage, London 2004, p.32-33.

[24] In an Italian context, the website www.scosse.org is relevant here.

[25] Pope John Paul II wrote in no. 37 of his Apostolic Exhortation *Familiaris Consortio*, "Education in love as self-giving is also the indispensable premise for parents called to give their children a clear and delicate sex education. Faced with a culture that largely reduces human sexuality to the level of something commonplace, since it interprets and lives it in a

national family planning policies, which—under the banner of reproductive rights—support massive campaigns of birth "control." [26] At the same time, we have sex education proposed as an *obligatory* subject in schools. So here *uniformity becomes control.*

Consider the Beijing Conference of 1995, characterized precisely by the concept of control over sexuality and fertility. Since that conference, UN agencies have advocated campaigns based on a trivialization of sexuality in order to spread contraception and abortion, simultaneously imposing a LGBT model and a dissemination of gender theory ideology. Parents are thereby dispossessed of their role and their educational responsibility when children's sexual education is placed under the "protection" of the State.

Yet in the Western tradition the family represents an intermediate institution between the person and the State. Welcoming life "is not only an offer of life, but the effectual place in which a life multiplies itself, opens up to what is different from itself via a movement essentially contradicting the immunizing logic of 'self-preservation.'"[27]

2. *Unum Velle*: The Difference that Makes Communion Possible

A person's relational structure is what renders identity and otherness complementary.[28] According to Ricoeur, between identity and otherness there is not just a relation of comparison but also of implication. Otherness is constitutive of identity itself.[29] Diversity does not presuppose lack of communication, but rather just the opposite. Since thought proceeds by distinc-

---

reductive and impoverished way by linking it solely with the body and with selfish pleasure, the educational service of parents must aim firmly at a training in the area of sex that is truly and fully personal: for sexuality is an enrichment of the whole person-body, emotions and soul-and it manifests its inmost meaning in leading the person to the gift of self in love. Sex education, which is a basic right and duty of parents, must always be carried out under their attentive guidance, whether at home or in educational centers chosen and controlled by them...In this context education for chastity is absolutely essential, for it is a virtue that develops a person's authentic maturity and makes him or her capable of respecting and fostering the 'nuptial meaning' of the body... In view of the close links between the sexual dimension of the person and his or her ethical values, education must bring the children to a knowledge of and respect for the moral norms as the necessary and highly valuable guarantee for responsible personal growth in human sexuality."

[26] See E. Roccella, L. Scaraffia, *Contro il cristianesimo*, Piemme, Milan 2005.

[27] R. Esposito, C. Galli, "Liberalismo"... p.113.

[28] F. Bellino, "Bioetica e principi del personalismo" in G. Russo (ed.), *Bioetica fondamentale e generale*, SEI, Turin 1995, p.92-102.

[29] P. Ricoeur, *Oneself as Another*, University of Chicago Press, Chicago 1995.

tions, where these are missing there can be no progress. Where there are no differences there is no precondition for understanding and communication.[30] Difference is not an "obstacle" to the search for goodness and truth but rather "an impelling condition to have access to the truth about what unifies the bodily, spiritual, psychological and semantic dimensions of mankind. Communion in diversity is the 'semeion' of man's truth, of an idea of humanity understood as human greatness."[31]

What really pits us against each other, obscuring and distorting relationships, is *alienation* from ourselves, from our being human. It is in this way that man becomes a "stranger." Conversely, when a common nature establishes relationship and dialogue, a "common criterion takes over and in this there is no violence as it ultimately awaits the truth. This does not imply uniformity. On the contrary, it is only when this happens that the opposition can become complementarity."[32]

Peace itself "is not just an absence of war, nor a balance of power between enemies, but rather is based on a correct understanding of the human person."[33] Peace is endangered not when it is impossible for everyone to do what they want, but more radically when "man is not given all that is due to him as a man, when his dignity is not respected."[34] Only a recognition of human dignity can make possible equality among different cultures and the common and personal growth of all.

While the defense and promotion of human rights are important contributions to the building of a peaceful society, their roots lie in the truth about human beings and their dignity. Justice is not a mere human convention because what is right is not what is determined by law.[35] Rather this is dictated by the identity of what it means to be human at its greatest depth.[36] Love in the objective sense of the term implies a *fundamental* difference between those involved, for whom attraction between persons of the same sex does not exist as a "mirror" relationship properly speaking, even if feelings exist

[30] I. Trujillo, "Bioetica, multiculturalismo, e verità" in E. Compagnoni, F. Agostino (eds.), *Il confronto interculturale: dibattiti bioetici e practice giuridiche*, San Paolo, Cinisello Balsamo 2003, p.69.

[31] G. Russo, "Eugenica e razzismo in bioetica" in G. Russo (ed.), *Bioetica fondamentale e generale...*

[32] J. Ratzinger, *Truth and Tolerance*, Ignatius Press, San Francisco 2004.

[33] Pontifical Council for Justice and Peace, *Compendium of Catholic Social Teaching*, Editrice Vaticana, Vatican City 2004, No. 494.

[34] *Ibid.*

[35] *Ibid.*, No. 145.

[36] John Paul II, Encyclical Letter *Solicitudo rei socialis*, No.202.

between them. Because love is no mere feeling. Rather it is a commitment packed with plans resting upon the truth about being with another. Being two different people with different personalities is not enough to be in a relationship of otherness if, in addition to this, the meaning of sexual difference is left unintegrated.

Following the approach proposed here, it is possible to take a stand against perspectives that are unilateral and reductive on the question of sexual difference and that, as such, are incapable of accounting for its proper human meaning. On the one hand, an affirmation of deeply rooted corporeal difference in no way implies subjection to rigidly biological determinants. This is so since, as can be observed, the human body always bears the imprint of spirit, and is marked by all that proceeds from it. That is, since the body is so rich in symbolic and cultural expressions, it is never purely inert matter alien to freedom of action.[37] On the other hand, the original sexing of the body precludes difference from being reduced to some mere socio-cultural construct. It cannot be deconstructed on the basis of subjective choices, completely jettisoning the structure of its biological foundation, to be viewed as irrelevant to sexual orientation and relegated to personal preference alone.

The position entitled "philosophy of sexual difference," which owes to Luce Irigaray's theoretical advances and has been embraced by other scholars as well (especially in France and Italy), offers more fruitful and positive developments. According to this position, the original differential status inscribed in the body is inseparable from its proper human meaning, rebuffs any opposition between nature and culture and addresses the demand for full appreciation of the peculiarities of each sex.[38]

In regard to the assumption that the person is not considered in his or her uni-totality of body, mind and spirit, a personalist anthropology asserts that the person not only *has* a determining sex but is either a man or a woman. Human sexuality is thus not attributable to a thing or to an object but rather is a structural form of the person, a structure that is meaningful prior to its having a function.[39] Here sexuality is a fundamental component of personality with its own way of being, manifesting, communicating with others, feeling,

---

[37] G. Salatiello, "L'essere umano femminile: chi è come funziona", *Studia Bioethica*, 3 (2014), p.10-17.

[38] *Ibid.*

[39] G. Miranda, "La sessualità umana: il valore e i significativi," in M.L. DiPetro, E. Sgreccia (eds.) *Bioetica ed educazione*, La Scuola, Brescia 1970, p.77-89.

expressing and living out human love.[40] This ability to love by giving oneself is then "incarnated" in the nuptial meaning of the body, wherein the masculinity and femininity of a person is inscribed. "The human body, with its sex, and its masculinity and femininity... includes 'a spousal' dimension. It is an ability to express love... right from 'the beginning.' Every form of love will always bear this masculine or feminine character."[41]

As two "selves" become one, "we" passes through a communion of wills that empowers the two "selves" to become one "we" (*unum velle*). Being sexed marks the human condition, a condition characterized by distinction while ordered toward convergence. So complementary factors specify when one acts as a mirror for another, wherein "all individuality is not an enclosed uni-totality but is rather a structured openness, as with any other human uni-totality. Where uni-totality is aimed at complementarity, a uni-duality is established in reciprocity."[42] In the description, and not in the analysis (as differences between men and women are so unequivocal, they can only be described), of female and male specificity there is no chance for any form of sexism. Emphasizing those lines of demarcation best demonstrates the complementary features that draw the sexes into dialogue.[43] The fact that man and woman are biophysically complementary provides a strong indication that a complementary structure is present and operant within the psycho-spiritual dimension: "attraction involves a complementarity that is not just physical; and this connotes a difference. This cannot be merely physical... Sexual difference already contains the constitutive requirement of a relationship in the form of reciprocity."[44]

But let us go further. To consider the two sexes distinct is not enough. Rather this is about comprehending the hermeneutic principle "Distinguish in order to unite" as one of uni-duality. The male-female relationship is unitary yet articulated and differentiated throughout its entire reality. All this depends upon being a person: "The person, because unrepeatable, says original sexuality, is from its origin combined with specific factors of its comple-

---

[40] Sacred Congregation for Catholic Education, "Orientamenti educative per l'amore umano", in *L'Osservatore Romano*, December 2, 1983.

[41] Pontifical Council for the Family, *Sessualità umana: verità e significato*, Libreria Editrice Vaticana, Vatican City 1995, No.10.

[42] S. Palumbieri, *L'uomo, questo paradosso*, Urbanium University Press, Rome 2000, p.200.

[43] R. Habaci, *Le Moment de l'homme : Commencements de la créature, la colonne brisée de Baalbeck* (Convivence) Desclée de Brouwer, Paris 1991.

[44] S. Palumbieri, *L'uomo, questo paradosso* ... p.205.

mentary 'Thou.' It says, in short, difference and relation, and for this reason is the only backdrop against which we can even discuss... gender equality within difference."[45] The *other* is a diversity that recognizes itself upon coming into contact with what is symmetrical with the Self. A male ego is self-perceived as such in the presence of a woman acting as a mirror, and thereby recognizes itself as different. Reciprocity thus means remaining different while effecting unity with the *other*. "This unity is not the absorption of one into the other, nor a cancelling out either of oneself or of another in some vague anthropological nirvana. Nor is it, as with bisexualism, merging into some neutral androgyny... Rather it is the constitution of a 'we' within a dynamic perception of differences consciously recognized, and those convergences seized and promoted by a will to cooperate."[46]

[45] *Ibid.*, p.207.
[46] *Ibid.*

GIUSEPPE MARI*

GENDER THEORY AND EDUCATION

In recent years references to gender have become commonplace, and gender theory's influence on education is frequently advertised. In this paper, after briefly treating what gender is, I will focus on the educational challenge involved in this phenomenon, especially in K-12 schools.[1]

1. Gender Theories: common identity, underlying assumptions and critical feedback

The word gender groups together some significantly different cultural orientations. However, they all share in common an underlying characteristic. They claim that the meaning of human sexuality—with regard to its symbolic interpretation—is totally attributable to mere socio-cultural practices, related to conventions and customs, and is therefore open to discussion.

The driving force behind the embrace of this perspective tries to remove any element which might imply distinction (viewed as discriminatory) between men and women. Obviously if everything is reduced to social conventions, such distinctions can be questioned, renegotiated, even changed radically. This is achieved by distinguishing the words "sex" and "gender." The first word alludes to a corresponding description of a male or a female's anatomical and physiological identity. The second refers to the symbolic meaning of gender difference. Only the first identification is common to all cultures, the second, as noted above, is treated as quite arbitrary.

Not surprisingly, "Gender Theories" use a "politically correct" vocabulary identifiable by the elimination of differences between men and women and the adoption of a strategic neutrality. In Italy this came about by substituting the expressions "Parent 1" and "Parent 2" for those of "mother" and "father."

---

* Professor of General Pedagogy, Catholic University of the Sacred Heart giuseppe.mari@unicatt.it

[1] For further information on the theme, see M.A. Peeters, *Il Gender*, San Paolo, Milan 2014 and the bibliography in the book. For a monograph on its pedagogical consequences, see *Studia Patavina*, 1, 2015, p.15-120. You also may see my book *Gender e sfida educativa* reviewed in *Rivista Lasalliana* 3, 2014, p.389-398.

Again, the goal is to promote the "undifferentiated nature" of sexual profiles to prevent discrimination. Yet here an obvious anthropological problem emerges. If the human being is structurally relational (as the Western cultural tradition has affirmed for over twenty-five centuries), this means being human implies a recognition of "difference" understood as "otherness." Yet if one adopts an "indifferent language" (i.e., a vocabulary that is undifferentiated), how can there still be a recognition of those differences required for the existence of intrinsic human relatedness?

Such is, in fact, the heart of the problem. It sprang from a desire to remove any discrimination that "being male" or "being female" entails. And so it adopts a strategy that—under the pretext of maintaining an indifference between the two sexes (in terms of their anthropological meanings)—denies precisely what it seeks to affirm. What is at stake is founded on the anthropological level—a symbolic interpretation joined at the hip with anatomical and physiological description.

Such a symbolic reading becomes possible due to the descriptive moment, one understood to express commonly-held knowledge. Still, it must be emphasized, of itself this would lead to insufficient knowledge at the levels of ethics and pedagogy. In fact, a criterion related to sexual difference—that of capabilities—does not automatically distinguish human sexuality from animal sexuality. In this regard, an ambiguity (one already expressed in the history of educational thought) now comes to light. About two centuries ago, it led many to recognize an alleged "neutrality" of values in scientific study bringing with them certain foundational guidelines. As is known, this was one of those points that led to controversy between positivists and Neo-Thomists. Today it occurs anew, albeit it be in a "softer" version.

The limitation of "the gender approach" is linked not just to a descriptivist reduction of human sexuality, nor to the elaboration of an alleged neutral interpretation of difference, but to the underlying problem connected to the distinction between "sex" and "gender." As we have seen, it assumes that only a "sex"-based approach offers a reliable orientation. It denies any interpretation at the "gender" level that goes beyond mere description, making it a value-neutral approach.

Yet this is fundamentally questionable. The existence of symbolic readings regarding human sexuality in the Prehistoric period cannot be explained (their archaism preceding acculturation) with the acquisition of extraneous socio-cultural conventions. The myth of the origin of the existence of the world from the union of "Father Sky" and "Mother Earth" necessarily bring us face to face with two explanations. Either we accept an incredible serendipity in the identical socio-cultural conventions expressed across diverse non-communicating cultures, or else what emerges is a fundamental anthropological construct common to all.

With this second explanation, there is meaning at the "gender" level that does not depend on socio-cultural conventions but in fact precedes them; and so we can evaluate them. Since the archaic semantization of male and female types presents them as essentially different, if similar in being life-giving, it follows that, symbolically, there is an original meaning to "being male" and "being female." This allows us to reject any discrimination based on dimorphism, yet without denying difference, indeed recognizing its ability to facilitate communication and sharing.

I concede the *motivation* offered by the gender approach (which, actually, is much older—we need only consider the Pauline passage in Gal 3:28 where "there is neither male nor female" precisely precludes discrimination based on sexual difference). Yet this passage can be viewed in the opposite light, as the semantization of differences and not their denial. I believe that such an approach is essential with regard to the educational challenge presented by gender.

2. *Gender and Education*

One cannot underestimate gender theory's impact on education. First, we must remember that humanity has always questioned the meaning of being male and being female, as we have seen in the myth of humanity's origin. The question of gender has always been linked to an answer regularly expressed in education.

No civilization ever neglected a "need" to teach junior members the goal of "becoming" men and women. Obviously, this practice also has resulted at times in unfortunate and questionable forms that in some specific cases should be rejected. Certain stereotypes in educational practices were adopted in a discriminating manner, often to the detriment of women. But this does not mean every category can be erased.

We must not forget that categories also answer a (necessary) logic of identification, which is—and must necessarily be—the simplification of a complex reality. Such simplification, though, is not necessarily negative. If it is uniformly negative, a stereotype must be corrected. Yet if the schematization it conveys does not adversely affect the dignity of persons and merely discloses harmless clichés, then such categories should be recognized for the role they express within human communication. The desire to deconstruct stereotypes is worthwhile only if, at the same time, it reconstructs them in a form that does not involve discrimination. Otherwise deconstructing merely serves to confuse those striving to become adults. For example, drawing attention to the fact that distinctions between male and female forms of dress are conventional has an informative and critical validity. Yet this should not lead males to dress as females, nor females to dress as males, as this disorients people who, precisely in order to mature, have an initial need to identify in precise patterns.

The issue of education is also important for other reasons, not the least of which is that it reveals the intrinsic limits of the gender approach. This approach professes the absence of any basic anthropological meaning, as this is usually attributed (reduced) to socio-cultural conventions. From a pedagogical standpoint, this question is of decisive importance. Educating inevitably means acting prospectively since it implies a constitutive link to freedom. It is also linked to the fact that being free, a human being must orient herself in a direction distancing her from some current factual condition. This means, concretely, that educating a boy involves respecting—theoretically, but in practice too—the man he potentially becomes. While educating a girl means to respect the woman she potentially becomes. Whenever a gender approach reduces all the anthropological significance of sexual profiles to mere convention, it rejects the ability to recognize original meanings. Everything is then reduced to one single meaning common to all. When we deviate from a descriptive approach, pure and simple, we wind up proceeding in an arbitrary manner.

Yet our problem is far from being resolved. Today, "to educate" in practice means to reject any ethical orientation derived from the pure and simple "physiological" fact of sexuality. In concrete terms this means embracing an indifference toward sexual behaviors (obviously excluding the illegal ones) that in practice translates into bisexuality, elevating a statistically limited behavior to the rank of a model for normative sexuality. One could instantly recognize the logical inconsistency of this approach, in which "politically correctness" operates as a propaganda strategy by offering a presupposed "neutrality." We must unmask the alleged neutrality of gender approaches by exposing how they orient themselves, and in so questionable a manner.

We can agree to campaign against homophobia, as an incitement to violence, and related unacceptable behaviors. But a campaign against homophobia must not morph into a Trojan horse for instilling indifference to sexual behaviors. We cannot deny the objective fact that there are specific differences in these and other behaviors that are subject to critical appraisal in the name of freedom of inquiry.

3. *School and Gender*

One context for which these facts should be kept especially in mind is schools.

As stated in the Constitution [of Italy, Article 30], parents bear the primary and, in fact, plenary responsibility regarding their children's education. Thus, the school, acting in a merely subsidiary capacity, cannot adopt rules that are not shared by the family. This is particularly true of the gender approach as presented for discussion in scientific and cultural contexts. It does not represent an interpretation that is widely shared (in public opinion), nor solidly confirmed (in science). This topic thus exceeds the school's responsibility. We should not forget that education has to interpret a series of guidelines that must be valid for both the civil and scientific spheres. In the case of the gender theory, it is controversial to say the least.

This issue is far from being settled, as demonstrated by the fact that such booklets as "Educating for Diversity" (produced by the Beck Institute and disseminated by the Italian National Office against Racial Discrimination [UNAR]), which was initially targeted at schools by way of promoting an anti-discrimination campaign, were not widely made known by the [Italian] Ministry of Education. This means the situation is as yet unclear, and prudence is needed before accepting these approaches as "approved" before they are verified.

So how might schools proceed?

Once the above-mentioned points are settled, I think the modality to follow is that of acting in the name of gender *personalization*; i.e., working to preserve the originality of the "masculine" and the "feminine" by bringing into focus behaviors and learning for boys and girls. I personally have made this the object of my attention, arriving at the conviction that this is the appropriate response to the challenge of promoting an awareness of gender identity within the context of recognizing the common dignity of males and females.[2] Moreover, there are many studies in Italy addressing the issue and worthy of consideration. Presupposing the category of "person," they assume

---

2 See G. Mari (ed.), *Comportamento e apprendimento di maschi e femmine a scuola*, Vita e Pensiero, Milan 2012.

a trans-ideological reference point that enjoys broad recognition in documents relating to schools in recent decades.[3]

Education is a delicate subject, and requires a careful approach. Constitutional guardrails framing the school as a "common" institution are sufficient to reject two trends—as equal as they are opposite—undermining gender identity. We must reject denying the problem, on the one hand, and framing gender identity in ideological terms on the other.

The recognition of difference (favored by the semantization of male and female profiles) and of the identical dignity of the sexes, together with the exclusion of any discrimination or violence against legally acceptable sexual experiences, should suffice for affective and sexual education.

[3] See G. Zanniello (ed.), *Maschi e femmine a scuola*, SEI, Turin 2007; A. La Marca (ed.), *La valorizzazione delle specificità femminili e maschili. Una didattica differenziata per le alunne e per gli alunni*, Armando, Rome 2008.

AN INTERVIEW WITH GIANFRANCO AMATO*

Today many people talk about "gender theories," but the fact is that the vast majority don't even know what they are.

A peculiar, curious fact I continue to notice at conferences I hold almost daily throughout Italy, is that the vast majority of people haven't the faintest idea of what the so-called "gender theories" are. This widespread ignorance on the subject is accompanied by an equally widespread confusion. Some confuse gender theories with sexual education, affirming young people's need to be properly educated in that area. Others confuse it with equality between the sexes, pointing to some need to overcome stereotypes according to which women and not men should supervise housework. Still others confuse it with homosexuality, stating that it is the right to respect those with a different sexual orientation. In fact, gender theory is none of the three things mentioned above.

It is hard to understand that this theory is based on the concept—as simple as it is absurd—that a person is male or female, man or woman, based not on objective data, i.e., on how the person is organically structured, but rather on the subjective perception of how he/she feels at the moment. The irrationality of this idea is self-evident. In fact, it is no coincidence that the pope, during his pastoral visit to Naples on March 21, 2015, called gender ideology "a mistake of the human mind that causes confusion." It was a colorful expression highlighting the ideology's utter absurdity.

Yet, despite its obvious irrationality, gender theory is seeping into the sphere of public opinion through a variety of channels

Yes, especially four: the legislative channel, via statute; the judicial channel, via case law; the cultural channel, via mass media; and the educational channel, via school indoctrination. Here are some concrete examples.

On July 9, 2013, the Justice Commission of the Chamber of Deputies for the Italian Parliament approved a unified text as the basic text of a drafted law called "Rules Against Discrimination on Grounds of Sexual Orientation

* President of Italian Association of Jurists for Life.

or Gender Identity." This is the so-called Scalfarotto Act, named for one its sponsors. Well, Article 1.B of the text reads: "For purposes of criminal law, 'gender identity' means the perception of belonging to the male or female sex a person has of himself or herself, even if this fails to conform to his or her biological sex." The consequences of such a legal provision are unimaginable.

The day after the Justice Commission approved the basic text, the Jurists Association for Life publicly denounced the absurdity of these legislative provisions, launching a petition to stop this juridical nostrum. The online Catholic publication *La Nuova Bussola Quotidiana* took the initiative of proposing an online public petition just two days later that garnered over 20,000 signatures in short order. Then other Catholic journal and websites joined the petition.

On July 15, a *Huffington Post* article, by way of reaction, entitled "Homophobia Law and the 'No' of the Catholic Right Wing," prompted a response from Jurists for Life. The next day, the Catholic world's attention to the petition was confirmed by an interview I gave as President of Jurists for Life, aired at the international television network Telepace in Rome, which was instituted at the express wish of Pope John Paul II in 1990.

On July 17, the protests of Jurists for Life finally found space in newspaper *CEI*. In fact, the newspaper *Avvenire* published an article entitled "Not So Fast, Jurists: A Trojan Horse Bill to Introduce Gender Identity into Italy." The following day, Vatican Radio interviewed the President of Jurists for Life about the petition. On July 22, 2013, as a result of media clamor about the petition, the bill's two sponsors, the Rep. Leone and the Rep. Scalfarotto presented a single amendment which completely replaced the text upon which previous discussion had developed, permanently canceling out any bias in favor of gender identity.

A major victory at first. Except that what went out the door came back in through the window…

While we managed to block that legal absurdum at the national level, the battle is still ongoing regarding a similar—perhaps worse—statute discussed by Trent's Provincial Council. It's a legislative proposal entitled "Law Enforcement on Interventions of Certain Sexual Orientation, Gender Identity or Intersexual Discrimination" (Article 2, Paragraph 1, A), and it literally defines "gender identity" as "the perception of oneself as male or female or an undefined condition." The discussion of this bill was stalled due to strong political opposition that seems to have been able to avert final approval.

On November 4, 2014, the First Civil Chamber of the Messina Court reached a verdict in case 2649/2014 reaffirming the principle that, "the gender identity of a person does not temporarily or permanently depend on surgery modifying his or her primary sexual characteristics." What had happened was obvious. A young man of twenty-one had gone to the Registry Office of the Municipality of Messina demanding that his ID should indicate that he was female. The official of the Municipality pointed out the law allows him to change his sex on his ID only if he is undergoing surgery.

The young man stated he did not want to undergo any operation, and explained that he is a woman because he feels he is a woman, and public authorities have the duty to certify his condition on the mere basis of his self-perception. Naturally, the Registry Office official was forced to issue a formal denial on the basis of current legislation. The young man brought the matter before the Court of Messina, who, according to their decision, found his request well-justified. In fact, in the explanation of their decision, the judges stated that, "a person's gender identity is constituted by three elements: one's body, one's self-perception, and one's social role." Analyzing the specific case submitted to them, they concluded that, in this case, the young man's body was somehow less important than the other two elements, which should thus be seen as dominant.

Given this sentence, the same Court ordered the Registrar of the City of Messina to change the boy's birth certificate and all subsequent documents. Today in Italy we have a man, a male, a holder of the XY chromosome, who according to law is a woman. If this man wished, for example, to take advantage of affirmative action according to sex (the so-called *female quota*) he might very well do so, with bureaucratic documentation to attest to his condition as a woman.

He could, in theory, marry another man. The controversial principle through which the Court of Messina embraced gender theory has unfortunately been recently reiterated by another surprising decision of the Court of Cassation. With a decision destined to become historical (Cass. First Sec., Sent no. 15138/2015 of 20 July 2015), the Court—in contrast to the clear pronouncements of the Court of Piacenza and the Appeals Court of Bologna—which had denied a right to obtain personal data rectification without surgery—has determined that, "the desire to actualize the co-incidence between soma and psyche, even in the absence of a surgical operation, is the result of a painful and personal processing of one's gender identity."

It is clear, therefore, how gender theory—despite the clamor of deniers—advances through the strong arm of the law.

And that's not all. This questionable jurisprudence is dangerously influencing the administrative sector. Resolution n. 27-1613 of the Piedmont Regional Council, June 23, 2015, which aims to achieve a "Gender Identity ID," is an excellent example. There is no doubt—nor could there really be any—that the LGBT lobby is pushing for the enactment of this administrative measure since, as the preamble to the resolution candidly admits, the Council has acted, "in view of the request received by the Piedmont Region LGBT Pride Cooperative of Turin to introduce its employees to the chance to receive an ID in accord with the gender chosen and which respects one's gender identity." Here for the first time (it seems), the new term "gender choice" coined by the LGBT lobby has been used in the bureaucratic language. We honestly did not feel need for it, but there it is. Gender ideology offers an enviable neologistic fantasy.

The resolution also offers some truly dramatic and even surreal passages. After recalling the norms on sex rectification governed by Statute No. 16414 of April 1982, the Council adopted a controversial (and minority) jurisprudential direction on the subject. In fact, in the resolution it says: "Whereas some judgments have proposed an interpretation of that legislation which, departing from the literal data, allows a registry for sex rectification even in the absence of genital reconstructive surgery."

As you know by now, Italy is slowly turning into a country of common law, with the "advantage" (unlike the Anglo-Saxon countries) that each can choose, at will, the precedent one likes best from among the contradictory and multicolored jurisprudence of the many judicial offices scattered throughout the national territory. As the Regional Government of Piedmont did.

So, this resolution ventures into the inaccessible area of "gender": "With consideration, finally, that there may be cases of person for whom there is no correspondence between gender identity and the biological body, so that the same persons feel they belong to a particular gender that does not correspond to the one attributed by birth."

What all this has to do with employee IDs is explained in the next step: "Given that, if on one hand the identification card has the function of being for clients a reference for the person who attends them in the public offices, on the other hand having an identification badge suited to one's gender choice can allow the same employee an improvement of his/her working conditions."

From here we derive the final conclusion: "The Piedmont Region, due to all of the above circumstances, has considered it appropriate that employees of the Employee Board are required to display their ID. For those whose physical sexual identity does not correspond to gender identity, there is the option, if specifically requested, to have an ID conforming to their gender of choice."

Do you believe that the mass media is contributing to the spreading of gender ideology? If so, how?

There surely is not enough space to describe how the mass media is striving to spread this theory, from television to print. I will just mention one case.

On May 5, 2015, after offering a lecture to the students of the Faculty of Civil Law at the Pontifical Lateran University, I hopped on a train to Milan and on my seat I found a copy of the magazine *Grazia* (No.2, Vol. 7 January 2015). It probably was left by the traveler who preceded me. I was flipping through the pages when I was hit by the image of a child dressed as an adult, in a black and white suit. The title intrigued me: "Generation UNISEX." The specific subtitle was: "She dresses like a boy, but calls himself 'John.' Shiloh Nouvel, Brad Pitt and Angelina Jolie's daughter, has become the most striking example of 'neutral' education, with no gender barriers. This is not an isolated case. From the United States to Italy, *Grazia* investigates."

In that article, *Grazia* explained on the side that "in fact, more and more parents, teachers and experts argue that we should educate children to be 'gender neutral.'"

It is easy to imagine the impact this message can have on public opinion if we consider the mimetic effects of celebrities' *modus vivendi* on normal people. So "neutral" gender is likely even to become trendy.

Not even the fashion world seems to be immune to the lobby's ideological attempt to impose gender theory on all levels. (Despite deniers' increasingly unbearable din.) To understand how they manage to deliberately lie, you can just take a walk around Oxford Street in London. The historic luxury store "Selfridges" is opening a store for neutral-gender shopping. The space devoted to the now obsolete men's and women's departments will make way for three floors of "gender free" fashion. All this to meet the demand of those who perceive themselves as male or female regardless of their biological sex.

So, a man who feels like a woman will have no problem buying a long evening dress, make-up or high heels to wear in the evening. The same goes for a woman who feels like a man. The old mannequins with masculine and feminine appearances have been scrapped as symbols of sexual difference, the products of supposedly obsolete stereotypes from the past. According to Selfridges, where you will see the most curious fashion shows, muscular guys dress up in heels and make-up wearing skirts with absolute ease, while a neutral mannequin represents the new frontier of the "gender free."

There is no lack of demand. Among Selfridges' customers, for example, are students from the prestigious University of Cambridge, who obviously can afford the wealthy level of shopping. Extravagance has always been a luxury inaccessible to the rest of us poor mortals. Nor do I mention Cambridge students at random. Breaking a centuries-old tradition, the British historical university has decided to succumb to the pressure coming from the Cambridge University Students' Union's LGBT+, changing the classic "dress code" for the graduation ceremony in force until a short time ago. For males this was a black suit, white shirt, bow tie, socks and strictly black shoes, and for females an elegant black dress and a white shirt. Now, thanks to the "gender free," things can easily be inverted. We have already seen big boys graduate with makeup, long dresses, and high heels, a beard notwithstanding, such as Conchita Wurst.

To the joy of Charlie Bell, president of the student CUSU LGBT+ and promoter of revolutionary initiatives, he's finally been able to claim that sexual difference is actually a simple socio-cultural variable, and that, according to the pervasive gender theory, one's self-perception should prevail over one's biological sex.

How does this reflect on the education and school system?

We might start with a document widely promoted by the Italian National Office against Racial Discrimination (UNAR) entitled *National Strategy for Preventing and Combating Discrimination Based on Sexual Orientation and Gender Identity* (2013-2015), implementing Recommendation CM/REC (2010)5 of the Committee of Ministers of the Council of Europe, to combat discrimination based on sexual orientation or gender identity.

According to the aforementioned National Strategy, repressing discrimination against LGBT people should be structured according to four axes: (i) Education and Instruction (II) Work, (III) Prison Security, (IV) Communication and Media.

At this point the first axis in particular, the one concerning education and instruction, deserves to be examined.

Here the strategy aims precisely "to spread the gender theory in schools, also through initiatives for students and teachers, for the purposes of the elaboration of their process of acceptance of their sexual orientation and gender identity." The aim to propagate the "gender theory" is explicitly declared.

However, to understand what is going on in several kindergartens and primary schools in our country, we can just read the dense document entitled *Standards for Sexuality Education in Europe*, sub-titled: *Framework for Policy Makers, School and Health Authorities and Specialists.* This document was drawn up by the World Health Organization's Regional Office for Europe and BZgA (*Bundeszentrale für gesundheitliche Aufklärung*). The WHO document created in Cologne in 2010 includes indoctrination per age group on topics that are rather illuminating, through information and educational activities.

Let's start with the first category: that from zero to four years. According to the *London Standard*, infants should be briefed on "early infantile masturbation," the "discovery of their bodies and their genitals," an ability "to acquire awareness of gender," "different family relationships," "the right to explore nakedness and the body" with curiosity, and to "accept the different ways of becoming a child within a family."

The second group includes children from four to six years of age. The children of this range must not only already be taught all the individual parts of their genitals (in detail) but also must nurture a "respect for difference" and "gender equity," learn to "consolidate their gender identity," to "promote" the belief that "my body belongs to me," to be aware of the possibility of "same sex relationships," to know "other family concepts," to accept differences and to become convinced that it is up to them to decide with "an open and non-judgmental attitude."

The third category is between six and nine years. Children of this age must be introduced to "the basic idea of contraception (how to plan and decide on your own family)" through an in-depth knowledge of "different contraception methods," "sexual relations," "children's sexual rights," and knowledge of "diseases related to sexuality." It is also mandatory that children, boys and girls six to nine years of age, learn to accept not just "the insecurities that come with the awareness of their own bodies" but also "diversity," in particular "same sex friendship and love," including education in absolute respect for different "values, lifestyles and norms."

The fourth group is that of children ages nine to twelve. At this stage, in addition to an already complete sexual knowledge (of ejaculation, abortion, menstruation, contraception, etc.) they must adopt a "positive attitude toward gender identity and equity," learn to try "same-sex friendship and love" and to accept, respect and understand diversity in sexuality and sexual orientation."

A fifth group includes teenagers ages twelve to fifteen years of age. They must be educated on "the role expectations and role behaviors of sexual arousal and gender differences," analyzing aspects of "gender identity and sexual orientation," including "coming out," and, of course, they too must "accept, respect and understand diversity in sexuality and sexual orientation."

The sixth and final category regards boys and girls of fifteen years and up. A more advanced training phase is needed. This includes, for example, the ability to create genetically designed babies, "a critical view of the different cultural / religious norms related to pregnancy, parenthood, etc.," to perform "coming out" in front of others (publicly admit to homosexual or bisexual feelings), more "acceptance of differences in sexual orientation and identity," the "transition from possible negative feelings, disgust and hatred toward homosexuality to acceptance and appreciation for sexual differences," and "changes in family structure" to analyze concepts of "homosexuality, bisexuality, asexuality and single parenthood," as well as an ability to "recognize violations of rights and to denounce discrimination and gender-based violence."

How does one explain the irrationality and danger behind such a document?

First, it is the expression of a culture that conceives of human sexuality as connected to the body alone, to genital experience and to narcissistic pleasure, leading to a loss of serenity—already during the early years of innocence—and emptying out into different forms of depravity.

Second, it introduces a deadly, toxic ideology of pan-sexualism to young people through hate-filled forms of propaganda and indoctrination from an early age, seeking to transform the anthropological conception of man as it's been known to our civilization for thousands of years.

Third, it disempowers the family—the privileged, natural sphere for education—of its formative task in the sexual field, disregarding the fact it's the family that offers the ideal environment for fulfilling the mission of securing one's gradual education into sexual life, prudently, smoothly and without major trauma.

Fourth, it clearly violates two fundamental rights recognized, guaranteed and protected by the Universal Declaration of Human Rights: in particular Article 18, which guarantees the freedom to express one's religious values in education either alone or in community with others, in public or in private; and Article 26 of the priority of parental rights in choosing how to educate one children. Yet it seems pretty significant that the latter principle was expressly declared in 1948, the year in which the Universal Declaration was signed. As a generally accepted and granted principle, it was not mentioned in any national or international legal document. The point is that it followed the Second World War, an experience tragically demonstrating how devastating, destructive and deadly the indoctrination of young people through the Third Reich state education system could be.

It became clear how public education could become a lethal weapon in the hands of power.

Returning to the present, it should be noted that the section on the "Standards for Sexuality Education in Europe," which could become devastating, is precisely the one related to so-called "gender identity," i.e., the theory that children should have the right to choose their sex. They must be able to decide whether to become boys or girls.

What's a barnehage and how has it been presented?

The Scandinavian gender *barnehage* model is increasingly becoming a trend in several kindergartens. In this model boys are dressed as girls and vice versa, and boys play with dolls and girls with cars. The terrifying thing is that political power is seeking to manipulate the most malleable individuals in any population—children from zero to six years of age—to inculcate a novel absurdist anthropology that brings to mind Pope Francis' implacable judgment: "a mistake of the human mind that creates confusion." Yet what seems incredible is that this attempt to indoctrinate children is faring well amid indifference and general unawareness. Worse than that: if anyone dares to oppose it or raise doubts, he or she is branded with the usual offenses: "Bigot," "backward," "medieval," "opponent of scientific progress"—ending with the inevitable insult of "homophobic" or "fascist," which is always good for any occasion. We are not even aware of the excesses achieved to date. Just consider Gonapeptyl, a hypothalamic blocker—approved by the British government—designed to delay puberty in children so as to give them more time to decide whether to become male or female…

The sternest, most implacable judgment was offered by the Roman Pontiff when, on the occasion of a speech to the representatives of the International Catholic Child Bureau (BICE), on April 11, 2014, he insisted that, "we must support parents' rights to educate their children and reject any kind of experimental education on children and young people, used as guinea pigs" in schools that more and more resemble re-education camps, and recall the horrors of educational manipulation already endured during the great genocidal dictatorships of the Twentieth Century, today substituted by the dictatorship of "Group Think." As well as when, on his return trip from the Philippines, January 19, 2015, when interviewed by Jan-Christoph Kitzler (a journalist for the German radio program "Ard"), Pope Francis, referred to gender theory as "ideological colonization."

Today young people are taught that everything is "opinion and instinct," to the point that to have the right to challenge even one's own nature, now reduced to spirit and volition, in a contradictory logic for which "the manipulation of nature, that today we deplore regarding the environment, becomes the choice of man toward himself," as Benedict XVI masterfully recalled in his speech to the Roman Curia held on December 21, 2012.

Perhaps the greatest danger is that of an anthropological vision that abandons a human being's truth and beauty.

This anthropological vision, in which man is conceived only abstractly, is truly dangerous: a being able to choose for himself something like his own nature, autonomously. In this way, as Pope Benedict always recalled, "man as a legal entity in his own right necessarily becomes an object, to which one has a 'right,' and who, as a subject of law, may be procured." When the freedom "to do" becomes freedom "to be," the inescapable conclusion is to deny not only the Creator, but the creature as well. Thus, man denies himself.

In addition, it's a real short-circuit of human reason to repress sexual difference from among natural indications so as to reduce sexuality to pure instinct, through the implementation of educational projects rooted in this vision.

PART IV

AN INTERDISCIPLINARY APPROACH TO SAME-SEX ATTRACTION

ALESSANDRO FIORE*

A PHILOSOPHICAL AND MORAL ANALYSIS OF SEXUAL BEHAVIOR

Many conceive same-sex attraction to be "a natural variant of human sexual behavior." This expression comes from the World Health Organization.[1] Is it still possible to state that same-sex behavior is "contrary to nature"?

The question is not of secondary importance. Sexuality is one of a person's most profound dimensions. Considering the World Health Organization's position, we must first understand the possible validity of such a judgment about same-sex attraction and, above all, what meaning the adjective "natural" has. What exactly do we mean by "nature" when we speak of SSA? Here, we want to distinguish the various fields of knowledge and retrace the reasoning that has led Christian philosophical (and theological) thought, in particular, to support the "non-naturalness" of SSA.[2] The term "natural" has a plurality of meanings.[3] For example, it may stand for "what you find in nature." In this sense, SSA could be called "natural" because it corresponds to a human condition (more or less) as old as man himself. However, in this sense pedophilia, rape, murder, etc. could also be considered "natural."

The observation that some same-sex behaviors are also present in the animal kingdom (even if the nature of this variant of practice is much disputed) and are therefore"natural" does not help much. Rape, necrophilia, devouring

---

* Managing editor of *Notizie ProVita*.

[1] "World Health Organization removed homosexuality from the international classification of diseases (ICD) in 1990. It was included in the category of "sexual orientation." ICD-10 specifically states that "sexual orientation by itself is not to be considered a disorder." However, "the ego-dystonic sexual orientation" remains cataloged among the disorders (F66.1). See WHO, *The ICD-10 Classification of Mental and Behavioural Disorders*, p.172-173, available at its official website www.who.int.

[2] In this reasoning, ample space is given to the concept of nature and the principles of morality as systematized by Thomas Aquinas (1225-1274). We are interested in examining whether these concepts and principles still retain substantial validity.

[3] Already Aquinas noted that the term "nature" and the derived adjective "natural" were analogous terms with a plurality of meanings: *Natura dicitur multis modis*. See *Contra Gentiles*, IV, c. 41, and *In III Sent.* D. 5, q. 1, a. 2.

one's partner following sexual intercourse, and other behaviors of this kind are also present in the animal kingdom.[4]

A definition of "natural," such as "what happens in nature," does not tell us anything about how humans should behave but only about how they behave (and often, very often, misbehave) *de facto*. Now, we are interested in the aspect of "duty," the moral aspect. It is mainly in the moral sense that same-sex behavior is defined as "disordered," "contrary to nature" or "abnormal." Organizations such as the WHO have a specific authority (not infallibility) to tell us what pathology is or is not for medical science. However, a pathology is not necessarily a moral disorder, and moral problems are not necessarily pathological.[5]

We intend to explore the properly moral aspect of "nature" and of human behavior and to specify the behavior, including same-sex inclinations (today we say "orientation") in line with moral principles. However, we are not directly interested in discussing whether same-sex behavior can be qualified as "pathology." There is evidence that it can be the cause of various diseases, which is "pathogenic" regardless of whether it is a pathology or not.[6] However, the moral discourse will remain central. First, we will define what "moral" (or "ethical") is. Morality or ethics is, in simple words, the knowledge of what a human being, as such, should or should not do. The first principle of this knowledge is the following: "Good is to be done, and evil avoided."[7] This principle is the moral action. But we need to understand what is morally right and what is morally evil, the good and evil that appeal to man's duty.

Let us now return to metaphysical principles. Good, in general, corresponds to a specific perfection that can be an object of desire and, ultimately, a fullness of being.[8] By contrast, evil is the absence of this perfection and this being. To be more precise, the "privation" of a perfection (*being*) constitutes evil. In fact, not every "absence of good" constitutes evil—only the "privation

---

[4] An exhaustive review of the bizarre sexual practices of the animal world may be found in popular books, e.g., L. SIGNORILE, *Il coccodrillo come fa: La vita sessuale degli animali*, Codice, Turin 2014.

[5] Some prominent examples: murder, theft and rape are not invariably linked to psychological disorders.

[6] It is the case of the extension or privileged transmission of certain diseases such as AIDS due to same-sex behavior. See Infra.

[7] "Hoc ergo est primum praeceptum legis, quod bonum est faciendum et prosequendum, et malum vitandum. Et super hoc fundantur omnia alia praecepta legis naturae...," *Summa Theologiae*, I-II, q. 94, a. 2.

[8] See *Summa Theologiae*, I, q. 5.

of good" constitutes it. Privation is the absence of a good that should be there: evil is precisely the absence or denial of a good.[9]

A few examples can help us understand. It is not an "evil" thing for a pig not to have wings, but it is for a bird. It is not bad for the oyster to be incapable of reasoning, whereas this inability is bad for a man. The same can be seen in artificial things. We would not say a knife is "a bad knife" because it does not broadcast images properly. Rather, we would judge a television that does not transmit images well a "bad" television. A bad knife would be one that does not cut—"being unable to cut" is, therefore, definitely "bad" for a knife.

So, to find the "good" of a being and, by contrast, the "evil," it is necessary to distinguish between what is simply "lack" of good and what is "privation" of good. This is to know when the good under consideration is a "due" good, and when it is not. Only in the first case can we talk about an "evil."

The secret lies in a single concept: finality. This idea may sound strange, even absurd, to the anti-metaphysical contemporary mindset. The final cause is the only element necessary (but not sufficient, as we shall see) to cross the alleged abyss that separates the "is" from the moral "ought." Referring to other works for a more detailed discussion of this issue, we rely on the reader's common sense. [10]

It is the final cause that tells us when we are facing a lack of good-perfection-being that is also a "privation," i.e., "evil." It is the final cause that tells us when the good is, in some way, "due." The pig's structure is not intended to fly, and thus it is irrelevant if it does not have wings. The bird should fly, so it should have wings. If it had no wings, it would be in a state of "privation." The oyster's structure is not made for reasoning, while the man should be able to reason. That is, its structure and its development are intended to exercise

---

[9] *Malum enim est corruptio vel privatio boni*, Aquinas, *Textus Petri Lombardi*, II, dist. 34.

[10] Modern philosophical thought finds it difficult to found ethics objectively, especially after the so-called formulation of Hume's law, according to which *one cannot derive an ought from an is*. That is, from a description of a thing's being one cannot derive how that thing should behave. Hume's reasoning is unassailable *if* we assume the empiricist worldview. After all, final causes are meaningless for empiricism. However, within a metaphysical view of reality that includes final causality, one could recognize a relation of *dutifulness*, which becomes *moral* dutifulness when the will is ordered toward the ultimate finality of human nature. On the possibility of escaping "Hume's Law," also called the "naturalistic fallacy," see E. Sgreccia, *Personalist Bioethics: Foundations and Applications,* The National Catholic Bioethics Center, Philadelphia 2012, p.44-60. Mons. Sgreccia sees in the "teleology derived from Aristotelian Thomism" one way of escaping the "grand division" of facts from values. From a natural law perspective, see R.M. Pizzorni, *La filosofia del diritto secondo S. Aquinas*, Studio domenicano, Bologna 2003 p.359-383.

that function. The knife is not made to transmit images, while the television is. It is its purpose. The perfection of "transmitting images" is, therefore, due to a good television, as that of "cutting" is to a knife, since that is its purpose.

In summary, evil is metaphysically defined as a privation of good, that is, as the absence of a "due" good. This statement of this "duty of good" is given by the final cause according to which the subject, the faculty, the action, and so on is ordered.

Therefore, evil cannot be reduced, for example, to pain. First, physical evil is much broader than just pain. There may have been a privation of good, absent consciousness and therefore absent pain. Think of a person that loses his legs and even his senses after an accident. That person may not experience pain but surely is not feeling "good." The same death, which is a privation of life, excludes pain at the moment it happens.[11]

Evil is thus the privation of good, a perfection that corresponds to the final cause of the subject, function, action, etc. Sickness is the deprivation of health (the organic balance and fulfillment toward which the entire subject and various faculties tend), blindness is the privation of sight (the eye's finality), and so on. It is important to note just one thing. It is easy to see how "good" and "evil" are realized differently depending on the being to which we refer. We have seen that good and evil are applied differently to a pig, bird, man, knife, etc. In other words, while maintaining the same definition, we adjust those concepts according to "what a certain being is," and "to what end it is directed."

Philosophically this is expressed in one word—the "nature" of things. "Nature," in its physical-finality sense, expresses this precisely[12]—the essence of a thing ("what it is") as ordered to its final cause.[13] An essence as a principle

---

[11] Even pain can meet the metaphysical definition of evil, however, to the extent that it is bad. And yet, pain can also be good in two senses: a) if it is identified with the awareness of a "privation" that afflicts us. If this awareness did not exist, we not would be aware of the evil that afflicts us, and we would not know how to react proportionally against physical (or psychological) evil, risking disintegration sooner or later. b) Pain could be a good if it is "aimed" at achieving a greater good. In any case, pain is bad as well because it implies an awareness of something we lack.

[12] This expression is found, for example, in R.M. PIZZORNI, *La filosofia del diritto secondo S. Aquinas*, Studio Domenicano, Bologna 2003, p.268. Based on *In III Sent.*, d. 5, q. 1, a. 2, the author distinguishes at least three different meanings of the term "nature": 1. nominal meaning; 2. physical-teleological meaning; 3. Metaphysic meaning.

[13] Aquinas explains that nature is "the essence of the thing as it is ordered to the operation of the thing itself," *De Ente et Essentia*, I, 3.

of activities and operations, with each having distinct finalities, contributes towards a being's overall and totalizing final cause.

At this point, we can begin to delineate the meaning of the expression "contrary to nature." Still, the logical path is not yet finished. We have to take a step forward. Assuming "good" and "evil" and their relationship with the "final cause" and "nature of things" are defined metaphysically, it is when we are in the presence of a specifically moral good or evil that "natural" and "contrary to nature" have an ethical significance. When do we enter the moral sphere?

Not every "good" and every "evil" (privation of good) in a metaphysical or physical-finalist sense constitute a moral good or evil. Moral good and evil are connected to a series of concepts, such as merit, guilt, punishment and virtue, that do not compete with other types of good and evil. The sun and water are good for plants as they contribute to their growth, but this good is not a moral good. The sun and water have no particular "merit" in the realization of this good, and if they stopped giving water or light, they would not be "guilty" of anything. If a dog were to bite a child causing serious injury, we would use similar terms to those we would use if the injury were deliberately caused by a person ("He's a bad dog," "He deserves punishment," etc.). It is clear that these expressions, although similar, are profoundly different if they refer to a person. The person who harms a child, perhaps for trivial reasons, is a bad person in a different sense from the dog. In fact, a dog does not face a trial, its "guilt" is not investigated, and its "repentance" is not required. The dog will not eventually go to confession, etc.

After all, the good and evil done by man are unique because they imply a fundamental reality: freedom.

In fact, if the (wrong) action were not freely willed (or at least allowed) there would be neither guilt nor punishment, even under the civil legislation. If the (right) action were not freely accepted, there would be no "merit" and therefore no right to a reward. The issue of free will is another point that deserves much ink. After Benjamin Libet's experiments, many today claim that in reality freedom is an illusion. We will explain why these claims are unfounded.[14] We will confine ourselves to an argumentum *ad absurdum*: if there were no freedom, if the human acts did not come from a will, if the

[14] We refer on this theme to a recent work that tells why the psychological and neurological arguments inspired by Benjamin Libet's experiments are entirely insufficient to exclude the existence of free will, which is, rather, an indisputable fact of common sense and personal experience. See A.R. Mele, *Free. Why Science Hasn't Disproved Free Will*, Oxford University Press, New York 2014.

actions were produced by unconscious, predetermined and necessary mechanisms, then there would be no morality. Merit, remorse, virtue, punishment and guilt would lose their meaning. Why judge as "evil" and apply a penalty to someone who could not have acted otherwise? What merit have those who could not have chosen differently? Without freedom, it would be meaningless to wonder what man should or shouldn't do. Without freedom, human action would be a mere overall result of conditioning and necessary causes. Without freedom, all moral principles would be pure illusion.

This is morality's first ingredient: the act is derived from free will. It could be morally good or evil only if it is stems from free will. Good or bad in the physical-finality sense acquires moral significance when it is the object of a free act. Not every action of the person is of moral importance, only the ones made with knowledge and will.

It is necessary to understand when a morally relevant act is qualified as "good" (which should or can be carried out) or "bad" (which should not be done). There is a further problem: not every freely done "physical evil" is a "moral evil." Sometimes the fulfillment of a "physical evil" may be a "moral good." Take for example the amputation of a limb. To amputate a leg is undoubtedly something terrible: someone is deprived of a good (the leg) that he or she should typically have. If this action were accomplished for revenge or trivial reasons, it would be a moral evil. However, if the amputation were done to save a life, it would be morally right. The goodness of an action depends on its end. Although the leg is a physical good, to amputate it can paradoxically be right in certain circumstances. These are exceptional circumstances in which the absence (amputation) of the leg allows it to achieve the final cause it typically aims to realize: the wellbeing of the whole organism.

This is a typical example of the principle of "totality": the parts exist for the sake of the whole.[15] If the presence of a part (due to illness or other reasons) contradicts its finality, causing the destruction of the whole, it is morally licit (at times a moral obligation) to suppress it in order to achieve the preservation of the person's total good (that is, the final cause to which the part is ordered). The suppression of a component is a "privation" only in a physical and not a moral sense, since its superior end—the good of the whole person (and not its parts)—is achieved by suppression of the member under the circumstance.

[15] On the principle of totality, also known as "therapeutic principle," see E. Sgreccia, *Personalist Bioethics: Foundations and Applications*, p.180-182.

This does not imply that all evil, desired for a right end, automatically becomes good. "The end does not justify the means," or more precisely, the end does not necessarily justify the means. Indeed, we can distinguish two types of ends: the agent's end, which is the further intention by which the agent uses certain means; and the end of the act itself, that is its immediate purpose or the object of the action. If the object of the action (the immediate goal, the means to the agent's end) is morally indifferent or sound, the act will be made right or better by an ulterior good end (or morally corrupted by an evil end). For example, driving a car (ethically indifferent) to visit and comfort someone in the hospital (ulterior right purpose) is a good act.

The (ulterior) end is still able to "justify" the means when, despite being the normally prohibited "means" (because it is usually bad), these are pursued precisely to achieve the goal to which the prohibition was ordered. It is the case of an amputation for medical reasons. (The prohibition to cut off a leg under normal circumstances is because the leg serves the body's function as its end. In this case, the end is achieved by the performance of a normally prohibited action). Similar cases occur every time you are forced to disregard the "letter" of the law if there is no other way to achieve the "ratio" (that is still the end) of the law itself.

The agent's end, however, does not justify "means" that are intrinsically immoral—these acts that are in themselves disordered because they contradict a finality that is in some way already "final" and not conditional.[16] The action can be "intrinsically immoral" or disordered because, for example: 1) it denies the person's good as such and as a "whole" (it denies the person's very existence; it implies treating him/her not as a person but as a "thing," etc.); 2) the faculty or the operation implemented contradicts its end, which is ordered toward the good of the person as such and as a whole; 3) the act contradicts, in any event, the ultimate ends of human nature (the existence or the common good of society, above all, in its transcendental sense, God Himself).

For example, concerning point 1 of the preceding paragraph, you cannot reduce someone to slavery to provide labor for critical public works even though they are necessary and useful (hospitals, schools, etc.); you cannot directly kill one innocent person to save two. The disordered carnal act, as we shall see, is part of point 2 of the preceding paragraph—the faculty of the complete sexual act is aimed at the good of the person as a whole (its ex-

---

[16] On the relation between the object of an act and the end of the agent, see *Summa Theologicae*, I-II, q. 19.

istence), and so perversions of sex (including, but not exclusively, same-sex acts) are not "justifiable" by ulterior ends.

These behaviors in their very dynamic (physical-teleological) structure, that is, in their relationship with the immediate end towards which they are directed, contradict an ultimate finality constituent of the human being as a whole and so are not conditional. The enslavement of a person denies in practice the nature of the person as such, degrading him/her to "a thing" and a mere means;[17] the killing of the innocent denies the very existence of the person as a whole; denying or hatred against God is opposed to the person's transcendent end; and the perversion of the sex act is also intrinsically immoral because the immediate object/end is the good of the person as a whole, comprising his or her very existence.

Like it or not, this is the nature of sexuality.[18] Human sexuality, being dimorphic and complementary, is at the origin of every single person and all of humanity. Human sexuality is organized into the masculine and the feminine—other conditions such as Turner syndrome, Mayer Hauser syndrome or hermaphroditism are sexual developmental disorders precisely because they do not express its natural finality. Human sexuality is dimorphic and complementary from a genetic point of view—the Y chromosome is the biological determinant of masculine features, while its absence produces feminization. It is dimorphic and complementary from a hormonal point of view, by virtue of the presence or absence of androgens. Sexuality is also dimorphic and complementary from a neurological and therefore psychological point of view. Male and female brains, despite certain plasticity, differ as to the lateralization of specific functions, such as those of language and reasoning—linear and discursive in males; circular, intuitive and emotional in females.[19] Human sexuality is dimorphic and complementary in its primary and secondary sexual characteristics.

The sex organs are complementary in morphology (the shape of the phallus and the vagina) and function (the production of sperm and eggs), aimed

[17] Although in our view, he was not able to find a solid objective foundation to the moral law, Kant explained the imperative as, "Act so that you treat humanity, whether in your person as in the person of any other, in the same time as an end and never merely as a means." See I. Kant, *Groundwork of the metaphysics of morals*, BA 67-68.

[18] To deepen the anthropological assumptions about sexuality and procreation, see E. Sgreccia, *Personalist Bioethics: Foundations and Applications*, p.384-399.

[19] On this issue, see also for the considerations concerning gender theory M. Gandolfini, "Identità sessuata e teoria di gender: dalla biologia all'ideologia," in *Notizie ProVita*, n. 27, February 2015.

at the transmission of life. All the mechanics (ejaculation and then reception, helped by the consistency of the cervical mucus that facilitates the passage and selects the sperm in the ovulatory phase) and chemistry (biomolecular compatibility of the ovum and the sperm, which interact chemically and provide "half" of their genetic patrimony) of sexual intercourse, and a thousand physiological details that characterize it, are there to witness to the otherwise unexplainable fact of procreation. Even some lesser known psychological traits indicate this. Women have increased sexual desire in their fertile days[20] and at the same time appear more attractive and desirable to men.[21] The urges, inclinations and orientations do not change in substance the natural sexual end in humans that we have described. For sexual nature, it does not matter if someone is (as they say) hetero-, homo-, bisexual or zoophile. The male in his whole being, is "made for" (or if you prefer, "has an end directed to") the female; the female is "made for" ("has an end directed to") the male.

It is also true that sexuality and sexual intercourse do not have only one purpose. Sexual intercourse profoundly unites us. It responds to a need for love and companionship. It is also "satisfying." That is, the pleasure procured by the whole relationship (momentarily) satisfies the erotic drive. And yet, as already explained above concerning the general principles of morality, the ulterior ends cannot justify the deliberate denial of the immediate end of the act, when it is the superior and ultimate end geared toward the good of the person (his/her existence). The final cause of procreation, as tension and openness towards a new life, has an indisputable ontological superiority, and in relation to the will, a moral superiority. In fact, the "existence" of a new person, which is the end of the sexual act, is the founding good compared to everything else. It exceeds all other goods such as companionship, pleasure or even affection, which, despite being great perfections, are incidental and secondary to existence.

The problem, therefore, is not pursuing the other sexual ends or goods. It is the search for these goods while denying the essential and unconditional one.[22] A will oriented in this direction overturns the order of values. A sex

---

[20] See S.J. Dawson, K.D. Suschinsky, M.L. Lalumière, "Sexual fantasies and viewing times across the menstrual cycle: a diary study," in *Archives of Sexual Behavior*, 41, I, 2012, p.173-183.

[21] See D.A. Puts, R.A. Cardenas, et al., "Women's attractiveness changes with estradiol and progesterone across the ovulatory cycle," in *Hormones and Behavior* 63, 2013, p.13-19.

[22] Moreover, a sex act that respects the procreative purposes but not the unitive, love and mutual gift between a couple, would not be morally ordered. To be such, the act must be

act that is closed to positively wanted life, is willing the deprivation of its greatest good, the person's integral good, and, therefore, is ultimately desiring a moral evil.

A word of caution: we are not speaking of a "physical" evil in the sense that the person's actual physical good is affected (at least not directly). At the moment the act is accomplished, the existence to which the act is ordered is that of a future existence. But the specificity of the moral order (and will) lies in this—that the "goods" and "evils" are not exclusively physical. The will can be "disordered" without or before any reference to an actual physical harm. Normally, the end is first in intention but last in execution. At the moment of an act, it often happens that the proximate or remote end has not been concretely realized.

A few examples will help. If I have the intention to physically harm an innocent person, my will is already disordered and bad even before the physical injury is done, before the physical evil is real. My will could be disordered regardless of any reference to a physical evil. For example, I may deeply hate a person, even in a general way, without thinking to do anything to that person. Again, blasphemy (even if interior) is undoubtedly a great moral evil that does not imply any physical injury. Finally, the pedophile who gropes a sleeping child surely commits an immoral act, even if no physical or psychological damage has been done to the child.

In these and many other cases, the immorality of the act is due to the direction of the will that leans toward the privation of a good—which could be material, immaterial or intentional—of the end (physical integrity, the glory of God, personal existence, modesty, etc.) of one's own being or of another person. In sexual disorders (be they "same-sex," "heterosexual," contraceptive or other disordered acts), evil consists primarily in an attitude of the will that does not recognize the order of values, denying the primarily directed good of sexuality. A good that, precisely because as an "end," is not conditional but always due.

At this point, someone could object to what we have said of the generative end of sexual intercourse. In this case, would all sexual relations during infertile periods be immoral? Is it morally necessary that all sexual acts lead

"whole" in its essential finality, "Malum ex contingit singularibus defectibus, bonum vero ex tota integra causa." T. Aquinas, *Summa Theologica*, I-II, q. 19, a. 7, ad tertium. See also the *Catechism of the Catholic Church*, n. 2352. "The deliberate use of the sexual faculty, for whatever reason, outside of marriage is essentially contrary to its purpose." Here sexual pleasure is sought outside of "the sexual relationship which is demanded by the moral order and in which the total meaning of mutual self-giving and human procreation in the context of true love is achieved."

to conception? No. The same natural finalities of sexuality require fertile and infertile periods. This corresponds to a good refined by human nature that is precisely the natural regulation of fertility. The nature of human sexuality is such that even though its elements (morphology, genetics, chemistry, sexual characteristics can only be understood by the generative end) are always aimed at procreation, the modulation of mechanisms through the interactions of these elements does not always achieve its final effect (conception).

To the extent that the same natural finality, of which the regulation of fertility forms a part, does not concretely result in conception, we cannot speak of a "privation of the natural order of sexuality" when sexual relationship does not achieve its final effect. The subjects do not intentionally impede the attainment of the good to which the sex act is directed.

To voluntarily have sex during infertile days, taking advantage of the knowledge of the physiological mechanisms (in natural methods of fertility regulation[23]), does not contradict the natural final cause (good)in itself, because the sex act remains in principle identical to any other potentially fruitful act. It is nature that has not pursued the effect of conception. In other words, it is not possible to pursue conception when nature does not pursue it.[24]

On the other hand, the use of additional devices (such as artificial contraceptives[25]) or unfruitful sexual unions (such as oral or anal sex) are free acts that manifest a desire to contradict the final cause of the sex act, independently of any natural regulation.

It is now clear why the same-sex act contradicts the finality of the sex act, the good of sexuality, and, therefore, constitutes a moral evil. That is, an evil that is not "justifiable" by the agent's additional ends because of the special finality of the sex act. Unfortunately, sexuality has been trivialized today. Its relationship with life has been overshadowed and minimized. In fact, it is precisely this relationship that constitutes its greatness.

It is important to make some distinctions in order to have a complete evaluation of SSA from a moral point of view. The adjective "same-sex" includes different realities that are not morally the same.

Same-sex inclination or orientation is an affective disposition that operates on the level of the psyche, and that leads to sexual desire for an individual

[23] On natural methods and regulation of fertility, see E. Sgreccia, *Personalist Bioethics: Foundations and Applications*, p.405-406, 409-411.

[24] We set ourselves here within the perspective of the object of the act and not of the agent's ulterior finality, which could also abuse the natural methods of fertility regulation.

[25] On contraceptives see: E. Sgreccia, *Personalist Bioethics: Foundations and Applications*, p.395-412.

of the same sex. By itself, it is not a fault, nor does it qualify a person negatively from a moral point of view. The inclination is not an act of the will, and the voluntary nature is the measure of morality. However, it is called "disordered" in regard to its relational aspect as it represents a tendency towards a voluntary same-sex act.[26]

Then there is the voluntary "same-sex act." It is inherently a moral disorder, for all the reasons we have mentioned. Contradicting the natural purpose of human sexuality, it is not "natural." It is "contrary to nature."[27] Notably, an act of this kind can also be committed by those who do not have SSA, and those who have SSA may not commit them.[28]

Finally, there is "same-sex vice" that, like every other vice, a stable disposition of the will to commit morally disordered acts and is produced (and strengthened) by the voluntary repetition of those actions.[29] We may also add that there is an "LGBT ideology" that aims to "naturalize" the inclination, justify the act and promote the vice.[30]

The same-sex act is not the only moral disorder in sexual matters. Heterosexuals perform many disorderly actions of this type. For example, oral and anal intercourse between men and women is a similar (but not equal) moral disorder to sexual acts between people of the same sex.[31]

---

[26] Also, the *Catechism of the Catholic Church* at n. 2358 presents same-sex inclination as "objectively disordered."

[27] The doctrine of the Catholic Church echoes and confirms natural ethics. "Basing itself on Sacred Scripture, which presents homosexual acts as acts of grave depravity, [Cf. Gen 1:1-29; Rom 1:24-27; 1 Cor 6:10; 1 Tim 1:10] tradition has always declared that homosexual acts are intrinsically disordered" CONGREGATION FOR THE DOCTRINE OF THE FAITH, Declaration *Persona Humana* 8. They are contrary to the natural law. They close the sex act to the gift of life. They do not proceed from a genuine affective and sexual complementarity. Under no circumstances can they be approved." *Catechism of the Catholic Church*, n. 2357.

[28] It is a severe injury to people's dignity to "define" them by their "orientations," thereby limiting them as if they are unable to rise above their inclinations, as if these inclinations were quintessential. The person who experiences same-sex inclination, like any other person, can (and should) avoid morally disordered acts, even if he/she feels psychologically inclined to commit them. The greatest demonstration of freedom, and then of "humanity, consists precisely in this.

[29] See T. AQUINAS, *Summa Theologiae*, I-II, q. 71.

[30] Today the supporters of this ideology identify themselves by the acronym (variable and extensible) LGBTIQ... They are not necessarily people with same-sex inclinations, just as there are many people with SSA who do not recognize themselves in this LGBT ideology.

[31] We could establish a sort of hierarchy between carnal disorders, because of the greater or lesser deformity of the action according to nature (in the moral sense). That is, because of the distance of the sexual act duly finalized. The first level of immorality and disorder is contraception, or any case in which the sexual act occurs between the two sexes (a man and a

Therefore same-sex acts are like any other act that contradicts the natural purpose of sexuality, and are morally disordered. They are primarily a moral evil and, in this sense, are contrary to nature. Any other disorder or adverse effect related to SSA is secondary. They occur as a consequence of the primary disorder, which contradicts the human being's natural (sexual) final cause. There are possible adverse side effects[32] of these acts which can be "signs" of sexual disorders (not necessarily or even primarily pathological). They are linked to same-sex acts but not necessarily derive from them. Usually, they derive from the repetition of these acts even though each act could at least lead to the "risk" of a negative effect.[33]

---

woman) but its purpose is deliberately impeded or frustrated. The second level of disorder is when the finality of the sexual act is defeated because it does not even occur among people of the two sexes (i.e., it takes place between two or more men or between two or more women). The third level of disorder occurs in the case in which the sexual act is between subjects that are even of different species, as in bestiality. See in this regard, T. AQUINAS, *Summa Theologica*, II-II, q. 154, a. 12, ad quartum.

[32] Just some indications on the question. Many studies and official statistics (e.g., WARD, DAHLHAMER, GALINSKY, JOESTL, "Sexual orientation and health among US adults: National Health Interview Survey," 2013, in *National health statistics reports*, no. 77, July 15, 2014, www.cdc.gov) indicate that in the LGBT population there are higher levels of problems like depression, anxiety, alcohol and drug consumption, suicidal tendencies, certain cancers, etc. LGBT sources confirm all this (see for example O'HANLAN, "Top 10 things lesbians should discuss with their healthcare providers," GLMA; SILENCE, "Top 10 things gay men should discuss with their healthcare providers," GLMA, both available at www.glma.org). These facts do not seem attributable, at least in an exclusive way, to the presumed "social homophobia," but also derive from causes intrinsic to the relationship or a same-sex inclination. For three reasons: 1. The substantial invariance of statistics in countries with little or no "social homophobia" (MATHY, COCHRAN, OLSEN, MAYS, "The association relationship between markers of sexual orientation and suicide: Denmark, from 1990 to 2001," in *Social Psychiatry and Psychiatric Epidemiology*, December 2009 and COWI, "the social situation concerning homophobia and discrimination on grounds of sexual orientation in the Netherlands," March 2009, available at fra.europa.eu site); 2. The verification in socio-psychological terms that some endogenous factors to the same-sex relationship are at the root of some psychological problems (e.g. A greater tendency to suicide: CHEN, LI, WANG, ZHANG, "Causes of suicidal behaviors in men who have sex with men in China: National survey questionnaire," in *BMC Public Health*, 15:91, 2015). 3. Some physical problems are not primarily related to possible external influences but are due to the physiological mode of same-sex acts. We refer to the higher incidence of sexually transmitted diseases (see following note).

[33] It is particularly true for the highest rate of STDs (sexually transmitted diseases) that disproportionately affect the male SSA population, mainly because of the physiological mode of anal intercourse. See the topic data and tables of the Center for Disease Control and Prevention US (available at www.cdc.gov/hiv/ site). "Risky sexual behaviors are the cause of most of the HIV infections in gay and bisexual men. Most of the gay and bisexual men acquire HIV

In summary, the human good is defined by the objective end inscribed in our nature. Those goods, those purposes, are the way we are. We enter the domain of morality when they meet freedom. In this sphere, good and evil do not correspond to immediate physical "perfections" or "privations." It is necessary to analyze the action related to the good of the person as such, particularly concerning the ultimate ends of human nature.[34] "Natural" in its moral meaning is not an appropriate adjective for SSA (especially as an "act"). Instead, the principles of natural ethics reveal to us its intrinsic disorder. It is a disorder that contradicts the deepest needs of the (sexed) human nature.

---

through anal sex, which is the riskiest kind of sex with regard to HIV transmission… Gays are at higher risk of contracting sexually transmitted diseases (STDs) such as syphilis, gonorrhea, chlamydia..."

[34] It is from this notion of "nature" that the notions of "natural law" and "natural right" have taken shape, especially in Christian philosophy. This is a different concept from the one handed down by a certain "doctrine of natural law." "Natural law," not in the biological sense but moral sense, is the reflection we have embarked upon. It is discovered as "duties" that oblige the human conscience when considering the finality of his nature. These "duties" are consequences of that original moral imperative of "doing good / avoiding evil." For a full discussion on the subject, see R.M. Pizzorni, *La filosofia del diritto secondo S. Aquinas*, Studio Domenicano, Bologna 2003.

GIANCARLO RICCI*

SAME-SEX ATTRACTION, PLURAL SUBSTANTIVE

There is a contemporary trend toward sanctioning behaviors and inclinations to make them instantly palatable. An oversimplification promoted by the media depicting same-sex attraction (SSA) as a "mainstream" social category erases distinctions within the vast, varied field of male and female SSA.

Producing uniformity—in an area where heterogeneity reigns—crushes subjectivity, and establishes an ideological vision that expands into a hypertrophy of rights.[1] What is at stake is beneath our daily gaze: an increase in gender lessons at schools, campaigns against "homophobia" and discrimination, a right to same-sex marriage and adoption by same-sex parents.

Thus, a normalized and normalizing conception of SSA is promoted culturally, socially and legally. A new anthropology also makes headway seeking to subvert foundational sex differences, the institution of the family and principles governing symbolic filiation. SSA ultimately claims several privileges and rights involving the entire social system. Presenting the face of victimhood, SSA lives off simplifications that elide subjective differences.[2]

1. Multiple forms of same-sex attraction

There are, in fact, multiple forms of SSA.[3] There is one type that is militant, blithely committed. There is another with compulsive behavior revolving exclusively around sex. There is same-sex attraction claiming desperately to seek love and affection. There is a form of SSA that attempts to repair a family situation wherein the Oedipus complex has taken a problematic turn. There is one with effeminate behavior proceeding from a male's identification with a woman. There is a type of SSA offered as a gift to a mother, or which

---

* Psychoanalyst, member of the Italian Association of Lacanian Psychoanalysis (ALIPSI), honorary judge for the Milan Court for minors.

[1] "The multiplication of rights, even the most socially aberrant appears as a result of the subjectivist paroxysm that seems to characterize post modernity." L. Antonini, *Il traffico dei diritti insaziabili*, Rubbettino, Soveria Mannelli 2007, p.5.

[2] See D. Giglioli, *Critica della vittima. Un esperimento con l'etica*, Nottetempo, Rome 2014.

[3] See G. Ricci, *Il padre dov'era. Le omosessualità nella psicanalisi*, Sugarco, Milan 2013, p.93-98.

manifests a maternal instinct by seeking out boys to love. There is a same-sex attraction consummated through the repetition of a perverse game. There is a vindictive type of behavior that hates women; or even hates a father or brothers and frantically seeks someone to humiliate and degrade as a consequence. There is SSA as a manifestation compensating for, and seeking to stabilize, a situation of psychosis. Besides an orientation toward the same sex, there can be questions about the category of membership.

The above list, though long, is just partial. Each type could be the title of a novel whose plot (from a psychological standpoint) would be extremely complicated. Though the plot grows thick and opaque at times, this does not mean it cannot be read. Each case falls within a singular psychological order, i.e., within a system in which various elements are interconnected, as well as strung together by numberless implications.

Each case is different. Every human subject is historically immersed within a psychological process, especially during puberty and adolescence, and comes to terms with sexuality in different ways, as well as with different accents.

In the following paragraphs we will present certain themes schematically from which different forms of same-sex attraction derive.

2. The family

In same-sex orientation the figures of the mother and the father have considerable relevance (one that sometimes is terribly decisive). Many forms of SSA are a response, a reaction to a clearly pathological trait in one or both parents. Often the child's only way to distance himself from a dysfunctional family is through scarring mockery, defiance and transgression.

This can happen not only through questioning one's sexuality but, practically, by desiring to wound a family's expectations. Another current debate is that of same-sex parenting, which questions the anthropological nature of human symbolic foundations. So, it may be difficult for a child to find a place in the family that recognizes him or her in a logic of filiation.

What follows is the fruit of clinical data. If there is no symbolic moment transmitted by the family that calls the child into existence, situating him or her in the world, the results can lead to a nihilistic end.[4]

In such cases the manifestation of SSA is a way in which the subject opposes what was received as a child, assuming that he or she received anything. The problem often is the latter. This manifestation is thus already visible in

[4] See V. Cigoli, E. Scabini, "Sul paradosso della omogenitorialità", in *Vita e Pensiero*, 3, 2013, p.109.

the parents who have little or nothing to "give" to their children, or who consider them as a casual, or occasional, added dimension in their lives, leaving them to a pre-ordained fate or else abandoning them to achieve their desires or narcissistic ideals alone.

We easily forget that the acquisition of sexual identity is marked by precise processes and stages succeeding, one upon another, within a period that extends over less than two decades. Along this path marked by physiological growth, through the body's metamorphosis and neurological development, on through the way in which the psychological life integrates and assimilates these changes, the symbolic position of parents is absolutely primary. The quality of their relationship and the place each of the couple gives to love and sexuality, to filiation, to the meaning of existence and of death, are decisive. This is no small thing. It is something vast, intangible and opaque. Sometimes it is something unspoken or hidden, like an unspeakable secret furtively sweeping over generations.

3. Neurosis, psychosis, and perversion

We will systematically present the criteria that broadly contextualize the different types of same-sex attraction. That is, in the following paragraphs we will contextualize the psychological, historical, subjective order in which the issue of SSA acquires substance and form.

According to clinical psychoanalysis, and to a well-established psychiatric tradition, there are three main psychological categories: neurosis, psychosis and perversions. Even SSA assumes different mental forms depending on the psychological order to which it belongs. In some way each configuration presents different manners of expressing same-sex attraction, situating the sexual object, and relating to a partner. We proceed by outlining the order of neuroses that may, in technical terms, be summarized as hysteria and obsession. According to Freud, a symptomatic dimension develops from an intrapsychic conflict within which the classical dynamics of repression and the return of the repressed, or the complex dialectic between ego, superego and id, predominate.

The manifestation of SSA finds itself here as the particular outcome of the sexing process, i.e., the way in which the subject has dealt with that long, complex symbolic process of his or her own sex and with that identification effort that leads to the construction of one's gender identity (becoming man or woman). In other words, in neurosis the ways by which a person assumes his or her sexual identity is problematic. In this case identification with a parent of the same sex remains incomplete, deficient or has only partially succeeded. All this implies a deep insecurity and fear when it comes to facing life and approaching members of the opposite sex. There is also difficulty in dealing with peers, or the overwhelming idealization of peers who are sometimes even eroticized.

It is not always easy to make appropriate evaluation and diagnosis of psychosis or highly dysfunctional personality disorders (borderline personality disorder, mixed pathologies, etc.). Here a manifestation of same-sex attraction, given its psychological complexities, must be considered very carefully. These are extremely problematic situations in which SSA (which often is practiced compulsively or even self-destructively) is the manifestation of the individual's need to hold together a divided, torn identity and prevent psychotic fragmentation.

The clinical complexity of these (fortunately uncommon) cases is found in those who, on the one hand, are exposed to real risks or unhealthy encounters. On the other hand, they help by promoting in some way an integration of the death instinct. This integration ensures the maintenance of a narcissism that would otherwise be exposed to the problematic "drift" of the self.

In cases of perversions—today called paraphilias—the situation is different. Perversions are a fixation on infantile sexuality, starting with castration avoidance.[5] An emphasis is insistently put upon pleasure. The kind of relationship one has with a sexual partner, erogenous zones, characteristics and practices, a frantic quest for pleasure with what is self-identical, sexual scenes ever repeated in the same way, and according to the same scenario, etc. Perversion, contrary to neurosis, knows no shame or guilt, while the other person is reduced to an object of pleasure and reified.[6]

Methodically aiming for immediate, complete gratification, always at the borderline of a fog, a perverse individual seeks to reproduce a lost paradise where, under the auspices of a maternal libidinal regime, he could take without asking or give himself bodily and blindly in response to a demand. A perverse person does not know how to give up this lost paradise.

When we speak in clinical terms of perversion or psychosis, we refer to a structure. In practical terms, in each individual case there is always a gap, a variation, a distinct turn such that, for example, a perverse or psychotic person sometimes exposes a failure point—namely a failure to act. It is an intriguing space indicating a breach, a potential path to take.

---

[5] See M. Magatti, "Dalla società dei consumi alla società generativa," in Aa.Vv., *Ho ricevuto, ho trasmesso: La crisi dell'alleanza tra le generazioni*, Vita e Pensiero, Milano, 2014.

[6] L.A.Salomé, *Anale e sessuale*, ES, Milan 2007, p.49.

4. Fantasy and action

Forms of same-sex attraction also differ depending on whether this is merely fantasized or fully practiced and acted out. In other words, they differ depending on whether this has been occasional, a contingent remedy to a sexual impulse, or whether it is sought out as one's only option. In this sense we have two polarities. On the one side, there is an imaginary field of fantasies, curiosities and beliefs proceeding mainly from a hypothetical child sexual theory, or from some fixation upon partial objects. On the other, there is a practiced SSA, repeatedly acted upon and, in some cases, acted upon tenaciously and not just occasionally.

A similar topological difference to that between fantasy and action exists between the register of a desire dominated by the phantasm of a certain logic, on the one hand, and enjoyment in which an encounter with reality is sought, on the other (J. Lacan).[7] These are two adjacent but separate registers. The variables are the body, the way in which it is driven by the flesh, the idea of enjoyment and the endless imaginary variants designed to achieve the most pleasure. Between these two poles each subject combines different phantasms.

In a course of treatment, it is important to identify at which point in the sexual development process SSA is manifested. It is important to evaluate the variants: whether they result from a "spontaneous" or a "solicited" origin; whether there was a particular incident; whether it started by with a game with peers or with "older" kids; whether it manifested itself as an imperious attraction toward someone; whether there was a kind of "initiation" into male sexuality; and whether it began after an episode of abuse or seduction by an adult, a brother or a stranger.

In this regard the issue of abuse and harassment often remains covert in the matter of same-sex attraction. LGBT leaders prefer to say that the tendency is "natural." The abuse issue is rather significant, however, as it represents the first way in which sexual pleasure is inscribed within the individual. Often that particular pleasure—experienced as violence during the abuse—is inscribed within psychological memory as a trait around which later the theme of repetition and the pursuit of pleasure with others is organized. For the first time in the individual's story a pleasure occurs and is inscribed upon the scene of the body involving specific erogenous zones. Themes of guilt and shame then step into either the background or the foreground.

---

[7] See E. Roudinesco, *La parte oscura di noi stessi: Una storia dei perversi*, Angelo Colla Editore, Vicenza 2008.

Traumatic effect involves, among other things, fears of sexuality, social isolation and difficulty when comparing oneself with peers, all experienced as arduous or even dramatic.[8] Often abuse is transformed into a shameful secret of devastating psychological weight. It can be so devastating that subsequent same-sex enactments often are viewed as ways of expiating a guilt considered unquenchable.

5. The mirror stage

In addition to considering how, there is also "when" same-sex attraction begins. Objectively identifying chronological criteria is not easy. Many factors are in play. Patients initially always narrate a reconstruction that is vague, even when this seems supported by certitude. The remotest memories easily overlap with imagination, such that any presumed reality is a reconstruction, an adaptation or a biased accommodation.

In that respect it seems significant to mention the mirror stage, formulated by Lacan, and subsequently accepted within the psychoanalytic community.[9] The mirror stage discloses a primary degree of precocity in which a subject (ages six to eighteen months) may experience a sense of uncertainty about his or her sexual identity. It can be a level so initial as to be confused with an organic or genetic factor.

The mirror stage is that process within which an infant for the first time recognizes him or herself as an autonomous individual separate from the mother.[10] This operation—the mirrored self-recognition—can occur if there is the *other* (mother or parents) serving as a guarantor of the symbolic. If this stage of recognition and authentication does not occur, the child perceives him or herself as a "fragmented body": the person appearing in the mirror is not seen as his or her own reflection, but rather as an invasive *other*, perceived as fragmented. The *other* constitutes us, and so is essential in the formation of identity of the individual.

Now here's the thing. This *other* directly or indirectly confirms for the infant his or her sexuality: I recognize you as a boy or a girl, and I locate

---

[8] See M. RECALCATI, *Cosa resta del padre? La paternità dell'epoca ipermoderna*, Raffaello Cortina, Milan 2011, p.51-54.

[9] "Pure trauma therefore is one which leaves the body intact. We could say the trauma's epicenter is a kind of brute implosion." P.L. ASSOUN, *La clinica del corpo*, Franco Angeli, Milan 2009, p.65.

[10] J. LACAN, "The Mirror Stage as Formative of the Function of the I as Revealed in Psychoanalytic Experience", in *Ecrits: A Selection*, trans. B. FINK, W.W. Norton New York 1977.

you as such within my (familial and social) speech. If this recognition meets complications, if the infant does not receive a complete confirmation of his or her sexual identity, then an uncertainty could easily be established at an early stage. This uncertainty will be experienced as a lack of distinction (e.g., bisexuality) in childhood and in early puberty, and can strongly resurface in the form of an inadequate sexual orientation or problematic sexual identity during adolescence.[11]

In general, we can say that any difficulties occurring in the mirror stage bring into play a mother's somewhat problematic desire toward the child.

6. The oral, anal, and phallic phases

What happened in childhood is often opaque and imagined. Impressions and phrases remembered often remain without a precise frame of reference. For example, there is no memory of the oral phase, of the experience of breastfeeding, except within the transposed modality of how orality, with all its conjugations and displacements, operates within the present.

The same goes, albeit with some difference, for the anal phase involving the child's control of stool. Anal eroticism cannot but constitute a return to maternal care of the child's body in the stage of early childhood. Anality calls the *other* into question, implicating or recasting him in moments of aggression or submission, embodying him in order to throw him away as useless residue, or else throwing oneself away as waste, as something "repulsive."

The phallic phase, which clearly involves a leap with respect to the previous two, is more complex as it introduces a period when one discovers the surprising anatomical difference between boys and girls.

Going through the three phases (oral, anal, phallic) of sexuality, the child sometimes stops at one of these stages reaching some sort of "fixation." Freud emphasizes the infantile tendency of favoring different body parts to obtain pleasure, by defining this as "polymorphous perverse." The child plays with the body, with his orifices, and with every possible pleasant feeling.[12] This is all part of a normal growth process contributing to the psychological construction of what Françoise Dolto called the "body schema."[13]

---

[11] "It is this moment that decisively tips the whole of human knowledge into mediatization through the desire of the other," J. LACAN, ... p.5, http://pages.mtu.edu/~rlstrick/rsvtxt/lacan.htm [accessed 17 November, 2017].

[12] See F. GIGLIO, *Il disagio della giovinezza*, Bruno Mondadori, Milan 2013, p.40-43.

[13] See S. FREUD, *Three Essays on the Theory of Sexuality: The 1905 Edition*, Verso, London-New York 2017.

The complications begin when one area prevails (normally the oral or anal). This is a "fixation," the inscription of a trait related to a particular pleasure, that, if it remains in its uniqueness, is no longer considered to be polymorphic but "homomorphic." It is from that original nucleus that all other sexual components will originate, and which then will insistently gravitate around this trait. Such a nucleus will form what psychoanalysis calls the original phantasm and remain dominant during adult sexual life. Ultimately there are different engravings within the body—different ways in which sexual identity is inscribed within the psyche, privileging and identifying certain places rather than others.

7. The timing of sexual development

We said nearly two decades is the time it takes an individual to reach his or her sexual identity, that is, to assume subjectively the gender that nature has assigned. Sexualization is an unconscious psychological process occurring parallel to growth and marking the various representations enabling someone to identify with his or her own sex, as well as to differentiate him or her from the other sex.[14]

This then is a complex process whose logic unfolds for males and females differently. Going a bit deeper, we should point out that sexualization starts even before birth when parents—each in a different way—express a wish to have a girl or a boy. Then something begins to happen with the unborn child. From that moment, in words, an act of existence begins to take shape—a woman and a man attribute meaning to their desire to become a mother and father.

Sexualization continues within the family when a paternal surname is assigned to the newborn (with cultural variation) simultaneously with the assignment of a baby's "proper" name, indicating whether this baby is a boy or a girl based upon his or her anatomical sex. This simultaneity between a father's name and the definition of biological sex is relevant from a legal point of view as well.

After this original inscription, the baby growing up will realize that he or she is called by a name that designates him or her as a boy or girl. The person's naming is like an indelible imprint remaining within the psyche and carried out over the years, building and forming itself throughout childhood, puberty and adolescence. In this way, the individual does not have the option

[14] See F. Dolto, *L'Image Inconsciente Du Corps*, Points, France 2014.

of changing the biological, physiological, anatomical evidence because it was already inscribed in the flesh at a remote time when the subject could not even say whether he or she existed or name him or herself with an "I."

Sexualization is completed when a person accepts his or her sexual identity and recognizes the other sex.[15] This is an unconscious acquisition, resulting in a precise differentiation between the sexes. Only from this moment onwards can a male subject honestly say, with everything it implies, "I am a male and you are a female."

According to Freud this process occurs "in two stages, in two waves."[16] The first stage begins between two and five years, followed by the latency phase when the child becomes silent or withdraws. This wave is marked by the infantile nature of sexual goals. The second stage begins with puberty and determines the definitive structuring of sexual life. The importance of this timing which clearly distinguishes between two periods is essential.

In the first stage, marked by childish autoeroticism, sexuality hinges on essential survival activities (oral and anal phases). Subsequently in the second stage when the phallic stage emerges during adolescence, the subject is pushed to face the significance of one's sex, male or female. The first involves a horizontal dimension within which the individual's survival and self-preservation are at stake. The second stage occurs courtesy of access to genitalia, a vertical dimension within which a heterosexual relationship ensures the survival of the species.

It is not difficult to locate same-sex attraction within the logic of sexualization, represented as a stumble, a denial or an avoidance. It indicates the subject has difficulty relative to his or her sexual status, and that the phallic function is not ordered in the direction of a drive toward the other sex.[17]

---

[15] See. R. Chemama, B. Vandermersch, *Dictionnaire de la psychanalyse*, Larousse, France 2009.

[16] "Besides the three pillars of Claude Levi-Strauss—incest prohibition, sexual division of labor, and a recognized form of sexual union—I would like to add another one absolutely essential to explaining the operation of the other three. This fourth element or, if you like, tie binding three pillars of the social tripod together is the differential value of the sexes." F. Héritier, *Masculin-Féminin I: La Pensée de la différence*, Odile Jacob, Paris 2002.

[17] "It seems that among all living creatures this process of sexual development in two stages pertains to humans alone, perhaps representing a biological basis for the human disposition to neurosis," S. Freud, *An Autobiographical Study*, W. W. Norton & Company, New York 1963. [Italian translation, Bollati Boringhieri, Torino 1978, p.106.] "The banner of the homophile trend is not so much an attraction to one's own sex as a repulsion for the other." S. Argentieri, *A qualcuno piace uguale*, Einaudi, Turin 2010, p.51.

It is as if, experiencing the phallic function as an obstacle or an inaccessible stage, SSA unfolds within a sexuality situated between the first and the second stages of sexualization—within that discontinuity psychoanalysis call the latency phase. Here one is neither male nor female, or else both male and female. It is at this level, in the gap between one sex and the other, that Freud situates bisexuality.

The genesis of all forms of transsexualism, transgenderism or queerness is locatable within this area. Ultimately this is a more or less mutable position—practically a gender identity having no clear position—within which a subject cannot, or is not, able to give up on infantile sexuality nor to access the mature genitality that masculine or feminine stature requires.

Same-sex orientation is the sign of a disorientation situated essentially within one of the many stages constituting the sexual development process. Faced with a difficulty in the second stage of sexualization, access to genitality, then, SSA folds in, or lingers, upon that first stage dominated by an autoerotic schema. In addition to this folding-in and lingering, the appropriate verbs to describe this would be those emerging in a clinical setting: to rival, temporize, circumvent, disavow, remedy, repair and find compensation, protection and comfort. Different forms of same-sex orientation correspond to each of these verbs.

GABRIELLA GAMBINO*

SAME-SEX ATTRACTION AND THE LAW

1. The demand for public recognition of same-sex unions

In recent years, the same-sex issue has assumed a growing public relevance, capturing in a new way the interest of the law.

Since the nineties, in fact, the LGBT community has organized social movements demanding the recognition of certain prerogatives in the name of the fundamental rights to equality and non-discrimination. Within a few years, this demand has become an explicit request for legislative changes aimed at protecting the interests of the "innovative" couple and family models. The new post-modern LGBT movement profile consists of the claim of "same-sex marriage" and adoption, as well as of other, similar forms of legitimate same-sex unions[1]. Several countries around the world have recognized same-sex unions in different ways. Sometimes they occur gradually—through "legal cohabitation," registered partnership and, finally, "marriage." Sometimes they happen by immediately extending the regulation provided for heterosexual marriage to any couple, regardless of their gender or sexual orientation.[2]

However, it is proper to make a distinction and some preliminary remarks. The political and cultural battle for the recognition of LGBT civil rights, as well as for guarantees to protect their physical and moral integrity, in the fight against homophobia and all forms of discrimination does not pose a legislative problem. The legal protection of persons with SSA, in fact, is not debated here, even though it remains an open political and cultural question

---

* Professor in Philosophy of Law and Bioethics, Università Tor Vergata.

[1] G. Gambino, *Le unioni omosessuali. Un problema di filosofia del diritto*, Giuffrè, Milano 2007.

[2] In many countries, the expression used is "egalitarian marriage" (i.e. equal in its effects and in its forms to what was traditionally heterosexual marriage). In 2015 the institute of "gay" marriage is in force in 21 countries: Spain, France, UK, Portugal, Belgium, Luxembourg, the Netherlands, Denmark, Greenland, Finland, Iceland, Norway, Sweden, United States (in the capital and in 37 states of the federation), Canada, Mexico, Argentina, Brazil, Uruguay, South Africa, New Zealand. In Malta, in Israel and in the Caribbean countries of Aruba, Curaçao and Saint Martin, while same-sex couples are not allowed to marry, it is possible to recognize and register same-sex marriages celebrated abroad.

in many countries of the world. Instead, the real complexity arises when SSA is no longer a personal matter, but as a relationship problem that challenges the meaning of a couple, marriage and family.

The question of marriage has particular bearing on the issue of parentage at the factual and legislative level.[3] It is a matter of logical consistency. Once marriage becomes accessible to same-sex couples, the law needs to address parentage for adoptive and artificial filiation.[4]

From this perspective, the demand for public recognition of same-sex unions raises endless problems regarding not only one's vision of SSA but also that of sexuality, family, children and one's *mode* of relating with the world. These changes are even more complex in the light of so-called gender theories, as they lead to the *deconstruction of personal identity*, making all sexual dimension of coexistence undifferentiated (including maternity and family) and all genders neutral and interchangeable. The gender thought, in fact, is based on the dual dialectics of male-female opposition, on the one hand, and sex-gender, on the other. As a result, individual freedom of choice is made absolute with regard to sexuality and gender roles in the family and in society. Disembodied, sexuality shatters into multiple orientations and subjective preferences, founded on existential choices that demand that the law recognize and institutionalize.

Yet, sexuality is anchored in norms, intended as the *order of things* in *nature*, starting from the sexed body: a non-deterministic but finalistic order—because it is authentic in the space of human freedom. To achieve it, human beings possess personal freedom. In this sense, sexuality has its own law, a structural dimension that arises as a challenge and as an existential question, to which human beings—immersed in the stress of modernity—are still called upon to respond.

To this end, we need a critical metaphysical reasoning. The order of things is not necessarily what emerges as a social need but rather what guarantees coexistence because it is structurally founded on anthropology. From this

---

[3] The theme of filiation—that is, the human being's rights as a child that has come into world—is today one of the most complex and sensitive issues for the law, the most affected by the implications of the disintegration of marriage and family in the existing social order: See G. Gambino, "Nuove tensioni nella filiazione", in *Atti del Convegno Internazionale di Studio «Nuove tensioni nel matrimonio civile»*, 23 gennaio 2015, Edizioni dell' Assemblea, Regione Toscana 2015.

[4] So, it is defined filiation, for example, in the new Argentine Civil Code (approved in 2014 and in force since 2016), which as well as the natural sonship, it has introduced into their legislation the concepts of adoptive and artificial filiation.

perspective, the first consideration is that *recognition* does not mean *foundation.* Public recognition of same-sex marriage is not in itself sufficient to establish and thus make this love objective. It remains a subjective feeling. In fact, no matter how important this recognition is, it *does not create conjugality* but merely guarantees it on a social, political or religious level[5]. On its own, conjugality is anthropologically founded. It springs from the sexual difference ontologically inscribed in the person, man and woman. It is rooted in the complexity of sexual identity and not in the mere sexual orientation or gender of individuals who love each other. Nevertheless, its recognition serves to subtract conjugality from a purely private dimension, projecting it onto the public experience, qualifying and socially corroborating the couples' *sexual* relationship which, precisely because it is inscribed in the structure of human relatedness, has a specific relevance for social coexistence.

In this sense, public recognition of same-sex marriage requires a specific reflection on SSA's relevance not only from a physical or cultural level but also from a social and legal point of view. Therefore, its demands must be based not upon a sexuality reduced to mere erotic physicality but upon a broader view of the issue. Sexuality is important for the law not as a product of pleasure but because the first and most significant difference is grounded in it, the male and female dichotomy. It is the difference that activates all our cognitive ability in the world.[6]

> For humans, the bipolar character of sexuality does not only have an exclusively *reproductive* function... but an essential *cognitive* function. Sexual difference is in fact the cognitive prototype of every perceptive possibility of difference in general, that is, of that way of knowing the world which implies a process of distinction of reality[7].

This perspective requires, therefore, an understanding of human sexuality not reduced to its functional-naturalistic reproductive dimension. On the contrary, not recognizing the difference as a co-essential dimension of existence is due to a difficulty in grasping the natural tensions and conflicts that the subject needs to understand his or her identity and exact position in the world. In this sense, modernity is *questioning the law's meaning*—as a constitutive dimension of coexistence—when it tries to manage sexuality while disregarding

---

[5] F. D'Agostino in F. D'Agostino, G. Piana (eds.), *Io vi dichiaro marito e marito. Il dibattito sui diritti delle coppie omosessuali*, San Paolo, Milano 2013, p.77.

[6] *Ibid* p.79.

[7] F. D'Agostino, *Sessualità. Premesse teoriche di una riflessione giuridica*, Giappichelli, Torino 2014, p.35.

sexual difference. It depolarizes human love, interprets sexual drive generically and indistinctively. It sees the *intervention of the law as merely extrinsic, instead of structurally belonging to the gendered dynamics of human beings.*

2. Sexuality and Same-sex attraction, family and the law

First, before any demand for public recognition, before the issuing of regulatory formulae, the law has the duty to research the sense of reality and evaluate it juridically to discover if it is *legally sound*. We must therefore ask what relevance sexuality and family have for the law, and if SSA in its relational dynamic can be a possible foundation for the family.

To answer this question, we must begin with two commonly known assumptions.[8] The first is that sexuality and family are inseparably connected. What binds them is their constitutive legal and relational dimension. In other words, law binds a human being's sexuality, understood as sexually structured *selfhood*, to the family dimension of his existence. The law is not intended to be a positive norm but, in a more specifically philosophical sense, an intrinsic normative order and the legality of a relational structure.

The second assumption is that human sexuality must not be taken in its purely naturalistic-phenomenological dimension, which only highlights its functionalist aspect, identifying it as a sexual activity, a form of pleasure and an optimal reproductive mode. It must rather be referenced to the totality of the person, aimed not only at the reproduction of the species but primarily at the same production of the "I."

Further development of these theoretical assumptions allows us to understand its anthropological importance and meaning in relation to the specific issue of the "same-sex family."

Sexuality is, first of all, intrinsically relational. In fact, it is not an end in itself but is expressed in behaviors and expressions that come into contact with others' subjectivity. Not only that, but sexuality is the *most significant* form of ego-relatedness on an existential level. First of all, every human being is expressed and relates to others through necessarily gendered modalities. Being a person means to be a man or a woman, not only biologically, but in the whole being of the person. In this sense, the sexed body is an indispensable mediator, a revealer of masculinity and femininity that pervades the whole individual. Each existential experience will therefore be a male or female one, filtered by ways of being and seeing the world according to sexual identity.

[8] F. D'Agostino, *Una filosofia della famiglia*, Giuffrè, Milano 2003.

This is not a reductive determinism, which binds the human being within the narrow limits of a life condemned by sex. On the contrary, because the ego reaches its maximum fullness when it can fully develop as being man or woman, adhesion to sexual identity is the condition for psychological fulfillment.

The person will achieve the development of her full identity if peculiar relationship dynamics happen, thereby showing her the existence of otherness and difference and leading her to the discovery of her sexual identity.

The relational setting where these peculiar dynamics occur, dynamics inherently fruitful in their ability to lead the individual to develop one's own existential *selfness*, is the family. It can be defined as—in the most general and universal terms possible and present in every society—"the more or less socially approved durable union, of a man and a woman and their children."[9] Family exists where there is at least one heterosexual couple and, possibly resulting from this, a socially recognized parent-child relationship.

Why does it necessarily have to be a heterosexual couple? Because, as we will see, it is only the presence of a "father" and "mother" that in principle allows for the full development of individual identity. Parental roles can only result from a sexual bipolarity. It is true that some recent legal systems seem to have lost their anchor to reality. Where same-sex parenting has been recognized and legalized, the words father and mother are replaced with neutral terms aiming to make the carnal and sexual truth—the origin of every child who comes to world—irrelevant. But from an anthropological perspective, these choices have no *raison d'être* and are only the expression of a functionalist and constructivist use of the law. Stripped of its objective and realistic basis, it becomes *quod principi placuit* (what the ruler wanted),[10] according to a concept of sovereignty in the hands of social practices and ideology we have already abandoned.

Sexual difference that naturally arises in the structure of human coexistence, and in particular within the family, is the difference between man and

---

[9] C. Levi-Strauss, *Razza e storia e altri studi di antropologia*, Einaudi, Torino 1967, p.147-177. In particular, the word "family" is used to denote "a social group with at least three characteristics: 1. originates in marriage; 2. consists of a husband, a wife and the children born from their marriage, even if we admit that other relatives integrate in this core; 3. family members are connected by a) legal constraints, b) economic, religious constraints, and other basic rights and duties, c) a precise network of rights and sexual prohibitions, and a set of variable and differentiated psychological feelings, such as love, affection, respect, fear, etc..."

[10] Digesta 1, 4, 1, pr. 0.

woman. *It is this structural constitution of sexual complementarity that forms the intrinsic juridical nature of human sexuality.*

At this point, we see the anthropological and ontological circularity among the triad sexuality-family-law. The family is based on the man-woman sexual complementarity, legitimized and made public because it has a socially and legally relevant dimension—the human possibility of having children. Sexuality, in turn, has its own intrinsic law from which the individual subjectivity (identity) cannot be separated from one's relation with other individuals in the world. Human sexuality is not an attribute that any person can choose according to their taste, but a way in which the ontological subjectivity manifests. It has an intrinsic normativity inscribed in its constitutive man-woman bipolarity, which is a natural and symbolic condition of the possibility of its functional expression—fertility, the transmission of life in its biological and psychological dimensions. The two orders meet in the expression of human fruitfulness, originating from the union between man and woman. Nature, whose end is reproduction, and the couple who express their love toward the fullest subjective realization.[11] If the person is an "I" open to a "you," the sexual body is the "sign" and the "place" of the opening, the recognition of the encounter, gift and dialogue. It is this bipolar complementary relational dimension inscribed in human sexuality that forms the law and justifies its substantial and constant presence in the issues of fertility, family and the parent-child relationship.

Being man and woman are two ways to express human sexuality, as they represent not only the biological condition of the human being but also the prior, anthropological condition. Only man and woman have fertility inscribed in them as a possibility of self-realization through the discovery of that difference which allows for complementarity. In the consciousness of his own corporeality, the man reveals to the woman her femininity and the woman reveals to the man his masculinity. The body inescapably reveals identity and becomes a mediator of the psychological identity in bringing it to fulfillment through the discovery of the difference. In this sense, there are not multiple sexualities. Just as there are not many forms of differences structurally inscribed in the human nature. On an epistemological level, therefore, one cannot speak of sexual diversity.[12] There is only one type of sexual difference: that between a man and a woman[13].

---

[11] K. Wojtyla, "Amore e responsabilità", in G. Reale, T. Styczen (eds.), *Metafisica della persona. Tutte le opere filosofiche e saggi integrativi*, Bompiani, Milano 2003, p.701-703.

[12] V. Baird, *Le diversità sessuali*, Carocci, Roma 2003.

[13] In the most recent philosophical thought some would like to use the term "diversity" instead of "difference" when referring to man and woman in an attempt to introduce a more

This understanding rejects the dualistic anthropological approach of "gender theory" that, in a constructivist perspective, divorces corporeity from sexuality, reducing it to sexual orientation.[14] The direct relationship between the anatomic-corporal and the subjective-relational identity is substantial. Compared to the uniqueness of the person, we cannot separate them except at the expense of a "fragmentation of the identity" of the entire person.

In this sense, the bipolar feature of sexuality has not only a reproductive function but also an essential cognitive one. It is the possibility of perceiving the difference, a prerequisite for self-knowledge.

That is why the birth of the family is deeply tied to the personal aspect of fertility expressed in the concepts of paternity and maternity. Fecundity needs the diversity of the other, someone different, in order to flourish, not only in its biological reproductive dimension. More importantly, on an anthropological and constitutive level, fecundity is aimed at the production of an "I," the subjective identities of parents and children.

In this sense, the terms that normally identify the various family subjects—husband, wife, father, mother, son, daughter—indicate not only socially constructed "family roles" through usage and customs but also authentic "family identities" structured within the relational dynamics that naturally develop between the subjects of the family.[15]

J. Lacan's contribution is valuable in this regard. He suggests that subjective identity structures start from the man-woman expression of sexual complementarity in the family. It is the "anthropogenic" process. In the relationship with their parents, the child gradually learns to recognize the presence

---

modern language able to put aside the difficulties caused by the "theory of difference". However, this diversity is not able to give account to the philosophy of difference. The latter, in fact, concerns the ontological dimension, the essence of the humanum, while diversity regards the many achievements of human nature through subjectivity: these are mutable and contingent, linked to history and time, and none of them can exhaust the entire human essence. The difference of male and female, however, is the only possibility that the human has to exist. The difference concerns the essence, so it is a constitutive principle, and as such should guide the practice. On the irreducibility of sexual difference, see G. SALATIELLO, "Verità della differenza sessuale", in A. Molinaro, E. Francisco, De Macedo (eds.), *Verità del corpo, Pro Sanctitate*, Roma 2008, p.113-128; L. IRIGARAY, *Essere due*, Bollati Boringhieri, Torino 1994; L. PALAZZANI (eds.), *La bioetica e la differenza di genere*, Studium, Roma 2007.

[14] See J. NORIEGA, "Homosexualidad: la ficción de una intimidad", in *Anthropotes*, monographic numer on "La questione omosessuale", 2, 2004, p.327-339; F. D'AGOSTINO (ed.), *Corpo esibito, corpo violato, corpo venduto, corpo donato. Nuove forme di rilevanza giuridica del corpo umano*, Giuffrè, Milano 2003, p.193-221.

[15] S. COTTA, *Il diritto nell'esistenza, Linee di ontofenomenologia giuridica* Giuffré, Milano 1991, p.123.

and the difference between the mother and the father, with whom she must identify so as to build her female sexed identity, corresponding to her biological identity. In other words, the symbiosis-release-recognition-identification symbolic dynamic, with the presence of a female figure and a male reference, is the anthropological norm that allows the child to build his or her own sexual identity. This process cannot be ignored, at the risk of not building balanced sexual relationships. In this sense, the sexuality of difference, with its inherent normativity, creates the possibility of making it a public experience acknowledged by the law. It assumes a symbolic and collective value not so much in practice as in its meanings.

Therefore, the normativity inscribed in the mother-father-child triad constitutes the inherent legality of the sexual polarity expresses itself within the family. It is the anthropological place of birth and acceptance of children—both their biological and psychological birth.

That is why the concept of the couple must be recognized by law only when it is anthropologically generative, in a way same-sex couples cannot be. The fact that today science can make anything artificially and outside personal relationships, such as through IVF, is irrelevant. The law, in fact, denies the reality of relational dynamics in such cases. Parenting as procreation is, therefore, the human setting in which the sexual difference is the most irreducible, precisely for its structuring. The division of sexuality both from its procreative finality written in corporeality and from its intrinsically ontological-relational dimension based on sexual difference, makes the subjective identity of parents and children irrelevant and threatens to destroy them. In a context of subjective individual actions that strengthen solipsistic closure, the person becomes indifferent to the presence of otherness involved in the sexual dynamic. The normative becomes self-referential, indifferent to co-existence and identity in a relationship. There is a real danger of de-relationalizing the law, starting from a de-subjectification of the person.

3. The function of law regarding human sexuality

The law is the guardian of the proper evolution of relationship dynamics. The law constitutively belongs to human sexuality, the relationship dynamics responsible for fecundity and family. The law must continue to protect the symbolic value of the family, a privileged place of fertility, as the site for the transmission of life and identity. Human sexuality, therefore, cannot escape from its internal normativity to become self-referential and reduced to a matter of subjective instinct. Just as the family has its structural symbolic dimensions, it cannot be reduced by law to a functionalist pragmatism for personal interest.

In this sense, the family remains the place where we cannot reverse generational and gender roles, including the prohibition of incest. It is structurally given the task of "personalizing the person" through specific processes of socialization. These are the conclusions Levi-Strauss expresses in his anthropological studies:

> The duality of the sexes is a requirement of marriage and of the building of a family... The structure of the family, always, makes impossible, or at least unlawful, certain kinds of sexual relations. Therefore... society belongs to the realm of culture while the family is the social emanation, of those natural requirements without which there could be no society, nor, ultimately, the human race.[16]

Same-sex relationships, therefore, cannot constitute a family for two main reasons. It involves an alteration of the identity of one of the two partners, which assumes the appearance or attitude of the missing sex, both on a horizontal and vertical dimension of the family. Since it is extraneous to heterosexuality, it is precluded from authentic parenting. The role of the father, in anthropological and symbolic terms, only takes shape in the presence of a mother who "recognizes" him as such in front of the child. She legitimizes his "name" and the power that this name has in the child's identity formation. In turn, the mother fulfills her role and reaches completion toward the child only in the presence of a father who intervenes in the symbiotic process to manifest the presence of a sexual diversity that the child must learn to recognize and identify. In a same-sex relationship, one of the two roles is inevitably lacking. The partner is placed in the ambiguous situation of *being-like* a husband, a wife, a father, a mother or a family. It is a mimicry, with possible unfinished outcomes in their respective familial subjectivity.[17]

One cannot overlook the fact that, paradoxically, the recent extension of marriage to same-sex couples, as well as the additional legalization of cohabitation (para-marital experiences), only show one thing. Namely, marriage is not a contingent historical or cultural expression of sexual polarity, as people would like to believe, but a structural dimension of the relationship between the sexes through which the human individual manifests. All these different experiences that they want to legitimize are nothing but attempts at imitating

---

[16] C. Levi-Strauss, *Razza e storia e altri studi di antropologia,...* p.147-177.

[17] F. D'Agostino, Una filosofia della famiglia,... p.140-150. See also S. Cotta, *Il diritto nell'esistenza,...* p.126.

the only true and authentic dynamic of coexistence, the one structured on the dialectic between the sexes through marriage.

Legal systems that recognize same-sex marriage and adoptions inevitably distort the structural truth of human communication and impose laws to recognize situations that do not reflect and anchor to reality.

If the Latin proverb *ius quia iustum* (the essence of law is justice) is true, then the law must treat equally what is equal and differently what is different. The law cannot approve beyond its function, calling "family" what pragmatically appears to work as a family, but structurally is not and cannot be. The law cannot be reduced to its positive function, to the position and formulation of subjective rights of flexible content. Otherwise, it would necessarily end up being a bio-legislation, bending to the ideology of extreme tolerance. It is a tolerance that does not respect diversity as such but strives to homologize the differences and remove the recognition of their specific diversity.

To this end, we start from the assumption that: a) there is an intrinsic juridical existence, inscribed in the anthropological premise of the law, in being human that is at the origin of his obligation; b) the law must guarantee the coexistence of the subjective identity in a just society, recognizing its universalizability as a law. It follows that only heterosexual marriage can guarantee the fulfillment of the human being through procreation, and develop his or her relational identity within the family.[18] In this regard, it is clear that SSA "is not a legal issue but instead: it belongs to one of those dimensions of mere factuality that characterize human existence, that law [and in particular the public law] cannot manage or regulate."[19] Same-sex attraction, precisely because it is a mode of relationship-with-the other that has no parallel in intrinsic legality of coexistence, does not have that inherently normative nature. There is no basis to raise it to a typical and universal modality of communication with the other, such as to be codified as law. The same-sex relationship does not hold an intrinsic legality, and so in that sense is not a question of the law. This does not exclude, however, that as a pure fact it can be considered by jurisprudence and interventions aimed at resolving disputes caused by unjust and discriminatory attitudes towards individuals with SSA. In such cases, these actions of criminal, civil or labor law do not imply institutionalizing SSA but instead guarantee respect for the person in specific areas of existence.

---

[18] G. DANESI, "La dottrina giuridica italiana di fronte all'omosessualità", in *Ragion pratica*, 19, 2002, p. 21-240.

[19] F. D'AGOSTINO, *Una filosofia della famiglia*, ... p.150.

This legal approach would exclude from the recognition of same-sex unions all merely sociological considerations based on specific situations and intentions, since they surpass the essential relational structure of sexual bipolarity, which family law is called to protect. Political, solidarity, egalitarian motivations as well as rights discourses are irrelevant because there is a structural problem of coexistence at stake which the law cannot ignore.

The content of the legal norm should merely offer a factual description of new cases, such as same-sex cohabitation, and take their public consequences into account. But the law must protect the truly relational structures, those which constitute the substance of human coexistence.

ROBERTO MARCHESINI*

THE CHURCH AND SAME-SEX ATTRACTION

1. *Persona Humana*

What is the Church's position on same-sex attraction?[1] Does the Church discriminate against people with same-sex tendencies? Does the Church consider SSA a sin? These are some of the questions that arise when dealing with the issue of the relationship between the Church and SSA.

Within the Church, among lay people, priests and even among bishops, there are different views on SSA. The official position of the Church on this subject is expressed in the Magisterium—the Church's teaching in matters of faith and morals.

The first document of the contemporary Magisterium in which the Church speaks of same-sex attraction dates back to December 29, 1975, the date on which the Congregation for the Doctrine of the Faith published a statement entitled *Persona Humana*: *Declaration on Certain Questions Concerning Sexual Ethics* (PH).[2]

This declaration opens with a statement that contextualizes the Church's view on human sexuality and its position toward gender ideology, which postulates a total independence of sex (the biological aspect of sexuality) from gender (the psychological, relational and spiritual component of sexuality):

---

* Psychologist and psychotherapist.

[1] List of abbreviations:

PH = *Persona Humana*

HP = *Homosexualitatis Problema*

SCC= *Some Considerations Concerning the Response to Legislative Proposals on the Non-discrimination of Homosexual Persons*

CRP= *Considerations Regarding Proposals to Give Legal Recognition to Unions between Homosexual Persons*

CCC = *Catechism of the Catholic Church*

ICC= *Instruction Concerning the Criteria for the Discernment of Vocations with Regard to Persons with Homosexual Tendencies in view of their Admission to the Seminary and to Holy Orders*

[2] For the prior Magisterium, see *the Council of Elvira*, 305 A.D.; *the Council of Toledo*, 693 A.D.; *the Third Ecumenical Council of the Lateran*, 1179 A.D.; *the Council di Nablus*, 1120 A.D.; Pius V, the Constitution *Cum primum*, April 1, 1566; Id., Constitution *Horrendum illud scelus*, August 30, 1568; the *Greater Catechism*, Rome 1905.

> According to contemporary scientific research, the human person is so profoundly affected by sexuality that it must be considered as one of the factors which give to each individual's life the principal traits that distinguish it. In fact it is from sex that the human person receives the characteristics which, on the biological, psychological and spiritual levels, make that person a man or a woman, and thereby largely condition his or her progress towards maturity and insertion into society. (§ 1)

The Church, however, takes note of the cultural situation that has changed traditional perception of sexuality to the point that many Catholics question the teaching of the Church. For this reason, the Congregation for the Doctrine of the Faith has considered it appropriate to reiterate the Church's Magisterium by publishing this statement. Among the various conceptions of sexuality that are contrary to the natural law, the Congregation cites some concerning SSA. We reproduce the whole of paragraph (§ 8)[3]:

> At the present time there are those who, basing themselves on observations in the psychological order, have begun to judge indulgently, and even to excuse completely, homosexual relations between certain people. This they do in opposition to the constant teaching of the Magisterium and to the moral sense of the Christian people. A distinction is drawn, with some reason, between homosexuals whose tendency comes from a false education, from a lack of normal sexual development, from habit, from bad example, or from other similar causes, and is transitory or at least not incurable; and homosexuals who are definitively such because of some kind of innate instinct or a pathological constitution judged to be incurable. In regard to this second category of subjects, some people conclude that their tendency is so natural that it justifies in their case homosexual relations within a sincere communion of life and love analogous to marriage, in so far as such homosexuals feel incapable of enduring a solitary life. In the pastoral field, these homosexuals must certainly be treated with understanding and sustained in the hope of overcoming their personal difficulties and their inability to fit into society. Their culpability will be judged with prudence. But no pastoral method can be employed which would give moral justification to these acts on the grounds that they would be consonant with the condition of such people. For according to the objective moral order, homosexual relations are acts which lack an essential and indispensable finality. In Sacred Scripture they are condemned

---

[3] Congregation for the Doctrine of Faith, *Persona Humana. Declaration on certain Questions Concerning Sexual Ethics*, Vatican City 1975. Editor's note: the term "homosexuality" and its variants have been replaced by the terms "same-sex attraction" or "SSA" throughout this book whenever possible, as it is the currently preferred formal terminology. In this chapter, when quoting the Church documents, the old terminology prevails but the substance of the explanation does not alter.

> as a serious depravity and even presented as the sad consequence of rejecting God. This judgment of Scripture does not of course permit us to conclude that all those who suffer from this anomaly are personally responsible for it, but it does attest to the fact that homosexual acts are intrinsically disordered and can in no case be approved of.

This section presents many claims which, in subsequent years, will come to form the complex and elaborate teaching of the Church on SSA.

Here there is a distinction between "same-sex" tendencies and same-sex acts: the first should be "treated with understanding," while "homosexual acts are intrinsically disordered," and "in no case may in no case be approved of." It also defines SSA as an "anomaly," one for which, however, people are not necessarily personally responsible.

Particular attention should be paid to the first part of the paragraph. Its content is clear. Some people (e.g., LGTB activists) argue there are two types of SSA: a "transitional" or at least "modifiable" one and an "innate," "non-modifiable," "natural" one. They use this distinction to justify the same-sex relationships of those who say they have a tendency pertaining to the second category. The statement does not make a distinction between "transient" and "innate" SSA. In line with its mission it does not comment on scientific issues. However, it denies that such a hypothetical distinction can ever justify same-sex acts, which "in no case in no case be approved of."

In spite of this, some people, even within the Church, took advantage of the complex phrasing of the document and completely reversed the meaning of this paragraph. Citing PH, they claim that the Magisterium distinguishes between two types of SSA, and they conclude from this distinction the very consequences that PH condemns, i.e., even a partial justification for SSA. This misinterpretation of the PH paragraph dedicated to same-sex attraction unfortunately will stalk all of the subsequent Magisterium, fueling ambiguous and misleading readings.

2. John Paul II and Joseph Ratzinger

During the pontificate of John Paul II, the Congregation for the Doctrine of the Faith published three specific documents constituting a single, coherent doctrinal corpus on SSA.[4]

---

[4] Also see *Angelus* of 20 February, 1994; *Angelus* of 19 June, 1994; *Discorso ai partecipanti della XIV assemblea plenaria del Pontificio Consiglio per la Famiglia*, 4 June, 1999; *Angelus* of 9 July, 2000.

The first of these documents was published on October 1, 1986 and is titled *Homosexualitatis Problema* or *Letter to the Bishops of the Catholic Church on the Pastoral Care of Homosexual Persons* (HP). It is signed by Cardinal Ratzinger, prefect of the Congregation, and presents Pope John Paul II's approval and order of publication at the bottom.

Responding to erroneous "interpretations," the Congregation, reiterating both the invitation to welcome persons with SSA and the definition of same-sex acts as "intrinsically disordered," clarifies that, "Although the particular inclination of the homosexual person is not a sin, it is a more or less strong tendency ordered toward an intrinsic moral evil; and thus the inclination itself must be seen as an objective disorder."

The letter then invites bishops to be active in their concern toward persons with SSA by offering them specific pastoral programs that display the richness of the Church's sexual ethic while warning them against the fallacy of gender theory.

The second document of this "triptych" is entitled *Some Considerations Concerning the Response to Legislative Proposals on the Non-discrimination of Homosexual Persons* (SCC), particularly topical nowadays as so-called laws against homophobia are being ratified. These prophetic considerations denounce the attempt to pollute the fight against discrimination against "persons with SSA" with the aim of promoting LGBT rights, such as, for example, same-sex parenting adoptions. These considerations deny that SSA can serve as the basis for specific civil rights because "sexual orientation" does not constitute a quality comparable to race, ethnic background, etc. with regard to non-discrimination (§ 10). In addition, a sexual orientation is generally not known to others unless someone publicly identifies himself as having this orientation, or unless some overt behavior manifests it (§ 14). So it is implausible to discriminate against same-sex orientation in itself.

The third and last document is entitled *Considerations Regarding Proposals to Give Legal Recognition to Unions Between Homosexual Persons* (CRP). This document is dated June 3, 2003, signed by Cardinal Ratzinger and, like HP, enjoys John Paul II's approval and order of publication at the bottom.

The judgment of the *Considerations Regarding Proposals to Give Legal Recognition to Unions Between Homosexual Persons* is very clear (§ 5):

> In those situations where homosexual unions have been legally recognized or have been given the legal status and rights belonging to marriage, clear and emphatic opposition is a duty. One must refrain from any kind of formal cooperation in the enactment or application of such gravely unjust laws and, as far as

> possible, from material cooperation on the level of their application. In this area, everyone can exercise the right to conscientious objection.

In support of this statement, different considerations on the order of right reason are added, namely, "The State could not grant legal standing to such unions without failing in its duty to promote and defend marriage as an institution essential to the common good." (§ 6); on the biological and anthropological order:

> Such unions [civil unions of persons with homosexual tendencies] are not able to contribute in a proper way to the procreation and survival of the human race... Homosexual unions are also totally lacking in the conjugal dimension, which represents the human and ordered form of sexuality... The absence of sexual complementarity in these unions creates obstacles in the normal development of children who would be placed in the care of such persons."(§ 7);

on the social order:

> If, from the legal standpoint, marriage between a man and a woman were to be considered just one possible form of marriage, the concept of marriage would undergo a radical transformation, with grave detriment to the common good. (§ 8);

on the legal order:

> Because married couples ensure the succession of generations and are therefore eminently within the public interest, civil law grants them institutional recognition. Homosexual unions, on the other hand, do not need specific attention from a legal standpoint since they do not exercise this function for the common good (§ 9).

3. The Catechism of the Catholic Church

With the Apostolic Constitution *Fidei depositum* of October 11, 1992, John Paul II promulgated the *Catechism of the Catholic Church* (CCC), "an exposition of the Church's faith and of Catholic doctrine, attested to or illumined by Sacred Scripture, the Apostolic Tradition, and the Church's Magisterium. I declare it to be a sure norm for teaching the faith and thus a valid and legitimate instrument for ecclesial communion."

It was, in truth, *an aeditio ad experimentum*, to which then a *Corrigenda* of content was added. The *aeditio typica* was promulgated with the apostolic letter *Laetamur magno opere* on August 15, 1997. Among the correct contents of the *aeditio ad experimentum* and *aeditio typica* are articles on same-sex attraction. These are the articles of the *aeditio ad experimentum:*

> **2357** Homosexuality refers to relations between men or between women who experience an exclusive or predominant sexual attraction toward persons of the same sex. It has taken a great variety of forms through the centuries and in different cultures. Its psychological genesis remains largely unexplained. Basing itself on Sacred Scripture, which presents homosexual acts as acts of grave depravity, tradition has always declared that "homosexual acts are intrinsically disordered." They are contrary to the natural law. They close off the sexual act to the gift of life. They do not proceed from a genuine emotional and sexual complementarity. Under no circumstances can they be approved.
>
> **2358** The number of men and women who present innate homosexual tendencies is not negligible. These do not choose their homosexual condition; for most of them it constitutes a trial. They must be accepted with respect, compassion, and sensitivity. Every sign of unjust discrimination in their regard should be avoided. These persons are called to fulfill God's will in their lives and, if they are Christians, to unite to the sacrifice of the Lord's Cross the difficulties they may encounter from their condition.
>
> **2359** Homosexual persons are called to chastity. By the virtues of self-mastery that teach them inner freedom, at times by the support of disinterested friendship, by prayer and sacramental grace, they can and should gradually and resolutely approach Christian perfection.

These are the articles of the *aeditio typica*[5]:

> **2357** Homosexuality refers to relations between men or between women who experience an exclusive or predominant sexual attraction toward persons of the same sex. It has taken a great variety of forms through the centuries and in different cultures. Its psychological genesis remains largely unexplained. Basing itself on Sacred Scripture, which presents homosexual acts as acts of grave depravity, tradition has always declared that "homosexual acts are intrinsically disordered." They are contrary to the natural law. They close the sexual act to the gift of life. They do not proceed from a genuine emotional and sexual complementarity. Under no circumstances can they be approved.
>
> **2358** The number of men and women who have **deep-seated homosexual tendencies** is not negligible. This **inclination, which is objectively disordered**, constitutes for most of them a trial. They must be accepted with respect, compassion, and sensitivity. Every sign of unjust discrimination in their regard should be

[5] The changes to the text of 1992 are in bold type.

> avoided. These persons are called to fulfill God's will in their lives and, if they are Christians, to unite to the sacrifice of the Lord's Cross the difficulties they may encounter from their condition.
>
> **2359** Homosexual persons are called to chastity. By the virtues of self-mastery that teach them inner freedom, at times by the support of disinterested friendship, by prayer and sacramental grace, they can and should gradually and resolutely approach Christian perfection.

As is evident, the changes are essentially two. The first is the elimination of the word "innate" in reference to same-sex tendencies in men and women, which is replaced by the words "deeply rooted." The change is not cosmetic, as "deeply rooted" is not a euphemism for "innate." Defining same-sex tendencies as innate means to make a scientific statement about the origin of same-sex impulses, which is not within the competence of the Church and which is not yet proven, shared and unanimously accepted. The second change is an explicit definition of SSA as an objectively disordered tendency. The importance of these changes is underscored by the fact that gay-friendly Catholic circles often cite the edition *ad experimentum* of the CCC (more favorable to LGBT instances) rather than the edition *ad typica*. It should be noted that another sentence in the CCC, in which the psychological genesis of SSA is described as "largely unexplained," has been instrumentalized. In this case the CCC wanders (inappropriately) into scientific issues not within the competence of the Magisterium. Above all, though, this phrase has been used as an excuse not to take a position on an issue that gradually has become more and more pressing. Indeed, we have read in some Catholic media statements such as: "If the Catechism, after years of consultations and subsequent versions of the text, concluded that the nature of homosexuality remains largely unexplained, then who am I to pronounce on this difficult and mysterious subject?"[6] This is stated as if the Magisterium of the Church has not said anything on the issue of SSA.

4. Other documents

In March 2003, the Pontifical Council for the Family published *Lexicon. Ambiguous and Debatable Terms Regarding Family Life and Ethical Questions.*[7]

---

[6] See M. Introvigne, R. Cascioli, "Omosessualità, alcuni punti da chiarire," in *La nuova bussola quotidiana*, 9 gennaio 2015.

[7] From the Pontifical Council for the Family see also the *Letter* to the *Presidents of the Bishops' Conferences of Europe on the Resolution of the European Parliament Re-*

In November 2005, the Congregation for Catholic Education published an instruction concerning criteria for the discernment of vocations with regard to persons with same-sex tendencies in view of their admission to the seminary and to Holy Orders (ICC).[8] An important innovation introduced into the document, of doctrinal importance and in line with HP, is an explicit reference to "gay culture." This document states that anyone who supports "gay culture," practices SSA or presents "deeply seated" same-sex tendencies cannot be admitted to a seminary or to Holy Orders (§ 2). The statement also appropriately distinguishes between same-sex acts and same-sex tendencies and adds that the first "cannot be approved under any circumstances." There are, however, some problematic points, the main one being a reference to two types of same-sex tendencies, one being "deep-seated" and a second "transitional" type. This note in the text refers to what was already discussed in PH (§8) to justify this problematic distinction. In practice, a hasty, superficial reading of this paragraph has led to an interpretation contrary to what the document actually says.

PH does not claim that there are two types of SSA, one "innate" and one "transitory."[9] PH claims that some people (easily identified with LGBT activists) argue that there are two types of SSA ("innate" and "transient"); that they wrongly infer this presumed innate SSA is "natural"; and that on the basis of these statements they justify same-sex unions.

The Magisterium does not take a position on claims made by these individuals (because, we repeat, it is not the task of the Magisterium to comment on scientific issues) but simply states that same-sex acts are intrinsically disordered and that under no circumstances may they be approved. ICC completely reverses the PH perspective, offering LGBT activists a basis for their claims.

---

garding Homosexual Couples, March 25, 1994; *The Truth and Meaning of Human Sexuality: Guidelines for Education Within the Family*, December 8, 1995, n.104-125; the *Declaration on the Resolution of the European Parliament Regarding Homosexual Couples, March* 25, 1994; *Family, Marriage and "De facto" Unions*, July 26, 2000, No.2.

[8] From the Congregation for Catholic Education see also *Educational Guidance in Human Love. Outlines for Sex Education*, November 1, 1983, Nos.101-103.

[9] Among other things, the words "innate" tendency that in PH are opposed to "transitional" have been replaced, in ICC, with "deeply seated," which is the phrase that, in CCC, has replaced "innate"; as if the substitution made between the two editions of the CCC was solely cosmetic.

5. A fundamental evolution

In the Magisterium there is an evolution in the use of the word "homosexuality," a major change that deserves to be emphasized.

The word "homosexuals" appears in PH (1975) where the word "homosexual" is used as a noun. The phrase 'homosexual persons' is used in HP (1986) where the word "homosexual" becomes an adjective. Cardinal Ratzinger, then Prefect of the Congregation, explained the change usage:

> The human person, made in the image and likeness of God, can hardly be adequately described by a reductionist reference to his or her sexual orientation. Everyone living on the face of the earth has personal problems and difficulties, but challenges to growth, strengths, talents and gifts as well. Today, the Church provides a badly needed context for the care of the human person when she refuses to consider the person as a "heterosexual" or a "homosexual" and insists that every person has a fundamental Identity: the creature of God, and by grace, his child and heir to eternal life. (§ 16)

In the ICC document of 2005, which speaks of "persons with homosexual tendencies," the word "homosexual" refers to the tendency and no longer pigeonholes people. Monsignor Livio Melina, President of the Pontifical John Paul II Institute for Studies on Marriage and Family, explained: "...it would seem appropriate to overcome the term 'homosexual' and replace it with that of "person with homosexual inclination," as an inclination that assumes significant meanings cannot exhaustively define the subject."[10]

The word "homosexual" moves further and further away, graphically and semantically, from the person. The significance of this change is clear: according to the Magisterium, "homosexuality" is, in philosophical terms, accident, not substance. There is no "essence" or "homosexual nature." There are no "homosexuals," but people with same-sex tendencies (SSA).

6. Conclusions

The Magisterium on SSA is complex and sometimes problematic. There are some points, constantly reiterated, that we would like to restate:

- The welcome and respect toward people with same-sex tendencies
- The objective disorder of same-sex attraction tendencies
- The inherent sinfulness of same-sex acts

[10] L. Melina, S. Belardinelli (eds.), *Amare nella differenza. Le forme della sessualità e il pensiero cattolico: studio interdisciplinare*, Cantagalli, Libreria Editrice Vaticana, Siena-Città del Vaticano 2012, p.25.

- The call for the bishops to be vigilant about the infiltration of LGBT ideology within the Church
- The requirement of the promotion of authentic pastoral care for people with SSA in the diocese
- Distrust of legislation that, with the pretext of combating discrimination, promote ideologies contrary to natural law
- The opposition against the legalization of same-sex unions

Yet there are also, as we have seen, hasty interpretations and undue stances on issues not directly related to faith and morals. There is also a constant attempt by LGBT activists to distort and interpret the Magisterium in their favor (this attempt is seen mainly with HP). Three basic things are needed in order to approach the Magisterium of the Church on SSA seriously:

- A thorough knowledge of the Magisterium on SSA[11]
- A thorough knowledge of LGBT ideology in order to detect and counteract distorted and tendentious interpretations of the Magisterium
- A knowledge as thorough and objective as possible of the phenomenon of SSA, both from a scientific and from an anthropological standpoint[12]

---

[11] See for example R. Marchesini, *Omosessualità e Magistero della Chiesa: Comprensione e speranza*, Sugarco, Milan 2013.

[12] See for example R. Marchesini, *Omosessualità maschile,* Ateneo Pontificio Regina Apostolorum, Rome 2011.

MIRIAM FIORE*

SAME-SEX ATTRACTION AND "REPARATIVE" PSYCHOTHERAPIES

In this chapter we will deal with the themes of same-sex attraction and of reparative psychotherapies. We will seek to respond to an initial need to understand SSA and to address this issue from an interdisciplinary perspective.

We will explore this frontier of bioethics not just in terms of the ethics of a form of psychotherapy so much spoken of but because this evaluation implies case by case observations, as well as analysis of relevant elements of the broader dynamics of same-sex attraction. Bioethical investigations into reparative psychotherapies do not only consider therapeutic procedures to verify whether these comply with the rules of professional conduct, but also seek to investigate anthropological assumptions and underlying ethical issues. This is because the very identity of specific individuals is at stake.

This analysis will consist in a scientific analysis of the most significant studies and reports. There are certain obstacles raised by ideological movements that address the issue of SSA from another perspective. They are particularly critical of reparative therapies, deriding it as a pseudo-scientific approach to SSA. Clinical practice continues to raise serious questions not often noted by the media. What emerges is not something we normally consider. The suffering of those who do not wish to embrace their same-sex tendencies; those with deep rooted wounds of identity who appear to lead ordinary lives.

Given the fact that we need to deal with those with such suffering, we cannot avoid the discussion of SSA and reparative psychotherapy. It requires tremendous intellectual honesty to investigate the topic in order to form an adequate judgment.

1. Same-sex attraction and psychotherapy: a problematic relationship

If we consider SSA as a normal variant of sexual identity or merely the result of a person's free choice, its relationship to psychotherapy is not imme-

* Ph.D. candidate for the Pontifical Athenaeum Regina Apostolorum, degree in Philosophy from the University of Palermo.

diately evident. The LGBT liberation movement has promoted a fairly precise image of SSA as being characterized by naturalness and immutability.

These two features render it a "mainstream" condition in which the only elements of conflict for a person with SSA would result from societal or individual rejection of the same-sex identity. Yet, contrary to an irenic view of the SSA phenomenon, the roots in the relationship between SSA and psychotherapy are much deeper than one would expect.

Since the inception of psychoanalysis, when methods for interventions in pathology were first developed, the phenomenon of SSA has been the subject of great interest for scholars.

All great psychiatrists and psychoanalysts, from Sigmund Freud to Carl Gustav Jung to Alfred Adler and Victor Frankl, regarded SSA as a deviation from an individual's normal development.[1] From Freud onward, the main psychoanalytic theories agreed that SSA is a pathological condition caused by an unbalanced relationship with one's parents, together with a failure to construct a sexual identity, to produce a change in the sexed individual.

In accord with this vision, methods of intervention were created over the years with the intention of returning subjects having same-sex tendencies to an original heterosexuality. The original intervention strategies were definitely defective, rooted as they were in Freud's Oedipus theory. Lacking a broader vision of individual sexuality, they aimed merely at reconverting the individual. Depending on therapeutic strategies deployed, success rates varied considerably.[2] Over time these therapeutic interventions underwent transformations as the theories improved with innovative contributions. These adaptations allow for the correction of specific fundamental errors within the original therapies, as well as a fuller consideration of the relationship between therapist and patient.

We will not dwell on these evolutionary steps. Instead, we will simply point out that these investigations and subsequent reparative psychotherapies

---

[1] In this compound the word "deviance" generally refers to the subject's deviance in its chosen object of love. See I. Bieber, *Homosexuality: A Psychoanalytic Study of Male Homosexuals*, Basic Books, New York 1962, p.3-18; T. Dean, C. Lane, *Homosexuality and Psychoanalysis*, University of Chicago Press, Chicago 2001; S.L. Jones, M.A. Yarhouse, *Homosexuality: The Use of Scientific Research in the Church's Moral Debate*, InterVarsity Press, Westmont 2000.

[2] See J. Nicolosi, Reparative therapy of male homosexuality, Jason Aronson, Northvale-NJ-Londra 1991. Among the scholars cited we note: Stekel (1930), Ovesey (1969), Mayerson e Lief (1965), Bieber (1962), Ellis (1956), Ross e Mendelson (1958), Monroe ed Enelow (1960).

have built their foundation upon a psychological perspective with very different assumptions from those of psychoanalysis.

The key concept of reparative psychotherapies, that of "repair," comes from psychoanalysis. It is necessary to clarify this term in advance as most of the misunderstandings regarding this subject are based on this concept. Reparative psychotherapies are often criticized on the basis of a fundamental equivocation of considering the adjective "reparative" in reference to an individual with same-sex tendencies as if the psychotherapist had to "fix" his patient, compelling him to return to heterosexuality.

To "repair" is actually a technical term in clinical psychology referring to a process initiated by the subject to remedy a damage inflicted on an object.[3] The term dates back to Austrian psychoanalyst Melanie Klein (1882-1960), who dealt with child psychoanalysis and was the first to describe a repair mechanism.[4] Melanie Klein thought the infantile psychological world initially to be dominated by anxieties and primitive defenses, by a clash among life instincts, death instincts and object relations. They are relationships to interior objects the child builds upon as a basis for perceptions of good and bad.

When the child begins to differentiate external reality from what is internal and begin to perceive external objects, he or she experiences the possibility of losing a fundamental object: the mother. Alongside this, the child experiences his or her own impotence, developing a depressive attitude Klein called the "depressive position." This is a sense of loss and despair experienced during times of absence and remoteness, which characterize a maternal adaptation. It is similar to an experience of mourning but exists in function of the progressive acquisition of a sense of the real. The child considers his or her aggressive impulses to be the cause of this loss, and from this springs a desire to repair any damage inflicted on the beloved object through love.

---

[3] The term "object" is to be considered in a psychoanalytic way. Please see a medical dictionary.

[4] See M. KLEIN, *Love, Guilt and Reparation and Other Works 1921-1945*, Simon and Schuster, New York 2002; M. KLEIN, *Scritti 1921-1956*, Bollati Boringhieri, Turin 2006; G. CLAUDE, *Mélanie Klein*, Editions Universitaires, Paris 1971. During this same period also Anna Freud speaks about "reparative" therapies (See A. FREUD, *The Ego and the Mechanisms of Defense: The Writings of Anna Freud* Revised Edition, International Universities Press, New York 1979; also see S. VEGETTI FINZI, *Storia della psicoanalisi*, Mondadori, Milan 1982. The concept of "repair" was then proposed by psychoanalyst and pediatrician Donald W. Winnicott, see D.W. WINNICOTT, *Through Paediatrics to Psychoanalysis: Collected Papers* (Karnac Classics), Karnac Books, London 1979; W. WINNICOTT, *Psicoanalisi dello sviluppo: brani scelti*, NUNZIANTE CESARO, V. BOURSIER (eds.), Armando, Rome 2004; C. GEETS, *Winnicott*, Jean-Pierre Delarge, Paris 1981.

The child constructs and gradually integrates the self within an alternation of aggressive and reparative actions. However, not all reparative actions are real and positive. Ongoing maladjustment due to a deficit in that encouragement needed for a child's delicate balance can lead to failed reparative operations, and can determine those forms of obsessive defense focused on illusion and a denial of reality. These defenses can be consolidated within mental life and subsequently influence the individual's future behavior.

Inspired by this theory, various authors have interpreted SSA as a reparative impulse, as an attempt to remedy an inadequate sexual identity. Consequently, they developed therapeutic strategies to tackle defenses constructed by the subject. This theory, which forms part of the psychoanalytic tradition and has been enhanced over time, considers same-sex attraction an attempt to remedy a lack of gender identity, to compensate for feelings of deprivation and unsatisfied sex-based emotional needs. SSA would be the repressive expression of a person whose identity, not having grown in masculinity, seeks this out at the biological level by merging with another man.

Bieber, in particular, has listed some of the main factors that, according to the psychoanalytic literature, are the determining causes of SSA.[5] Just to mention a few: a lack of virility in the father; immaturity and poor understanding of sexual impulses generally; shyness, innate or acquired; strong attachment to a man; feminization through dressing in women's clothes; occurrences such as venereal diseases rendering heterosexuality unpleasant; disillusionment in marriage; being treated as an equal by persons with SSA; a persistence of childhood conceptions that sexual activity is something forbidden, dirty, painful, humiliating, degrading or mutilating.

Modern psychoanalysis gradually moved away from Freud's concepts. It afforded a growing importance to the subject's relationships, specifically focusing on those with the father and mother, thereby offering a more psychodynamic model.

However, the latest psychotherapeutic guidelines have attributed a greater importance to environmental, familial and social factors. A particular vision of the self and the formation of habits resulting from specific interactions with parents and peers seem to be decisive.[6] This explanatory psychodynamic model of SSA is the basis of all reparative psychotherapies.

---

[5] See I. Bieber, *Homosexuality. A Psychoanalytic Study*… p.11. We also recall among the psychoanalysts who support this theory Ovesey, Rado and Socarides.

[6] See G. Zuanazzi, *Omosessualità: Aspetti psicologici*, in G. Russo (ed.), *Enciclopedia di Bioetica e Sessuologia*, Elledici, Turin 200), p.1314-1315.

We use this word in the plural as it is well known that psychotherapies are a complex of therapeutic interventions within the psyche, which center on a relationship between therapist and patient and on their communication. They differ regarding the methods and tools employed according to the underlying theory.

All reparative therapies agree that same-sex attraction has an environmental origin and that it is not an innate tendency. Instead, they suggest that it arises and is acquired through the influence of factors external to the individual, such as family, education or society. This brief analysis concerns male SSA alone, which has been studied most. It will mainly focus on the approach of Joseph Nicolosi. He was the best-known psychotherapist engaged in this form of therapeutic support, co-founding a known scientific and professional association called NARTH, the "National Association for Research and Therapy of Homosexuality."

First, we will seek to understand how SSA can be psychologically explained and then investigate the mechanisms of action of reparative psychotherapy.

2. Same-Sex Attraction Origin: a Psychological Explanation

According to Nicolosi, a SSA state is the symptom of an inner conflict of a sexual nature.[7] The origin of the conflict usually begins in childhood and places the pre-SSA boy in the condition of feeling differently from other boys, sabotaging the development of his sexual identity.

The concept of "symptom," typical of all reparative therapies, should be understood according to its psychoanalytic definition. It thus should be understood as a formation in the unconscious developed to provide a solution to something the individual perceives as "unbearable." For this reason, it is something set aside, remaining unresolved. In other words, a symptom is that means by which an individual seeks to rationalize and confer meaning upon psychic conflict, in a substitutionary and defensive, as well as reparative maneuver. It is a compromise aimed at achieving satisfaction even as it generates evident mental suffering when latent conflict is repressed rather than confronted.[8]

So SSA would be the symptomatic manifestation of a psychic conflict intervening during the process of sexual development, hindering and blocking the

---

[7] On Nicolosi's works see: J. Nicolosi, *Reparative Therapy of Male Homosexuality…*; Id., *Healing Homosexuality. Case Stories of Reparative Therapy*, Jason Aronson, Lanham 1993; Id., *Shame and Attachment Loss*, InterVarsity Press, Downers Grove 2009; J. Nicolosi, L.A. Nicolosi, *A Parent's Guide to Preventing Homosexuality*, InterVarsity Press, Downers Grove 2002, second edition Liberal Mind Publications 2017.

[8] See G. Ricci, *Il padre dov'era. Le omosessualità nella psicanalisi*, Sugarco, Milan 2013, p.119.

process of assuming and identifying with one's own sex. Nicolosi believes the vast majority of individuals with persistent same-sex tendencies experience a problem with gender identity. Several factors impede the subject's identification with his masculinity, from the individual's character/disposition to specific family dynamics and relationships with peers. This would result in a rejection of his masculinity, lived out defensively, so that he would subsequently feel attracted to someone appearing to possess what the subject himself feels he lacks.

The relationship with parents is a decisive factor in developing sexual ambivalence, according to English psychoanalyst and pediatrician Donald Winnicott (1896-1971) who studied parental influence on children.[9] Nicolosi reintroduces his "Triangular System" theory. This theory suggests that it is the mother-father-child system, combined with a very loving but domineering and possessive mother, and a very weak and almost absent father, which can trigger a SSA development.[10] According to Nicolosi, the family in which a son with SSA develops is one which has not adequately fostered the child's male identification process, nor has encouraged him sufficiently during formation of his gender identity. This seems to occur most frequently within a typical model with a "triadic narcissistic" family, characterized by parents' seeming insensitivity to the child's emotional needs at various stages of his growth.

The mother has a distinctly narcissistic attitude, which causes her to pour her needs into the child, in effect stifling him. The son is her special confidant; often he is especially sensitive and helpful, someone on whom she focuses possessive and even intrusive attention. This special role assigned to the child almost always follows upon a sense of dissatisfaction with her husband, with whom compatibility issues persist, and of whom she constantly complains to her son. The child in this way becomes an object of love as an alternative to her husband. This holds significant value for Nicolosi because such maternal criticism becomes foundational for the construction of a negative view of men and masculinity. The figure of the father, meanwhile, is often weak. The father either is distant and uninvolved in family life or else, if he has a "strong" character, is critical and hostile towards the child.

This family pattern may lead to a fracture in the child's bond of attachment during early childhood years. He then experiences deep humiliation

---

[9] See D. Winnicott, *The Maturational Process and the Facilitating Environment*, International Universities Press, New York 1965.

[10] Beginning with Bieber's research of 1962, many authors have argued for this thesis, describing recurring family dynamics in the history of men with same-sex tendencies. For a review, see. J. Nicolosi, *Male Homosexuality*... p.65-66.

and real trauma, with the potential to activate defensive dissociation.[11] This is characterized by a state of inattention and indifference to reality, as well as a strong sensitivity to any form of disapproval or rejection by those people most important to him. The child thus arrives at the second phase of his development—the "gender identity phase"—insufficiently and even disadvantageously equipped.

At this point the father emerges in all his fundamental importance. The son develops a defense against emotional attachment to the bond with his mother and now turns to his father. If the father is able to support and encourage him, he will solve the child's problems by acting as an object of compensatory attachment. If instead he is emotionally unhelpful and distant (if not critical and hostile), the child will remain in his dissociative state, completely withdrawing into himself. That is why the father turns out to be, in the end, the key figure for the balanced development of the child. Persons with SSA, more frequently than heterosexuals, often have a relatively distant, cold, inscrutable father. He could be a bit on the authoritarian side, one who does not bond with the son emotionally.[12] An analysis of case studies seems to demonstrate a dearth of persons with SSA who have had a loving father in childhood.

This confrontation with the father's negativity triggers a trauma in the child, setting off a series of chain reactions. His desire for affirmation and male attachment is frustrated, so he experiences a deep shame that throws him into a state of humiliation and frustration. The son has been wounded by his first major narcissistic injury. However, the child does not feel angry towards his parents for the humiliation received. Instead he is angry with himself for having saddened and disappointed them. He then internalizes the message that he is wrong as a male, that he is weak, defective and unworthy of love. The child then

---

[11] Nicolosi assumes John Bowlby's attachment theory, which was developed in the twentieth century. This theory describes family relationships and parental functions from the first months of a child's life, integrating yet surpassing the dominant theory in Freudian psychoanalysis. Freud explained the child's bond with the mother in terms of drive theory, i.e., a mere satisfaction of sexual instincts. The bonds of childhood attachment are derived instead from a need to receive protection and security against the dangers of the outside world. Bowlby describes this push to attachment as a primary thrust toward survival, such that the loss of one's attachment is equivalent to death. These bonds also allow the child to build "internal working models," i.e. internal representations of his or her relationships, which, once developed, are maintained over time so the experiences of past life can affect relationships and future behaviors. See J. Bowlby, *Maternal Care and Mental Health,* World Health Organization 1952; J. Bowlby "The Nature of the Child's Tie to His Mother," in the *International Journal of Psychoanalysis,* 39, 1958, p.350-373; J. Bowlby, *Attachment and Loss*, Volumes 1-3, Penguin, Harmondsworth 1985.

[12] Nicolosi relies on this in numerous studies: see. J. Nicolosi, *Male Homosexuality...*, p.40.

abandons any desire for attachment to his father, and, as his masculinity was nipped in the bud, he symbolically "returns" to his mother, with whom he takes shelter. He simultaneously detaches from his father as a defense mechanism, rejecting both him and all that he represents, starting with his masculinity. This leads, however, to an increasing hostility and a burning rage against his father—a fairly common attitude among those with same-sex tendencies.

This defensive detachment will have significant effects upon relationships with other boys. It is pretty common among pre-SSA children to find difficulties in establishing friendly relationships with same sex peers during pre-adolescence.[13]

Due to the humiliation experienced, the child uses compensating defense mechanisms, particularly those of narcissism and the development of a false "self," which, according to Nicolosi, are essential conditions for pre-SSA. These defenses maintain the subject in a state of constant emotional isolation as he is unable to relate effectively to other people. In this way he falls into what Nicolosi calls the "Grey Zone," a condition of loneliness, discouragement and impotence. His expectations of others are continually disappointed, and he thus feels weak, humiliated and unworthy. When the subject is trapped in this depressive situation, all conditions for the emergence of a same-sex attraction are in place, as it is a frequent response to this state of affairs.

Shut out and practically exiled from the world of men, a child experiences a growing admiration toward those mysterious and, at the same time, alluring features he feels he still lacks. This is a feeling that can evolve into real erotic attraction. During adolescence he will explore, through same-sex behavior, satisfaction for those emotional needs left unfulfilled in childhood.

It is on this basis that Nicolosi adopts the theory of SSA as repair. This impulse toward the same sex is expressed by an individual's effort to win the love, to absorb the virility, of the object feared (apparently the father figure). While at the same time, he is making contact with his own gender—to act like, and be regarded as, a male.

The same-sex act expresses an individual's unconscious attempt to resolve a profound mental conflict, to heal an open wound, to finally achieve the ful-

---

[13] This aspect has been effectively described by Gerard van den Aardweg, who considers the interwoven relationship with one's similar at the beginning of adolescence crucial for the development of homosexuality. See G.J.M. Van den Aardweg, *Homosexuality and Hope*, Servant Publications, Ann Arbor-Michigan 1985; Id., *The Battle for Normality. A Guide for (Self-)Therapy for Homosexuality*, Ignatius Press, San Francisco 1996; Id., *On the Origins and Treatment of Homosexuality: A Psychoanalytic Reinterpretation*, Praeger, New York 1986; Id., "Parents of Homosexuals: Not Guilty?", in *American Journal of Psychotherapy*, 38, 1984, p.180-189.

fillment of a desire for success, and of being self-possessed once and for all. It is a quest that remains unspoken. He is fed by the narcissistic illusion—narcissistic because the partner is an object for achieving this purpose—of having revenge on those who have hurt him. He gains the respect and acceptance he needs but without confronting traumatic events, such as a loss of attachment, in an authentic and constructive way. Thus, he continually re-creates and re-proposes this scenario in a ritualized way through erotic activity. The subject is overcome by shame and the fear of being once again defeated and humiliated in his attempt at masculine self-affirmation. Nicolosi focuses in particular on the topic of shame, a paralyzing force that inserts a real barrier within the ego separating the individual from his gender identity.

To conclude, this analysis of the origins and development of SSA refer to a multi-dimensional explanatory model that ought to be considered. It not so much views social environment as a *unicum* but rather seeks to explain multiple aspects of the phenomenon under examination. It is a model that acknowledges the relevance of biology and that responds to certain negative inputs from the social environment. This can be seen in subjects having a highly sensitive temperament—fairly frequent in subjects developing SSA.

3. Reparative Psychotherapy

Reparative psychotherapy is frequently sought by a number of individuals experiencing conflict over persistent same-sex tendencies. These individuals refuse to integrate this orientation with their sexual identity. They perceive it as extraneous to their authentic self, as it induces a strong discomfort or malaise, affecting their daily lives and social relationships. Speaking of his patients, Nicolosi used the expression "non-gay homosexuals." Others instead speak of "ego-dystonic" persons with SSA.

If ego-syntonic persons with SSA accept their tendencies and live in accord with these sans difficulty, then ego-dystonic are those who reject and are rather ashamed of these tendencies, living in profound conflict with themselves. Despite appeals to "come out," such individuals reject the gay lifestyle and, far from wanting this to form part of their identity, live their sexual orientation in a painful and agonizing way. They view "affirmation" (supposedly the only way to be more authentic and genuine) as a fundamental obstacle.

Reparative psychotherapists respond to requests for help by proposing a therapeutic approach that is not restricted merely to those with same-sex tendencies. Rather than a change in sexual orientation being the goal of reparative psychotherapies, the goal is a maturation of gender identity. From this standpoint, the development of stable same-sex tendencies flows from a self-identification problem to the point of a defect in gender identity. To achieve its purpose, reparative therapy works on both past and present. For Nicolosi, the patient is accompanied through a self-discernment process, leading him first to understand his relationships with his parents and peers. At the base of persistent erotic attraction to same-sex individuals there are unmet childhood emotional needs, along with attachment trauma. This is why psychotherapy focuses on feelings, motives and moods, aiming to reactivate the subconscious emotional development repressed by defensive mechanisms.

At the same time, the patient is invited to question those reasons that have led him to eroticize relationships with other males. Therapy is not mere reflection but rather aims at launching new behaviors, especially the creation of intimate nonsexual male friendships. In this way it also acts upon the present. When a person begins to detect hidden needs lurking behind unwanted homoerotic behaviors—needs for attention, affection and approval—he comes to understand that these cannot be satisfied erotically. The goal of therapy is a transformation of meaning that empowers the patient to realize what he truly desires *is not* sexual behavior with another man but rather to heal his own masculinity. This therapy proposes to initiate a more global process of change aimed at the maturation of the subject's personality. A change in sexual orientation is but one potential effect in the recovery of general emotional stability.

From these premises, we can understand how reparative therapies differ from a strictly psychoanalytic approach that confines a patient within his psychosis and past conflicts in order to pursue conversion as the fundamental task. The change sought is not imposed upon a passive subject from above; rather, the patient *becomes* the primary agent of the therapeutic process, called to live out transformation with himself. In this respect reparative psychotherapies draw on cognitive-behavioral therapies.

From the behavioral perspective, a problem's symptoms are related to behavioral patterns previously learned and maintained over time. These may develop into cognitive structures unsuited to confronting the stimuli of external reality in the present. Various conditioning techniques are employed to change learned, and previously stored, responses, exposing the subject to new ideas and fostering the learning of new behaviors and skills.[14] Cognitive therapy focuses on a correlation between emotions and behavior, on the one

[14] See M. Durante, P. Orifiammi, F. Rovetto, "Comportamentismo e psicoterapia comportamentale," in F. Del Corno, M. Lang (eds.), *Elementi di psicologia clinica*, Franco Angeli, Milano 2005.

hand, and an individual's perception of events on the other, while aiming to achieve behavioral change.[15] Even when trying to trace the origins of cognitive distortions and dysfunctional ideas—common mental errors associated with psychological disorders—cognitive therapy offers an outlook on the present aimed at "cognitive restructuring," or a modification of beliefs effecting a change in emotion and behavior.

First, we must stop to consider that a patient with unwanted same-sex tendencies is in a mourning "pathological situation." There is an unresolved experience of grief caused by injury over attachment, as well as narcissistic wounds inflicted during the pre-SSA phase, accompanied by self-destructive feelings.

The goal of psychotherapy is to help the patient confront the reality of this loss, to help him dislodge it, and to thus transcend the constructed defenses. Nicolosi first proposed a "therapy program focused on feelings" (Affect-Focused Therapy, AFT) in response to attachment trauma.[16] Since SSA is viewed as an attempt to repair an insecure attachment to one's father, this therapy aims at a reconstruction of attachment through a harmony between patient and therapist.

Constructing a relationship of trust with the therapist ensures that the patient develops a growing self-confidence, stepping away from emotional closure and into emotional openness with his defenses gradually eroding. This relationship is the patient's remedy for emotional betrayal endured in childhood, a repair for a lack of parental harmony. In this way the patient experiences the closeness of a man who really does care about him and who looks out for him. The therapist seeks to establish a connection with the patient from the outset of therapy. He keeps a dialogue with the patient alive so as to encourage him to verbalize his innermost feelings.

Nicolosi's therapy follows the model of so-called Intensive Short-Term Dynamic Psychotherapy (ISTDP). This approach, developed by Davanloo in the 1960s, is based on English psychoanalyst David Malan's and American psychiatrist Karl Menninger's studies on defense mechanisms. According to these authors, defense mechanisms are developed in a recurring pattern

---

[15] See J.S. BECK, A.T. BECK, *Cognitive Behavior Therapy: Basics and Beyond*, 2nd Edition, The Guilford Press, New York 2011; F. WILLS, *Beck's Cognitive Therapy: Distinctive Features (CBT Distinctive Features)*, Routledge, New York 2013.

[16] See J. NICOLOSI, *Gender Identity...*, p.10ff. In developing this therapy Nicolosi was prompted by Habib Davanloo's clinical studies with their reference to attachment theory. See H. DAVANLOO, *Basic Principles and Techniques in Short-Term Dynamic Psychotherapy*, Spectrum, New York 1978.

called the "Triangle of Conflict." Certain emotions inspire negative reactions from people, namely, anxiety and shame, and in response they construct defense mechanisms to avoid the initial emotions. A session begins by asking the patient to report one or more events that occurred the previous week. This provides the original material for the session's work. The therapist aspires to detect an "identified conflict" from this, a problem experienced by the patient that triggers such negative reactions as anger, sadness or frustration. The goal is to identify the moment of conflict, the one producing the strongest feelings and even the most intense physical discomfort.

A new phase begins once the patient is able to identify a fundamental affection, and is ready to express his feelings, gradually lowering his defenses. During this stage the patient constructs cognitive connections between his present and past relations, discusses the past, discusses figures from his life and achieves a greater understanding of his emotions. During this phase the patient also explores his relationship with the therapist, which ought to mature into an active and dyadic involvement that Nicolosi calls "dual containment."

Dual containment is a strategy used to contrast the typical situation of a triadic narcissistic family, referred to as "double bond." In this type of bond, a child feels a discrepancy between a parent's words and the way that message is transmitted, which would seem to suggest a content different from what is explicit. For the child this is a source of confusion as he does not know which message he should believe, the verbal or the non-verbal one. He knows that if he follows his somatic and emotional reaction, he will experience humiliation from his parents because he has not trusted their messaging and, instead, sensed something beyond it. However, if he believes his parent's words he will feel accepted by them. The choice not to disobey explicit verbal messages is in some way imposed by the relationship of dependence on his parents. When this double bond becomes a habitual situation, it ends up creating a double separation within the subject: one within the self, one with others. With the passing of time the individual recognizes a need to detach his feelings and somatic reactions from any implicit message that he intuits in another person's tone or expression so as not to lose his personal agency. At the same time, he internalizes these feeling of shame that this manner of communication arouses in him due to the state of helplessness and paralysis to which he feels condemned. In addition, the subject feels a growing distrust in human relationships, which he suspects will always center on this double bond.

In contrast, dual containment creates a "virtuous circle" in which the therapist, ensuring the patient's emotional closeness and "containing it" in the suspension of the present moment, encourages the expression of his feelings. Finding a response in the therapist, the patient slowly opens up and, before the experience of being regarded and accepted by another, undergoes an emotional expansion. He is then able to unlock his defenses and achieve comprehension of his conflicts. Dual containment also enables laying the foundation for non-erotic male bonding, which is one of the primary goals of the therapy.

The beneficial effects of dual containment appear to be confirmed by insights into neurobiology. The presence in the brain of neuroplastic zones can change with learning and experience, as well as with the impact of interpersonal communication upon the brain that may, of course, be either positive or damaging.[17] If the double bond causes a disconnect between the brain's right hemisphere and left hemisphere due to an explicit message recorded by the left brain at odds with an implicit message registered by the right hemisphere, empathic harmony nurtured by the therapist may facilitate unification of the two hemispheres. This occurs by (metaphorically) "binding" the hemispheres of the patient's brain. In this regard, and if specifically requested by the patient, Nicolosi uses another treatment based on studies by Francine Shapiro, Eye Movement Desensitization and Reprocessing (EMDR),[18] which operates on symptoms produced by the trauma.[19]

Nicolosi's use of EMDR for the trauma of gender shame and unwanted sexual arousal in the past is based on the neurophysiology of traumatic experience. Its origin is traced back to a sort of neural disruption in the memory circuits, the result of the internalization of stimuli too painful for the subject. Therefore, at the base of a trauma there is a problem of processing information, stored in a non-functional way and "frozen" in the form of anxiety lived by the body, which causes a number of variable disorders. The EMDR aims to create neurological connections necessary to bring to light the non-processed memory, so that the subject can turn back to the event that caused the trauma and reach its solution. What emerges is that the attuned relationship between therapist and patient is able actually to change the neurological structure of the brain by creating new neurological pathways.

---

[17] Nicolosi relied on the following studies in particular: Schiffer (1998); Schore (1991), (2003); Stern (2002); Siegel (2002).

[18] See F. Shapiro, *Eye Movement Desensitization Reprocessing: Basic Principles, Protocols and Procedures*, Guilford, New York 2005.

[19] For a thorough explanation of such therapy, see J. Nicolosi, *Identità di genere...*, p.336-342._

The development of these connections, which Nicolosi called *insight* to emphasize the appearance of a sudden "awakening," should be the outcome of this cognitive process, and they should result in a transformation of meaning. While in this situation of double containment, the patient can relive the early trauma and attribute to the conflict its true meaning. He understands that his same-sex behavior is an expression of a need for attention, approval and affection from men that, however, cannot be satisfied erotically, but only through the gradual internalization of masculinity. It is a process that had been interrupted during his childhood and teenage years and that is now activated through new behaviors and new relationships with others. This change in meaning triggers a series of positive effects on the patient, while a decrease of erotic attraction towards other men also eliminates the distressing sensations connected to it. This way the patient finally discovers that authenticity and vitality from which he had till then felt excluded. This is, in short, a genuine maturation of the patient's personal identity as, learning to relate to his inner self, he also learns to build healthy and authentic relationships with others. This is the real change sought.

The positive effects from which patients have benefited are reflected in a number of studies. We will briefly cover controls used to screen the efficacy of reparative psychotherapies for purposes of ethical evaluation. When addressing the results of reparative psychotherapy, we must not conclude that the potential for failure invalidates therapy as each treatment, involving an individual person, inherently bears such a possibility. Nor can sexual orientation change be used as the only parameter since what interests the patient is a path to growth more globally. Among the various works that have been selected,[20] we will cite Stanton Jones and Mark Yarhouse's research on 98 people, followed by the Robert Spitzer's study.[21]

The first is a longitudinal and prospective study, conducted with psychological standardized tests intended to verify whether a change of sexual orientation is possible. It yielded the following results: 15% of the sample experienced

[20] For a review in Italian, see P. Petrini, E. Lambiase, "L'orientamento sessuale egodistonico: La deontologia vigente," in T. Cantelmi (eds.), *Cattolici e Psiche*, San Paolo, Cinisello Balsamo 2008; R. Marchesini, *Omosessualità maschile*, ... p.150-163.

[21] R.L. Spitzer, "Can Some Gay Men and Lesbians Change Their Sexual Orientation? 200 Participants Reporting a Change from Homosexual to Heterosexual Orientation," in *Archives of Sexual Behavior*, Vol. 32, No.5, October 2003, p.403-417. [Editor's note: There are reports in the news that in 2012, the author again retracted his position. However, this study has not been formally retracted by the journal editor even though the news reported that he had wished to do so.]

a change of sexual orientation, with the emergence of heterosexual attraction; 23% felt same-sex attraction decreased (subjects control it but have embraced chastity); 29% of the subjects experienced a reduction of same-sex attraction and then continued treatment; 15% are "indecisive," as they have not experienced any response to the treatment and do not know whether to continue it or abandon it; 4% did not reveal response to the treatment and decided to abandon it; 8% abandoned the therapy and have formed their own gay identity.

Spitzer's study caused a great stir in the context of the American Psychiatric Association. It is common knowledge that in the 1970s Spitzer supported the decision to remove SSA from the list of mental disorders in the Association's Diagnostic Manual. After carrying out research to investigate the possibility of a change in same-sex attraction in 2001, he admitted that he had changed his view on the issue. He in fact affirmed that a modification of sexual orientation is possible, and also that it is not sought out by the patient due to strong social pressure but rather due to a profoundly rational motivation. Spitzer interviewed 200 subjects (143 males and 57 females) by phone using a structured format of 114 questions that assessed various aspects of sexual orientation. The subjects interviewed had felt a predominantly same-sex attraction for years until the beginning of therapy and experienced lasting changes in sexual attraction (for at least five years) following the therapy. One year after the conclusion of therapy, 67% of males and 44% of females met the criteria of "good heterosexual functioning," meaning that they had found a stable and significant heterosexual attraction.

Even those who had seen limited changes considered the therapy extremely beneficial, as participants benefited from improvements in other dimensions not directly related: a decrease in depression; a greater sense of masculinity in males and of femininity in females; and the development of intimate relationships of a non-sexual nature with persons of the same sex.

Such effects were likewise confirmed in studies by Van den Aardweg analyzing the effectiveness of such treatment.[22] Based upon an extended follow-up of three-to-five years, he concluded most patients in ongoing therapy undergo actual improvement. He observed that, out of 110 subjects in care, 60% arrived at a satisfactory state vis-à-vis same-sex tendencies and affectivity generally over an extended period of time. Improvements noted were not merely in relation to SSA obsessions and their weakening, nor to contingent manifestations of heterosexual feelings, but in relation to overall personality, which became less neurotic such that lifestyle and even physical appearance

[22] See G.J.M. Van den Aardweg, *Homosexuality and Hope...*, Id., *The Battle for Normality...*

were positively affected. Even those experiencing little progress still improved due a reduction in same-sex encounters (ethically and physically problematic in light of sexually transmitted diseases and the consequent life expectancy among persons with SSA).

Numerous studies uncover a link between same-sex relationships and increased risks to human health.[23] There is a greater risk of contracting infections and sexually transmitted diseases within the demographic of SSA active men. This is mainly due to a high degree of sexual promiscuity, or sex addiction, characterizing the subjects, as well as the frequency of "open" or even transgressive relationships, as well as various forms of prostitution, along with voluntary exposure to sexually transmitted diseases.

Yet risks also affect mental health. Epidemiological studies reveal that these patients have a higher frequency of psychological and psychiatric disorders compared to heterosexual individuals: higher levels of anxiety, depression, schizophrenia, borderline personality disorder, narcissistic personality disorder, and suicidal ideation and temptations, as well as suicides.

In response to the alleged dangers of reparative therapy, which, on the contrary, has been proven to benefit so many people, it is our duty to ask whether it is ethically permissible to propose and encourage, as "affirmative" therapy does, a lifestyle and identity that harms the subject's health and life. Caring about the patient means caring for his health, first and foremost.

4. SSA pain

Nicolosi denounced psychiatry's neglect of non-gay persons with SSA, ignoring the wrenching conflicts experienced by such individuals and inflicting such heavy frustration upon them. They might be called victims of reverse discrimination.

If at some point psychiatry meant to oppose a social discrimination experienced by persons with SSA, it ended up discriminating against those dissatisfied with the SSA condition by rejecting reparative psychotherapies *in toto*. The fact is that despite traditional theories of SSA as a reparative response, the 1960s witnessed a progressive weakening of the pathologizing of traits commonly associated with same-sex orientation, together with a progressive advocacy of its "normalization." This evolution may be seen across successive editions of the most authoritative manual on psychiatric diseases, the *Diag-*

[23] For a comprehensive review, see C. Atzori, *Il binario indifferente: Uomo e donna o GLBTQ?* Sugarco, Milan 2010, p.88-94.

nostic and Statistical Manual of Mental Disorders (DSM) published by the American Psychiatric Association (APA).[24]

The original 1952 edition included "homosexuality" among sociopathic personality disorders, while the second (1968) version of the manual included it in a group of "other non-psychotic mental disorders." In 1973, a revised version of the DSM-II placed SSA in a new category of "sexual orientation disturbance." Yet it specified this applied solely to individuals experiencing a conflict with their own sexual preferences and thus willing to change sexual orientation. SSA itself was not considered a psychiatric disorder, being treated instead as one more form of sexual behavior.

The Manual's third edition (DSM-III), published in 1980, introduced an important innovation. SSA was still found among such mental disorders as "ego-dystonic homosexuality" (as distinct from so-called "ego-syntonic" homosexuality). Yet this distinction was shelved in the *revised* text of 1987 (DSM-III-R) in which ego-dystonic homosexuality was no longer considered a disorder in its own right. Rather, *any discomfort* associated with the condition was considered an evolutionary and adaptive disorder, one mostly caused by an internalization of social hostility. In later versions (DSM-IV in 1994, revised in 2000), reference to SSA is still found as a 302.9 disorder, i.e., a "sexual disorder not otherwise specified," wherein is found mention of a "persistent and intense distress *about* sexual orientation."

A different classification is often invoked within the context of the SSA debate, one proposed by the World Health Organization (WHO) in its International Classification of Disease (ICD). In its current version ICD-10 cites SSA among those "psychological and behavioral disorders associated with development and sexual orientation" (F66). This F66.1 disorder in particular is related to an "ego-dystonic sexual orientation," associated with those situations where there are no doubts regarding an individual's gender identity or sexual preference. Still, when these situations cause psychological or behavioral disorders, an individual who wishes may seek treatment.[25]

Thus, we see SSA gradually tending to disappear from classifications of disorders. If any distress remains, it is referred to an individual's non-acceptance of this tendency and thus to a subjective imbalance not attributable to SSA itself. The real problem for patients who choose the therapy would be a

---

[24] See R. Bayer, *Homosexuality and American Psychiatry. The Politics of Diagnosis*, Basic Books, New York 1981; revised edition Princeton University Press, NJ 1987.

[25] See http://apps.who.int/classifications/icd10/browse/2010/en#/F66 [Editor's note: In the upcoming 2017 edition of the ICD 11, there is a proposal to declassify ego-dystonic sexual orientation as well. See http://www.who.int/bulletin/volumes/92/9/14-135541/en/].

complex feeling of guilt almost always induced by society. The only truly effective treatment would be to induce the patient to rid himself of these feelings of guilt by attuning to a same-sex orientation. This is what Gay Affirmative Therapy (GAT) proposes, the most widespread therapeutic approach today.

The problem concerns the motivations for such profound and sudden change in official diagnostic classification of SSA advanced among weighty reservations. Ronald Bayer, Professor of Socio-Medical Sciences at Columbia University's Mailman School of Public Health, has written how the issue of classifying SSA in early versions of the DSM became the main polemical target of the Gay Liberation Movement at the end of the 1960s.[26]

Activists organized picketing and obstruction at the Annual Convention of the American Psychiatric Association, breaking into convention halls to disturb lecturers with shouting and insults regarding the treatment of SSA. Representatives of different groups demanded the declassification of SSA in the DSM, and a chance both to attend and participate in the conference's work. The demand was swiftly conceded by certain APA members. While impossible to reconstruct the debate that broke out within the APA here, the DSM's subsequent revision was achieved following an internal referendum in which the association's most influential members pressured the APA Committee on Nomenclature's decision to exclude SSA from the list of mental disorders.[27]

Several studies, including Alfred Kinsey's research, were presented in support of this decision, reflecting the influence of the Sexual Revolution. Two influential studies on SSA individuals' mental health were published by Eli Robin, Marcel Saghir and Evelyn Hooker.[28] However, as both studies presented obvious manipulation and methodological errors, their validity was undermined.[29] There was thus no scientific evidence demonstrating the normality of SSA in mental health terms. In view of powerful external pressure, opportunity and convenience combined to lead the world's most influential psychiatrists in a novel direction so as to avoid any risk associated with considering SSA a pathology.[30]

---

[26] See R. Bayer, *Homosexuality and American Psychiatry...*, p.67.

[27] These events have been reconstructed in detail by Roberto Marchesini. See R. Marchesini, *Omosessualità maschile*, Pontifical Athenaeum Regina Apostolorum, Rome 2011, p.175-184.

[28] E. Robins, M.T. Saghir, "Male and Female Homosexuality: Natural History," in *Comprehensive Psychiatry*, Vol. 12, No.6, November 1971, p.503-510.

[29] E. Hooker, "The Adjustment of the Male Overt Homosexual," in *Journal of Projective Techniques*, No.21 (XXI) 1957, p.18-31.

[30] See J.B. Satinover, "The 'Trojan Couch': How the Mental Health Associations Misrepresent Science," http://narth.com/docs/TheTrojanCouchSatinover.pdf [accessed

Psychological theories on the origins of SSA came to appear dangerous, correlating as they did the emergence of such trends with a complex of problems related to the sexual identity of the subject. The progressive downplaying of SSA in the DSM for researchers' attention was exchanged for explaining the origin of SSA in biological terms.

In spite of the great enthusiasm for this trend in subsequent years, to date there is no scientific evidence demonstrating a hormonal, neuroanatomical or genetic correlation for SSA. Arguments presented as scientific evidence have turned out to be hypotheses advanced arbitrarily, or even just-so stories constituting advocacy research by the studies' authors.[31] To date, then, the psychological hypothesis remains the only plausible explanatory model of SSA, addressing as it does most factors arising in clinical practice.

However, the influence of political and ideological factors has led most professionals to state their position on a patient's potential, or even *obligation*, to embrace uncritically a same-sex orientation and to integrate this into a gay identity. This is accompanied by a rejection of reparative psychotherapies, which now stand accused of effecting a form of "homophobia," and as such are attacked as manipulative nature and even dangerous. The hypothesis of reparative therapy's danger must be taken seriously since, if verified, this would cast a shadow over its possible benefits. When evaluating a therapy *primum non nocere* is the primary criterion.

It should be noted that despite fierce and numerous voices of opposition to reparative therapy, it has rarely been explicitly prohibited.

In August 2009, a document presenting the results of research performed by the Task Force on Appropriate Therapeutic Responses to Sexual Orientation was published. The working group had been set up by the American Psychological Association to analyze the scientific literature on attempts at changing sexual orientation (Sexual Orientation Change Efforts, SOCE).[32] Many accepted this document as the final chapter of a long debate on reparative therapy, presenting it as definitively rejected by the international scientific community because it is ineffective and harmful.

The working group set out to investigate three key issues: the effectiveness, the potential risks, and the potential benefits of SOCE. However, it as-

05/06/2015]; Id., *Homosexuality and the Politics of Truth*, Baker Books, Grand Rapids 1996; R. Marchesini, *Omosessualità maschile...*, p.175-184.

[31] It is public knowledge that many of these studies were conducted by researchers sympathetic to gay advocacy, i.e., Bailey and Pillard, Hamer, LeVay. A review of the most important studies is found in G. van den Aardweg.

[32] See www.apa.org/pi/lgbt/resources/sexual-orientation.aspx, [accessed 3/14/2017.]

serted that, beyond personal experience and the participants' individual perceptions, available research did not permit the drawing of conclusions as to the efficacy or safety of these therapies. Neither the benefits nor the alleged damage reported by subjects in therapy were to be attributable to SOCE in the strict sense.

The text contains a number of principles to guide therapists with clients experiencing problems in their sexual orientation. Ultimately, the report mostly references the previous position with respect to SSA's being considered a neutral variation of human sexuality and thus not a mental or developmental disorder (much less a possible cause of negative consequences for the individual's life). This document repeats what was already expressed by two previous documents: those of the American Psychological Association in 1997,[33] and the American Psychiatric Association in 1998.[34]

These documents offer principles therapists should follow in response to problems related to sexual orientation. The first is essentially a warning to avoid any representation of lesbian, gay and bisexual people as mentally ill due to sexual orientation. The second document contains more direct references to so-called "conversion therapies."

The text begins by recalling how the American Psychiatric Association, after removing SSA from the DSM in 1973, even decided to exclude ego-dystonic SSA from its third revised DSM edition of 1987, based on evidence that it is not a mental disorder. The APA claims not to have an official position on "reparative therapies" due to a lack of evidence, yet expressly disclaims any psychiatric treatment based on the assumption that SSA is a mental disorder or on an a priori assumption that a patient should change his or her same-sex orientation. The tone of these positions is clear. If, in the manuals, there is still left a trace of possibility for a patient to change his or her sexual orientation, this is probably due to a need to preserve, at least ostensibly, those basic values considered in patient care. When considering the diversity of treatments and the autonomy of patients, those values must be enshrined for reparative therapy as well.

On the other hand, the scientific literature supplies no evidence of a "danger" of such therapies. For example, though psychiatrist Paolo Rigliano re-

---

[33] See AMERICAN PSYCHOLOGICAL ASSOCIATION, "Resolution on Appropriate Therapeutic Responses to Sexual Orientation," www.apa.org/about/policy/appropriate.aspx, [accessed 3/14/2017.]

[34] See AMERICAN PSYCHIATRIC ASSOCIATION, "Position Statement on Psychiatric Treatment and Sexual Orientation," http://www.psychiatry.org/advocacy--newsroom/position-statements, [accessed 4/06/2015.]

ported six works claiming the danger of so-called reparative therapies,[35] it has been convincingly demonstrated that these studies do *not* prove what they wish to, being merely a collection of testimonies possessing no scientific value.[36]

First, most of the authors mentioned are LGBT activists. We refer to psychotherapist Lee Beckstead, history professor Martin Dubermann, psychologist Douglas Haldeman and psychologist Richard Isay. Second, they relate tales of personal feelings or negative states that cannot be directly linked to reparative therapies. In addition, Lawrence Hartmann's article is merely a suggestion of alleged damages that remain undemonstrated.

The most relevant work is that of Michael Schroeder and Ariel Shidlo. The authors aim to document negative effects and damage of reparative or "homophobic" therapy. It was financed by an association that fights for the affirmation of LGBT rights (the National Gay and Lesbian Task Force), and was conducted by interviewing 150 people recruited through an advertisement posted on gay magazines and websites.

What remains is a number of testimonials from people who have dropped out of a reparative therapy and generic accusations made by members of the LGBT community—certainly not any scientific evidence of the reparative psychotherapies' danger. The possibility of positive changes in the patient due to such therapies instead remains unproven and undocumented.

In spite of this fact psychotherapists today engaged in this form of psychotherapeutic support are subjected to pressures and threats. If compliance with the code of professional standards is maintained, and a strong therapeutic alliance built in the course of therapy reinforces this, then this rejection is unwarranted in the scientific sphere. From the brief analysis offered we can indeed affirm reparative psychotherapy is eminently realistic in light of the help it offers a patient honestly confronting his or her problems. What is more, by shifting focus from an individual's instincts and sexual behavior to his or her emotional needs, reparative psychotherapy is mindful of a patient's authentic good as it appears to him or her multi-dimensionally. After all, it offers authentic educational value to the extent it encourages positive change and growth.

On the other hand, the authentic good of patients ought not to be sought through a sympathetic cheerleading for every conviction, nor through the

---

[35] See P. Rigliano, "Le terapie riparative tra presunzioni curative e persecuzione," in P. Rigliano, M. Graglia (eds.), *Gay e lesbiche in psicoterapia*, Raffaello Cortina, Milan 2006.

[36] See R. Marchesini, *Omosessualità maschile...*, p.165-168.

victimization characterizing such convictions, but rather by utilizing a realistic, scientific approach that goes straight to the heart of a problem—the deficits and unresolved traumas that prevent a patient from seeing things as they are. It would seem that homoerotic behaviors serve a merely narcotic function insofar as they numb the pain temporarily, offering the individual a sensation of self-dominion, on the one hand, and of power over others on the other. This remedy is merely illusory, though, since, through continuous repetition of the act, it hurls the individual into an ever deeper despair, nailed to his self-defense and his shame.

An approach that encourages same-sex orientation or exacerbates gay identity thus loses sight of the real problem and threatens to devalue the patient's identity, first by compromising his sexuality. There is a danger that sexuality is demoted from constituting a fundamental dimension of the person (one involving all his or her basic dimensions) to merely pure instinct. In this way it is depersonalized. What these patients seek, by contrast, is an understanding and emotional proximity that requires a respectful response to a suffering affecting the hidden level of emotions, those of a devastating discomfort harming the person in his or her very identity.

The greatest risk experienced in this area is that the suffering of patients seeking change remains unheard, overshadowed by gender ideology. This unfortunately has occurred in the fields of psychology and psychotherapy, which somehow feel threatened by attempts to change, and even by the very presence of patients seeking change.

Interestingly, the deep suffering affecting this demographic is confirmed not only by the direct testimony of therapy subjects, but even from surveys by some scholars of openly gay men and women that arrive at some surprising conclusions.

Psychiatrist and professor Antonio M. Persico, who has recorded and compared scientific articles on the topic since 1999, reveals the presence of a deep psychic pain that emerges in a consistent manner among those with same-sex tendencies, beginning with the initial appearance of a SSA drive.[37]

---

[37] See A.M. PERSICO, *Omosessualità tra scelta e sofferenza...*, p.11ff. refer to the following studies: D.M. FERGUSSON, L.J. HORWOOD, E.M. RIDDER, A.L. BEAUTRAIS, "Is Sexual Orientation Related to Mental Problems and Suicidality in Young People?" in *Archives of General Psychiatry*, 56, 1999, p.876-880; ID., "Sexual Orientation and Mental Health in a Birth Cohort of Young Adults," in *Psychological Medicine*, 35, 2005, p.971-981; S.D. COCHRAN, V.M. MAYS, "Lifetime Prevalence Of Suicide Symptoms and Affective Disorders Among Men Reporting Same-Sex Sexual Partners: Results from NHANES III", in *American Journal of Public Health*, 90, 2000, p.573-578; S.E. GILMAN, S.D. COCHRAN, V.M. MAYS, M. HUGHES, D. Os-

This pain later will be accompanied by incidences of anxiety, depression, alcoholism, drug addiction, suicidal ideation and suicide attempts – twice as much as those recorded for heterosexuals.

Persico confirms this state of affairs on the basis of his professional experience. These percentages seem to exclude the "normality" of a SSA condition in terms of individual well-being and adaptation, so much so that Persico considers them, among the patients he meets in clinical practice, to suffer the most.

It is this suffering that demands a rethinking of SSA from a realistic and scientifically grounded view of this phenomenon and of the human person rather than from views motivated by presupposition.

TROW, R.C. KESSLER, "Risk of Psychiatric Disorders Among Individuals Reporting Same-Sex Sexual Partners in the National Comorbidity Survey", in *American Journal of Public Health*, 91, 2001, p.933-939; T.G.M. SANDFORT, R. DE GRAAF, R.V. BIJL, P. SCHNABEL, "Same-Sex Sexual Behavior Psychiatric Disorders—Findings from the Netherlands Mental Health Survey and Incidence Study (NEMESIS)," in *Archives of General Psychiatry*, 58, 2001, p.85-91; R. DE GRAAF, T.G.M. SANDFORT, M. TEN HAVE, "Suicidality and Sexual Orientation: Differences Between Men and Women in a General Population-Based Sample from the Netherlands," in *Archives of Sexual Behavior*, 35, 2006, p.253-262; M. KING, E. MCKEOWN, J. WARNER, A. RAMSAY, K. JOHNSON, C. CORT, L. WRIGHT, R. BLIZARD. O. DAVIDSON, "Mental Health and Quality of Life of Gay Men and Lesbian in England and Wales—Controlled, Cross-Sectional Study," in *British Journal of Psychiatry*, 183, 2003, p.552-558.

AN INTERVIEW WITH DINA NEROZZI*

"Gender theory" and same-sex attraction anchor their arguments in an egalitarianism that identifies sexual difference as a pretext for discrimination. This approach becomes as much a wall as a strategy, forestalling inquiry into the questions of SSA. Are we still allowed to inquire about SSA today?

Same-sex attraction understood as a prevalent and persistent attraction toward people of the same sex has become a difficult topic to discuss accurately, above all because it has been politicized. At a time when political considerations enter into science, which aims at understanding human and social phenomena, it becomes difficult, if not impossible, to create a shared platform since all research will then be compared to either similar or opposing data. In this situation the studies, including the most serious ones, end up being marginalized, leaving the decision to politics. The task then becomes one of standardizing social phenomena according to a worldview regardless of scientific results.

This is the mechanism behind "political correctness," which stands in sharp contrast to a reality based upon principles of objectivity and non-contradiction. This is also the reason why it is preferable to address the issue on the basis of fundamental considerations of an anatomical and physiological nature. The physiological basis of human sexuality has been obscured by the smokescreen surrounding the issue of SSA. This impedes the correct setting for dialogue in the scientific field, though this does not mean purely biological notions are, of themselves, able to explain the complexity of this human and social phenomenon.

The most debated issue concerns whether same-sex attraction is a purely biological fact. Is it?

It is perhaps worth recalling that the human being is a mystery in his or her complexity. It is thus a mistake to consider it possible to circumscribe human behavior, itself the result of numerous factors, within the bounds of

* Professor of Psycho-Neuro-Endocrinology at Roma Tor Vergata University, child psychiatrist and endocrinologist, as well as consultor of the Pontifical Council for the Family.

some esoteric equation. Like all complex behaviors, even attraction towards people of the same sex is multifactorial. Thus, it is neither exclusively biological nor exclusively psychological or environmental. It would be more accurate to say that it is the result of a hard-to-quantify mix of differing factors involved during critical stages of development: genetic, environmental and cultural, as well as the results of individual choices.

That is why it is preferable to speak of people having a same-sex orientation in some broad sense since what motivates a person to prioritize one behavior over another is multiple and difficult to verify within some single formula. Thus, every person with a same-sex orientation has his or her own story and motivation that must be understood individually.

How has same-sex attraction passed from being considered a deviation to a neutral "variant" of sexuality?

SSA persons are nothing new in the social landscape. They represent a reality that has always existed and always will exist. What changes over time is the interpretation of this phenomenon, as well as social reactions to it.

In the past it was framed as a perversion of the sexual instinct, and not without some reason since the sexual instinct is the indispensable means for achieving the conservation of the species, and no one doubts that the sexual and reproductive apparatus have procreation as their ultimate terminus. If you look at the anatomy and physiology of the human body, you see a sexual and reproductive system (male and female differences with their complementarities) that is not the same as, say, the gastro-intestinal system (the same for both sexes). This explains why male SSA has been considered a distortion of human physiology. Given the morally negative connotation of the term perversion, a signal of greater social tolerance toward this reality was indicated when we moved to its medicalization. In other words, this phenomenon was classified as a disorder of the sexual instinct, to be corrected by psychological or medical intervention. A further decisive step toward social acceptance was made when SSA was no longer classified as a pathology but rather as an individual life option. In a more "liberal" society, everyone is free to choose how to live out one's sexual gratification. Behavioral sciences established the non-existence of sexual deviations, redefining these as different lifestyles.

According to a psychologist specializing on this issue, if humans were left to express their sexual orientation, culture would change and any behavior would be accepted by society and considered normal. According to this cultural vision, different lifestyles represent merely a matter of social definition, so some behaviors are considered acceptable while others are condemned. This vision forgets that anatomy and physiology are not insignificant details of the human body and cannot be easily set aside.

When it comes to people experiencing same-sex feelings, not everyone automatically employs the term "gay." Could you clarify the meaning of this term?

The gay movement was born alongside the sexual revolution of the late 1960s.

Being "gay" meant a happy and carefree lifestyle proper to people with SSA and had also become a political symbol meant to claim the liberation of humanity from the "stereotypes" of binary sexuality. The "gaiety" of the LGB liberation movement was in crisis by the 1980s when the reality of sexual liberation emerged: the AIDS epidemic, which mainly concerned the LGB world and the world of drug addiction. The prior definition of gaiety had to be abandoned when people with same-sex orientation began to demand the right to have children and be considered a "family." At that point "gay" was no longer the previous banner of gaiety, but now came to mean "just as good as you are," according to the egalitarian criterion imposed by a now politically correct (but scientifically questionable) world.

Some studies strive to indicate the existence of a genetic basis for same-sex attraction. What validity do they have?

The liberal cultural approach had failed in its task of ensuring LGBT people were considered "mainstream" in the eyes of the general public. To achieve full acceptance of same-sex attraction, a whole "scientific" literature flourished in the 90s claiming they were born that way and, therefore, SSA was a "natural" fact just like heterosexuality. By that point, having SSA had been transformed into a constitutive part of the person, not a behavior soliciting a response. Though subsequent studies denied the scientific validity of the "born that way" theory, falling into a mutual de-legitimization game, there is one element that should cause us to reflect on deterministic views of the phenomenon. While "born that way theory" was invoked for male SSA persons as a biological justification for a lifestyle, the position regarding female SSA changed radically. The latter slogan became "Biology is not destiny"—precisely the opposite of the former position. This inconsistency of positions was due to the simple fact the aim of the research conducted was not to discover the laws of nature, or even the reason for the deviance. Rather, researchers working in this field were motivated solely by a political end, namely, to advance their own social claims.

Do male and female same-sex attractions have the same matrix or do they differ, since man and woman are differently sexed?

Before answering that question, it is necessary to make some introductory remarks. Sexual instinct is an irrepressible force of nature that combines the pursuit of pleasure with the conservation of the species. In the animal world it is a pure instinct and, as such, not subject to censorship. For human beings, on the contrary, the sexual drive is tempered by a rational nature to help characterize it. A human being is not helpless before instincts but rather, as a rational being, can evaluate the consequences of his or her actions and implement self-censorship. The rational person can avoid implementing behaviors that may offer fleeting pleasure, but for which the consequences can be painful and long-lasting.

Proponents of sexual and same-sex revolutions assume that a human being is just like an animal, denying the existence of a moral value attributable to different behaviors. They demand freedom for everyone to act according to one's wishes. For the progressive liberal world, all behaviors are considered equal; the difference consists in the basic motivations behind male and female same-sex behavior.

Male same-sex behavior seems to be mainly dictated by a need to give free rein to the sex drive and, at the same time, to avoid its possible physiological consequences—the creation of a new life. So pleasure is sought without fear of the responsibility deriving from it. This kind of attitude might also include a sign of respect for the physiology of the female body which one may not wish to violate, well aware that the result of the sexual act can mean bringing a new life into being.

In nature there are also people born with a drive originally and specifically directed toward people of the same sex, but these would be a small minority representing a biological and psychological mystery within the current realm of knowledge. It is difficult, in fact, to understand motivations because the elements involved in such a complex behavior are varied and difficult to fathom. Whatever motivation leads toward same-sex behaviors, biology does not prevent the occurrence of sexually transmitted diseases. This happens because the organs involved do not have the protection mechanisms—glandular, muscular and immune—necessary for such physiological interaction.

Female same-sex attraction seems to have different motivations and can primarily be identified as a refusal to follow the rules of biology, by which females may get pregnant following sexual intercourse with males. Females with SSA escape from this intolerable inequality by choosing to have sexual enjoyment with a same-sex partner. Although the reasons can differ, this seems to be the most appropriate interpretation of our time, when this phenomenon assumes a swathe of political and social claims.

From these two positions one can also understand why there are different cultural settings at the base of male and female claims: "Born that way" for the former and "Biology is not destiny" for the latter.

What are the historical and cultural origins of LGBT claims?

With *The Origin of Species by Means of Natural Selection, or the Preservation of favored races in the Struggle for Existence* by Charles Darwin in 1859, a new interpretation of reality was born. Living species were not fixed in their creation, as they had been viewed for thousands of years, but rather were subject to an evolutionary process. Nature provided a selection of stronger individuals through sexual selection to the detriment of inferior ones. It is essential to turn back to Darwin and Lamarck to understand the cultural setting of our time, one that provided the adaptation of species to the environment in which they lived and worked. Without understanding the root of the liberal progressive movement, it is impossible to understand the demands that come from that world.

Though the Darwinian hypothesis has never been proven beyond scientific doubt, it has entered the textbooks of the natural sciences and represents the scientific legitimacy of the liberal progressive political movement. According to the evolutionary approach, we can maintain "the magnificent and progressive fate of human beings" with a constant, unstoppable trajectory. We can predict its direction and facilitate its implementation.

Darwin applied his theory of evolution to plants, animals and humans, an evolution that was intended not just biologically but also psychologically, morally and socially. So-called social Darwinism in the last century was used as a scientific basis for the theory of racial superiority, the consequences of which we are familiar with.

And in the psychological field?

Sigmund Freud was a follower of Darwin as well as the researcher who made the biggest effort to understand the mysteries of human sexuality.

Freud pointed out a common and real element involved when sexuality is lived in a "free" way: fear of unwanted pregnancy. This is a reality a majority of humans in adulthood confront and is the reason Freud once said humanity would have reached one of its greatest achievements when it invented something that would prevent the consequences of the sexual act. (In fact, he believed that mental disorders were the result of the repression of sexual impulses.) In the modern world this goal has largely been achieved, albeit without the result anticipated and desired by Sigmund Freud—a population with fewer mental disorders.

His prediction of the reduction of mental disorders as a consequence of sexual liberalization[1] was wrong, as was the subdivision of sexual maturation into three stages: oral, anal and phallic, greatly debated and studied by many psychologists and psychiatrists over the past hundred years. The phases of sexual maturation developed by Freud are nothing more than a development of Ernst Haeckel's three stages of embryonic evolution. According to Haeckel, "Ontogeny is a brief recapitulation of phylogeny," in which ontogeny means the body's development and phylogeny the development of that species to which the individual belongs.

What we are witnessing in the postmodern world is the restoration of social Darwinism adapted to the current circumstances. Everything evolves, including biology, psychology, morality and, through these mechanisms, society. Given this fact, from Malthus onwards, the greatest danger humanity faces is alleged to be the excess of population, with the evolutionary process proposing a reduction of planetary population. If the planet's good requires a reduction in population, then evolution must promote all those sexual activities that are naturally sterile. This reduction in population is achieved not just through a reduction in birth rate but also through an elimination of persons who absorb economic resources and so represent a burden for society. In such a situation euthanasia is a useful way out of this problem, due to both the waste of resources and an excess of population.

In summary, the question of same-sex attraction ought to be framed within a coherent worldview attuned to reality and not to the ephemeral majority of current policy. In this task, we should allow science and not political correctness to dominate, something that has not been happening in this specific area for far too long.

---

[1] Editor's Note: On the one hand, Sigmund Freud's daughter, Anna Freud, did not believe her father intended a program of sexual liberation. On the other hand, Jerome Neu of the University of California at Santa Cruz has chosen to disagree. E.g., see his chapter "Freud and Perversion" in J. Neu (ed.), The Cambridge Companion to Freud, Cambridge University Press, Cambridge UK 1991.

PART V

THE FAMILY AND EDUCATION

FURIO PESCI*

THE FAMILY AND AFFECTIVE EDUCATION

1. "Creating Families"

According to Maria Montessori, young people must, by the end of adolescence, have set themselves a life goal of "creating families."[1] Taking Montessori's proposal seriously, we can contextualize countless problems pertaining to relations between the sexes.

Framing it within an anthropologically and ethically adequate perspective can foster a harmonious conception of female-male difference, as well as address all those opportunities this can offer for a just society. It is an opportunity in which such a difference does not become warped into a pretext for either unwarranted disparities, nor arbitrary abstractions.

Maria Montessori's words facilitate the relation of two curiously concurrent phenomena. Today, on the one hand, young people, at least in mostly Western countries (though, via globalization, more or less everywhere), enjoy an autonomy that previous generations did not enjoy. On the other hand, this autonomy is lived out and enacted in ways that offer several parallels to immature trends and attitudes. Young people are allowed to manage their time and relationships with others, especially peers, availing themselves of very broad freedoms. Yet their emotional, cultural and economic conditions scarcely differ from those of childhood. Economic crises have diffused and prolonged this situation, which can last up to the age of thirty, or above.

These are not just the musings of a "conservative" spirit. One can find similar analyses even among such significant landmarks of secular progressive culture as Hannah Arendt[2] and Nel Noddings.[3] While dutifully distinguishing

* Furio Pesci is Associate Professor of the History of Pedagogy in the Department of Psychology of Development and Socialization Processes at La Sapienza University in Rome. He is President of the Scientific Committee of the Montessori Foundation in Italy, as well as a member of scientific committees for the publication of *History of Education* and *Children's Literature* and *Ethos*.

1 M. Montessori, *Dall'infanzia all'adolescenza*, Garzanti, Milan 1949, p.158. [English edition: *From Childhood to Adolescence*, The Clio Montessori Series, ABC-CLIO, USA 1994.]

2 H. Arendt, *Between Past and Future*, Viking, New York 1961.

3 N. Noddings, *Happiness and Education*, Cambridge University Press, Cambridge 2003.

tints and shades between these scholars, one notices a united concern about increasing "autonomy" given by parents, teachers and adults to young people.

This concern primarily proceeds from the fact that the autonomy left to the youngest is almost always an "end in itself," rather than empowering them to achieve maturation. Through experiences lived in the name of such autonomy, relationships between the generations fray or even snap, owing mainly to endless economic dependence. Meanwhile, the timeline for assuming adult responsibilities—the only thing that truly catalyzes a person's full and sensible freedom—remains distant, confined to an abstract horizon without any relationship to the present.

As Maria Montessori notes, we are left with a generation of young adults who still live like "kids." We are training a generation of teenagers who will be succeeded by future generations following in the footsteps of a "prolonged adolescence" of temporally indeterminate boundaries. There is an absence of authority characterizing parental and educational relationships alike. In addition, in the prospect is poor that young people will exercise personal responsibility fully and concretely towards oneself and others.

Statistical data shows that this lack of responsibility contributes to genuine emotional insecurity. About out one of every two marriages ends in divorce. In addition, among divorced people who remarry the experience of divorce is repeated twice over on average. This is a novel phenomenon even for countries with a long history of divorce. Introduced in the late nineteenth century as "innovative legislation," couples in crisis had not resorted to widespread divorce the way they have these last twenty years. According to Bauman, the divorce phenomenon seems unstoppable now that people everywhere have begun to think in terms of precariousness, flexibility and change—even attributing a positive significance to such "magic" words.[4] This ideology of "change" is especially difficult to confront in education.

2. The Historical Roots

Our starting point for reflection on education can be the analysis of the contemporary social situation we mentioned above. Yet knowledge and awareness of current events beg for historical analysis, that is, for looking at how modern subjectivism and individualism influence ethics and education.

This historical account begins with the seventeenth century as the age of subjectivism, both theoretically and ethically. All modern thought has a

[4] Z. Bauman, *Liquid Love: On the Frailty of Human Bonds*, Polity Press, Cambridge 2003.

subjectivist character insisting that an objective truth does not exist, to the point of denying the existence of objective reality itself. It assumes human understanding of reality, indeed of any truth, to be conditioned and linked to perceptual capacity. Kant distinguishes the world of ideas in themselves from the world of phenomena. In Kantian thought phenomena alone have real consistency. Only that which appears to the subject is "true," and there is no truth apart from the subject.

This context does not emerge from "anywhere." Within an interpersonal context it exists in function of certain social and economic dynamics. Coincidentally, the great philosophers of the seventeenth and eighteenth centuries were largely members of emerging classes in the worlds of commerce and manufacture, which had displaced the nobility's preeminence in social and economic life and ultimately fought their way to political recognition.[5] The Enlightenment was not just an ideological movement. It was a political movement decanting into the great democratic revolutions. The French and the American revolutions were also partially motivated by economic considerations. One might call liberalism an application of Enlightenment economics.

A constant in the last two centuries, from the nineteenth century onward, is the profound transformation of thought. First, it was of lone intellectuals, then it progressed to large swathes of the population. Subjectivism took some time to develop. During the seventeenth and eighteenth centuries, the idea of individual initiative and freedom was established in all fields of society (speculative matters, morality, politics, economics). The foundations of contemporary individualism are found in the minds of the great British empiricists Locke and Hume and in those of French thinkers.[6]

Charles Taylor describes in detail the history of these ideas and their social impact.[7] We must take into account the individualistic component of Western thought from the seventeenth century till now in order to understand the force of secular or secularist positions in bioethics today. For example, the

[5] C. Lasch, *The True and Only Heaven: Progress and Its Critics, Norton*, New York 1991; *The Culture of Narcissism*, Norton, New York 1979; *The Minimal Self*, Norton, New York 1984; *The Rebellion of the Elites and the Betrayal of Democracy*, Norton, New York 1995.

[6] See MacIntyre's precise reconstructions of individualism's historic progress in the modern era. E.g., A. MacIntyre, *After Virtue*, University of Notre Dame Press, Notre Dame IN 1981; Id., *Whose Justice? Which Rationality?* University of Notre Dame Press, Notre Dame IN 1988; Id., *Three Rival Versions of Moral Enquiry: Genealogy, Encyclopedia, and Tradition*, University of Notre Dame Press, Notre Dame IN 1990.

[7] C. Taylor, *Sources of the Self. The Making of Modern Identity*, Harvard University Press, Cambridge, MA 1989; *The Ethics of Authenticity*, Harvard University Press, Cambridge, MA 1992; *A Secular Age*, Harvard University Press, Cambridge, MA 2007.

moral arguments for justifying euthanasia or assisted suicide can be understood by reference to the individualistic visions of man and the world.

According to "official" modern education theory, the first task that each individual must fulfill is to realize him or herself. It is not only legitimate but even a moral duty that we raise children to become autonomous. In keeping with prevailing theory, autonomy is the primary goal of education. For too many specialists, children must become as independent and creative as possible, the sooner the better.

Creativity can be as insidious an idea as it is sacrosanct. How should it be defined? Despite their vagueness, such key words are also found in official documents of the European Union—not just in educational treaties but also in policy statements. Professionalism means working in order to acquire a certain level of wealth (or well-being), and with these resources you can create the life you "want." All the efforts of educational activity in school, and often in the family, are focused upon this as a coherent whole.

3. Returning to Fundamental Questions about Happiness and the Virtues

There would likely be a profound change if we were to reestablish the links between ethics and happiness, and between virtue and happiness.

A moralistic approach has prevailed in modern ethics due to the weakening of ethical foundations caused by a subjectivist hegemony and moralistic approach. In other words, this approach is deprived of its vital link to the roots of "classical" ethics. In modern and postmodern pedagogical vocabulary, one speaks of "law" and "duties" (in education we usually talk about "rules"). They all exist for a reason, but rules are not merely constraints. Ideally, they proceed from a positive, personal attitude of awareness that rules can guide one towards a personal pursuit of happiness. Only in transcending the rule can one tell the difference between true happiness and false happiness. Otherwise, it is undeniable that one can also be happy while violating the rules.

This conception of "duty," so greatly magnified in philosophical thought, was established during modernity in order to balance the moral consequences of subjectivism. Kant, for example, maintains that before the demands of the categorical imperative, happiness itself is not a moral goal. To seek happiness is immoral; rather, duty should be followed even in opposition to happiness itself. It is on this basis that Kant erases the idea of virtue. He did not believe that a greater good can be achieved through independent actions without recurrence to universal principles and maxims.

Faced with such an impasse, recent moral and practical philosophy has brought the idea of virtue back to the center of attention, demonstrating that the realization of a desire for happiness involves a philosophical dimension of considerable depth. This in turn extends to an existential understanding of what philosophical tradition calls the "transcendentals"—that truth, beauty, justice and goodness are the "substance" of which all goods are fashioned and are found in all objects of human desire.

To understand the nature, goals, and current problems facing education, we begin with an anthropological and ethical analysis of educational work. The foundation for this perspective can serve as the background for what some philosophers call "dynamic action."[8] The background of classical philosophy is retrieved within such a perspective that roots ethics in virtue, understood as that which facilitates correct human action appropriate to the place and time. The virtuous person is one who does the right thing at the right time. This ability demonstrates a transcendent dimension, since a virtuous person has the virtue of constitutive openness toward others like herself.

All this is true at the psychological level since the actual self, as much as the ideal self, develops through interaction with others. An individual learns what is good within a community. To achieve such awareness, there need to be flesh and blood models. Such models are usually found in the family, mainly parents and family members. This "rule" also applies to negative models. It is easier to become a smoker in a household that smokes or to become a drug addict in a group of drug addicts, even though such conditioning is not mandatory.

René Girard's mimetic theory views this process as non-deterministic given that each person assumes a "stance" toward others. This is to say that when we assimilate the behavior of another person perceived as a role model, we assume a stance toward him or her. We hope to be or not to be like that model.[9] Positive influences can occur beyond family boundaries due to interaction with other people.

4. Evolution of the Moral Subject

Surprisingly, many people find it very difficult to admit nowadays that certain decisions could have absolute values. As we find in Wojtyla's philosophy, eternity is seized and fulfilled in the present moment. The very signifi-

[8] E.g., see the aforementioned MacIntyre and Taylor.

[9] R. Girard, *Des choses cachées depuis la fondation du monde*, Grasset & Fasquelle, Paris 1978.

cance of ethics itself consists precisely in an awareness of this eruption of the Absolute and Eternal into the flow of life and history.[10] While it is true that considerations must always be contextualized with respect to individual condition and concrete situation, people today do not seem to be aware of this deeper reality. Even if the accumulation of available options is indefinitely large and complex, they should still recognize that their fundamental choice for the good—which gives real meaning to life in the broadest sense—is exclusive and absolute.

While culture can offer valid values and meaning to existence in an absolute sense and can shield it from mere individual caprice, educational experience teaches us that personal choice is unavoidable.

This absoluteness is not taken for granted, as human beings are characterized by radical freedom. At the pedagogical level, there is always the typical risk of each new generation of youth wanting to follow the proposal of the adults. On the other hand, there is dialectic such that a multiplicity of particular goods, with an identifiable absolute good or priority, may find their "synthesis" in the fundamental meaning ascribed to existence.

These considerations can be applied to individual developmental stages, albeit with the inevitable qualifications. Above all, we need role models, people who to some extent embody those goods so as to point out the meaning of life, as well as showing others the means to achieve them.[11]

Regardless of its nature and context, education is a relationship between a subject and a role model in light of the good itself. The question arises regarding the nature of the good, its authenticity or inauthenticity. The same learning process is presented here in a form that is anything but linear. It becomes comprehensible only under the light of a conscious dynamic involving the constitutive temporal dimension of human life and its changing experience.

To escape from the relentlessness of this precarious and uncertain condition, mainstream pedagogical traditions have always presented models to be "normative," to be perceived by others in this way. Educational relationship implies recognition of an asymmetry that, instead of creating distance, offers direction and positive experience by those who adapt it.

In the formation of personality, the individual is confronted by (and produced by) a triadic dialogue in which the subject, a self-same individual, cor-

[10] K. Wojtyla, *Metafisica della persona*, Bompiani, Milan 2003. Other significant philosophical works of Wojtyla used for this essay include *Love and Responsibility*, 1961, and *Person and Act*, 1969.

[11] This question deserves more extensive commentary. Here I will continue to refer to MacIntyre's and Girard's works, at least to indicate the broad outlines for what follows.

responds to a role model. The role model is a bearer of the community's tradition and instantiations, embodying these and giving life to them, directing attention to specific goods and values, sharing in meanings the community itself holds, and serving as a guarantor of its identity.

Regardless of the variety of forms through which this delicate game of permission and prohibition is reflected in the history of Western culture, ethics so outlined—in light of basic ideas of good and virtue—has served as a foundation for education from time immemorial. Even today learning processes are characterized by an ethic of permissions and prohibitions, role models, values and shared meanings.

Any historical realization and embodiment finds echo in the awareness that the education of desire in view of some good (the real one) is education in "the virtues." A state of life is valid inasmuch as it is characterized by these virtues, i.e., those effective dispositions empowering one to live according to a shared model.

The Judeo-Christian spiritual tradition, for example, clearly states that the final objective of education, in view of happiness and the fulfillment of desire, is the gift of oneself in love. Paradoxically, the man who would "fulfill" himself must put his will aside in order to "transcend himself," to use an expression dear to Viktor Frankl. It means to go outside oneself in order to find the path to one's authentic fulfillment.[12] It is only in surrendering one's will that one can find happiness and not otherwise.

The alternative to this road, which promises full happiness and the blessedness of which the Gospel speaks, is a life at the mercy of desires caught up within a jumble of impulses that an intelligence void of direction cannot contain. Thus, the opposite of virtue is Girard's mimetic paroxysm, shaped by envy, jealousy and pride, according to the Christian catalog of vices. This vision incorporates a wisdom tracing back to classical culture itself.

It can be argued on this basis that there are two basic paths claiming to offer self-fulfillment. One way is self-centered and lacking in a future, the other decentralized and aimed at the complete fulfillment of oneself through dedication. This claim establishes a system for negative patterns (those who are self-centered) and for positive patterns (those directed toward something else—people and objects—ultimately toward the *Other*), in accordance with

[12] V. Frankl, *The Doctor and the Soul*, Vintage Books, New York 1980. For a specifically pedagogic perspective of Frankl's logotherapy, see D. Bruzzone, *Autotrascendenza e formazione*, Vita e Pensiero, Milan 2001.

pedagogical views that had characterized the central core of education in Western Christian countries.

5. Family Life According to "Character Education"

This anthropological and ethical perspective has been contextualized for education by the Character Education Movement, especially strong in the United States, and serving as a vessel for principles we can identify with. Lickona's reflection on family educational needs begins with the eminently realistic consideration that it is not necessary to be perfect parents. An American scholar and the director of a major university center in New York, Lickona has written books enjoying broad influence, such as *Character Matters* and *Educating for Character*. What follows is a brief presentation of principles and best practices for parents' day-to-day behavior.[13]

According to Lickona we must first become aware that the family is the first "school" where virtues are learned. From this standpoint family life is clearly invaluable. While love is naturally inherent in the human soul, the ability to care and effectively educate children is not.

Wise considerations and advice can be extremely useful, recognizing, first, that children do not need to see a "perfect" model, but simply someone *striving* to do his or her best. An insistence on removing any anxiety over perfectionism, as well as any fear of failure as a result of one's own inadequacy, is a recurring theme in Lickona's works. Parents do not "create" their children, they can only put them on the right track. The final shape of one's personality remains in the hands of that person.

As a result, the basic principle to follow in character education is knowing what constitutes good character, and to make its development a top priority. Lickona talks about ten essential virtues defining good character: wisdom (the ability to judge well); justice (as expressed by the golden rule); inner fortitude; self-control; love (the ability to give and sacrifice oneself for others); positive opening to others; ability to work hard; integrity (honesty and sincerity towards oneself); gratitude; and humility (the desire to improve).

Character (personality as a whole) serves to achieve positive results, consisting of giving the best of oneself in what one does and developing the moral conduct required for the most beautiful relationships. To make the development of personality a priority, a long-term perspective is required—understanding that parents themselves are adults who are growing. Adults who are

[13] T. Lickona, *Educating for Character*, Bantham Books, New York 1991; *Character Matters*, Simon and Schuster, New York 2004.

treated over-indulgently as children have difficulty coping with life's hardships, because they have distorted the sense of commitment it takes to do well in work and interpersonal relationships.

It is therefore necessary to be open to a family culture centered on character education and firmly committed to avoiding habitual complaining, excuse-making, lying, cheating, stealing or harming others. Positively put, what is required is learning from one's mistakes; working to be mentally, physically and spiritually healthy; being committed to the growth and development of one's individual potential, with an attitude of utter gratitude and ethically justified joy, as much as it is on the level of personal religious faith.[14]

6. The moral aspect of education

The second principle to which Lickona refers is the care of personal faith.[15] Religion has a strong impact on personality. American statistics show that teens who regularly observe the practices of their religion are more involved and engaged in pro-social service activities, less prone to steal, to violence, to the use of drugs and alcohol, and to risky sexual behaviors. Adults must openly manifest what they believe and why. Children seek and need accurate, well-argued answers concerning God, whatever the religious choices of those adults who care for them.

The third principle for an effective education is simply to live a happy marriage founded on love, respect and trust. Lickona realizes that there are numerous single parents at the present time. In each case, though, it is necessary to support children emotionally. One should be firm but not cruel in discipline. The parent should know where the kids are and what they are doing. These indications may seem difficult to achieve, if not atypical. Yet in descending to concrete details, Lickona suggests consistently scheduling face-to-face time with one's spouse on a daily basis, not necessarily to contest differing perspectives or tough decisions but just to stay "in touch" with each other, sharing the thoughts and feelings of the day. We need to work on communicating, understanding one another's needs, understanding the reasons behind conflict. ("Active" listening as a useful practice between spouses is recommended.)

One aspect Lickona highlights is the moment of reconciliation and forgiveness. Harmonious families have rituals to quickly forgive and overcome differences, thanks to an ability to seek forgiveness, embrace, make peace, etc.

---

[14] "Character" means personality.

[15] From an ecumenical as well as a confessional perspective.

Parents must work together in this, sharing parenting concerns, supporting each other, and, if differences arise on how to handle a situation with their child, discussing this privately—not in front of the children.

A fourth basic principle is to love children by supporting them, giving them time, talking to them and sacrificing oneself for them. In practical terms, this principle is reflected in supporting their interests, which is an authentic way to love and respect them. Appreciating and cultivating children's sports, talents or other interests helps young people to develop their personal identity. To prevent children from rebelling against their parents due to a lack of understanding, we must help them develop their interests and identity, ensuring that praise exceeds criticism. It is always good for parents to tell their children what they love and appreciate about them, the way they have seen them grow during the previous year, and the talents and energies they have seen emerge.

Psychological intimacy and time spent face-to-face with children is needed as well. Activities, games, sports or other pastimes—even when enjoyed together—do not fulfill these needs.

Every week we should find ways to spend family time doing something everyone enjoys together. It is fundamental to take care of communication, with respect to which Lickona offers readers and listeners extremely practical means for triggering a virtuous circle that helps kids open up. Talking together over lunch or dinner about positive things that happened during the day, the experiences of having helped someone, things to be thankful for, or daily problems, and the support that family members can offer in this regard are other experiences that can be easily practiced within the daily life of most families. Reading Lickona's words, one wonders if the society to which he refers has lost all common sense, to the point of needing "expert" help in suggesting activities to mitigate the relational difficulties that wind up choking family relationships.

Hence Lickona's call to sacrifice, motivated by his observation that the most important thing parents can do for children is to love them and spend time together.

7. Parent-child relationship

The fifth principle enunciated by Lickona includes an invitation to authority. Parents should have a strong sense of their own moral authority, as well as of the right to be respected and obeyed. Lickona recalls Diana Baumrind's research on parenting "styles": authoritarian, permissive or authoritative. Authoritative parents are characterized by a style that unites love, confident authority, reinforcement of rules, reasoning in adapting to them, attention to children's feelings when expressed with respect, parents having the "last word," and the encouragement of an appropriate self-confidence. Those granted the most trust and responsibility in every respect are those who have authoritative parents. In general, his advice is never to tolerate disrespectful speech or behavior.

In fact, children ought always to speak respectfully to parents, both in content and in tone, thinking "ahead" about the consequences of disrespectful behavior. Lickona's constant advice is to insist on respect, courtesy and kindness in all relationships within the family. One ought not to tolerate disrespect or disobedience toward parents, rough manners, nicknames, insults, nor any failings in kindness toward siblings.

The sixth principle is to teach by example. The stances we take define the values we believe in. Parents need to ask themselves whether their children really understand the stances they take, the way they think about respect for life, about poverty, about the environment or war.

This principle is also linked to the seventh: the effective management of a moral environment. For example, informed supervision of children's activities can never be underestimated. The more teenagers are motivated in their school work and exercise responsible behavior, the more difficult it is to indulge in risky behaviors. Children should develop warm, engaged relationships with parents who in turn must set clear expectations and monitor their activities in an age-appropriate way. The reason for this is that they are influenced by the friends they hang out with—to the point that a teenager can literally morph into his or her friends. So, it is useful to raise the question regarding what a "true" friend is, and how he or she differs from a false friend, by sharing life stories between parents and children.

Another factor to take into serious consideration is the critical influence of the media. It is estimated that in the United States (but similarly elsewhere) a child views about a hundred advertisements a day on average and the usage of electronic devices among the young averages seven hours daily. In many Western countries three-quarters of middle school aged boys have a television in their own room. In the midst of this situation we encounter results from scientific studies claiming that children viewing violent television programs are also the most violent among their peers and lack empathy towards others as a result of exposure to violent actions and behaviors. Analogously, teens regularly viewing pornographic content become sexually active more easily.

It is necessary to set precise limits to media usage in the day-to-day lives of children. Such usage should be a privilege, not a right. It is a privilege requiring parental permission; media must affirm family values; the viewing of programs contradicting such values must not be allowed. Night time should be a calming time of day spent without television. To watch television should be a special family event, not a normatively private pastime. It is likewise beneficial to establish reasonable limits to the Internet, video games, even telephone usage, as well as for all the many technological tools now available. Confronted with the media's moral decay, rules and expectations should be explained till it is clear that one does not allow films with sexual or violent content. You should insist they abide by this out of respect for you, since you take care of them and do not wish them to assimilate mentally unhygienic material any more than you want their bodies ingesting harmful foods. Lickona recommends considering the possibility of not having TVs in the home, given that children—by definition—are not grownups.

Supervision and control of the media should be clearly recognized by children as being for their good; their online activities should be monitored; they should be encouraged to inform their friends of this arrangement.

7. Specified Emotional Education and Relating to the Opposite Sex

The eighth principle concerns the use of teaching and discussion for the development of an awareness that takes years and years of constant teaching and careful self-examination. In large part this is a matter of consistency. It is necessary to practice what one preaches.

Yet the reverse is also true: what is practiced should be verbalized and its value explained. For this reason, it is as useful as it is appropriate to instruct the young in empathy. Positively, and in concrete terms, this means it is important to elicit honesty, recommending that one not lie, cheat, steal, complain in adverse moments when things go wrong, or produce excuses and self-justifications. Lickona recommends a non-coercive approach wherein parents, rather than offering statements of principle, use questions and dialogue and have children arrive at the correct conclusion themselves.

The same approach can be used to discuss fundamental issues. You can ask children why it is wrong to cheat, for example. Or you can collect and appreciate feedback on the seriousness of breaking trust as an injustice toward the honest, or in recognition of the fact that falsity reduces the self-respect of those committing such actions. Yet discussion can also be used to argue about the negative reasons of emerging behaviors among young people, such as substance abuse, drawing ethical and existential considerations from such examples.

Lickona claims that this is the way one successfully resolves the increasingly controverted question of sexual abstinence. Sexuality is such a special aspect of human life that it demands its own environment. When one is married sexual intimacy expresses the total involvement of oneself with another, and this complete intimacy depends upon the absoluteness of a mutual commitment between the spouses.

U.S. statistics indicate the attempted suicide rate as six times higher among girls ages 12-16 years who have had sexual intercourse than among their virgin peers. Teenagers themselves can recognize advantages and benefits to waiting: increased self-respect; respect for others; a clear conscience; no guilt; no remorse; as well as developing a personality type that incorporates such virtues as respect, self-control, modesty and strength, which attract people possessing the same characteristics and virtues. Lickona also advises raising questions regarding the truth about love, helping young people examine whether their love is real love, posing questions about mutual respect and kindness, about the expectations and confidence one is able to place in another, about sharing the same principles, as well as about the actual will to marry and have children.

The ninth principle described by Lickona consists of a wise discipline based on consistent rules regarding normal daily activities: helping clean up after meals; answering the phone politely; not yelling across rooms; drawing closer to the person (e.g., one's spouse or child) with whom one wishes to speak; not leaving clothes out of place but hanging them in the closet, reaching out to others with courtesy ("May I ...?" is preferable to "I want..."). When children do something wrong, you can invite them to apologize, explaining why the reason is due to their actions, as well as how to do something to make amends. It is also important to have them reflect on the consequences of actions performed.

The tenth principle is to provide opportunities for children to practice the virtues. Teens develop a personality through what they see, feel and are inclined to do routinely. Responsibility must be taught. The reward and execution of small activities and tasks is one way to contribute to family life and should not be rewarded with cash. Children should, however, also perform services outside the home. As you see, this practical advice is very useful, simple and easy to apply in any family situation where common sense prevails.[16] Reading several of Lickona's proposed interventions one gets the impression that, if today academic experts must provide information on the management of those relationships that should be the most natural to all human existence, then parents have largely lost or forgotten what once was common sense. Still, these are the times in which we live, and we must not be shocked by anything, nor incline toward that kind of moralism that, left to itself, will always be sterile.

8. A new and disquieting question

Unfortunately, the current situation suggests new problems that, some years ago, could not even be imagined, at least in our country, and that require a discussion (however brief) within these pages.[17] The introduction of gender theory into Italian schools poses a series of pedagogical questions not easily ignored, though the current political climate and public opinion do not seem engaged in any thorough discussion of them.

First, recent events have highlighted that any initiative on this issue not agreed upon and shared within a school by its multiple constituencies (primarily parents, teachers and pupils) is likely to produce negative—even perverse—results. However, organizations promoting gender theory—essentially LGBT associations among others—have seized upon a diversity of paths for penetrating schools.

Gender has been transformed into a topic for confrontation offering little benefit to Italian education, and producing far from positive results. We are obliged to say the process of its introduction into Italian schools is completely ideological, answering to indoctrination requirements rather than to genuine education. What is the purpose of putting lipstick on boys' lips in nursery schools? Or of reading stories that instill doubts as to whether their parents are have latent same-sex attractions, or whether surrogacy is a form of charity toward people who "desire" a child?

The open support provided by some politicians and governmental groups to the position papers of LGBT organizations, as well as the arrogance with which they have tried, at times even by fraudulent means, to propagate pro-gender initiatives, can only be judged negatively and as constituting an obstacle to the education of the young people of our country.

---

[16] For more on Character Education see: L. Nucci, D. Narvaez (eds.), *Handbook of Moral and Character Education* Routledge, New York 2008.

[17] See other specific contributions in this book.

The deployment of significant financial resources in this area is one of the most puzzling elements of this anti-educational design. While millions of euros are invested in such projects, which are void of any scientific reliability and lacking any trace of experimental verification, our schools are forced to raise funds needed for their most pressing needs through informal fundraising by parents "off the books."

In addition, the space offered to "anti-homophobia" programs during school hours is a loss of valuable time that ought to be used for academic activities. It is curious to note how supporters of "secular" schools—allegedly neutral in terms of values and aimed exclusively at academic preparation—now strive to make them an arena for outright ideological indoctrination leading to questionable outcomes—at least judging from students offering course feedback.[18]

There is one point upon which we can agree with those who disseminate these projects. That is, it is a just opportunity to combat bullying, especially in its "homophobic" variant, where it manifests itself in more or less seriously and in more or less open ways. In such cases, of course, intervention should be authoritative and clear, as all authentic advocates of human love have always believed. Still, such considerations apart, in regard to recent events there are many other issues that deserve to be considered with cool and calm appraisal, primarily regarding the definitely negative impact that certain projects under development and their implementation will have on Italian schools and on the younger generation.

First, the history of gender ideology is not taken sufficiently into account, nor its far from indisputable scientific validity. It is an idea originating in somewhat vague sources that have not been clearly formulated, and supporters of the idea are often, if not at odds with each other, at least still seeking a definition shared by them all. The very fact that the LGBT acronym is constantly morphing and is subject to additions, supplements and various muta-

[18] "You are born heterosexual. You are born homosexual. You are born bisexual. You are born pansexual. You are born asexual. You *become* a homophobe." A Lazio high school student wrote this on his school blog, apparently without lacking knowledge of the matter or of the ethical issues entailed after assisting an anti-homophobia class funded by the province. (What does "pansexual" mean anyway?) See *http:// eraorameucci.it/cronaca/77-la-vera-malattia-e-l-omofobia*. On the same site one can find a curious comment on the flyer distributed by a family association opposed to school-based gender programs: http://eraorameucci.it/cronaca/89-cosa-none-la-teoria-gender-in-475-parole). In Italy, the climate is at a point where one can no longer express ideas different from those claiming to be gender-friendly without being heavily criticized. Any free exchange of ideas seems to encounter several obstacles in this regard.

tions shows that it is still at an embryonic stage and that it is not a genuine scientific construct.

The idea of "gender" was born after World War II in a feminist context, and we can say it owes much to Simone de Beauvoir's work, in particular to her famous assertion that, "One is not born a woman but becomes one."[19]

It is a phrase that made considerable headway and encountered great good fortune when it made its appearance, contributing mightily to guide the theoretical development of militant feminism throughout the West during the protest years.

It could be argued that both the most recent radical feminists and LGBT organizations have latched onto this quote out of context. The author was referring to the fact that certain "feminine characteristics," such as patience, humility and even intellectual skills, long considered lower in women than in men, are acquired from one's environment and not congenital.

In this sense one cannot but agree with de Beauvoir. There is substantial equivalence between males and females regarding all the great events of the psychological, intellectual and emotional life, and society should do everything to remove obstacles preventing recognition of this equality and the exercise of equal rights (in particular to education and work).

The use subsequently made of this ideal of equality, as well as of de Beauvoir's reflections on women's status and feminine nature, however, constitutes a true and proper manipulation. Knowing de Beauvoir herself practiced a form of bisexualism and that she considered a person's natural characteristics as secondary compared with those acquired socially, does not mean their alleged subordination must be held as inconsistent—natural characteristics still exist and are an essential basis of personal identity—nor that the opinion of this one influential thinker and writer must be regarded as scientific truth.

This manipulation was accomplished by LGBT organizations that, on one hand, engage in tight strategic alliances with those of radical feminism while, on the other hand, attempting (with considerable media success) to pass off the opinion of celebrity intellectuals as real "science." The primary result has been an extension of the idea that social influence determines the formation of sexual identity and that, for this reason, SSA possesses the same legitimacy as heterosexuality.

The history of gender theories, in work by scholars who have developed and disseminated these ideas the most, confirms the non-scientific nature of this idea.

---

[19] S. de Beauvoir, *Le Deuxième Sex*, Gallimard, Paris 1949.

9. From Ideological Truth to the Beauty of True Love

If the arbitrariness of such positions is self-evident, another aspect that makes it extremely undesirable to introduce sex education and emotion-based programs founded on gender ideas and ideology is that the topics discussed far transcend the issues to which they claim to respond. For example, to combat homophobia, they deal with such issues as latent same-sex attraction in bisexual parents and heterologous fertilization.

All programs focusing on such issues, both by their evidently delicate nature and by the fact that these are still controversial matters, should not be presented in schools for a variety of reasons. In addition to paradoxically violating the principle—so often insisted upon in other contexts by those sponsoring such organizations, of a school's alleged neutrality regarding ethical and political values—these programs wind up supporting an (at best) respectable philosophical "stance." But they cannot be the basis of an educational program, given that no educational program should be built upon any purely theoretical point of view.

Moreover, one can legitimately protest the complete lack of empirical and experimental data confirming the validity of any education based on gender theories. The fact that this experiment is promoted through such programs should inspire substantial concern, allowing as it does for such experimentation to act as the proverbial "Sorcerer's Apprentice" with no regard for future consequences.

Finally, the materials produced by organizations interested in propagating gender theory in schools are extremely deficient from a pedagogical standpoint. Any careful, unprejudiced analysis of several such materials in circulation brings to light a number of defects revealing them as unsafe for use. In particular, the stories told—and the way certain value judgments are presented—impede, rather than facilitate, the formation of a personal point of view when gender theory positions are presented as axiomatically constituting the only correct ones.

In conclusion, it may be useful to recall how the whole idea itself was born of that meeting for which this book presents the history. Recent events have witnessed the appearance of Catholic associations of teachers and parents sharing a dual concern: the likely approval of laws known to be dangerous to the family and the introduction of inadequate sexual and emotional programs in Italian schools.

In particular, as we know, this concern regards the Scalfarotto and Cirinnà bills—designed to introduce gender ideology in the battle against homophobia—as well as proposals for rendering equivalent states of affairs in questions of law concerning married couples, cohabiting couples and gay couples in our country.[20] The texts so subtly introduced through government offices, the spreading of publicly funded programs and of clearly out-of-the-ordinary content regarding the fight against homophobia, along with early proposals expounding an ideology that drastically equates heterosexual and same-sex love, are aimed at children of both primary and secondary schools. All these events have united many teachers and parents in the shared task of taking the initiative and openly proposing an alternative to the increasing spread of this content, as well as an alternative to the unreflecting consensus now surrounding them due to indifference or disinformation.

Hence the initiative at Regina Apostolorum University in March 2015, which aimed to develop a clearer position on the questions raised, without the overt polemics of gender theory proponents, as well as without the fear of presenting content that today could be questioned by anyone yet which rests its validity upon an ancient awareness rooted as much in a tradition of common human wisdom as in scientific research.

The central point is a need to maintain that heterosexuality and SSA cannot be placed on the same level—neither from the perspective of the development of human affectivity, nor at the jurisprudential and legal levels. It is therefore necessary to support positive reasons for heterosexual love, as well as an education oriented around the harmonious development of children and adolescents, without confusing such educational intent with so-called "homophobia," so strenuously combated today despite the absence of concrete motives or even a precise definition of what this is supposed to mean.

Within this context an educator's priority should be to reiterate reasons for the irreducible "preference" for heterosexual love as a principal goal of education, one corresponding to the needs of both individuals and society as a whole. Such reasons are related not only to the "biology" of human reproduction but also to the genuine nature of love. The fullest and most complete gift of oneself is fulfilled in human love, and its most absolute form (even the most "romantic") is that which aspires to give birth to new lives through the unique and irreplaceable union between a man and a woman.

Those who still believe in faithful and lasting love should prophetically proclaim the ethical absolutes of this truth, which must not be forgotten in the affective education of today's youth.

---

[20] Still being discussed in Parliament at the time of the author's writing.

GIANCARLO CERELLI*

THE FAMILY AND THE LAW

1. What is Law?

Once upon a time the law was not written at the command of a prince, or written down in an authoritative text,[1] but rather it was inscribed in the very order of things. It was in the physical and the social, where, with a humble eye, it could be read and translated into rules for life.[2] First there was the law, and then there was political power.

The essence of political power consisted in *ius dicere*, or communicating the law. This was meant as a pre-existing reality, which power did not create, which it did not pretend to create, and which it was not able to create. Rather, it could be merely spoken, or "proclaimed."[3] The content of the *lex* was substantial, enjoying priority over the editors of the *lex*. Its editors could not act at will but had to draw upon an underlying, pre-existing reservoir, which was the legal order itself. That was the complex of rational rules compliant with, and congenial to, nature—and thus to God's will, the only true creator of law, the only true legislator.[4] The *lex*—according to Cicero *est ratio summa, insita in natura, quae iubet ea quae facienda sunt, prohibetque contraria.*[5]

---

* Court of cassation lawyer and canonist. Vice President of the Central Union of Italian Catholic Jurists.

[1] Our Western civilization has experienced a time—the Germanic Roman society, also known as Middle Ages, that we could substantiate in the fifth and fifteenth centuries—where "the law is ontic, it belongs to an objective order, it is within the nature of things where it must be found and read" see P. Grossi, *Mitologie giuridiche della modernità*, Giuffrè Editore, Milan 2001, p.23; P. Grossi, *L'ordine giuridico medievale*, Editori Laterza, Bari 1997; O. Brunner, *Il concetto moderno di costituzione e la storia costituzionale del medioevo*, in P. Grossi , *Per una nuova storia costituzionale e sociale*, Vita e Pensiero, Milan 1970 and M. Villey, *La formazione del pensiero giuridico moderno*, Jaca Book, Milan 1986.

[2] See G. Duby, *Lo specchio del feudalesimo: Sacerdoti, guerrieri e lavoratori*, Editori Laterza, Bari 1980; see also P. Grossi, *L'ordine giuridico medievale*, p.80-85.

[3] See J. Vallejo, *Ruda equidad, ley consumada. Concepción de la potestad normativa* (1250-1350), Centro de Estudios Constitucionales, Madrid 1992, p.308, 312-314.

[4] See P. Grossi, *L'ordine giuridico medievale*, p.136.

[5] Cicero, *Rhetorica, De legibus*, Liber I, 18. "The *lex* is naught but an expression of reason inherent to the nature of things which imposes or prohibits behaviors."

Thus, the law was not a will, was not linked to the subject that held the political power, but rather was an objective reality. It was a prescriptive rule that found its source and legitimacy in nature. In a few words we can say that the formal precept came from a natural *datum*. The precept had an objective content, which consisted of order, which was exclusively entrusted to reason. To order, in fact, is the act of arranging parts. The notion of order is to be appreciated because it allows dealing with the underlying reality, which facilitates compliance with all the complexity and plurality of reality.[6]

The *ordination* was once a predominantly cognitive activity, which humbly acknowledged an existing, objective, inescapable order within which to insert the content of *lex*. There was a categorical identity of law and morality not found in the material contents of one or the other, but rather in the common principle of intelligibility.[7]

1.1 The Law Betrayed

From the year 1300 onward—and with an ever more decisive march—a transformation of a mentality propitious to a new order of fundamentally different things was underway and reached its climax in the twelfth and thirteenth centuries.[8]

The law as what is right, despite being a perspective as ancient as the Roman jurists, virtually disappeared from the fourteenth century onward, replaced by subjectivism (the right as a subjective right) and then by normativism (the right as a rule), which is still a dominant theory[9].

This great historic process[10] was completely aimed at unbinding the individual from that sacral contemplation of the universe to which he or she had, till then, been oriented.[11]

There thus now appears a deft distinction between the logic of the law and the logic of ethics.[12]

In that era the morality of the law was identified as public morality (the "reason of state") upon which a system of social actions was built as objective

[6] See F. VIOLA, *Autorità e ordine del diritto*, Giappichelli, Turin 1987.

[7] See F. D'AGOSTINO, *Filosofia del diritto*, Giappichelli, Turin 2000, p.28-29.

[8] See J.HUIZINGA, *Autunno del Medioevo*, Sansoni, Florence 1989.

[9] See J. HERVADA, *Cos'è il diritto?*, ESC, Rome 2013, p.13.

[10] See P. CORRÊA DE OLIVEIRA, *Rivoluzione e Contro-Rivoluzione*, Sugarco, Milan 2009, p.46-55. See F. D'AGOSTINO, *Filosofia del diritto*, p.31.

[11] See P. CORRÊA DE OLIVEIRA, *Innocenza primordiale e contemplazione sacrale dell'universo*, Cantagalli, Siena 2013.

[12] See F. D'AGOSTINO, *Filosofia del diritto*, p.31.

and verifiable. These actions are meant to be coordinated and reciprocally cultivated, supported by the possibility and application of sanctions. On the contrary, traditional ethics recognizes an eminently private nature, devoid of a real operational value.[13] It is the transition from certain indifference toward general legal areas to the psychology (on the part of the new "Prince") of a watchful attention. It was a pushy attitude towards an increasing involvement in the production of law.

The law is no longer understood in its multivalent sense of *lex*, dear to St. Thomas, which tended to blur into *ius*. Rather it moved to the strict sense of *loy*, law in the modern sense. It became the authoritarian volition of the holder of a new sovereignty characterized by attributes of general sweep and rigidity.

If classical thought (Greco-Roman and Christian) had determined the essence of law within the framework of the just versus unjust, and moral versus immoral, while affirming the morality of the legal category according to its correspondence with human nature, the thought of modernity solves the problem of legal qualification by recurring to the notion of "amorality."

That is, a common truth unique to human beings is denied. Typologically, the law becomes an amoral category isolated from any reference to value or an understanding of man with respect to his ontological nature.

Respect for the law is thus no longer founded on righteousness, but on efficiency. It is based on an ability to establish itself and be obeyed through its coercive force alone. Awareness of the ontological foundation of relatedness proper to human beings, the ego, ethics and the law are interpreted within the horizon of what Sergio Cotta has defined as the "metaphysics of the absolute subject."[14]

1.2 The Law Used as a Means to Manipulate Reality

In this perspective, the law is transformed from a science that reads nature, i.e., that grand reality where the canons of right are inscribed, into a tool for manipulating reality. The advent of modernity thus affirms freedom understood as self-determination of the will conceived as *dominium*.

The essential mark of modernity lies in the disclosure of a new state of affairs, which, leaving any natural order aside, claims to be based on individuality. Relativism becomes the cultural background of our time; it may be easily observed how "ethical polytheism" is one of the most expressive manifestations of nihilism.[15]

---

[13] *Ibid*, p.32.

[14] See S. Cotta, *Diritto, Persona, Mondo Umano*, Giappichelli, Turin 1989, p.283.

[15] See F. D'Agostino, *Diritto e Giustizia*, San Paolo, Cinisello Balsamo 2000, p.121.

One of the leading figures in contemporary bioethics—who claims the inevitability of ethical polytheism—consequently affirms how necessary it is for people to become mutually accustomed to considering the *other* as a "moral stranger." That is, we can live physically close, without being together, because no one is bound by any basic, common, shared values. It prevents us from speaking the same ethical language.[16]

1.3 From Law to Human Rights

A wide-open road is paved under the guise of "rights," offering what are actually anti-rights, as they are contrary to the objective natural order.

The foundation of such new human rights lies exclusively within the subject's freedom of choice, in absolute self-determination, in the transformation of every free act, or of any act consented to by the subject, into a "human right." There is a tendency to extend "human rights," intended as an unlimited exercise of freedom, while denying their foundation (i.e., an objective natural order spontaneously recognized by the intelligence).

2. Family and Marriage

Also, the family has been affected by this cultural and legal transformation. Christianity has given a previously unknown dignity to the family. Even pagan cultures knew the value of marriage.

2.1 Marriage is understood as a matter of nature

Since ancient times marriage has been considered a fact of nature, and classical culture has highlighted three essential and inseparable elements:

- *Venus*: sexual attraction
- *Eros*: affective and emotional longing

Sacramentum: the commitment to a stable union, open to children, which is not yet a "sacrament" as Christians understood it. It indicates that, even in ancient societies, marriage is somehow sacred, involving the whole person's intelligence and will and not merely the emotions and senses[17]

[16] See H. Tristram Engelhardt, *Foundation of Bioethics*, OUP, NY 1995.

[17] A popular definition of marriage dating from the first half of the third century A.D., offered by the jurist Modestinus, reads, "*Nuptiae sunt coniunctio maris et feminae, consortium omnis vitae, divini et humani juris comunicatio.*" ("The union of man and woman, a lifelong communion, sharing what depends on human and divine law.") This definition, preserved

Christianity, by elevating marriage to a sacrament, was able to build a civilization founded upon the family. Thus a new civilization came into being—Christendom.[18]

3. The Revolution Attacks the Family

A process of destruction of all natural and Christian bonds that permeated European civilization began with the decay of the Middle Ages. This process was called "Revolution" by the Brazilian thinker Plinio Corrêa de Oliveira.[19] He has divided it into distinct stages. It is a process that immediately attacks the family.

3.1 First Revolution: The Protestant Reformation and the Renaissance

With the Renaissance and Luther's Reformation many European countries introduced divorce. Luther and the Protestant Reformation—the latter symbolically begins with the posting of Martin Luther's 95 Theses on the Wittenberg Cathedral door on October 31, 1517 attacked the sanctity of marriage proclaimed by the Catholic Church.

In his *De Captivitate Babylonica Ecclesiae* Luther permitted divorce, later re-affirming it with greater strength in his *Sermon on Marriage*, which lists three reasons for divorce—impotence, adultery, and rejection of spousal duty.

Luther did not hesitate to consider marriage merely an agreement of human nature, the objectives of which fail when they can no longer be pursued. Protestant divorce theorists tend to bracket the sacrament—the institutional element—by insisting instead on *eros* as understanding and concord between the spouses. Thus one of three pillars constituting marriage is put into question.

---

in the *Digest* (23:2:1), promulgated in 533 A.D. by the Emperor Justinian—is taken, almost verbatim, in the Institutes of Justinian (1:9:1), also published in 533 A.D. For quotations from the Roman rhetoricians offering similar definitions, see P. LANFRANCHI, *Le definizioni e il concetto del matrimonio nei retori romani*, SDHI, Rome 1936, p.3-12. A few years prior to Modestinus Ulpian said of this *coniunctio*, "which we call marriage," that it was a natural law, because "taught by nature to every living thing on land, at sea and in the air" (cf. Ulpiano, *Institutions*, Book I, D. 1:1:1:3). The work dates from the reign of Caracalla (A.D. 212-217). With this he took a *topos* of the Roman doctrine of natural law. See CICERO, *De Off.* 1:40:11, "*Commune autem animantium omnium est coniunctionis appetitus procreandi causa et cura quae dumeorum, quae procreate sint.*" ("Common then to all living beings is the mating desire to procreate and to take care of those who have been begotten.")

[18] See M. INTROVIGNE, *Sì alla famiglia! Manifesto per un'istituzione in pericolo*, Sugarco, Milan 2014, p.31-35.

[19] See P. CORRÊA DE OLIVEIRA, *Rivoluzione e Contro-Rivoluzione*.

3.2 *Second Revolution: The Enlightenment and the French Revolution*

With the Enlightenment and the French Revolution divorce is introduced into new countries. Intermediate bodies interposed between the individual and the state—among which stands the family—are considered harmful and abolished by the Loi Le Chapelier of 1791.

It is during the Enlightenment, in particular, that the family goes from being the basic unit and foundation of society to fertile legal soil for initiating a societal transformation.[20] We find confirmation of this in Cesare Beccaria's *On Crimes and Punishments*, where an openly ideological perspective on the "traditional" family model is showcased:

> Fatal and authorized injustices were approved by even the most enlightened men, and exercised by the freest republics considered society as unions of families rather than as unions of men. There are a hundred thousand men, or else a hundred thousand families each composed of five persons including the head that represents them. If the association is made for families, there will be twenty thousand men and eighty thousand slaves. If the association is one of men, there will be a hundred thousand citizens, and no slaves.

Beccaria continues by stating that,

> the first case there will be a republic, and twenty thousand small monarchies composing it. In the second, a republican spirit will cause inspiration not only in the streets and in national meetings, but also in the home, where much of the happiness or misery of men is to be found.[21]

These statements condense the Enlightenment lawyers' and philosophers' claims to free man from the institution of the family, criticized for its hierarchical structure, challenging the husband and father's authority. Moreover, they demanded the emancipation of women and children, as well as claiming the related demand of free choice in love. They desired the assimilation of natural children to their legitimate liberty under the principle of equality. They deleted any element that could somehow reflect the religious spirit of marriage, by considering it solely a legal transaction that bent individual interests to the needs of family institution. Many of these claims were echoed

---

[20] Jean Bodin clearly defined, in the *Déclaration royale* of November 26, 1636, registered in parliament on December 19, "that marriages are the arable land of the States, the source and origin of civil society and the foundation of families make up the republics," in A. Lefebvre-Teilhard, *Le mariage en France du XVI e au XVIII e siècle: l'emprise croissante de l'Etat*, Paris 1996, p.256.

[21] C. Beccaria, *Dei delitti e delle pene*, Giuffrè, Milano 1964, p.121.

during the Revolution of '68, confirming the unity of the revolutionary process we will see later.

It is also true that a complete break between civil and religious marriage arrived with the French Revolution.[22] The revolutionary effort, bent on change (and thus on weakening the social and family structure), took an interest in relationships between parents and their children. Wrapped within a pretext of alleviating an alleged social inequality, the revolutionaries concealed their goal of undermining all social authorities, beginning with the parent. A class struggle *ante litteram* appeared for the first time within the family itself.

With the Decree of August 28, 1792 paternal power was abolished and replaced by the joint supervision of both spouses together in the interests of the children. The goal was to deprive fathers of their authority in connection with the reform of the inheritance system, along egalitarian lines.[23]

The loss of the father's power to freely dispose of his assets engraved itself deeply upon the relationship between parents and children. Fathers lost not only the right to disinherit but also the freedom to make a will favoring certain children at the expense of others. From this moment onward, a structural transformation of the family began, with consequences of increasing aggression up till the present day. The family thus lost its importance as a social institution in favor of the rights of individual members.

The revolutionary regimes of the late eighteenth century, emancipated completely from religious power, began to rule on the question of divorce. The French Constitution of 1791 declared that the *loi ne considère le mariage que comme contrat civil*, and divorce by mutual consent was introduced the following year. The Code Napoléon regulated it. At this historical juncture, *eros*—one of three elements holds marriage together—is now no longer understood as harmony, but rather as a sentimental affection.[24]

3.3 *Third Revolution: Communism*

Marxism latches onto the Gnostic utopia of the French Revolution in order to build a new world. Marx says that "the history of any society that has existed so far is the history of class struggle."[25] Historical materialism "sci-

[22] See D. Lombardi, *Storia del matrimonio dal medioevo a oggi*, il Mulino, Bologna (2008), p. 193.

[23] See M. Cavina, *Il padre spodestato. L'autorità paterna dall'antichità a oggi*, Laterza, Bari 2007, p.242.

[24] See M. Introvigne, *Sì alla famiglia! Manifesto per un'istituzione in pericolo*, ... p.32.

[25] See K.Marx, F. Engels, *The Manifesto of the Communist Party: Authorized English Translation Edited and Annotated by Friedrich Engels*, Charles H. Kerr & Co., Chicago 1906.

entifically" ensures that history marches towards communism. Man is given the task of contributing to historical development, consisting of a negative phase—the destruction of all organizations opposed to communism (family, religion, property, social authority). This is followed by a positive phase—the Communist Eden, a kingdom of happiness in full equality.[26]

In the mid-nineteenth century the fathers of communist ideology theorized about the thesis—formulated by Friedrich Engels and fully shared by Karl Marx—that women's liberation is "the measure of universal emancipation."[27] For the revolutionary this large social group was numerous enough to constitute, or exceed, half of the total population. It was a social group that had suffered under "autocracy," and thus awaited "liberation." Such are the women who bore up under male oppression within the walls of domesticity. Such class struggle within the family had already been theorized upon and had roots in the French Revolution.

Revolutionary Russia in the 1920s pursued the liberalization of marriage and sexual behavior while attenuating the State's intervention in the private sphere, thereby anticipating trends that have gathered strength in several Western European nations in recent years.

Responsibility for marriage and divorce was diverted from the Russian Orthodox Church, and divorce was authorized on the basis of one simple question from the public registrar. Cohabitating unions were treated as registered marriages. Equality between men and women was proclaimed, all distinctions between legitimate and illegitimate children abolished, and abortion was decriminalized. The family codes of 1918 and 1926 respectively proposed an alternative family model to bourgeois patriarchy. It was one founded on the union of "a couple of free and equal workers," and it was a union which could easily be dissolved.[28]

In such a situation even the sentimental dimension of *eros* was lost, reducing marriage to the undiluted satisfaction of sexual desire. It is worth mentioning that socialist Russia—which in 1926 made divorce an absolute right for each spouse and by 1935 had nearly one divorce for every two marriages—was forced to change its policy for demographic and military reasons, subsequently subjecting divorce to more stringent conditions with the Decrees of June 27, 1936.[29]

[26] For more on these concepts, see F. OCARIZ, *Il marxismo ideologia della rivoluzione*, Ares, Milan 1997; A. DEL NOCE, *Lezioni sul marxismo*, Giuffrè, Milan 1977.

[27] See MEW, 20, 242 and 32, 583.

[28] See D. LOMBARDI, *Storia del matrimonio dal medioevo a oggi*, p.235.

[29] See J. GAUDEMET, *Il matrimonio in occidente*, SEI, Turin 1989, p.317.

3.4 Fourth Revolution: 1968

The Fourth Revolution appeared with the student riots of '68, a cultural revolution proclaiming the primacy of desire. Free abortion and contraception, legalized drugs, and the rejection of any sexual morality became the watchwords of the student movement. It is with this Fourth Revolution that the disruption of marriage and family arrived in Italy.

Italy had resisted revolution against the family with greater resilience than other European countries, thanks to the strong presence of the Catholic Church.

Compared with other European Constitutions, the text of the Italian Constitution defined the structure of the family quite strictly. Article 29 of the Italian Constitution recognizes the rights of the family, defining it as a "natural society" and identifying its foundation as marriage. While affirming a principle of equality between spouses, it also authorizes the legislature to place limits on equality for the sake of "safeguarding the family unit." By calling it a "natural society," the Constitution means that the family, in its deep structure, is not created by the State but pre-exists it. It is thereby subtracted from the State's manipulative will. It is not subject even to the "spirit of time."

Until the mid-twentieth century (and in Italy till the 1970s), the family was protected as a "group" and bearer of a "superior interest" for individual members. It was important to safeguard the family's stability for the good of the whole society. With 1968, however, a number of "egalitarian" reforms significantly affecting the institution of the family were implemented in various European countries.

4. The Fourth Revolution in Italy: The Law as the Revolution's Tool

Italy ultimately gave way to such "reforms."

A series of legislative actions of liberal inspiration contributed decisively to redefining the idea of family in Italy. The Law of December 1, 1970, No. 898 introduced the divorce concordat (or rather the dissolution of marriage, or termination of the civil effects of marriage) and was later confirmed by referendum in 1974. This happened more than four centuries after the UK, and almost two centuries after France, inflicting a final blow to the principle of marital indissolubility. There was the reform of family law, the Statute of May 19, 1975 No.151, to which we will return later. The Statute of July 29, 1975, No.405, on family counseling, which under the pretext of ensuring conscious and responsible reproduction, propagated a massive spread of contraceptives.

It revolutionized behavior and made Italy one of the countries with the lowest birth rates in the twenty-first century. Last but not least was the Statute of May 22, 1978 No.194, which introduced abortion and which was later confirmed by referendum in 1981.

4.1 The Family Law Reform of 1975

The family reform law, entitled Statute May 19, 1975, No.151, changed the organization and structure of the family significantly. The family model prior to the 1975 reform privileged the "institutional" aspect of family relationships. It still identified and protected the family model as a social "group." Following the reform, it favored a subjective and individualistic interpretation. Primary importance was given to the rights and interests of individual family members at the expense of the interests of the family as a group. In this sense, the organization of the family structure changed its appearance. Before the 1975 reform the hierarchical aspect based on the marital and parental rights of the householder was primary. A father was responsible for keeping the family group together. By contrast, the 1975 reform favored a diarchy, forcing the legislature to provide for the intervention of the judiciary to resolve any conflicts between spouses that this new family structure might produce. A judge's intervention was designed specifically to protect the child's interest as supreme.

4.2 The Child's Interest and Filiation Reform

With the 1968 revolution the "interest of the child" became an imperative even in legal terms. It was a concept of fundamental importance in current family law. Although too imprecise and susceptible to so many varied interpretations, it acquired a central role that it previously never had. In the regulation of relations between parents and children, primacy of place was no longer given to parental rights but rather to their duties to care for and educate their children. "Parental authority" was thus replaced by "parental responsibility."[30]

---

[30] Before the implementation of the 2012 reform, which occurred with the Statute of December 28, 2013, No.154, with the term *potestas* indicated, the allocation of *potestas* in relation to a person vis-à-vis another, who in turn assumes, thereby assumes a position of "respect." Parental authority was a functional authority whose finality was the begetting of children, who are minors. This recognized in parents a set of functions which—precisely due to the nature of *potestas* itself—was of a personal nature, not being delegated to third parties.

Filiation reform, with its underlying purpose of devaluing the family as a family group, verbally reformulated the terminology of "parental authority" to be a character of "office of private law," which the doctrine had already assigned this same power.[31] In this way, it finally abandoned the configuration of authority to the terms of individual rights.

4.3 *Individual autonomy and the right to self-determination*

As noted above, family law reform encouraged individual autonomy and a satisfaction of individual human needs in the face of group interests. This perspective likewise opened a path to the exercise of a "right to self-determination" on the part of each family member. [32]

To understand this reversal of perspective which the family has undergone, it is useful to note how legal separation is understood by the legislator—namely, as a tool for the spouse's self-protection. The spouses may ask to separate when they can no longer stay together, even if there are no specific subjective reasons.[33]

---

[31] The Statute of December 10, 2012, No.219 "proclaimed the principle of the uniqueness of the state of filiation," thus blurring any distinction between legitimate and illegitimate children. The removal of this distinction, hailed by many, favors weakening marriage as an institution, however. It divides filiation and marriage in relation to the child's legal status, protected, in any order of relations, as an autonomous value independent of any bond that may exist between the parents. Dividing filiation from marriage enacts a program aimed at weakening marriage as an institution. Actually, there was a precedent to this — namely, when the Statute of February 19, 2004, No. 40, on the regulation of assisted reproduction, covered, under its Article 5, "life partners" seeking access to medically assisted procreation techniques. A vision of marriage as the locus of procreation was thereby ideologically defeated, with near total indifference.

[32] A right to "self-determination" was coined for the first time by the feminist movement in the 1960s. They claim full autonomy for women in sexual and reproductive choices, including abortion. Currently the right to self-determination within the family is associated with the pursuit of "self-realization," self-interest and one's own happiness. It is a right to self-determination often exercised to the detriment of other family members. This right appears as a founding principle of Civil Cassation Judgment No. 2183/2013, recognizing the protection of an individual family member's rights, rather than those of the family community itself, representing a fundamental pivot away from previous case law, which instead protected the "family community." According to the Supreme Court (of Italy), one spouse's disaffection and, in particular, a felt need, after years of unhappy marriage, to pack up and demand separation is sufficient to demonstrate the impossibility of domestic partnership provided in law, and so to allow a constitutionally guaranteed freedom for a spouse to dissolve the union.

[33] See P. UNGARI, *Storia del diritto di famiglia in Italia*, il Mulino, Bologna 2002, p.249.

So the absence of conjugal affection—which occurs when the will to end domestic partnership can be inferred from the behavior of at least one of the spouses—is sufficient for a right to separate and, later, divorce.[34] The consequence of this over the years has been an increase in the number of separations and divorces, thanks to legislation oriented toward permitting termination of marriage more easily.[35] The introduction of divorce, together with the reform of family law, has achieved a "privatization" of the marital relationship.[36] It becomes an interrelationship linked to the permanence of ongoing *consensus*,[37] aimed at fulfilling individual rather than the family's primary interest.[38] Article 8 of the European Convention of Human Rights and the Charter of Fundamental Rights of the European Union Article 7 reaffirms

[34] See E. QUADRI, *Divorzio nel diritto civile e internazionale, in Digesto, Discipline privatistiche, sezione civile*, UTET, Turin 2012.

[35] This is the case of the recent Italian law No. 55 of 2015, which came into force on May 26, 2015. Accordingly, the dissolution of the civil effects of marriage with the application of the new short-term for the divorce takes just six months if the separation was consensual, and twelve months if the separation was of a judicial nature. Up to this point, separation time that had to pass from the separation to the request for divorce was three years. So-called "easy divorce" must not be neglected, as it essentially privatizes the pathological moment of marriage. It is possible to divorce—under D.L. 132/2014, converted into l. 162/2014—without going through the courts but instead proceeding to so-called assisted negotiation with the aid of attorney, or by going alone to the registrar of the municipality of residence.

[36] In common law countries the privatization process of marriage has been the subject of extensive debate. See M. GROSSBERG, "How to Give the Present a Past? Family Law in the United States 1950-2000," in KATZ, EEKELAAR, MCLEAN (eds.) *Cross Currents: Family Law and Policy in the U.S. and England*, Oxford U.P., UK 2000, p.21; N. KATZ, *Individual Rights and Family Relationships*, IBID, p.621; J. EEKELAAR, *The End of an Era*, IBID, p.637; G. DOUGLAS, *Marriage, Cohabitation, and Parenthood from Contract to Status?*, IBID, p.211; W.J. WADLINGTON, *Marriage: An Institution in Transition and Redefinition*, IBID, p.235; D.D. MEYER, "The Paradox of Family Privacy," in *Vanderbilt Law Rev*, 2000, p.527. In France, I. THÉRY, *Le démariage, Justice et vie privée*, Paris 1996; ID., *Couple, filiation et parenté aujourd'hui, le droit face aux mutations de la famille et de la vie privée*, Paris 1998. In Spain, see E. ROCA, *Familia y cambio social (De la "casa" a la persona)*, Madrid 1999.

[37] See L. CARRARO, "Il nuovo diritto di famiglia," in *Rivista di diritto civile*, I, 1975, p.96. More recently, favor a revolutionary take on reform, see L. BARBIERA, "L'umanizzazione del diritto di famiglia," in *Rassegna di diritto civile*, 1992, p.264.

[38] In this sense see E. RUSSO, *Le convenzioni matrimoniali ed altri saggi sul nuovo diritto di famiglia*, 17, Milan 1983, p.45. See also for further considerations and references, A. JANNARELLI, E. QUADRI, "La rilevanza costituzionale della famiglia: prospettive comparatistiche", in A. PIZZORUSSO, V. VARANO (eds.), *L'influenza dei valori costituzionali sui sistemi giuridici contemporanei*, I, Milan 1985, p.29. Cf. as well V. POCAR, P. RONFANI, *La famiglia e il diritto*, Bari 1998, p.7; M. SESTA, "Privato e pubblico nei progetti di legge in materia familiare," in *Studi in onore di Pietro Rescigno*, II, 1, Milan 1998, p.817; L. MENGONI, "La famiglia

this conception of family life as protection of the interest of privacy and freedom of self-determination.

4.4 The Courts of Justice and the attempt to redefine the family

In this regard, however, it should be noted that the European courts of justice[39] have attempted to redefine the family by means of "creative"[40] judicial decisions, paving the way for an ideological route to interpret Article 12 of the European Court of Human Rights (ECHR). The latter had provided a man's and woman's right to marry and found a family—in the light of the provisions of Article 8 ECHR, enshrining a right to respect private life and family life.[41] This right, however, is viewed by the courts as an elastic concept unmoored from any natural foundation, which thus ends up having no boundaries whatsoever.

To confirm this, the well-known judgment of ECHR, Schalk and Kopf v. Austria, June 24, 2010 is paradigmatic.[42] Here the Strasbourg Court considered it artificial to support heterosexual couples, whereas same-sex couples cannot enjoy family life in accordance with Article 8 of ECHR. Article 8 of the ECHR has become the pillar of the Strasbourg judges' creative jurisprudence and is understood as an elastic concept, an umbrella under which all those

---

nell'ordinamento giuridico italiano", in *La famiglia crocevia della tensione tra "pubblico" e "privato."* Milan 1979, p.286.

[39] This pivot has taken place, first and foremost, in the European Court of Human Rights, which, as we know, is not an EU institution and whose judgments are not directly binding on the Member States.

[40] The creative aspect of the law is, in fact, recognized and theorized as such by authoritative representatives of the European Court of Human Rights. Of particular significance for this mentality is the following passage from a lecture by Christos Rozakis at the World Conference on Constitutional Justice held in Cape Town, South Africa, January 22-24, 2009. In this lecture, entitled "The Interaction Between the European Court of Human Rights and the Other Courts," Rozakis, who served as Vice President of the European Court of Human Rights till 2011, says that in the absence "of a legislative and an executive power at the central level, the Courts are almost obliged assume the role of the legislature." The full text is available at: www.venice.coe.int/WCCJ/Papers/ECHR_Rozakis_E.pdf [accessed 5/20/2017.]

[41] The Court informs us that the "notion of 'private life'… is an elastic concept that includes the right to self-determination and elements such as... sexual identity, sexual orientation and sexual life, and the right to compliance with the decision whether to have or not to have a child" (ECHR Judgment SH and others v. Austria, April 1, 2010).

[42] In that case, according to ECHR, the right to marry would not necessarily be limited to marriage between persons of opposite sex but must be understood in the sense that every man and every woman has a right to marry, without limits and constraints with respect to the spouse's sex.

who have relations can find as a basis the constitutive, but scarcely legal,[43] category of "affection" for shelter.[44]

Marriage is not a "love contract." The proof of this is that a loveless marriage can still be a legally valid one.[45]

The work of the courts of justice is also crucial in the redefinition of the family. The interpretation that courts give to Article 14 ECHR cannot be neglected. That provision, which deals with prohibitions on discrimination, is interpreted not so much as a protection from persecutory behaviors as a right for everyone—whatever one's subjective and changing sexual orientation—to everything. It includes those institutions, such as marriage and family, that, by their foundational scope as a social consortium, demand objectivity and stability.

In line with this trend, the Charter of Fundamental Rights signed in Nice in 2000, and enforced in 2009, removed all references to the natural datum. Article 9, in fact, guarantees a right to marry and to found a family but without specifying who may do so.

Such endeavors of decomposition and deconstruction of the natural family[46] are implemented with a view to rebuilding it on a new basis, however, contrary to the natural law.[47]

4.5 The Influence of Gender Ideology

To pursue its objective, the anthropological revolution makes use of the weapon of law.[48] One of the main architects of this revolution—fully embed-

---

[43] Affection bears no legal significance, being, like friendship, unprovable, unquantifiable, and unmeasurable. If the foundation of marriage and family was affection only, this would legitimize, as unfortunately happens, the ending of a marriage relationship when affection is no longer present.

[44] It not only considers the natural fact irrelevant. It is contrived, since the only legally relevant reality is the individual's desire, the mere affection, sufficient to attribute the character of family to any union, regardless of the component's gender identity and sexual orientation (ECHR judgment Gas and Dubois, March 15, 2012).

[45] See G. Dalla Torre, "Una Carta chiarissima," in *Avvenire: quotidiano di ispirazione cattolica*, June 3, 2015, p.1.

[46] P. Donati, *La famiglia nella società relazionale*, Franco Angeli, Milan 1994, p.392, speaks of an "emptying" (*svuotamento*).

[47] See M. Ronco, "La tutela penale della persona e le ricadute giuridiche dell'ideologia di genere," in *Cristianità*, anno XXXIX, n.359, Jan.-March 2011, p.23-44 and "Identità sessuale e identità di genere" in *Quaderni di Iustitia*, F. D'Agostino (ed.), Giuffrè, Milan 2012, p.65 ff. See also F. D'Agostino (ed.), *Identità sessuale e identità di genere*, Giuffrè, Milan 2012, p.1.

[48] See M. Ronco, "Il diritto al servizio della vita o contro la vita?", in *Cristianità*, 328 (2005), p.5-14.

ded in the Fourth Revolution—are the promoters of gender ideology[49] and LGBT ideology,[50] both pursuing a formidable symbolic goal.[51] Namely, to render officially same-sex unions equivalent to marriage, which, according to natural law and fundamental constitutional recognitions (Article 29 of the Italian Constitution) constitute the family.[52] The legal strategy so often adopted seeks to impose through judicial decree what is not covered by the statue.

Under the pretext of overcoming alleged gender inequalities, gender ideology profoundly wounds the beauty of sexual difference, substituting for this a sterile neutrality of social roles and relations between the sexes that, at a deep level, rejects that wealth which a human being carries within him or herself.

We mentioned earlier how the law has been transformed from a science that reads nature, the great reality where the canons of right were written, into a tool to manipulate reality. This is achieved by opening the arbitrary road that presents as "rights." These are authentic anti-rights that are contrary to the objective natural order.

---

[49] For a clarification of gender theory, see M.A. PEETERS, *Il Gender. Una questione politica e culturale*, San Paolo, Cinisello Balsamo 2014; L. PALAZZANI, *Identità di genere come problema biogiuridico, in Identità sessuale e identità di genere*, Giuffrè, Milan 2012, p.7; F. D'AGOSTINO, *Sessualità. Premesse teoriche di una riflessione giuridica*, Giappichelli, Turin 2014, p.67 ff., *La teoria del gender e l'origine dell'omosessualità*, San Paolo, Cinisello Balsamo 2012; L. PALAZZANI, *Sex/gender: gli equivoci dell'uguaglianza*, Giappichelli, Turin 2011; D. O'LEARY, *Maschi o femmine? La guerra del genere*, Rubbettino, Soveria Mannelli 2006; L. PALAZZANI, *Identità di genere? Dalla differenza alla in-differenza sessuale nel diritto*, San Paolo, Cinisello Balsamo 2008. See also, for a clarification of the psychological mechanisms, dynamics, and evolutionary stages affecting the construction of gender identity, J. NICOLOSI, *Shame and Attachment Loss: The Practical Work of Reparative Therapy*, IVP Academic, Downers Grove 2009.

[50] See J. NICOLOSI, *Reparative Therapy of Male Homosexuality: A Reparative Approach*, Rowman & Littlefield, Oxford 2004. Also on this theme, see G. GAMBINO, *Le unioni omosessuali. Un problema di filosofia del diritto*, Giuffrè, Milan 2007, p.83-114.

[51] On the symbolic recognition of same-sex unions, see *Sulla valenza simbolica del riconoscimento delle unioni gay*, F. D'AGOSTINO, Riconoscere le convivenze? Le scorciatoie delle provocazioni, "La verità sulla famiglia. Matrimonio e unioni di fatto nelle parole di Benedetto XVI", in *Quaderni dell'Osservatore Romano*, No.77, Vatican City, p.73-74. See also G. ROSSI BARILLI, *Storia del movimento gay in Italia*, Feltrinelli, Milan 1999, p.211-212.

[52] It is useful to point out that gays, unlike persons with SSA, are those who identify themselves with a socio-political ideology, according to which SSA is not just normal but fully comparable to heterosexuality. Not all people with same-sex tendencies, however, identify themselves with the LGBT movement. Gays are still a minority, albeit a loud and highly visible one. See R. MARCHESINI, "L'identità di genere," *I Quaderni del Timone*, Ed. Art, Milan 2007, p.51-52. For detailed discussion of gay thoughts and problems underlying the recognition of same-sex unions and the terminological difference between gay, non-gay and queer, see G. GAMBINO, in particular p.33-40, for a deeper understanding of the semantic meanings of SSA.

4.6 The New Paradigm of Human Rights

Beginning in the 1950s, a new paradigm of "human rights" was promoted with the support of the World Health Organization and the World Bank[53] and found a new impetus for implementation at the United Nations Conference of 1994 in Cairo and the United Nations Conference of 1995 in Beijing.[54]

The Cairo Conference laid the foundations of the new ethical model of the "right to reproductive health." The Beijing Conference proposed the concept of "gender" as the normative, political, social and economic pillar of a new world order, inviting governments to "spread the Gender agenda" in every political program, and in every public or private institution. As Mary Ann Glendon has noticed, two factors globally contribute to the rapprochement among systems of family law—the empowerment of women and the affirmation of human rights for the international agenda.[55]

4.7 Can Same-Sex Marriage Exist?

It is by deploying this approach that powerful lobbies have managed to institutionalize same sex marriages and unions in several countries, often with the support of courts of justice at the top of the judicial apparatus.

Same-sex marriage is permitted by the laws of different countries now.[56] Same-sex marriage is one of the primary demands of LGBT lobby. This policy stems from a desire to eliminate legislative differences in the treatment of heterosexual marriages and same-sex unions on the assumption that sexual relationships are an expression of sexuality, and that the right to marriage is an inalien-

---

[53] See M. Ronco, "Il diritto al servizio della vita o contro la vita?"

[54] See M.A. Peeters, *La mondialisation de la révolution culturelle occidentale*, Institute for Intercultural Dialogue Dynamics, Paris 2007, especially p.111-196, which masterfully describes this process and the support provided to it by international UN bodies. See D. O'Leary *The Gender Agenda: Redefining Equality*, Vital Issues Press, Lafayette LA 1997.

[55] M.A. Glendon, *The Transformation of Family Law: State, Law and Family in the United States and Western Europe*, University of Chicago Press, Chicago 1997.

[56] As of this writing two persons of the same sex can marry in the following countries: Argentina, Belgium, Brazil, Canada, Denmark, Finland (in early 2017), France, Greenland, Iceland, Ireland, Luxembourg, Mexico (in the capitol and two states of the Union), the Netherlands, Norway, Portugal, South Africa, Spain, Sweden, the United Kingdom (in much of the country), the United States (in the capitol and in 37 states of the Union), Uruguay and New Zealand. Also, in Malta, Israel, and in the Caribbean countries of Aruba, Curaçao and St. Maartens, although same-sex marriage is not allowed, same-sex marriages conducted elsewhere are registered. Many countries have different ways to render same-sex unions legal. Allowed to marry or not, gays often have access to these kinds of civil union.

able right of the person.[57] This political demand, which has caught Parliament's attention in Italy,[58] conceals a powerfully ideological and symbolic value. It claims, from a perspective dear to "gender" ideology, to overcome sex differences as bearers of inequality and to undermine sexual differentiation, proceeding from its claim to render equivalent the union of a man and woman based on marriage to a union of two persons of the same sex. Among other things, such same-sex unions also make one last symbolic claim—that of rendering same-sex parents by law. The laws of countries governing same-sex unions and marriages also provide same-sex partners with a right to adoption—and when they do not, law courts do so. In such cases law is used as a tool to artificially change both the natural *datum* and the cultures of peoples.

An attentive observer can surely see how community institutions and judges in Strasbourg are forcibly projecting a color and a shade onto the EU Member States' national laws regarding the subjects of marriage and family as well as (given their intimate connections with the same) filiation, fertility and education.

One example is the European Parliament Resolution of May 24, 2012, on the battle against homophobia in Europe, which "believes that the fundamental rights of LGBT people would be better protected if they had access to legal institutions, such as domestic partnership, registered partnerships or marriage. It highlights the fact that sixteen Member States offer these opportunities, and calls on other Member States to consider them.

The real distinction, then, is between gender-friendly legislation and non-gender-friendly laws. This likewise applies to those countries wishing to join the

---

[57] See S. Riondato, "Diritto penale della famiglia," vol. IV, in Paolo Zatti, (ed.), *Trattato di diritto di famiglia*, Giuffrè, Milan 2011, p.88.

[58] The Cirinnà Bill on same-sex civil union, which in essence is a para-marriage, is being examined in Parliament as of this writing. While employing the term "civil unions," however, the Cirinnà Bill expressly refers in its articles to what our legal regime reserves for matrimonial arrangements. Among other things it contains reversibility of appeal and inheritance rights. It is even expected that so-called stepchild adoption offers a possibility granted same-sex partners to adopt a child who is the adopted child a partner. The only right not provided by the bill is full adoption, but European courts have long established that once an EU state approves a law on "civil unions," they are assigned the same status as a marriage between a man and a woman. Through any form of recognition putting them on the same level as marriage, comparable situations must conform to the same regime, with all that this implies. In other words, until the registered partnerships are not introduced into the system, there will be no conditions for Strasbourg judges to invoke respect for the prohibition of discrimination between comparable situations (recognized and marital unions). The risk, then (as has happened in other countries), is that once a step toward civil unions is taken, the slide towars same-sex marriage eventually will be imposed by judicial fiat.

European Union, which are obliged to ratify the Convention on Human Rights and, thus, to deal with the creative interpretations of the Strasbourg Court.

Gender should be understood as a new pillar around which not only the discipline of marriage and the family are being reshaped but also adoption, fertilization and educational programs, by introducing a species of neo-legal language ("Parent A" and "Parent B" instead of "father" and "mother"; "gestation for others" instead of "rent-a-womb"; egg "donation" instead of egg "sale" etc.)

It is within this context that anti-homophobia laws have gained such importance in several countries while pursuing a dual goal. On the one hand, the laws aim definitively to remove the perspective of family law anchored in the natural *datum* and, on the other, to prohibit discrimination such that everyone has a right to everything, reassuming, as in recent slogans, the "right" to a wedding and a child for everybody.[59]

4.8 The Redefinition of Marriage

As noted earlier, we are witnessing the privatization and redefinition of the family as an institution. This means that the institutional aspects of family and family status, which have a public significance, are losing ground to a subjectification of the family and marriage, which are considered more and more a private affair.

This leads us to a family prototype that we can define as "on demand." You can freely decide to take and leave one type of family for another, chosen among many models, according to your taste and desire, as often as you like.

It seems we are proceeding toward a type of "liquid" family within an increasingly fluid society, one lacking any points of reference. [60] Increasing emphasis is put on emotion-based relationships, predisposing laws that favor these. As we move towards legislation favorable to a type of marriage based on the tyrannical inconsistency of emotion, there will be no reason for this to be permanent or even limited to two people.

4.9 What is Marriage?

This situation doubtless weakens the family as an institution. In fact, marriage is a peculiar form of union and a lifestyle with basic characteristics that

---

[59] See D. Airoma, Omofobia, "unioni civili e 'matrimonio' gay nel quadro europeo, consultabile su," http://comunitambrosiana.org/2013/11/01/ omofobia-unioni-civili-e-matrimonio-gay-nel-quadro-europeo-di-domenico-airoma.

[60] See Z. Bauman, *Liquid Modernity*, Polity Press, Cambridge 2000, and *Liquid Love: On the Frailty of Human Bonds*, Polity, Cambridge 2003.

do not depend on individual or cultural preferences. In essence, marriage is intended as a union comprising a union of will (through consensus) and of the body (through physical union).[61] It is a union thoroughly ordered to procreation and thus the total sharing implied in family life.

A State thus recognizes a family based on marriage when recognizing that its protection is in the public interest, as an institution bestowing intergenerational order and acting as a source of relationships and status. These principles are all the more relevant at a time when lobbying pressure is intensifying in Italy. They demand the approval of a law governing relationships between persons of the same sex, insisting on the false claim that Europe is seeking to conform Italian legislation to other countries because Italy is discriminating against gay people.

In its decision No. 2400/2015[62] the Italian Court of Cassation claimed that a failure to extend the marital model to same-sex unions could be damaging to the integrated parameters of human dignity and equality.

On the other hand, American journalist and leading activist Michelangelo Signorile lets us in on the "real" reason for pressure in favor of same-sex marriage. Signorile encourages people involved in same-sex relationships to "reclaim the right to marry not as a way of adhering to a social moral code but rather to debunk a myth and radically alter an archaic institution."[63]

Signorile insists people should "fight for same-sex marriage and its benefits and then, once granted, redefine the institution of marriage completely, because the most subversive action that lesbians and gay men can undertake... is to entirely transform the notion of the family."[64]

It is hardly necessary to point out that in the Western world such ideas usually become political programs, with all that this implies.

For this reason, the recognition of same-sex relationships would have negative consequences for the common good, not so much in conferring benefits on these relationships so much as that a redefinition of marriage would take hold in public opinion. A law recognizing the legal status of such unions would transform the family's unique character. If such changes take root in our cul-

---

[61] See S. Girgis, R.T. Anderson, R.T. George, *What is Marriage? Man and Woman: a Defense*, Encounter Books, New York 2012.

[62] Court of Cassation February 9, 2015, n. 2400, the sentence states that Europe and the Constitution do not require the legislature to extend the bond of marriage to persons of the same sex, who instead have the right to a protective statute, already operated, with rights and duties of partnerships.

[63] M. Signorile, "Bridal Wave" *Out* 42, December-January 1994, p.68-161.

[64] *Ibid.*

ture, then the ordinary relationships implied by marriage would disappear. They would not disappear immediately. Rather they would be transformed into a different form of society expressing one of the many forms of existing ties, and these bonds would be much more easily dissolvable. In a nutshell, it would change the meaning of marriage itself.[65] Legally married couples would be increasingly defined according to what they have in common with same-sex relationships. Marriage as a basic human good would be more difficult to achieve.[66]

5. A Return to Reality

We began this chapter defining what the law is. Namely, an order inscribed upon physical and social realities that, assuming intellectual humility, can be read and translated into rules for living. At present, though, we have arrived at such a darkening of reason as to think that it is laws which establish the truth of things. It demands that dreams become rights.

In today's highly pluralistic society even the most basic ideas are questioned.[67] The notion of "human good" has been blurred to the point of confusing an individual's desires with the person's fundamental rights. The law cannot grant institutional recognition to simple sexual or emotional attraction but only to a project of life together—something that does not deny the dimension of sexuality and feelings but rather integrates them within an organized and structured whole.

A legal system that would confer rights of marriage upon same-sex unions would commit an injustice because it would treat two different situations as equivalent. Legal systems that equate the two cases have used the law in a technocratic way as a reality-altering tool, yet a law which betrays reality is unjust. The law cannot ignore reality. We must hope for a return to reality.[68] The law cannot deny that its essence is justice, summed up in the maxim—render each according to his or her due. Nobody and no majority can, or should, act otherwise. Otherwise, we betray the law.

---

[65] See J. Raz, "Autonomy and Pluralism," in *The Morality of Freedom*, Clarendon Press, Oxford 1988, p.393.

[66] See S. Girgis, R.T. Anderson, R.T. George, *What is Marriage? Man and Woman: a Defense*, p.59.

[67] See J.Hervada, *Cos'è il diritto?*, p.17.

[68] See G. Thibon, *Ritorno al reale, Prime e seconde diagnosi in tema di fisiologia sociale*, Effedieffe, Milan 1998.

DONATELLA MANSI*

AFFECTIVE-SEXUAL EDUCATION FOR THE YOUTH: THE *TEEN STAR* PROGRAM

1. *Teen STAR*: To Love and Be Loved

Teen STAR (Sexuality Teaching in the context of Adult Responsibility) was devised by Dr. Hanna Klaus in the United States in the 80s, and has immediately proved to be an effective tool for the affective-sexual education of young people. It was so successful that it has spread to more than 40 countries in the last 35 years.[1]

Research carried out in December 2014 and published in the U.S. under the title "What Works for Adolescent Sexual and Reproductive Health" verified the results achieved by 100 sex education programs conducted on young people under 18. Teen STAR is one of the first seven programs evaluated positively.[2]

Today a prevailing pansexualism proposes adult behaviors to younger people, when sex drive is still biologically in a latent stage or when teenagers have not yet achieved interpersonal and emotional maturity and lack the skills needed to consider their choices freely. Reduced to purely genital expression within a differentiation between the sexes that is ambiguous, sexuality becomes an end in itself and promises a pleasure that fails to match the depth of one's desire to love and be loved.

The *Teen STAR* educational method is contained in its logo—a star with five points indicating the inseparable aspects of a person's unity—physical, emotional, intellectual, social and spiritual. In order to grow harmoniously in all these personality dimensions, an adolescent must integrate a newly blossoming sexual ability and a profound desire to love and be loved with his or

* Pedagogy specialist. Director of the *Teen STAR* program in Italy.

[1] The program has operated in Italy since 2004, and collaborated with the Center for Athenaeum Studies and the Family Research Center at the Catholic University of Milan since 2010. As of this writing it is directed by Pilar Vigil, a professor at the Catholic University of Santiago in Chile and formerly a member of the Pontifical Academy for Life.

[2] A. Stewart Trust, M. Stewart Trust, *What Works for Adolescent Sexual and Reproductive Health*, Child Trends 2014, in www.childtrends.org/wp-content/uploads/2013/03/Child_Trends-2008_05_20_FS_WhatWorksRepro.pdf.

her ongoing process of identification. This is a challenge no integral education can ignore.

2. The inductive method: discovering the body

The affective and sexual education implemented by the *Teen STAR* program is characterized by an inductive method. It is an educational process responsive to the mode of knowledge and action characteristic of recent generations.

The journey begins with the discovery of biological rhythms within bodies specified by masculine and feminine differences respectively. Even the brain, dating back to intrauterine existence, is "modeled" differently by hormones acting in the formation of brain areas. Sexuality is inscribed within all dimensions of human experience—reason, freedom, affection, etc. Sexual education means educating the whole person to discover love and to recognize and respect the *other* as well as his or her value and dignity.[3]

Experience is the common thread that combines self-awareness with the determination needed to guide behavioral choices. Education, understood as a process of the transmission of experience from person to person, requires accompaniment and a personal relationship. A *Teen STAR* Tutor is an indispensable figure for this process.[4]

A Tutor has the task of accompanying adolescents in the discovery of their biological rhythms as essential tools to live a mature experience of sexuality in a free and responsible way. This discovery permits the acquisition of a balance built upon the recognition and integration of those layers forming the personality (bodily, sensorial, emotive, imaginative and cognitive-verbal). Through the proposed activities teenagers discover the beauty of reciprocity in love. They grow in the knowledge that the Other is the subject of an encounter, to whom I give myself and from whom I receive the love that helps shape my humanity.

---

[3] L. Melina, S. Grygiel, *Amare l'amore umano*, Cantagalli, Siena 2007.

[4] A tutor accompanies young people towards awareness about their choices. Sexuality is presented as a factor that affects the whole person in his or her physical, emotional, intellectual, social and spiritual dimensions. Young people discover the value of their own corporeality by means of a gradual process. *Teen STAR* organizes training courses for Tutors aimed at teachers, educators, parents, social workers who work with young people upon request http://teenstar.org/page.asp?DH=12.

3. How has the world changed in the digital age?

To understand the uniqueness of *Teen STAR* within the current educational landscape it is necessary to observe the way in which adolescents create relationships through social networks.

Engagements with reality have changed, such that adults are often mere spectators, unaware of the consequences impacting their children on the emotive and experiential level.

Until about 20 years ago (the mid-1990s), the cognitive process was deductive and objective, based on universally recognized axioms. Communication included voice, words, expression and gestures, and occurred through relationships in specific physical locations accumulated over time. The physicality of relations radiated emotions, consolidated experiences and affirmed or denied values such as trust, respect, affection, appreciation, dignity, courage, as well as contents learned through an osmotic process more often nonverbal than not.

In the developmental age learning was always mediated by relationships that prescribed value for people and things, empowering a process of identification. Self-discovery occurred through the *other*, who was physically identifiable, and with whom a dialogical process in the recognition of values was developed. Self-determination was dictated by a hierarchy of priorities clearly situated in social life. This enabled one to make necessary discernment of mature and responsible choices. Education in love was the result of universally recognized, necessary axioms for the purposes of guiding ethical conduct.[5]

The paradigm of cognitive process has morphed in the digital age. New generations "know" inductively. The cognitive process is linked to the subjective experience of each individual. Relationships are disregarded and communication occurs in a "non-place" where the corporeal dimension fades. The mind extends beyond the body's boundaries to withdraw into a screen, far from the tangible modalities of any relation to reality.[6]

Nevertheless, the body continues to present a number of needs, exerting a powerful lure. Teens are "emancipated" on an intellectual level while all the more disoriented, at the mercy of their own disruptive impulses and emotions on an interpersonal and affective level. They lack emotional competence. They do not know how to identify and describe their emotions, and they cannot distinguish between feelings and sensations. Their expressive modes deploy a

---

[5] See M. Benasayag, G. Schimt, *L'epoca delle passioni tristi*, Feltrinelli, Milan 2004.

[6] See A. Bandura, *Self-Efficacy in Changing Societies*, Revised ed. Edition, Cambridge University Press, Cambridge 1997.

concrete, practical and externally-oriented cognitive style that does not foster interior reflection.

In this sense youth identity manifests as an ethereal, constantly evolving and multifaceted identity that changes depending on context and environment. Even when parents experience a similar sense of loss, it is unlikely that a teenager can identify herself through the eyes of the adult who supports her in the growth process.

Frightened and bewildered, they do not take steps to accelerate their transition process, and remain poised between being no longer small but not yet qualifying as "adults."[7]

4. *Teen STAR*, how it works. The subjects covered and the results achieved.

The program is presented by a Tutor, first to parents and then to teens. When parents are not present, teenagers can choose to join by signing a consent form and eventually seek approval from a parent or educational referee.

Taking into account the different developmental stages, the Tutor sequentially develops those units described in the manual and slides received during training.

The knowledge of their biological dynamics induces an introspective reading, which is followed by a confrontation and dialogue through the teaching units that develop these themes:[8]

- Physiological differences between men and women
- Development of reproductive systems
- Observation of male and female fertility signs
- Sexual desire and behavioral choices
- Desire to love and be loved
- Fertility and the miracle of life
- Cultural influence of ideas and attitudes regarding sexuality
- Stereotypes and media messages about femininity and masculinity
- Sexually transmitted diseases
- Natural fertility regulation and artificial contraceptive methods

Teenagers learn to perceive the harmony governing the rhythms of their bodies, its natural laws, its limitations and its inescapable boundaries inscribed in our being from conception. In observing and describing male and female in their absolute difference, from brain formation to behavior, teens

[7] See E. Scabini, R. Iafrate, *Psicologia dei legami familiari*, Il Mulino, Bologna 2003.

[8] The contents of the program differ according to different developmental stages.

discover the presence of that fertility potential inherent in the structure of the person and learn to perceive the order and beauty of an exquisite biological balance.[9]

These findings require a period of accompaniment (which can vary due to age) over a four to seven month period. The time factor is critical for testing the inductive method's effectiveness. Time is required to begin a process of awareness about choices and to experience change. Through activities (described in detail, with instructional sequences in the manual) they come to realize they cannot separate the body from the deep desire to love and be loved that they find in their hearts.

During the final segment of the program each person shares his or her experience. This segment demonstrates that *otherness*, in its absolute difference, implies a mutual enrichment, a challenge and a resource that emerges in every relationship.

4.1 Educating to live sexuality

Young people who have spent a year participating in the sessions are trained to perceive sexuality as an organic whole involving all the dimensions of human experience (reason, freedom and affection). This corrects the tendency to separate the affective dimension from bodily impulses, as well as the notion that actions can imply external resonance with no impact on the psycho-affective dimension.

Reality is the foundation of education. This includes learning to recognize the signs of fertility and all signals that accompany it in one's own body. It includes discovering how deeply related everything is, to the point of discovering the knowledge that human fullness corresponds to the depth of one's desire. This comprises:

- Recognizing fertility through knowledge of biological rhythms
- How to make decisions in a way that is free, independent and self-aware
- How to open up new channels of communication and dialogue with one's parents
- How to be aware of behavioral choices
- How to decrease the teen pregnancy rate
- How to acquire the knowledge needed to decide when to give themselves to another

---

[9] See M. Ammaniti, V. Gallese, *La nascita della intersoggettività: Lo sviluppo del sé tra psicodinamica e neurobiologia*, Cortina, Milan 2014.

- Teens who attend the *Teen STAR* begin sexual activity later than their peers.

5. But what do they think?

Here are some comments made by students at the end of the course:
Sixteen-year-old:

"What comes to my mind when talking about a 'relationship'? The relationship between parents, the relationship between child and parent, relationships between friends, sexual intercourse, same-sex intercourse, one's relationship to religion… In this frantic life how many of us have been able to stop and think about it for a moment? How many teens have never talked with their parents because they were embarrassed? *Teen STAR* gave me a chance to break down the wall of 'shame' so I can freely express any doubt and uncertainty regarding different kinds of 'relationships,' helping me greatly at this stage of life called adolescence."

Fifteen-year-old:

"Well, good evening, Professor. Do you remember me? I was in 3-B. I wanted to thank you (although a bit belatedly) for those lessons. I happened to find myself in a simulation in the classroom during your period... Last night I went out with friends, and at one point two friends offered us a 'drag' of something. Some accepted, then it was my turn. I thought back to your lesson, and I said no. I just wanted to thank you, again. Good night."

AN INTERVIEW WITH FRANCO NEMBRINI*

Beauty attracts humanity, and this is why there is a driving force that pushes us toward good and beauty. Can we say that beauty possesses an educational value?

Indeed, perhaps we could even say that in some way *only* beauty educates. In the sense that it is beauty, the beauty of reality, of a gesture, of a way of living, which attracts human beings, that educates them, draws them out of themselves, inspires them to come out of themselves and encounter something bigger, more beautiful, that is, to grow. As Dante says in a famous passage of the *Convivio,* humanity comes from heaven, from God, from the supreme beauty, and is created to return there. In every object one sees, even in the smallest thing ("an apple, a little bird," writes Dante), one is seized by the reflection of God's beauty and is attracted to it. Education is precisely this path leading a human being to his fate, from beauty to beauty. We forget this too often, thinking we can educate with threats, reprimands and punishments. Then we wonder why our kids fail to follow what we teach. But it doesn't work that way. It is only attraction to the beauty of a good life that moves the human heart and inspires one to live up to his potential. One of the most shocking experiences I've had in recent years has been the reading of Dante aloud in prisons, where inmate groups are performing wonderful shows. What has prompted change in convicts and murderers? A speech? Just an experience of beauty someone offered them, even behind bars.

In some educational approaches there is the risk of implicitly accepting the Gnostic doctrine of self-sufficient human development, viewing human beings as not needing anything, even education. So what role does education play within the constitution of the human person?

Yes, the Gnostic idea of a *divus,* a god-man who should simply be left to himself to develop harmoniously, was established during Renaissance hu-

---

* Professor of Literature. President of *La Traccia* free school. President of the Federation of Educative Works (Federazione Opere Educative FOE). Member of the National Council of Catholic Schools and National Council of School Pastoral Activity of the Italian Episcopal Conference (CEI). Member of the Commission for School Equality of the Ministry of Education. Author of *El Dante.*

manism and continues through today. It was an idea that later in the twentieth century became a common mindset. Beware of prohibiting anything, of setting a higher standard, and the next thing we know we have fifteen-year-old savages, we have no idea as to how to recover, and we're having bullying prevention classes... But if it's true that the ultimate goal of education is a person's development, then the way (the "method" as the Greeks would say, evocative of steps along a journey) is an encounter with reality. It is only through a serious, systematic commitment to reality in all its aspects, with something other than oneself, obliging an effort to change, that the human personality grows. "To always live reality intensely" is the supreme formula for education. At this point an educator's task is to accompany a child in his or her evaluation of reality, supporting him or her in the necessary effort, suggesting to the child a hypothesis to answer those questions that contact with reality raises, and helping the child to verify experientially whether and how the hypothesis suggested "holds together." Each person undergoing education must verify through first-person experience.

Does education in the masculine and the feminine possess any validity in view of the development of a person's sexual identity? Is it possible to define the positive and negative aspects of so-called "differential" education?

It is a delicate question. On the one hand, for the most part there is no difference. The core of education is the same—to accompany each student through the discovery of reality and, therefore, of his or her own heart, as well as the basic requirements of the person's heart—are the same for males and females. Not surprisingly, from the earliest days of Student Youth (*Gioventù Studentesca*) in the 50s, Father Giussani educated boys and girls together, even if this choice attracted a lot criticism from a mentality that considered segregation indispensable. On the other hand, one cannot disregard that differences in temperament, sensitivity and rhythm of maturation exist. An education faithful to reality cannot ignore this. From this point of view, a certain mentality now claims to undo these differences and reduces them to a cultural conditioning to be fought and overcome. It is the result of an ideological position striving to erase reality in the name of preconceived notions, whereas the golden rule of education itself—faithfulness to reality—requires recognizing the differences that exist, to accept and value them as different paths toward the same objective.

In light of the urgent educational crisis, more and more parents want to see their rights as the primary teachers and their freedom to educate respected. In Italy, La Traccia educational center is a "free" school. What does that mean?

Well, a "free" school is kind of a redundancy of terms. By nature, the school is a path for discovering truth, so it cannot but pass through the teacher's and student's freedom. All schools, from the medieval universities to the founding of religious orders, are expressions of free initiatives by socially-minded individuals. Naturally, in a context of the last two centuries in which the state monopolizes and strives to impose an educational regime for all, the term "free school" has taken on a new meaning. It is an expression of a social reality that the founder experiences, and, on that basis, the founder decides to establish freely a school structure to communicate a particular culture or conception of life. Here, I believe that beyond its legal or structural aspects, a free school is one in which a person freely proposes a hypothesis or an interpretation of reality to students (and parents). They, in turn, are invited to stake their liberty on comparing the proposed hypothesis with what I mentioned earlier—the structural requirements of the human heart.

Finito di stampare nel mese di marzo 2018
da IF Press srl (Roma, Italia)

Stampato in Italia - Printed in Italy